The art of *light* + *space*

The art of light + space

Jan Butterfield

Artists' Portraits by Jim McHugh

Abbeville **modern** art movements

This book is lovingly dedicated to Henry Hopkins and Julia Butterfield, who have always been there for me and who continue to be supportive of my scholarship.

Partial funding for this book has been provided by the National Endowment for the Arts, a federal agency, and by the California International Arts Foundation.

Cover design: Scott W Santoro
Front cover, upper left: James Turrell, *Orca* (left) and *Kono* (right), installation at Capp Street Project, San Francisco, 1984
Front cover, center: James Turrell, detail of drawing for *Ronin*
Front cover, lower right: Robert Irwin, Corpus Christi, Texas, 1972
Back cover: Maria Nordman, exterior of *12839 Washington Boulevard (at Beethoven), Los Angeles, California,* 1979
Back cover, top: Eric Orr, *Prime Matter,* 1981

Editor: Nancy Grubb
Designer: Scott W Santoro/Worksight
Production Editor: Sarah Key
Production Manager: Matthew Pimm

First edition

Library of Congress Cataloging-in-Publication Data

Butterfield, Jan.
The art of light and space / Jan Butterfield.
p. cm.
Includes bibliographical references and index.
ISBN 1-55859-272-5
1. Visual perception. 2. Light in art. 3. Space (art)
I. Title.
N7430.5.B88 1993
709'.13'09045—dc20 93-9130
CIP

Contents

Preface

Because of the subjective nature of Light and Space art, it initially seemed essential for me to limit this survey to works that I had personally experienced. After a decade or so of research, however, it became clear that such a restriction was impossible. As these artists matured, their exhibitions and commissions multiplied and scattered; it was no longer feasible for any one critic to track their projects across the United States and Europe. Therefore, some of the pieces here have been described by quoting the responses of others whose perceptions I trust—particularly Melinda Wortz, Ronald Onorato, Peter Plagens, and Kenneth Baker—each of whom has, of course, been credited in the text and endnotes.

One of the most difficult aspects of the art investigated here is the most obvious one: there is often no physical object. Unlike a painting or a sculpture that can be dated from the moment of its completion, these works may have no beginning and no end. In the early stages of Light and Space art, the few exhibitions that were held often included work that still had some objectlike qualities, even though the artist had progressed beyond that point by the time a show opened. The written record thus sometimes skews the actual chronology of creation. In addition, documentation is scarce, and memories not always reliable; as a result, accurate dating remains problematic. For the purposes of this book, I have used dates provided by the artists and by the institutions where their work was shown.

Because of the many difficulties with (and in some cases, taboos upon) photographing this work, it is important to note the sources of the photographs reproduced here (specific credits appear at the end of the book). Most came directly from the artists. Many came from the archives of the Los Angeles photographers Frank Thomas and Malcolm Lubliner, who had been chosen by the artists to document their work. Others were obtained from the museums or galleries that mounted the various exhibitions. I endeavored, in all cases, to obtain the permission of the artists. The only one who has chosen not to grant her approval is Maria Nordman, whose works are more sparsely documented as a result.

It is crucial to recognize that photographs in no way capture the full presence of this work. Many, in fact, bear little relation to it. They are being published for documentation only and should be accepted in that spirit.

Perception does not give me truths

like geometry but presences.

Maurice Merleau-Ponty

The object of art may be to seek an elimination of the necessity for it.

■ **Robert Irwin and James Turrell**

Introduction

In the mid-1960s a small cluster of artists in Southern California began intense investigations. Aware of each other but not yet interrelated or counterinfluenced, each of them began to discard selected truths about art and to build a structure within which new or (for them) more "real" truths could be examined. This work did not become known to the larger art world for some time, but now that nearly thirty years have passed, it can be seen as a major development in the history of modern art.

The terms *art* and *object* are virtually synonymous, yet for a decade and a half these artists produced essentially no objects. Light and dark, sunlight and shadow, time and space, sound and silence, fire, smoke, scrim, and string were their original materials. Eventually they began to utilize far more complex media and methodologies, and over the years their materials have included di-electricoated glass, luminescent or phosphorescent materials, Plexiglas, polyester resin, cast acrylic, fiberglass, neon, fluorescent lights, high-intensity xenon projectors, and so on. The results could not be easily collected, exhibited, or even transported to a locale other than the one for which they had originally been conceived. In most cases the artist's intent was to offer a tabula rasa on which the percipient could inscribe his or her specific experience. The Mondrian was no longer on the wall—instead the viewer was in the Mondrian.

Key among the artists making such work are Robert Irwin, Jim Turrell, Doug Wheeler, Maria Nordman, Larry Bell, and Eric Orr. There are others—such as DeWain Valentine, Bruce Nauman, Hap Tivey, Susan Kaiser Vogel, and Tom Eatherton—whose investigations, while not precisely parallel, at times intersect with the concerns of the first group. More recently a new generation has started, with Lita Albuquerque and Peter Erskine. Work by these artists has been variously termed experiential, situational, phenomenal, phenomenological, site-specific, ambient, or simply Light and Space, despite the fact that all of the artists have avoided such designations. The similarity of their investigations in no way indicates cohesiveness; in fact, to understand the work of these artists it is crucial to recognize that they constitute neither a group nor a movement. There is no manifesto. Yet even though they have never banded together, they have given each other strength, and an astonishing amount of each artist's work has been seen by all the others. Their independence and their egos have not crowded out honest admiration for the contributions of their peers.

The artists to be discussed here acquired their knowledge through trial and error, weighing this against that and that against something else, until what felt right resulted in what was right. In this sense many of them are as much philosophers as artists. Robert Irwin, for example, has said: "Any one of us, when we sit down...and ask 'Why am I here?' 'What do I mean?' 'What is my life about?' is being a philosopher. That is the whole point about being a philosopher...examining your existence in the world, your moment in the world....The real beauty of philosophy is the examination of your own moment, your own being in circumstance."[1]

This procedure comes close to an illuminating description of phenomenology proposed by Axel Madsen:

> Phenomenology was...a movement trying to understand the way man thinks and to redefine his relations with himself and the world....Phenomenology wanted to go back to basics by describing things—phenomena—without trying to explain or analyze them, and from the narrowed notion of thinking moved forward to a new, more intuitive grasp of our sense of being. Phenomenology meant to stand back and suspend all judgment and to try to grasp things and ideas with a kind of primal intuition.[2]

How we see has been a crucial aspect of art since its beginning. Cavemen knew that painterly gestures depicting a head, four legs, and a tail would mean "horse" if they were put together in a specific way. The invention of one-point perspective in the Renaissance provided illusions of depth for the first time. Three hundred years later the Impressionists' application of scientific color theories yielded new sensations of color and movement. The Cubists sought to convey an even more sophisticated visual concept: the simultaneous representation of multiple facets of an object from different points of view.

In our own time, changes in attitudes about time and space brought about by the new physics have radically altered our

The history of modern art is a radical history. We had a perfectly formed figurative art which worked not only philosophically and poetically, but in a larger religious sense. The art of the last hundred fifty years has gradually abandoned that art, essentially by examining "What do we mean by 'painting'?" "What do we mean by 'reality'?" "What do we mean by 'truth'?" and so on. Slowly, by degrees, we have dismantled the whole process. My view of modern art history is that it has been a process of doing the only thing it can do—which is to start with what it has, and begin to examine the system and the structure itself and dismantle it. This step-by-step process threw out pieces and parts of that structure all the way down to the point where we are now left with being and circumstance and the setting of intention.

■ Robert Irwin

thinking yet again. In addition, an increased comprehension of and tolerance for Eastern philosophies have led to a deeper understanding of humans as metaphysical beings. These expanded attitudes have resulted in an expanded art; it is no longer an art of illusion or even of abstraction but one that is possibly more human than either of them, because it takes shape only through the viewer's directed perception.

To comprehend this new art requires examining existing attitudes based on the idea of art as illusion. Centuries of learned logic have encouraged a willing suspension of disbelief: we have learned to accept the illusion because we have been conditioned to do so. And yet it is not simply mathematical perspective, the seeming veracity of the image, or the painterly stroke that appeals to us. It is the search for truth, for a different state of being that causes us to find a given work compelling. It is this reality and not a literal one to which we respond. As Gaston Bachelard has noted, "The soul employs reverie to apprehend the poetic image."[3] It is in this state of reverie that the participant in a work of Light and Space slowly lets go of rational, structured reality and slips into an altogether different perceptual state. In this "double depth of the dreamer and the world," the *presence* of light, the *sense* of color, and the *feel* of space merge, becoming far more real than any literal representation of them could be.

The history of modern art has encompassed a progressive reduction of imagery and of gesture. The Russian Suprematist painter Kazimir Malevich wrote in 1915: "Over the past millennia, the artist has striven to approach the depiction of an object as closely as possible, to transmit its essence and meaning; then in our era of cubism, the artist destroyed objects together with their meaning, essence and purpose. A new picture has arisen from their fragments. Objects have vanished like smoke, for the sake of a new culture of art."[4] It seems that Malevich's explorations and those of other Russian artists, such as El Lissitzky, would eventually have led to an art without objects. However, the calamitous October Revolution cut short their breakthrough investigations, and the possibility of a new art of being rather than seeing was swept away with the storming of the Winter Palace.

After the Suprematist movement was derailed, it was some time before the original impetus was recaptured in new works of a phenomenal nature. In the intervening years there were numerous handcarts on the main track. Wassily Kandinsky took the journey, and so did Piet Mondrian. Later Ad Reinhardt, "The Black Monk," produced a body of work that made clear his comprehension of the route. But it is Suprematism that provides the most important frame of reference for the phenomenal art of Light and Space.

At the same time that Malevich and El Lissitzky were proclaiming a new art with metaphysical implications, the de Stijl artists in Holland, led by Mondrian and Theo van Doesburg, were attempting to create a new, universal language of art. Each group was utopian in its beliefs, and each attempted to integrate art into all aspects of life. Out of these attitudes evolved the room environments that are the antecedents, philosophically at least, of many of the Light and Space installations.

Emptiness, chaos, the unnatural, become space, that is: order, certainty, plastic form, when we introduce markers of a specific kind and in specific relationship to each other. The structure and the scale of the group of markers give the space a specific tension. By changing the markers, we alter the tension of the space, which is formed from one and the same emptiness.

■ **El Lissitzky, in Sophie Lissitzky-Küppers, *El Lissitzky: Life—Letters—Texts* (Greenwich, Conn.: New York Graphic Society, 1968).**

El Lissitzky (1890–1941)
Proun Space, 1965 reconstruction
of 1923 original
Painted wood, 118 x 118 x 102 3/8 in.
(300 x 300 x 260 cm)
Van Abbemuseum, Eindhoven,
the Netherlands

The most important of these was by El Lissitzky, who began to develop what he called *Prouns* in 1920–23. *Proun* is an acronym for "Project for Affirmation of the New," which has been defined as an "interchange station between painting and architecture."[5] El Lissitzky's *Proun Space*—originally created for the *Greater Berlin Art Exhibition* in 1923 and reconstructed by others in 1965—is roughly a nine-foot cube. Light enters it through a translucent panel in the ceiling. On each wall is a different grouping of two- and three-dimensional Suprematist elements: horizontal and vertical rectangles, intersecting bars, a small ball, and so on, some reaching nearly floor to ceiling. As the percipient moves around the room, it soon becomes apparent that there is no one fixed position; all six sides of the cube have become part of a whole. Even the translucent ceiling is integrated into the work by virtue of a single black bar that marks off a quarter of its space.

At first the room appears to be architecture rather than painting or sculpture, but it is really a brilliant amalgamation of the three, and as such clearly has links to the site-specific, architecturally involved work created by the Light and Space artists. Indeed, Boris Brodsky has claimed that "all subsequent experiments in modern art which include the viewer in relation to an environment derive from this first attempt."[6]

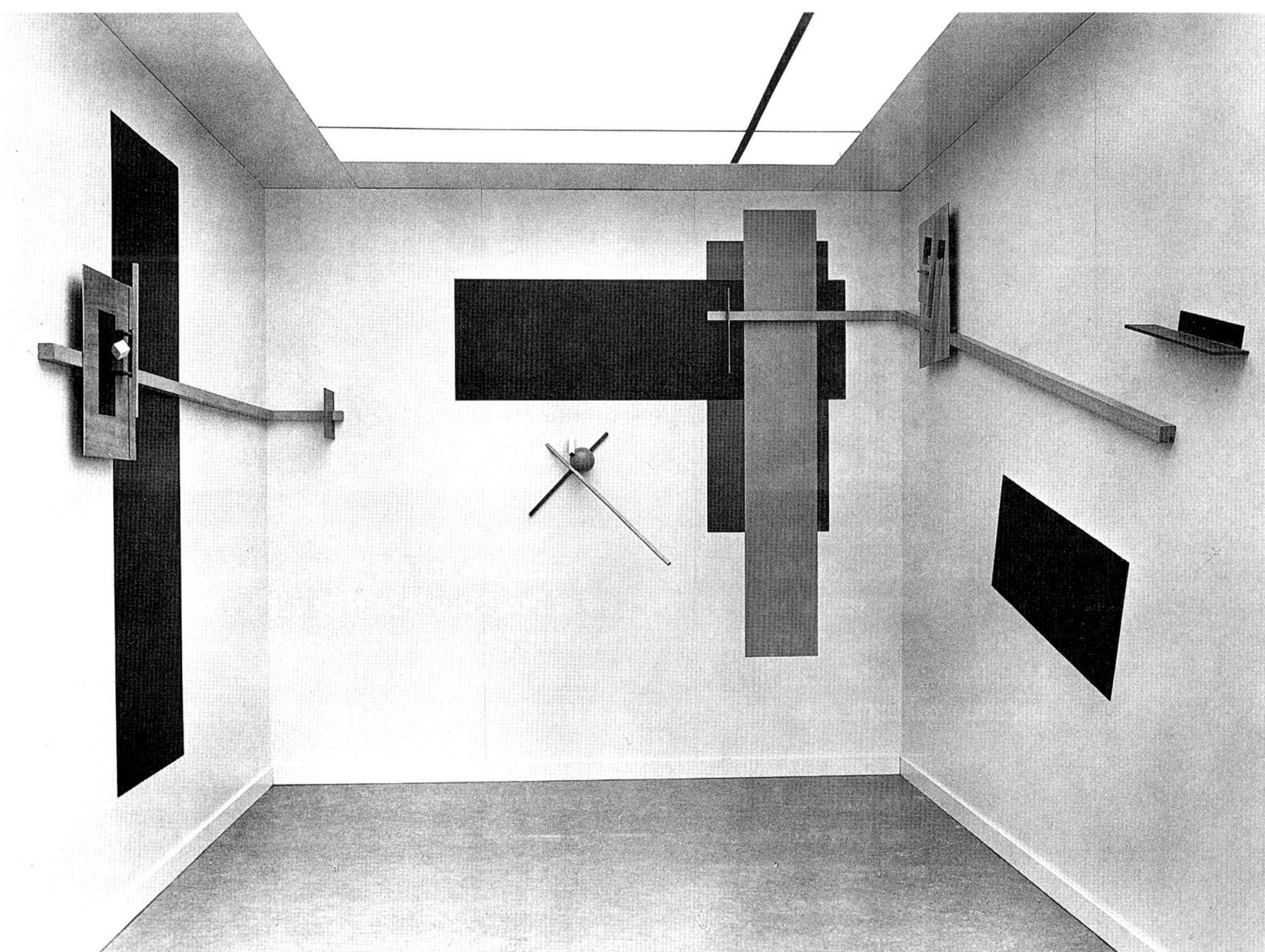

Let artists give their entire attention to relations of equivalence in forms and colors and their effects will never be poor, even though the expression depends, to a great extent, on the materials used. But for this to take place on a large scale, social life itself must first be purified; from social life so purified, a new beauty will rise in the most natural way.

■ Piet Mondrian, "Natural Reality and Abstract Reality: An Essay in Dialogue Form, 1919/1920," in Michel Seuphor, *Piet Mondrian: Life and Work* (New York: Harry N. Abrams, 1956), p. 330.

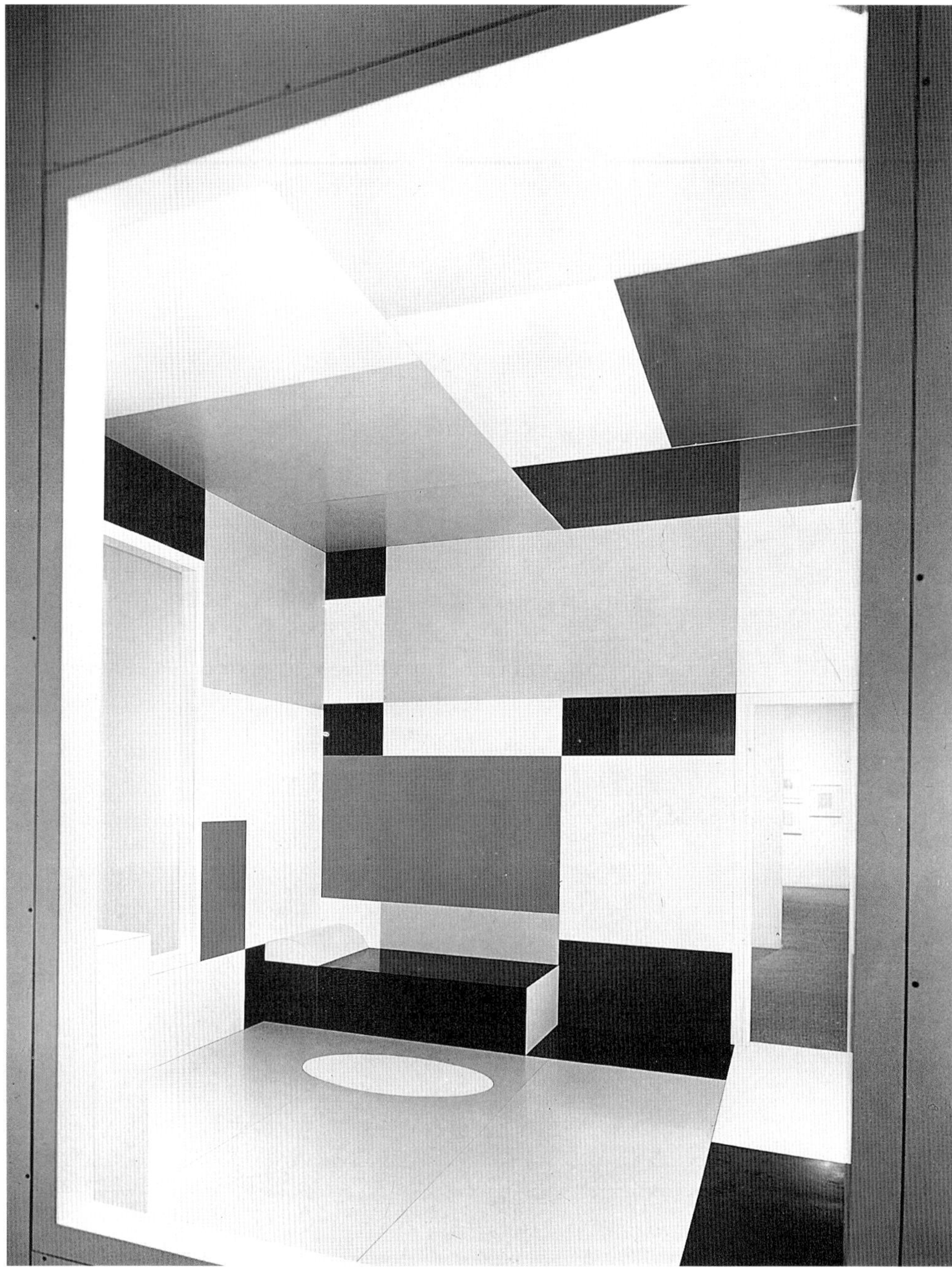

A second room-environment work of critical importance as an antecedent is Mondrian's *Salon de Madame B. à Dresden.* His designs for it were made in 1926, but the room itself was not executed until a 1970 show at Pace Gallery in New York. The room was more successful as a six-sided application of Mondrian's concepts than as an actual living environment. Mondrian intended that it be derived from the sense of space in his studio, which served as his living and working space. Michel Seuphor, a frequent visitor to the studio, described it well:

> The room was quite large, very bright, with a very high ceiling. Mondrian had divided it irregularly, utilizing for this purpose a large black-painted cupboard, which was partially hidden by an easel long out of service; the latter was covered with big grey and white pasteboards. Another easel rested against the large rear wall whose appearance changed often for Mondrian applied to it his Neoplastic virtuosity. The second easel was completely white and used only for showing finished canvases. . . . He had two large wicker arm chairs, also painted white, and, on the scrupulously clean floor, two rugs, one red and the other grey.[7]

Opposite
Piet Mondrian (1872–1944)
Salon de Madame B. à Dresden
Constructed in 1970, based on
Mondrian's 1926 plans
Formica on wood, 10 x 12 x 14 ft.
(3 x 3.6 x 4.3 m.)
Pace Gallery, New York

Below
Craig Kauffman (b. 1932)
Untitled, 1968
Sprayed acrylic lacquer on
vacuum-formed Plexiglas,
44 x 89 x 17 in.
(111.8 x 226.1 x 43.2 cm)
Asher/Faure Gallery,
Los Angeles

The Light and Space artists belong to another tradition as well—the use of literal light in art, which the scholar Willoughby Sharp refers to as Luminism. "Luminism," he says, "was born on St. Thomas Day, December 21, 1734, [when] Father Louis Bertrand Castel (1688–1757)... demonstrated, to a small group of friends gathered in his Paris study, his 'clavessin oculair,' the world's first color organ."[8] This was a five-octave harpsichord keyboard connected to a series of transparent tapes through which candlelight glowed.

From that beginning until the late 1950s, light works featured a machine-centered, spectacle-oriented aesthetic, with an element of kineticism in that virtually all of them at least flickered. These characteristics distinguish the work of those early artists working *with* light from that of the Light and Space artists, who generally were unaware of their predecessors' efforts. The many technological experiments that followed, such as the work produced collaboratively through the Experiments in Art and Technology program, had little or no influence on Light and Space art. (Robert Irwin and James Turrell, however, were important participants in the *Art and Technology* exhibition at the Los Angeles County Museum of Art in 1971.) The fascination with spectacle and state-of-the-art hardware did not provide the serenity or the philosophical ramifications desired by the Southern California artists, though many of them have found sophisticated technology to be a source of materials they have used in a more sublime way.

During the 1960s a number of major artists working in Southern California began to use materials such as fiberglass, cast acrylic, polyester resin, and glass—an informal movement that was soon dubbed "L.A. Glass and Plastic." The transparency and the seeming immateriality of these materials made them ideal for conveying in a highly sophisticated yet subtle fashion the local concerns with light, space, and color. This work, though still object based, became very experiential, particularly as successive refinements started to take place.

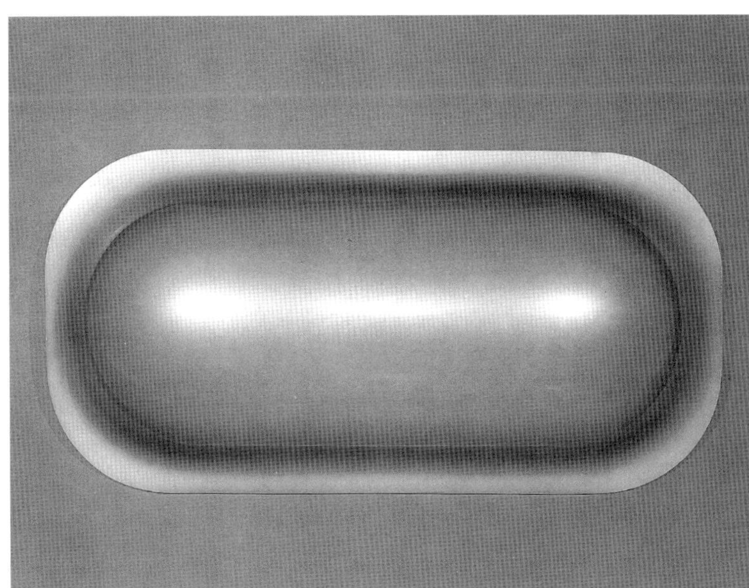

With this widespread involvement in glass and plastic, the boundaries between painting and sculpture began to dissolve. Many of the painters produced works that were in some way sculptural, and virtually all of the sculptors evidenced painterly concerns. Among the Southern California painters dealing with these media were Chuck Arnoldi, Ron Cooper, Ron Davis, Laddie John Dill, Craig Kauffman, Ed Moses, and Helen Pashgian. Each explored the opacity or translucence of plastic as well as its capacity for carrying opalescent color. (The classifications get somewhat confusing, because Pashgian has produced sculpture as well as painting, and Kauffman's early plastic works are more accurately identified as sculptural wall works than as paintings.) Among the sculptors were Peter Alexander, Larry Bell, Guy Dill, Doug Edge, Fred Eversley, Robert Irwin, DeWain Valentine, and Doug Wheeler.

(This list is somewhat misleading as well, because up to that point Irwin had been a painter, and the acrylic columns he executed in the late 1960s were the first objectlike sculptural works he had done.)

By the beginning of the 1970s it had become clear that L.A. Glass and Plastic, initially misunderstood as expensive baubles for the rich, could be seen as a crucial stepping stone to an art of far greater sophistication. The technical know-how behind those works, derived from engineering and the aerospace industry, was put to use to produce works far more subtle, more resonant, and perceptually much richer than those of the preceding decade. The new work was also far more difficult; in many cases it seemed almost invisible.

Although arising out of different ideas, the glass and plastic works produced by West Coast artists shared some elements with Minimalist sculptures being made on the East Coast at roughly the same time. The seductive surfaces and colors of the West Coast works disqualified them from orthodox Minimalism; yet, like the Minimal work, these were statements reduced to an essence. But the East Coast artists wanted the object and the material to be inseparable, whereas those on the West Coast sought to make the statement separate from any object; they wanted to suggest the ripple of sunshine on water, the flicker of light through trees, a spill of moonlight. As Melinda Wortz put it: "The illusions found in these Southern California works—of solid forms dissolving through reflected or projected light...all result from an interaction between the ambient light and the objects themselves. In other words, these works incorporate the light and space of the place they are in rather than painting the illusion of colored light on a canvas."[9]

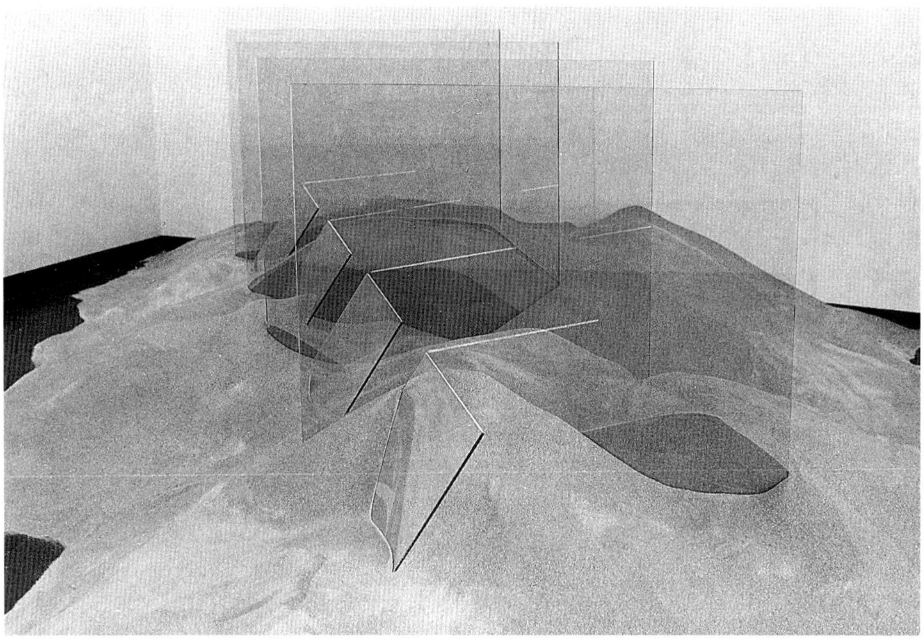

The Light and Space artists are primarily concerned not with color itself but with the perception of color. When color is utilized, it is never for color's sake alone; its use is based on the belief that color can be not only visual information, not only metaphor, but a physical presence. In the beginning only Turrell and Hap Tivey used color extensively, though Turrell has also made works with little or no color. Tivey is now concerned with a variety of phenomena, all of which include color. Irwin used color early on as a hook on which to hang his paintings, but he soon dismissed it as extraneous. Most recently he has come full circle: leaving two decades of pure, "white" work behind him, he has purposefully reintroduced color as an integral part of his work. Larry Bell has misted color across the faces of his cubes and coated his important *Iceberg and Its Shadow* (page 185) with a transparent blue the color of sapphires. Maria Nordman has used color in a number of pieces, such as *6/21/79, One Day Only, Dawn to Dusk,* in which the sun poured through

Laddie John Dill (b. 1943)
Untitled, 1975
Neon, glass, and sand,
dimensions variable
Courtesy Sonnabend Gallery,
New York

colored windows (pages 107–9). With Doug Wheeler, color is no more than a halation that results from the fact that not even "pure" white is really white. Eric Orr has concentrated on the noncolors of lead and gold—materials that have mystical implications related to his interests in alchemy—and on the color of his own blood. Bruce Nauman has used color in his *Green Light Corridor* (page 139) and in his Duchampian neon works, such as *Window or Wall Sign* (page 133). DeWain Valentine has used color prismatically in his room-environment pieces. And exquisite color is crucial to the power of Susan Kaiser Vogel's work.

The effect of California itself on Light and Space art must not be ignored. The sunny skies, sparkling water, and soft sand are as much a part of the feeling of the place as subways, skyscrapers, and gridded streets are of Manhattan. To live in Southern California is to be conscious of curiously softened color and vast space. The quality of the light is striking. Even smog has its positive visual attributes: the striations of soft pink, yellow, and turquoise in the inversion layers are more spectacular than any clear-sky effects ever seen there. When the noise and the traffic become unbearable, there is always the desert, whose vast stretches calm, reassure, and restore.

Hal Glicksman—whose professional stints at the Pasadena Art Museum, Los Angeles County Museum of Art, Pomona College, and Otis Art Institute have brought him into close contact with all of the artists discussed here—takes issue with the idea that California's light has been central to their work:

> Artists in Southern California investigating light phenomena were *not* reacting to the specific quality of natural light here. Most artists were working primarily with artificial light and only later did they extend their investigations to situations of controlled external light. The work is definitely *not* a response to the bright, lucid light of Southern California. In fact, it would have been more logical for all this to have occurred in New York, for instance, where everything is oriented to the interiors. The interest in light phenomena relates, rather, to the interest in oriental mysticism. . . . [and] to the earlier art forms illustrated by Wallace Berman and others which emphasized spirituality and meditation, and to the presence in the area of the aerospace industry.
>
> The scientists in the aerospace industry were working on a variety of perceptual problems which would confront an astronaut in a spaceship. These scientists were studying meditation in a very scientific way, almost trying to put Zen Buddhism in a test tube. The basis of mysticism had always been that one could not prove anything or even describe it very well. The scientists, with their explorations in brain-probes, sensory deprivation, etc., attempted to specify and quantify mystical phenomena to enable them to experience subtle introspective phenomena and reach a state of calm where one's perceptual systems become more acute. Artists were working on similar and parallel issues at the same time and through a variety of programs were in communication with these scientists.[10]

People are always trying to lay that guru stuff on me . . . which I never set up. And using the word *Zen* in relation to my work only clouds the issue. It is a problem with linguistics—when you hear the word *Zen* you get Alan Watts on a houseboat in Sausalito. There is nothing wrong with either Alan Watts or Zen Buddhism, but for the moment they have a lot of "mystical-twistical" implications which have nothing whatsoever to do with my investigations.

■ **Robert Irwin**

Although much of what Glicksman says is true, I think his own involvement with the Art and Technology Project (A&T) may have made Zen Buddhism and aerospace (a curious combination at best) loom rather too large in his view. It is important to remember that the explorations by many of the phenomenological artists were well under way before their connections with either Experiments in Art and Technology or A&T. Many of the Light and Space artists were aware of Buddhism, too, but most of them have investigated its spiritual tenets in a decidedly secular fashion. None except Tivey (who spent some time living in a monastery in Japan) is a true practitioner. Most remain intellectually curious about it but vehemently deny that their art has any spiritual overtones.

I think this business of history is not inconsistent with producing perishable things. Traces and remains and memories of what is done can be entered precariously into those historical stakes.... Who knows what way history turns? Artists spend too much time thinking about it. It's a way of consuming yourself completely. Al Held says, "History is the devil and all artists are Faust."

■ **Patrick Ireland, "Projects for PCA," a panel at Philadelphia College of Art, April 1976.**

We do these artists a great disservice if, in an attempt to understand their work, we link it with what it is not. It is essential to acknowledge from the start that Light and Space art is not a pastiche but something uniquely different. The inheritance left by earlier artists—whether Suprematists or Luminists—has in a sense been spent, and the Light and Space artists have gone on to accumulate their own aesthetic capital.

During the 1960s, '70s, and '80s the East Coast press remained relatively unaware of and uninterested in their work. Few definitive articles on major California artists appeared in East Coast publications until the end of the 1970s, when the importance of Light and Space art could no longer be ignored. (Ironically, many of these artists achieved international status long before they were recognized in this country, and far more of their major exhibitions have taken place in Europe than in the United States. One sees that situation at last beginning to change.) This lack of critical interest had a curiously positive effect. The fact that California artists have been left alone to develop slowly and thoughtfully has been a major factor in their remarkable individualism.

Many of the profound changes in art over the past twenty years or so have yielded a new awareness of how context plays a crucial role in the process of perception. Placement of a work of art in a museum or gallery has traditionally certified or authenticated it: three beautifully proportioned boulders encountered on a wild seacoast do not communicate the same message as similar stones in a sculpture garden by Isamu Noguchi.

Either the artist is in conformity with the past and regards it as his heritage which he feels called upon to perfect; or he discovers that he has a spontaneous indefinable aversion against established and generally acclaimed art. And as in the first case he will be pleased to settle down in the customary forms and repeat some of their sacred patterns, thus he will, in the second, not only deviate from established tradition but be equally pleased to give to his work an explicit note of protest against the time-honored norms.

■ **Jose Ortega y Gassett, *The Dehumanization of Art* (Princeton, N.J.: Princeton University Press, 1968), p. 43.**

Irwin has posed the idea of art as "an act of inquiry." In this view, private investigations undertaken in the desert, the forest, a vacant lot, or the privacy of the studio are no less real, no less viable, no less important than works of art put on public view. Investigations that never yield a tangible art object may serve to enrich the matrix from which other works will develop. Such investigations may actually be even more important than tangible works of art because they offer ideas before the inevitable condensation that occurs when an idea takes finite form.[11]

Melinda Wortz has termed the Light and Space artists "architects of nothingness":

> The most remarkable level which the "architects of nothingness" touch is that which transcends the material. By reducing the physical and visual incident in their art to almost nothing, or at least creating the illusion of nothingness, they challenge us to share in these perceptions. And they are important perceptions, which go beyond common sense experience of ineffable states of consciousness, giving us access to the unfamiliar, the unknown, or those levels of knowing that cannot be translated into words. *These are precisely the states of being least addressed by our culture at large.*[12]

The willingness of the phenomenal artists to ask these questions and, in the words of Irwin, "to set the questions for the subsequent period,"[13] give their work more than just aesthetic value.

Robert Irwin

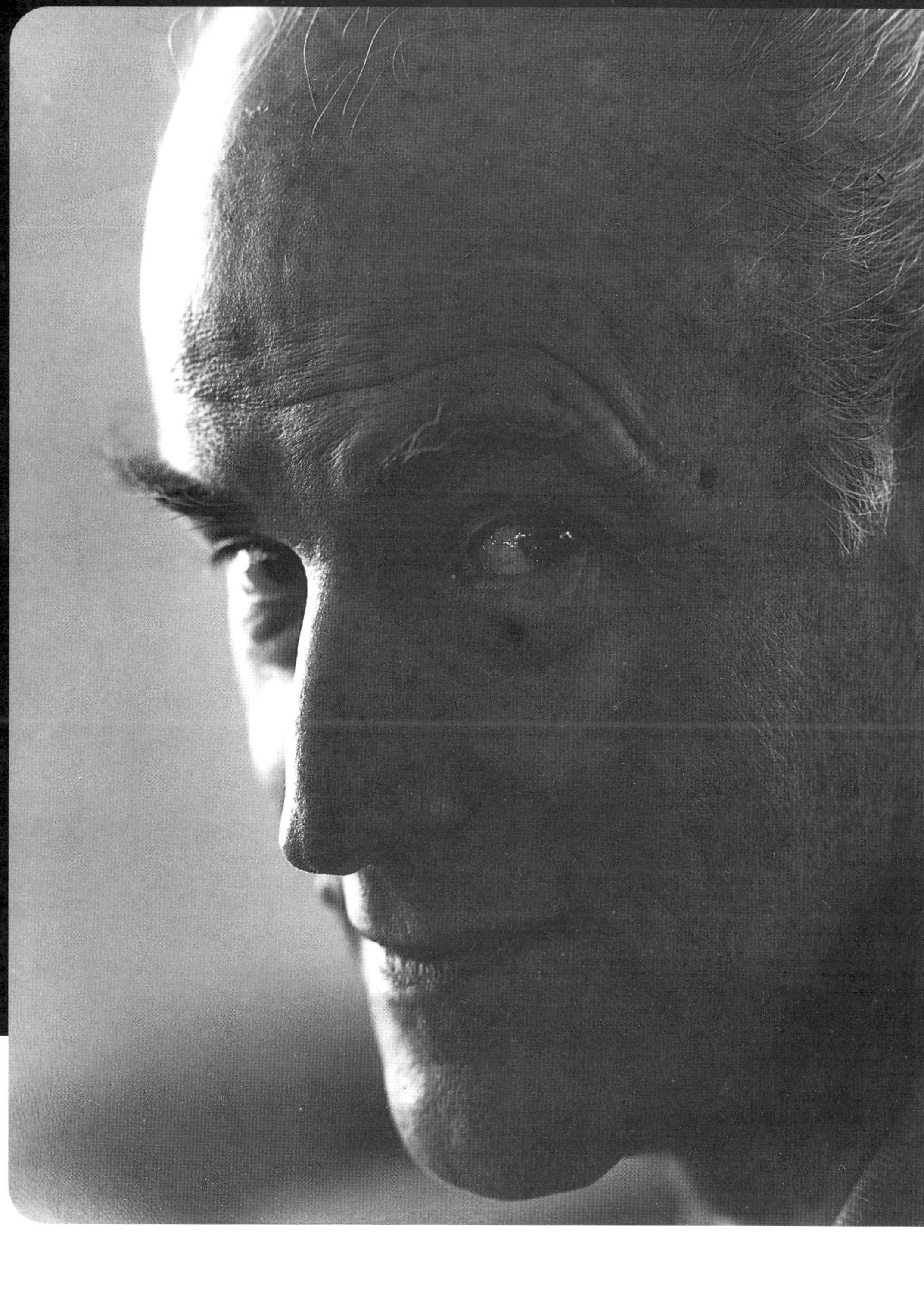

Love the questions and perhaps you'll

live your way into the answers.

Rainer Maria Rilke

The intention of a phenomenal art is simply the gift of seeing a little more today than you did yesterday.

■ Robert Irwin

Robert Irwin

The extender/inquirer in any primary discipline—is the anomaly, in that the movement of all the other intentions within that discipline is toward function and the collective whole, the movement of *inquiry* begins with the very question of intention as source . . . often suspending what is ordinarily accepted so as to summon the obscure questions of doubt and curiosity.

■ Robert Irwin, *Notes toward a Model* (New York: Whitney Museum of American Art, 1977), p. 30.

For the past thirty-five years Robert Irwin has raised questions and posited theories about the nature of art itself. His aesthetic background was traditional, but even as a painter he began to question the "why" of the mark, and eventually of art itself. Curiosity, which continues to be the prime catalyst for his investigations, led him to this questioning of his powerful, energy-filled early canvases. "Did *I* put the lines on, or were they . . . a product of the environment and education of my consciousness to reflect a conceptual norm for order?" Eventually, he "slowly dismantled the act of painting to consider that no thing ever transcends its immediate environment." His curiosity about the meaning of the mark led him to the conclusion that ways of seeing have been handed down through history as cultural constructs and that how we see is a result of complex learned logics. About figurative art, for example, he has said, "It takes a very elaborately developed *logic* to see a window where there never was a window." By the same process, he reasoned that a mark surrounded by a frame is no more meaningful than a mark outside the frame, except that our eyes and senses have been trained to see it as so.

In dialogue with himself, with painting, with art history, and eventually with philosophy, Irwin gradually gained a perspective that allowed him to eliminate the edges of his paintings and then to create works based on the phenomenon of perception. To "perceive oneself perceiving" became more important than to look at a group of marks representing the progressive refinements of centuries of painting history. "Art history," Irwin states, "is not art. History is a cultural method involved with the measurement of the cultural effect of those distinctions or definitions made in the name of art."

Irwin's earliest paintings date from the late 1950s. These powerful Abstract Expressionist canvases have energized surfaces of coursing marks that cluster in the center and then drift off the canvas like matter from a nebula, leaving the strongest of the marks hanging in space between the wall and the viewer. The thick paint is rich with soft creams and brilliant red oranges that pulse against angst-filled blacks, browns, and ochers. Even in the earliest works there is little concern for the framing edge; the heavy concentration of energy often swirls to the upper edge and almost beyond the frame.

The concentrated energy of Irwin's work came in part from interest in Philip Guston and Willem de Kooning and in part from interest in Ad Reinhardt—an interest that stems more from that artist's philosophy and writings than from his imagery. Reinhardt's statement "Art is art as art" (from *It is* magazine) is a crucial part of Irwin's own theory, and Reinhardt's interest in ridding the canvas of all unnecessary elements made a strong impact on Irwin.

In 1961 something else began to happen in Irwin's work. The markings became linear: "a straight line having the least possible literate meaning." The energy in these paintings was more subtle, the intersecting marks were organized and structured, and the ground was dry and flat. Then, in 1962, Irwin's early line paintings began to emerge—paintings that, in their reductiveness, are radically different from the preceding works. Their curious colors—olive green, cream, dulled orange, mustard yellow—possess a muted intensity. The ground, again, is dry and flat, toothy but utterly devoid of incident; the thin lines seem to float above it.

The late line paintings, done in 1964, are even more spartan. The ground appears still flatter, and the lines have been reduced to two, virtually the same color as the ground; they run like a narrow zip of light horizontally across most of the canvas. In Paul Klee's words, "The line no longer imitates the visible: it 'renders visible.'"[1] In the earlier works there had still been a concern for painterly problems such as composition and points of focus. In the late line paintings, however, the lines have no more actuality than the ground. Further, Irwin faced head on the questions posed by the framing edge, using it to shape and balance the work. Their sparseness and their impeccable surfaces make these paintings notable. Conducting his visual experiments with a fastidiousness that is half that of a fanatic and half that of a scientist, Irwin feathered each stroke into the next, gradually, so that no incident, however minimal, intruded into the visual field.

I painted all the way through the sixties, and [yet] the whole dialogue of the sixties simply assumes that I didn't exist, because what I was doing was not an affirmation [of what was going on at the time]. . . . I believed in the Abstract Expressionists, and considered them my fathers—[but] I did not consider my actions to confirm them by imitating them, or by resolving their performance, but really . . . addressing myself *to their questions*. . . . I started out as a painter totally *without* the question of *not* being a painter, and ended up *not being a painter.* But that was not my [original] intention. When I fell out of being a painter, I was as surprised as everyone else.

■ Robert Irwin, "The Spirit in Art," seminar at Graduate Union Theological Seminary, Berkeley, California, April 21, 1979.

Irwin began to recognize the sensitivity of the eye to apprehending perceptual subtleties. Making the lines slightly thicker with each successive painting (but increasing their thickness by no more than that of a piece of paper), he found that not only was the difference discernible but that even such a minuscule change affected the entire structure of the painting. With this recognition came his awareness that we perceive much more than we are ordinarily cognizant of and his increasing interest in perception as a critical process. As a result of these works Irwin began a new inquiry that was to deeply affect both his work and his thinking.

The next step, the dot paintings, took place in 1964–66. These paintings, which were exhibited at the VIII São Paulo Bienal (September 4–November 28, 1965) marked the beginning of Irwin's Light and Space involvement. The first year was spent developing a canvas that is almost imperceptibly bowed to form a convex square, set out slightly from the wall. The ground is white and totally flat. The mark per se has been discarded. At first glance, these paintings appear to have no image, but when the viewer allows his focus to soften, they begin to throb with energy—energy created by thousands of small red and green dots placed side by side, moving out from the center. The dots jump as the red and green interact in the eye, producing a field of energy surrounded by a halation of either one color or the other. (The red dots provide a green afterimage and vice versa.) In viewing these paintings it is not *what* is seen, but *how* it is seen that becomes critical. The viewer is left with a sense of presence rather than image. "Here," Irwin says, "two plus two actually make five, and what I did was to minimize the objective means, i.e., 'two plus two,' and focus on the energy of the addition (five)."

These works can be seen as the first step on the road to an "art without artifice." The real breakthrough came with Irwin's well-known discs, which he began in 1965:

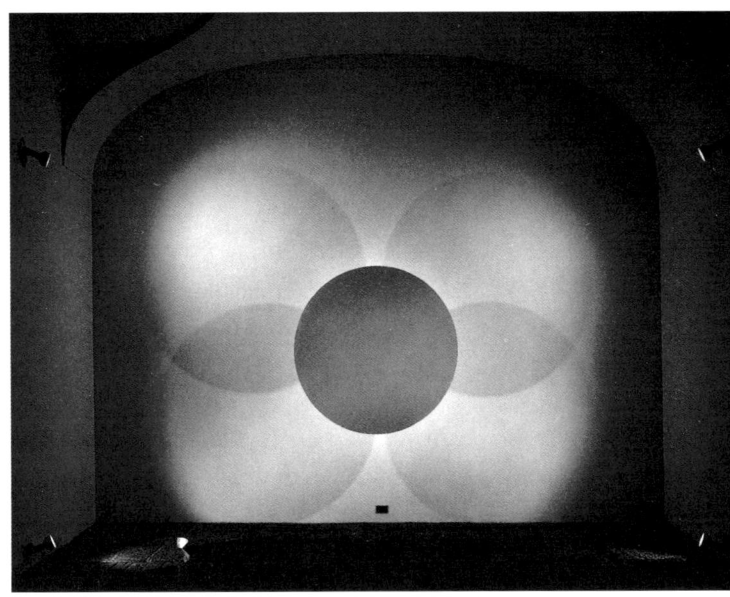

Robert Irwin (b. 1928)
Untitled, 1966–67
Spun aluminum, diameter: 53 in. (134.6 cm)
Giuseppe Panza di Biumo, Varese, Italy

> *I began with a slightly convex circle (simply because it was less demanding as a physical form), and, using automotive paint (acrylic lacquer) and certain techniques (a spray gun) in a simulated old master technique (egg tempera glazing), I sprayed on thin, transparent layers of color over a silver-white metallic ground. These transparent layers of color (50–100) were subtly blended from white in the center to gain both interacting hues and a value change at the edge. The surface was achieved by spraying from just enough distance to cause it to become slightly grained. This grain in turn faceted and diffused light to create a matte finish, as opposed to a hard, shiny automotive surface.*[2]

The convex shape of the spun-aluminum disc is held away from the wall by a short tube or cylinder, causing it to project into the viewer's space. Light is part of the medium as well, for the first time in Irwin's work. "I employed light directly in the making of those paintings," he has stated:

Robert Irwin
Untitled, 1968
Cast acrylic, diameter: 60 in. (152.4 cm)
Courtesy
Daniel Weinberg Gallery

by extending the common gallery source of floodlights on the ceiling (two) and matching them with two floodlights placed directly beneath on the floor. The four lights formed a symmetrical pattern, which caused the circle form (which was extended from the wall) to cast its own shadow on the wall—forming an overlapping pattern. That diffused the edge of the painting, blending it into its environment and achieving the effect of a painting with no formal beginning or end, the central area of which had a field density that operated on the eye in much the same way as a Ganzfeld [an undifferentiated space].[3]

Irwin explained his decision to utilize a circular configuration:

I had a big white canvas sitting on a wall and the question of confines began to be really critical for me. How can I begin to break the edge? How can I make a painting that does not begin and end at this edge? What I did was to use a circle (incidentally, everyone wants to call it a "mandala" or attach symbolic overtones to it and turn it into some mystique or another) but I used it very simply because the circle did not have the critical corner points and became less demanding as a form.[4]

The next step was obvious. Forming his subsequent discs of clear acrylic rather than spun aluminum, Irwin used the transparency of the new medium to full advantage. "I sprayed out from the center, working from an opaque white through a translucency until they became transparent around the edge—thus achieving an immediate integration of painting and environment."[5] Eventually the previously open center was replaced by a smoky band, which was dark at the center and slowly faded into transparency at the edges. With the exception of that band, which provided a point of focus, only energy is left behind—energy that seems to vibrate in front of the work. A shift of focus is demanded, but once one has learned from the early works, this letting go is easier and the rewards even greater. As the disc slowly slips out of focus, only the floating, silvered band of color takes on a real presence.

These exquisite paintings were exhibited in a small show at the Pasadena Art Museum (January 16–February 18, 1968). In spite of this modest recognition, Irwin refused to allow himself to linger over the sensuous beauty of these pieces. Had it not been for his driving need for further questioning, he might well have trapped himself in an aesthetic cul-de-sac and, like the final stages of Impressionism (or color-field painting, for that matter), his work might have dissolved into merely virtuoso effect. As extraordinary as the discs were, they represented questions rather than answers for Irwin, who has repeatedly made the point that "the art of any period either contains the questions for the subsequent period, or is a performance on the questions of the previous ones."

In 1970 Irwin executed a number of prismlike cast-acrylic columns. Still objects in the literal sense of the word, they are nevertheless virtually invisible when correctly installed in oblique, out-of-the-way spots and allowed to slip into the periphery of sight. Like Irwin's late line paintings, which used lines to attain the aspired-to "no mark," these columns aspired to "no-objectness" while still taking the form of an object. But, coming as they did at the end of the wave of L.A. Glass and Plastic, the choice of material obscured their real questioning. Nonetheless, the increasing nonobjectness of the work that was to follow clearly indicated where their questions had led. The columns were the last portable art objects

As one educated and practiced as a painter, my first hint (intuition) that the world of my perceptual and aesthetic concerns might not begin and end at the edge of my canvas was something that had no tangible reality. But my question would not go away and was soon joined by others. What kind of "reality" was this that allowed itself such abstraction as to demand that the world end at the edge of my canvas? Yet what kind of a world would it be if there were no such limits? And is not the idea of a non-object art a contradiction in terms? What would this art be *made* of? Where would it exist? And how would we come to know it, let alone judge it? Yet again, if we are to continue to take the words "aesthetics" and "perception" as having a serious bearing on art, can we simply continue to hold the dialogue of art to be subsumable to the making of objects? The surprise for me, when I stopped painting, was not the loss of something to do with my hands or the loss of my visibility (viability) as an "artist," but rather the loss of my thinking form (loss=gain?), the realization that painting had been both my process for selection and ordering of things and my philosophic method, and that the reality that had come to order my paintings was the reality that had come to order my life.

■ **Robert Irwin, *Being and Circumstance: Notes toward a Conditional Art* (Larkspur Landing, Calif.: Lapis, 1985), p. 12.**

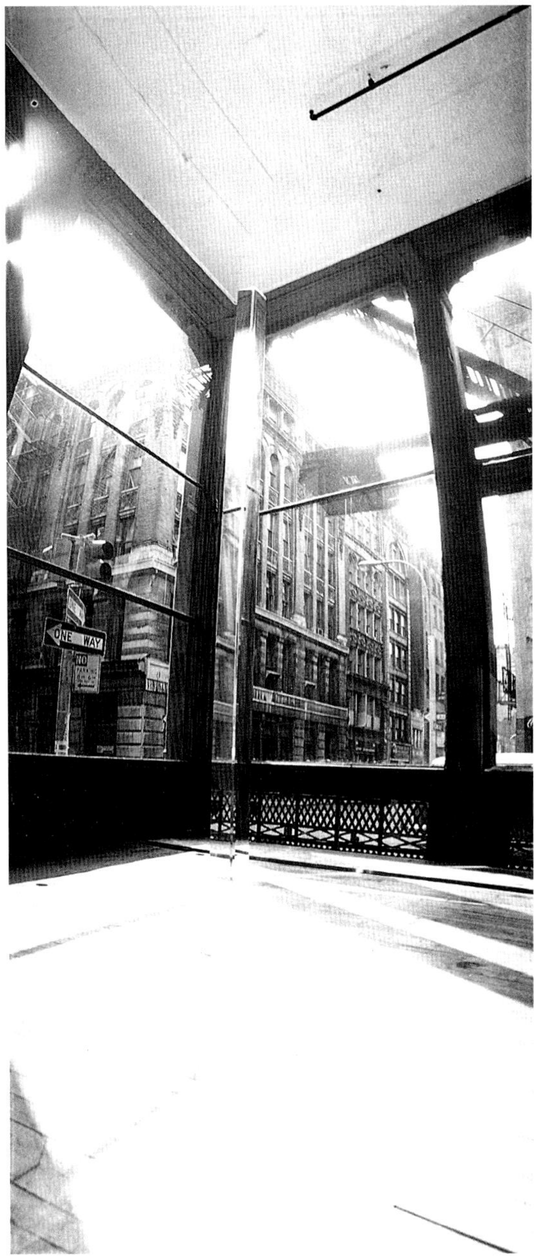

Above
Robert Irwin
Acrylic Column, c. 1970
Cast acrylic, height: 12 ft. (3.6 m.)
Installation, Donald Judd's studio,
Spring and Greene streets,
New York

Opposite
Robert Irwin
Fractured Light—Partial Scrim Ceiling—Eye-Level Wire
Installation, Museum of
Modern Art, New York, 1970–71

Irwin was to make. "I wanted to make an art without an art object, but I didn't know how to do that," he has recalled. "The columns acted as the bridge for me. At first, working sculpturally seemed like the obvious first step, but in fact, the same learned logic that confined painting to the canvas... confined sculpture to the object."

Fractured Light—Partial Scrim Ceiling—Eye-Level Wire
Museum of Modern Art, New York
October 24, 1970–February 16, 1971

The initial response to many of Irwin's works has been that there is nothing there. Many of his pieces, including the MoMA installation, have comprised only the barest and least substantial materials, such as string, scrim, and what Irwin calls "givens"—light, space, ambience. The burden is almost entirely on the viewer to perceive the piece and to distinguish its properties. The shape and presence of these pieces varies with the individual, and no two participants are apt to have the same response to any work. Some, indeed, never manage to perceive the work at all.

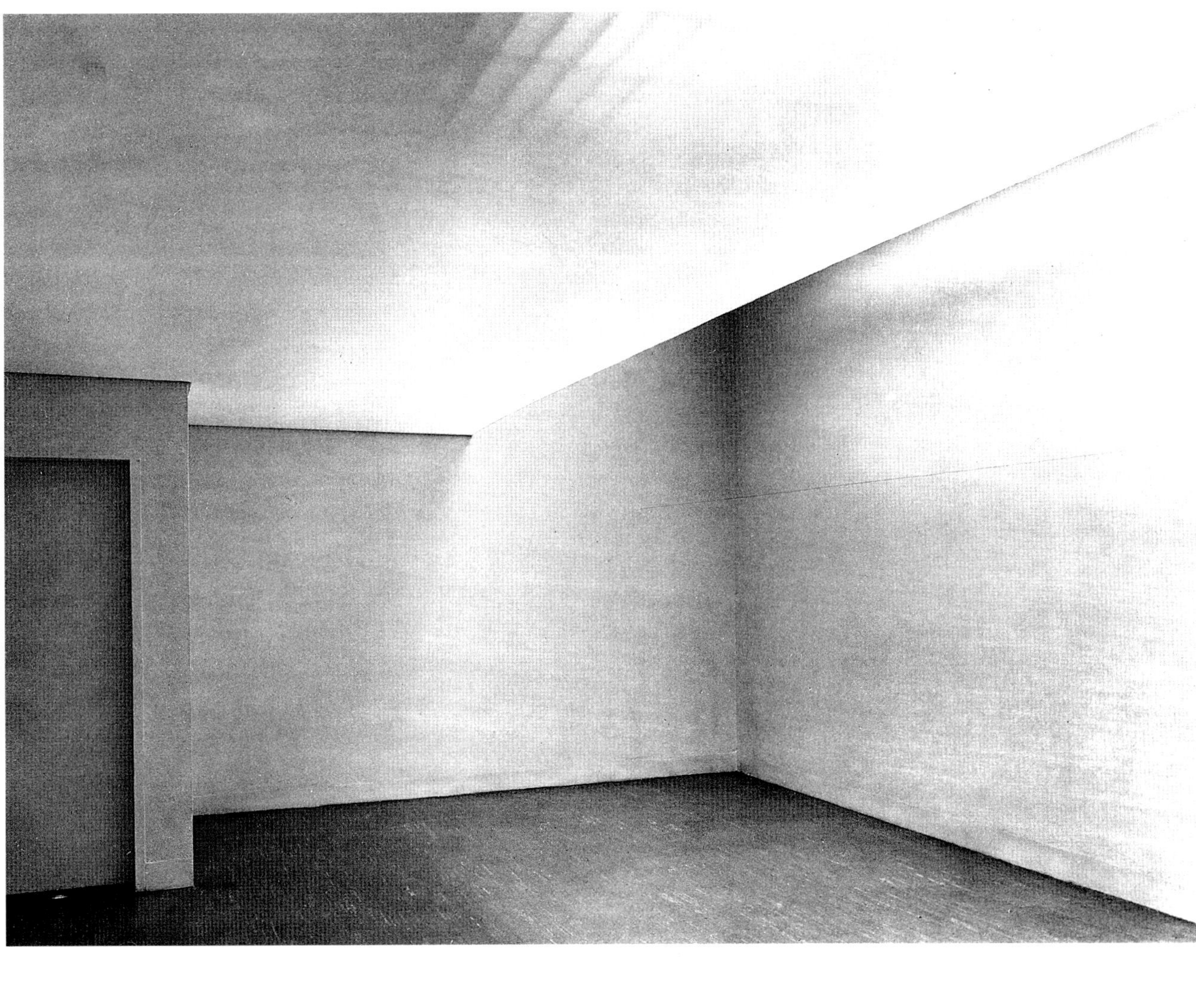

The MoMA exhibition, as Irwin explains it, was somewhat bootlegged:

> *I had been making experiments in the studio for a while with nowhere to go, and then strangely enough the first public installation was at the Museum of Modern Art... and they never acknowledged it.*
>
> *One person at the museum, Jenny Licht, asked me to come. She said, "We have an unprogrammed space, it hasn't been authorized, and I have no money, but would you be willing to use the room?" I said sure, and I went to New York, paid my own way, arrived at the museum—and the workmen would not let me work because of their union. They said, "Look, it's our job and we are getting paid to do this one, so you can't do it, and we are* not *going to do it. Okay?" So... I gave each of them fifty dollars and I came in at six o'clock each night, and I stayed in the museum all night, and then at the end of a period of time, I finished the piece.*
>
> *They never announced it; they never acknowledged it. But they wanted to put up a label so people wouldn't think it was an empty room. Jenny would go in each day and she would take the label down.... One of the things that [the room] did was challenge you at every level. You would walk in there, and the first question [you had] was: "Is this intended?" Then "Is it finished?"—even* before *you got to the question of whether it was Art or not. The question was whether or not it was even* there, *and on what grounds it was there.*[6]

Although not intended that way, the presentation had all the hallmarks of an experiment in perceptual psychology. And it marked a turning point for Irwin:

> *Up to that point I had always been involved with beauty. I had... always tried to make everything as beautiful as I could. I have never been about provoking people or making social issues or whatever. I have always made things just as pretty as I could make them. Up to that time, I had a tendency to want to transform everything that way.... And I got into that room... and the thing that really struck me [was that] the room was really an unhappy space. And that part of really just paying attention to the world is paying attention to the fact that this* was *an ugly room....*
>
> *There was this funny slot that went the length of the building.... It was an old skylight, hadn't been cleaned in years. It had some fluorescent fixtures running the length of the slot, and on the surface of the ceiling it had an old "egg-crate" light filter—you know, those old 2 x 2 x 2" egg-crate grids. I cleaned the skylight and I put up alternating cool and warm fluorescents. The grid fractured the light, leaving a kind of subliminal rainbow in the space. People would go in there, see nothing, leave and go into the next gallery, the one with the Brancusi sculptures, and say, "I never noticed how bad the light is in here—there are lights and shadows all over the sculptures." And then they'd walk away. No connection was ever made. But* I *went away feeling that a point* had *been made and the point had to do with simply paying attention.*[7]

The MoMA installation was the first of what later became a series of exhibitions Irwin titled Projects. Not until several years later did he begin to find out that the MoMA show, which had seemed to sink like a boulder rolled into a lake, actually produced some interesting ripples, and over a decade it produced waves too pronounced to be ignored. By 1981 site-specific works had become a known entity, and artists on both coasts had begun to experiment with altered-room-environment pieces—influenced by, or at least aware of, Irwin's room-environment pieces.

Irwin-Turrell collaboration, in process 1969–70
on view at the U.S. Pavilion, Expo 70, Osaka, Japan
March 15–September 13, 1970
and at *Art and Technology,* Los Angeles County Museum of Art
May 11–August 29, 1971

The Art and Technology Project (A&T) matched more than seventy-six major artists with an even larger number of scientists, mathematicians, technicians, and engineers from major corporations and industries, largely based in the Los Angeles basin and surrounding areas. The project was the major statement in a zeitgeist that seemed to favor a rapid integration of space-age concepts and technology with the intuitive attitudes and methods of art.

Jane Livingston, then associate curator at the Los Angeles County Museum of Art and central to A&T, wrote about the Irwin-Turrell collaboration in the telephone-book-size catalog that documented the exhibition:

> There can be no doubt that Turrell had suggested to Bob [Irwin] many of the concepts he was exploring with Don Christiansen at Lockheed and with Dr. Feynman [a Cal Tech physicist]. Significantly, he attached to his outline for Christiansen a bibliography compiled by Turrell of books and articles on perceptual psychology. Turrell, having had considerable academic training in psychology at Pomona College, had more direct access to literature in the field, and had a greater understanding of experimental methodology than did Irwin. Bob, however, had for years been intuitively dealing with certain subtle aspects of the psychology of perception through his work. When the two artists met and entered into a period of intense dialogue, they both felt a sense of extraordinary potential—it was as if each found in the other an ideal complementary source of information. Irwin brought to the relationship his long experience as an artist and highly evolved esthetic sensibility; Turrell had an intellectual background, and thus a verbal knowledge of theory and technique, which could open wide possibility for application by Bob or both artists together.[8]

The museum initially contacted Irwin, who then connected with Turrell and Wortz. Livingston wrote of their first encounter: "It was immediately evident that Dr. Wortz's interest and field of research were precisely parallel to those of the two artists. Wortz has a Ph.D. in Experimental Psychology from the University of Texas.... The nature of his work at Garrett [Aerospace] is directly concerned with human perceptual responses in special conditions."[9]

It is typical of Irwin that his first response to the project, in the words of the catalog, was to "express skepticism" and to "question the structuring of the program." (Expressing the phenomenologist's *epoche,* or carefully considered doubt, and examining structure form the basis for all of Irwin's undertakings.) Nevertheless, as Livingston stated with prescience in 1970, "his involvement developed into a virtual life commitment. Indeed, the ramifications of the 'Irwin/Turrell/Garrett Project' so far transcend the parameters of A&T that it is not possible for us to know, much less to document, every phase or outcome of the ongoing work set in motion by the original A&T project."[10]

The original project involved two six-month periods. The first was to be devoted to "the development of an overall perceptual thesis between the principles, Dr. Edward Wortz and artists R. Irwin and J. Turrell, the basic perceptual research to begin in January, 1969."[11] During the second period that thesis would be given physical form: "Having arrived at the basic format and physical plan, a space will be leased to build and then refine the actual working space, methods of entrance, exit, control of elements, input of stimulus, etc."[12]

Initially the participants conceived this working space as an isolated and acoustically deadened room at the Los Angeles County Museum of Art. This darkened anechoic chamber (a room heavily insulated against outside noise and stimuli) was to provide a neutral arena in which the percipient—only two or three people would be allowed in at a time—would have a "lingering anticipation and a form of participation [so that] his sense of isolation and his focus should fall back on his own phenomena. These phenomena were to consist of the sounds of his own system, retinal and color fields, etc." Further, plans began to be specifically formulated not only for an anechoic chamber but also for another chamber in which a Ganzfeld could be experienced. The artists also toyed with the idea of using a speaker system to broadcast loaded words that would be only subliminally perceived.

As the project continued, Irwin and Turrell drew up statements that defined, to some degree, their philosophy. These statements are the closest thing we have to a manifesto of phenomenal art. Keep in mind, however, that they were written by only two of the Light and Space artists and that Turrell's eventual abdication from the project implies disagreement even between these two.

Robert Irwin (foreground) and James Turrell (background), demonstrating an anechoic chamber, 1970

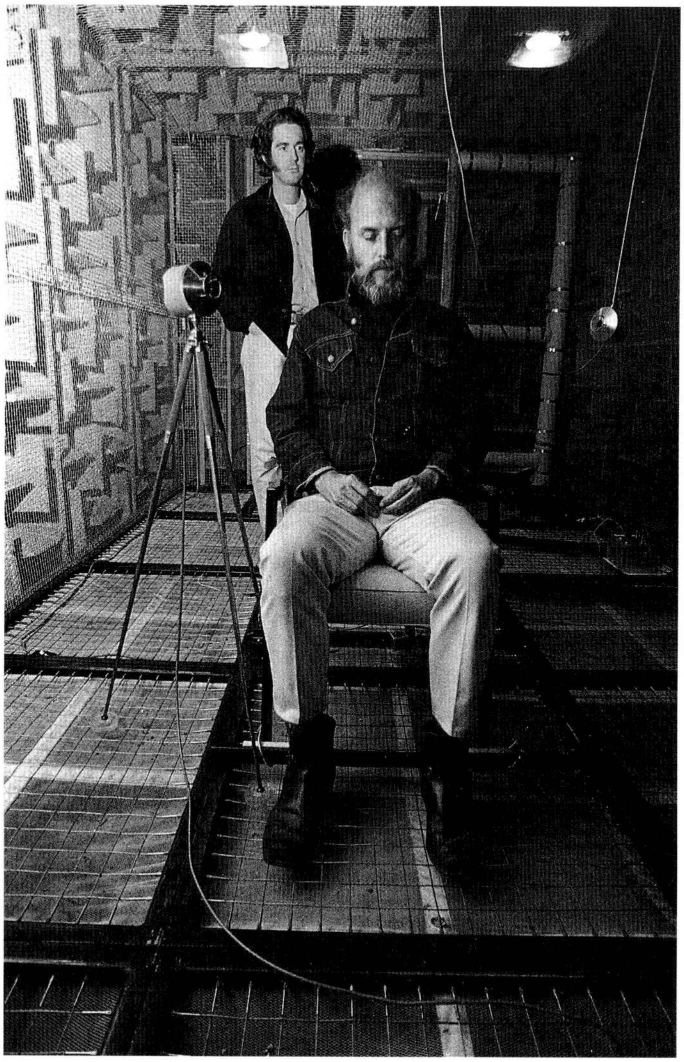

This project, we believe, is an extension of our work, just as our work is an extension of some mainstream of modern art. A problem may arise with this project in the minds of the art community who may regard it as "non-art"—as theatrical or more scientific than artistic or as being just outside the arena of art. Although it is a strong alteration as far as methods, means, and intent, we believe in it as art, and yet recognize the possibility of a redefinition needed to incorporate it into the "arena."

The necessity for this statement stems from the fact that this project will ultimately be dealt with by the art world, not so much the scientific world, though this might not be unwarranted, and therefore we are held to the dialogue of the art community and are subject to its reviews and criticism. Thus we feel we must make our position clear, that we feel the project is not inconsistent with what has come before (how can it be?).

[illegible] *of the realm of experience, we can assume that after a viewer looks at a* [illegible] *because the "art" has been experienced.*

[illegible] *—not, for instance, with the limits of painting. We* [illegible]

[illegible] *everyday experience. The object of art may be to seek an elimination of the necessity for it.*

Time is illusionary; events make time. There is no such thing as modern art, there was art that was done then, and art that is done now; art is equal.

All art is experience, yet all experience is not art. The artist chooses from experience that which he defines out as art, possibly because it has not yet been experienced enough, or because it needs to be experienced more.

All art-world distinctions are meaningless.[13]

Irwin and Turrell investigated meditative states and corresponding awarenesses of taste and tone and of tone and color perception as well as alpha-wave conditioning (considerably prior to its broad public appeal) and biofeedback mechanisms. As a result, the project began to change. Both artists became deeply involved with (one might even say seduced by) the subtle personal aspects of perception, and their experiments satisfied their curiosity in a way no object could have. The discovery that there was no longer any need for an object constituted the most important "eureka" phenomenon of A&T. It was, however, a discovery that did not sit well with the museum, which ended up making a regrettable decision: instead of exhibiting evidence of the Irwin-Turrell-Wortz investigations, the museum put on view one of Irwin's acrylic columns, which did not represent the artist's ideas in 1971 and thus unfortunately skewed the art historical record.

[illegible] **what looked for all the world like a diminishing horizon—the art-object's becoming so ephemeral as to threaten to disappear altogether—has, like some marvelous philosophical riddle, turned itself inside out to reveal its opposite. What appeared to be a question of object/non-object has turned out to be a question of seeing and not seeing, of how it is we actually perceive or fail to perceive "things" in their real contexts. Now we are presented and challenged with the infinite, everyday richness of "phenomenal" perception (and the potential for a corresponding "phenomenal art," with none of the customary abstract limitations as to form, place, materials, and so forth)—one which seeks to discover and value the potential for experiencing beauty in everything.**

■ **Robert Irwin, *Being and Circumstance: Notes toward a Conditional Art* (Larkspur Landing, Calif.: Lapis, 1985), p. 29.**

The project had provided an opportunity for the participants to chart unknown territory, but because the territory was unknown, Irwin and Turrell approached it differently. About his own involvement Irwin stated:

All this kind of information has very strange social connotations. . . . It's not a verbal experience. . . . Wortz and I operate out of common experience. We would do various experiments together and then begin to talk about them afterward. But when you spend this long playing with non-verbal forms, it gets hard to talk. You don't have a desire *to talk about it. It doesn't work and it doesn't feel right.*[14]

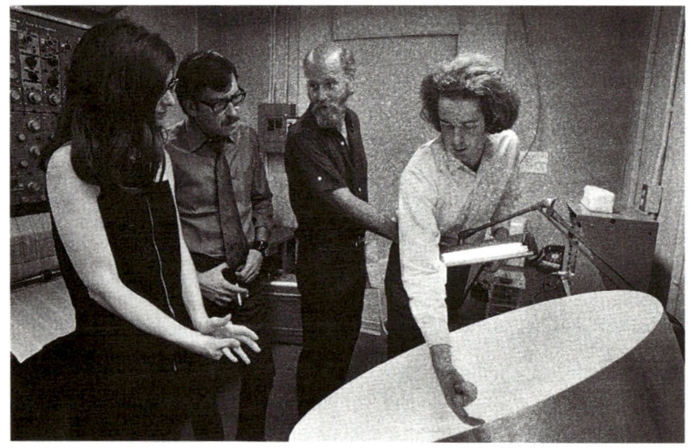

James Turrell (far right) demonstrating the Ganzfeld effect to (from left): Gail Scott, Maurice Tuchman, and Robert Irwin, 1970

Several years later Irwin elaborated on this statement:

One of the things that Wortz and I . . . played with, which was very interesting, was to put yourself in a room . . . in an anechoic space, for long periods of time, isolated in total darkness with no sound. . . . The thing for me that was really striking . . . was that when you came out of this space and walked down the same street that you'd walked down coming in, that the world really did look different . . . and it did for a number of hours afterwards; I mean it looked radically different. *It had a much stronger sense of color, a much stronger sense of movement, a much stronger sense of textures. . . . Now nothing* actually *changed out there, it was just perceived differently. And the simple observation was that in being in this so-called "sensory deprivation" situation for a while with no visual or audio input, you relied more on your sense of touch and smell . . . altering your sense threshold and your sense dependence . . . and consequently your reality.*[15]

During the decades since A&T, Irwin has become increasingly sophisticated in perceptual psychology, philosophy, theory, and methodology. If at one time he prided himself on never having read anything in those fields—wanting to preserve a kind of epistemological innocence—he now reads voraciously, often working on three or four major texts for months on end, compulsively underlining crucial passages with his ever-present red pen.

Although the Irwin-Turrell-Wortz portion of A&T produced no objects, the knowledge engendered by the project was of such a profound nature that it altered the lives of all the participants. Edward Wortz changed careers; Irwin ceased to make objects and began to pursue a phenomenal art; and Turrell dropped out of sight for a time, then continued his involvement with nonobject work.[16]

The collaborative process so often undertaken in the scientific community seems to have few parallels in the art world, and when exceptions occur they are usually between scientist and artist, not artist and artist. Most artists seem to have a consuming need to pursue their investigations alone, without input or interference from another individual whose goals, almost by definition, must differ. The strong ego of the artist—without which he or she cannot function—just about prohibits real collaboration and seems, in fact, to be diametrically opposed to it.[17]

Retinal Replay Volume
in *Works in Spaces,* San Francisco Museum of Modern Art
February 9–April 8, 1973

The 1971–72 period was a particularly rich one for Irwin, during which he produced a number of major scrim pieces, works that were magnificent, unparalleled, profound. But now that his art had become ephemeral and "invisible," Irwin was faced with a problem of his own making: just how invisible was his work and what did that invisibility mean in terms of its public accessibility? A classic example from that period is *Retinal Replay Volume.* Writing about it in *Artnews,* the Bay Area critic Thomas Albright quoted Irwin's description of the installation procedure:

The difference between obscurity and elitism is availability—I may be obscure but I am not elite.
■ Robert Irwin

> *First I conditioned the light to an even, low ambience in the day by changing the skylight and at night by floating cool green and daylight fluorescent above the translucent glass ceiling. I covered the baseboard so that the walls would dominate the floor pattern. I removed or covered fixtures, plugs, outlets and so on, all of which were not to be seen in any objective sense. I then placed a string the width of the gallery slightly above eye level for the purpose of suspending your focus in space, caught between the string and the wall plane, allowing for the viewer's attention to hold on to the retinal afterimage that he would experience from the [Stephen] Antonakos and the [Dorothea] Rockburne pieces located in rooms to either side.... Isn't that as real as if I had put in fixtures and done a light show? But most people missed those events and tried to focus on the string as the only object of art.*[18]

The work was not titled during the exhibition (Irwin's early works seldom were—the titles are assigned afterward simply for the sake of identification), and viewers were not told that the piece dealt with retinal afterimages. Irwin often talks about his art as being "in the realm of pure research," and it seems clear that this piece operated in that arena.

The San Francisco piece was, to all intents and purposes, nonexistent. It consisted of a pure white room with a single string across it. There was no object and no focal point. The work consisted of the play of afterimages from Antonakos's light work in the next room and the sense of throbbing images from Rockburne's gallery on the other side. The most interesting aspect of the entire piece was that people saw only the white room and a piece of string—if they saw that—and they ignored the afterimage altogether, "reading it out." "People attempted to take the piece seriously," Irwin says of this work, and every day the guards dutifully lined people up to have them contemplate the string—thus "identifying the finger instead of the moon."

Irwin still talks about that piece. He loves it. Though he feels that it was extremely successful in relation to his own expectations for it, he does acknowledge that it was a failure on a cultural level. ("Art," he notes, "is a matter of cultural agreement.") He realized then that he was going to have to effect an interface of sorts between his expectations and those of the public.

Sometime in 1972–73 Irwin stopped making art and began a period of serious thinking that was to coincide with a period of wandering. As I noted in 1974:

> "Art" as it has been traditionally defined, even contemporarily, is no longer meaningful or useful to him. At this stage, he finds himself questioning its functions and purposes, as well as its ability or inability to function inside or outside "the system."

By current definition, Irwin is, in effect, no longer an "artist." By virtue of his own extended definition, however, he is. Whether or not our existing social structure can encompass an art form which produces no objects remains to be seen. His art will continue regardless.[19]

The following exchange in *Arts Magazine* in 1972 examined his quandary:

Butterfield: How are you personally planning to transfer information without objects and without words? This seems to me to be the crux of your dilemma.

Irwin: *I don't know. I do know that if I continue to work as I have, I will respond to the same stimuli as before and be exposed to the same possibilities. I need the perspective of distance, and time is my only tool right now. This is why I am not, at this point, doing anything.*

How I manifest *what it is I am thinking, or, more to the point, what I am* feeling *is separate from what I am* really *doing and* not *the crux of the issue. What I am doing is trying to find out more about what it is that I sense. When I am interested in that direct (temporary) social contribution, I will confront the questions of how I communicate.*

Butterfield: So what will you do now?

Irwin: *Nothing. It's obvious, isn't it? To do* anything *as we recognize it and presently define that right now is to go backwards.*

Butterfield: But you are only halfway through your creative existence—what are you going to do for the rest of your life?

Irwin: *That's an interesting question.*[20]

Irwin went on the road. Divesting himself of his studio and all other possessions, he began an extended period of wandering that was to take him to colleges, universities, and museums across the country. Aware that his works were becoming increasingly obscure, he sought to make his ideas more accessible by making himself more accessible. Irwin has always gone to a given locale in response to a request, never on his own initiation. There was a ripple and then a groundswell, and by the time he stopped counting, sometime in 1981, he had spent time at more than one hundred fifty institutions. This activity not only gradually built a matrix of new information within which Irwin's art could be examined, but it also gave him a valuable sounding board.

Irwin is lucid and highly organized, with a multivalent intelligence and an insatiable curiosity. Intuitive and essentially self-educated, he terms himself a rustic. It was with great excitement that he went into universities where he encountered scientists, psychologists, theoreticians, philosophers, theologians, and historians whose thinking served both as feedback and as springboard for his own ideas.

Irwin passionately needs an audience. He thinks best on his feet, when challenged. He has become so good at this particular form of presentation that more than one critic has chosen to review his personality rather than his art. For example, Hilton Kramer, reviewing Irwin's 1977 exhibition at the Whitney Museum of American Art in New York, commented:

Anyone who has ever heard him on the platform will attest, I think, to the special spell he is able to cast. With his relaxed manner and striking good looks, and gifted with a mellifluous speaking voice that imparts an air of sanctity and sweetness to whatever it is he is saying, he makes a very appealing and persuasive figure. His message too—to the extent that it can ever be separated from his performance—has "spiritual" appeal. For Mr. Irwin casts himself in the role of esthetic saint, who, having renounced the world of material art objects, has found salvation in a higher realm of perception.[21]

During his period of wandering—sometimes en route to a lecture, sometimes simply "on the road," sometimes in the desert, sometimes in cityscapes—Irwin created scores of works he calls "Sight Lines." These private works were for his education only and were intended to remain in obscurity. Writing in the catalog for Irwin's 1975 exhibition at the Museum of Contemporary Art in Chicago, Ira Licht commented that the Sight Lines were "categories of artistic activity idiosyncratic to Irwin." Licht noted that there were then more than forty-three of them in Arizona, California, Colorado, Nevada, New Mexico, Texas, and Utah. He continued:

> Irwin will drive into the desert from time to time for several days seeking the special atmospheric conditions peculiar to that environment, particular effects of light and space, the almost hallucinatory quality of the desert. Most of these manifestations are transitory and ephemeral, occurring only in rare coincidences of climate. Irwin notes them, sometimes setting a marker or pointer to direct attention mutely in the proper direction. These are the "places," and "sight-lines." No other information exists; there is no guide, no guarantee that the phenomena will reoccur. But this is the situation toward which Irwin has been aiming; pure perception of the transformation of our environment through the actions of light and space and without the intrusion of the identity of the "artist." It no longer seems necessary to physically mark these events; their existence and/or awareness of them can be carried philosophically by the dialogue of immanence.[22]

Irwin also continued making scrim pieces, each one with a different presence determined by the site, and he began his involvement with walls, frames, and portals. This consuming interest in the framing device stems from his desire both to expand the parameters of painting and to explore the traditional idea of the painting as a "window on the world." Since Irwin's activity from the mid-1970s to the present has been far too extensive to document in its entirety, an overview of some of his major installations and exhibitions must suffice.

Eye-Level Room Division
in _Robert Irwin,_ Pace Gallery, New York
December 1–28, 1973

Soft Wall
in _Robert Irwin: Installation,_ Pace Gallery
December 7, 1974–January 4, 1975

Irwin's first commercial gallery installation in New York was at Pace Gallery in 1973; he followed it with another at Pace in 1974. They both were difficult and uncompromising works, primarily because they had no parallels with other art experiences. As Larry Rosing explained the 1973 installation: "Irwin transformed this . . . gallery space into a magical environment by building a solid wall, its top just above eye level, which bisected the gallery and left the far side fascinatingly inaccessible. Like the discs and the scrim pieces, it was carefully lighted; like them it induced a quiet meditativeness."[23]

I suspect that few viewers encountering a long white wall in an empty gallery perceived the way that the walls, floor, ceiling, light, and shadow formed a multidimensional space with a Mondrian-like symmetry and balance. The work had an otherness that was quietly compelling.

Robert Irwin
Eye-Level Room Division
Installation, Pace Gallery,
New York, 1973

For those willing to spend time with it, the piece took on a heightened three-dimensional presence. What to some looked initially like a sculpture or object could be seen as an environment with an uncanny presence: "We organize our perceptions of the physical world into abstract structures," Irwin said. "What we see is what we seek to see. There is little place in our frame of reference for 'not seeing.'"[24]

This "not seeing" was even more critical with Irwin's *Soft Wall* at Pace in 1974. He stretched a floor-to-ceiling scrim the length of the gallery's longest wall, approximately two feet away from the back wall. Evanescent and softly lit, the scrim took on ethereal qualities totally different from the geometric angularity of the 1973 work. The gallery lights played down the surface of the scrim, dematerializing it. Those of us following Irwin's development began the slow move toward "not seeing"; once accomplished, it changed the process of perceiving radically and irreversibly.

I begin to see things which are in themselves contradictions to the whole logic of seeing. Since we perceive through a system of reference points that we have been conditioned to believe are real, we allow ourselves small room for expansion. Some things are meaningful and some things are meaningless to you, so actually you have a structured way of looking at the world that means certain things probably are totally invisible.

■ Robert Irwin, in David Rush, "Robert Irwin," ***Artweek*****, February 15, 1975, p. 4.**

Wall Division—Portal
in *Robert Irwin: Installation,* Mizuno Gallery, Los Angeles
January 29–February 23, 1974

Scrim Veil
in *Robert Irwin: Installation,* Mizuno Gallery
October 21–November 15, 1975

Wall Division—Portal, which consisted of a long white wall inset with a low, rectangular portal, was seen to best advantage just before sunset. The soundlessness of the room created an ambience in which the real wall and room seemed to slip away, leaving behind a presence, a force, and a strong, blinding sensation of light. (One of the more interesting aspects of sensory deprivation is that when the light is blinding or intense it is impossible to hear well.) In this work the distinctions between walls, floor, and portal vanished. The shadow on the underside of the portal (like the ephemeral smoky bands on Irwin's late discs) became the only real image, hovering somewhere above eye level. The participant who let go was able to "perceive himself perceiving."

Irwin's next installation at Mizuno Gallery was at once empty and loaded with information. His now-familiar scrim, stretched tightly from the ceiling, had an almost blue tonality. Held taut by a black metal bar, the scrim ended somewhere below the participant's eye level. A mirror image of that black band appeared on the floor beneath it, extending up the walls to the edge of the scrim and thus forming a transparent rectangle. The space above the black bar would come into shape perceptually as a solid, then suddenly slip out of focus, causing the void below to become the true reality. The piece changed continuously throughout the day as the light, at first pale and yellow, became cooler and then slowly turned soft mauve as the light disappeared.[25]

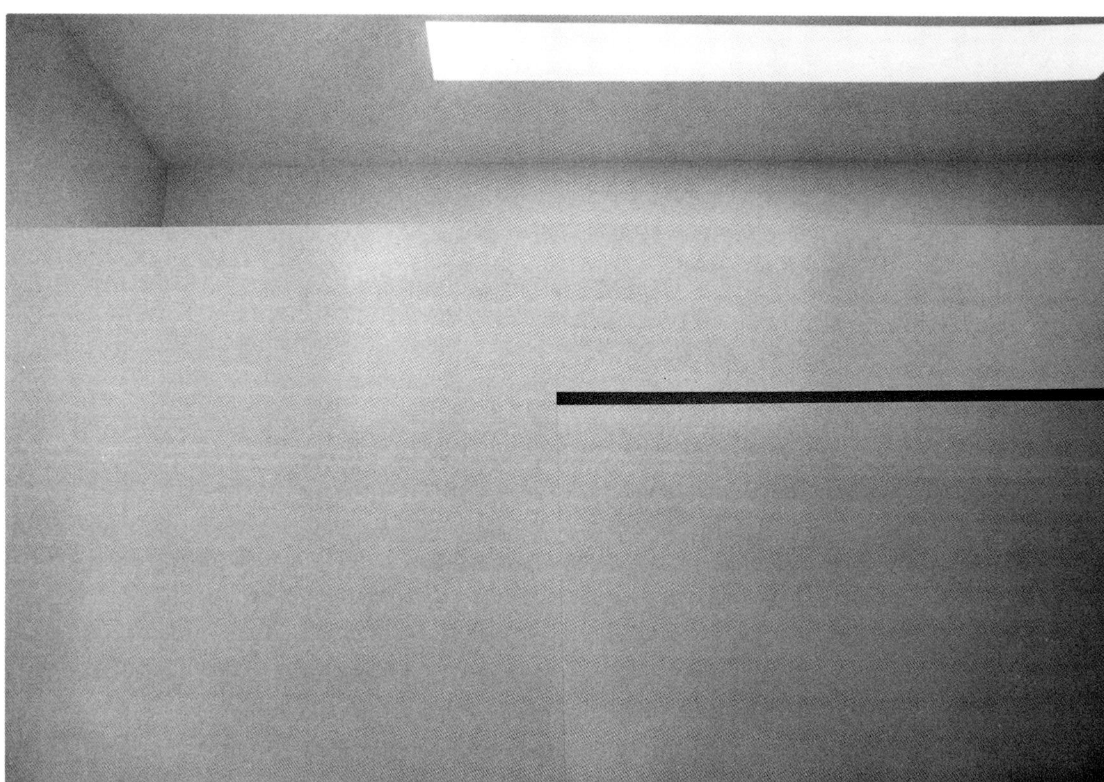

Robert Irwin
Wall Division—Portal
Installation, Mizuno Gallery,
Los Angeles, 1974

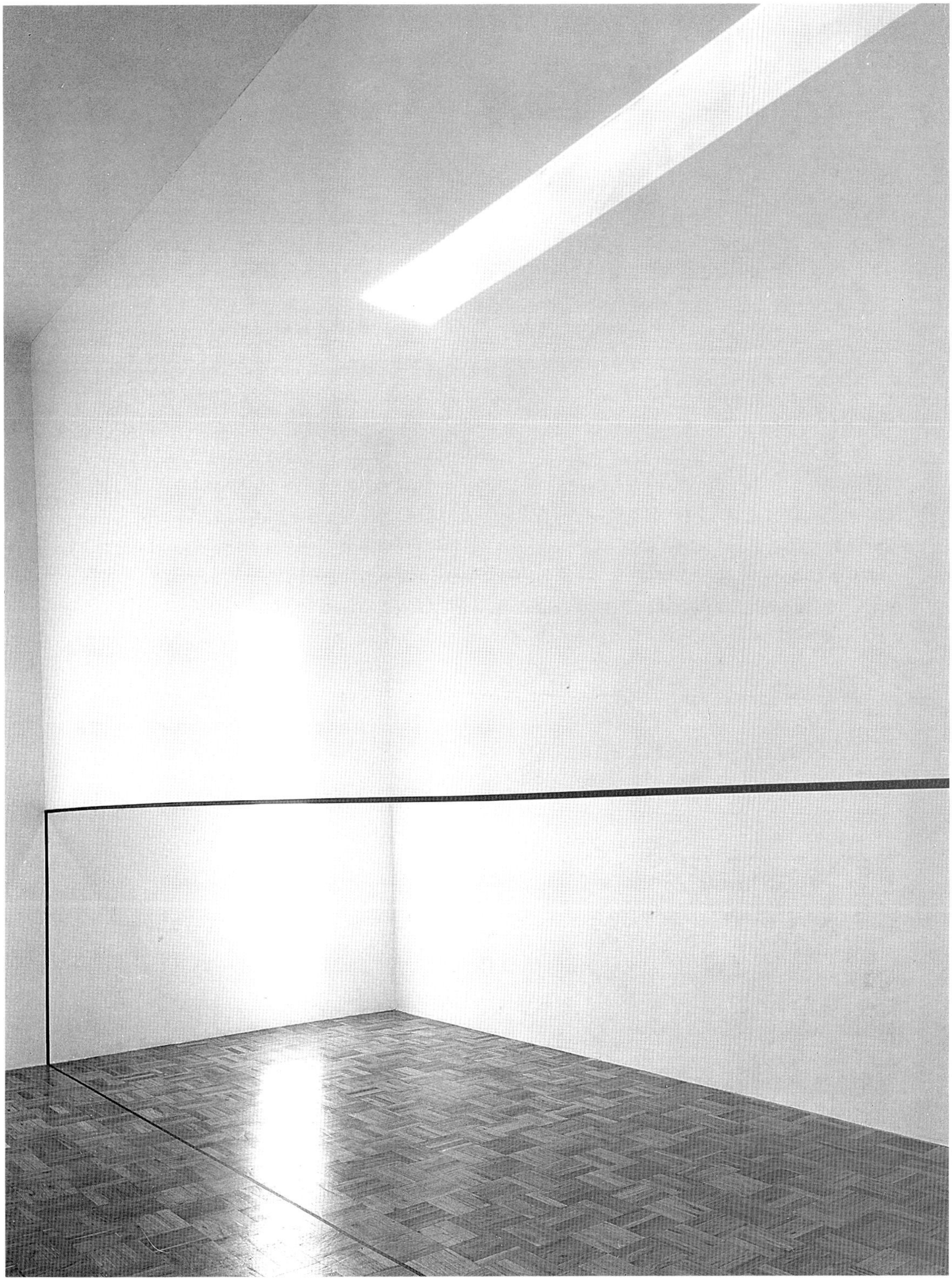

Robert Irwin
Scrim Veil
Installation, Mizuno Gallery,
Los Angeles, 1975

Passage Window—Outdoors
in *A View Through,* Art Galleries, California State University, Long Beach
September 22–October 19, 1975

This simple yet powerful piece has become the logo for the Art Galleries. Irwin created a large-scale white frame outside the art department, filling the entire breezeway between two buildings. His structure measured just over nine by sixteen feet and had an aperture of slightly more than six by nine feet. Clearly a frame, it forced a shift in focus from real to pictorial to real space. Looking through it, one saw the winding paths of the campus, the green lawns, the large trees that it framed. One became aware of looking only at the activity within the frame and ignoring everything outside it.[26] The work was very much about questioning one's system of focus—an essential part of Irwin's ongoing inquiry.

Portal Room, 1973, and *Window Room,* 1973
Giuseppe Panza di Biumo, Varese, Italy
installations completed 1975

In an eighteenth-century Italian villa, an hour and a half by train from Milan, is a secret garden. In the old stable area, behind great wooden doors, Count Giuseppe Panza di Biumo has installed a series of individual "rooms" by Irwin, Maria Nordman, James Turrell, Doug Wheeler, and others. As each of these spaces is unlocked, a microcosm is unveiled. Experiencing the Light and Space portion of the collection has an extraordinary dreamlike quality. The intense blue of the Italian sky, the green garden dotted with bright rosebushes, the ageless stones that line the corridor and form the arches of the stable colonnade make a curiously appropriate setting for experiential art. In this context one realizes with a shock that this work is not contemporary. It is not that it lacks the "shock of the new," for it certainly has that. But it is not an art of now, tied to this particular moment. For those fortunate enough to view Count Panza's collection in situ, the timelessness and historicity of this art become clear—and oddly reassuring.

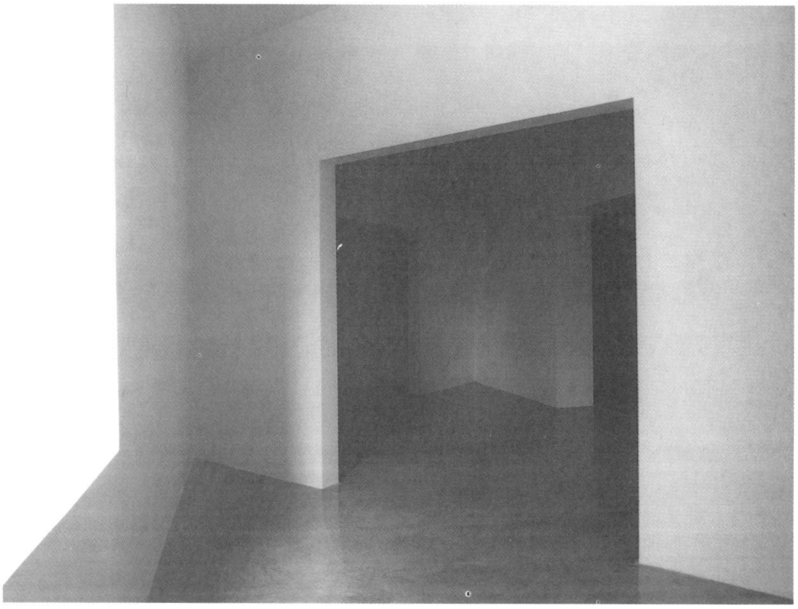

On the day I visited the collection, the caretaker had pinned his underwear to a clothesline he'd hung in an arch of the colonnade. Neither the count nor his polite caretaker apologized for the laundry, and it obviously had as much right to be there as the art. Panza's collection (only a very small portion of which is exhibited in the old stable area) is extraordinary in its inclusions and impeccable in its installations (the housekeeping required by these immaculate white spaces must be considerable), yet it is almost unbearably unpretentious. Here is art that is a part of life, that is lived with because it is loved and understood, and that is offered to the visitor in the same spirit.

Robert Irwin
Portal Room, 1973
Permanent installation, Giuseppe
Panza di Biumo, Varese, Italy

Robert Irwin
Window Room (exterior), 1973
Permanent installation, Giuseppe
Panza di Biumo, Varese, Italy
This corridor, which has scrim
running lengthwise at right, leads
to *Window Room.*

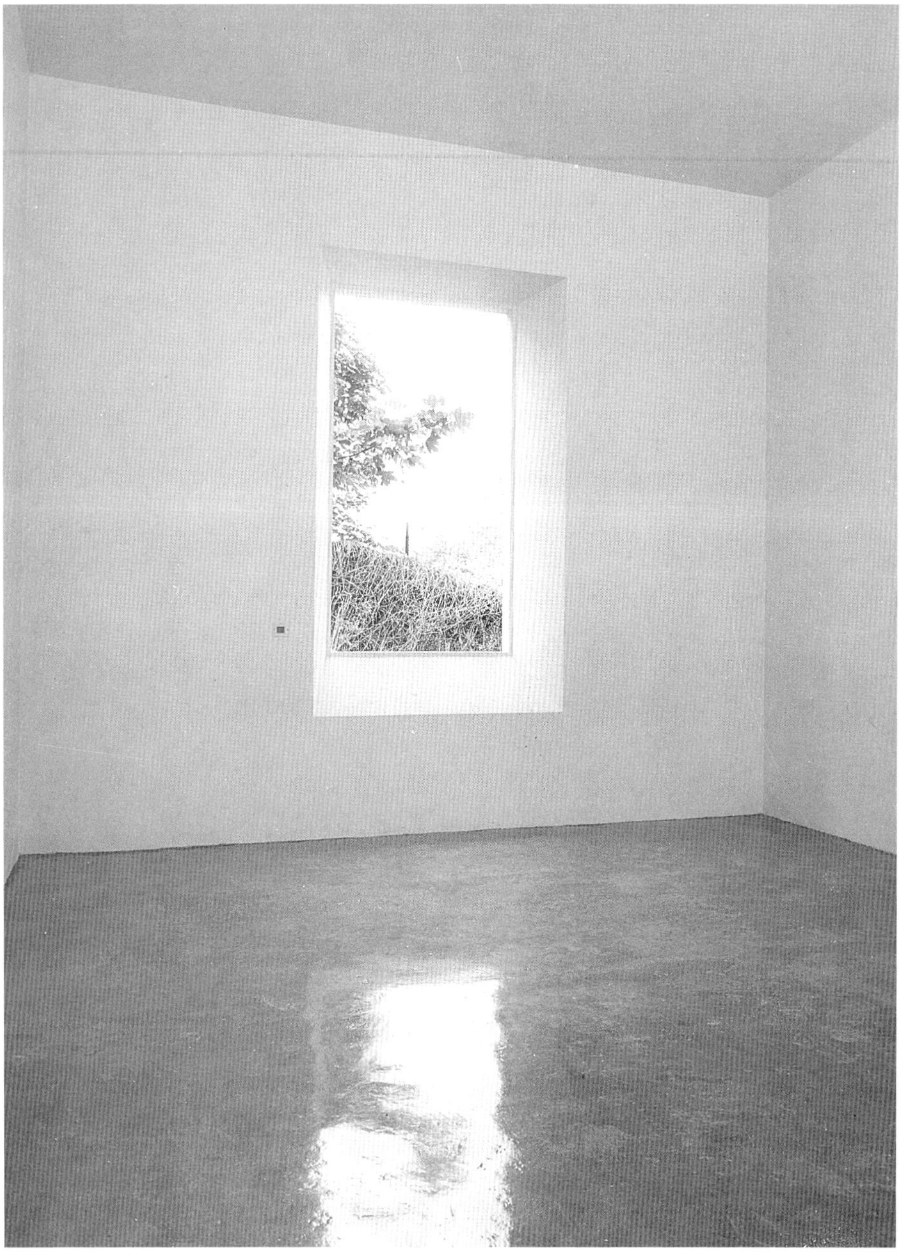

Irwin's two window pieces in Panza's collection are classic examples of his portal works. The pieces were conceived in direct response to Irwin's first experience of the collection in Varese. "You arrive via a high-walled, corridorlike street with bits of Italian gardens visible through gates. Once you're inside the villa, Panza walks you slowly through the collection, unlocking one room after another—vaultlike rooms, airless spaces, which are filled with works by Don Judd, Robert Morris, and so on." Repeated time and time again, the experience became claustrophobic for Irwin, and the idea of opening up the space to the outside and letting in the soft light and natural sounds seemed to him to be the perfect antidote.

Irwin's first window, empty of glass and open to the outside world, is set into the wall of a forced-perspective room entered through a large portal. With tongue in cheek, Irwin has presented a classical Italianate painting, complete with a Tiepolo sky, dark cypress trees that drape the frame in Baroque fashion, and a church tower in the distance. By framing reality in this and his other Varese piece, he provided answers to his much-quoted rhetorical questions: "Can there be art without artifice?" and "Can art lie equally in the incidental?" By simply framing what was already there, he answered those questions by creating an art without artifice.

Irwin's second window piece in Panza's collection is approached through a long, scrim-walled corridor that leads into a small room bathed in light. The room is open to the elements; blue sky and dark green trees beckon from outside. Sunlight streaming through a window on the facing wall pours across the floor and drifts through a scrim, which emits a softened halation that gradually fades down the corridor.

Robert Irwin
Window Room (interior), 1973
Permanent installation, Giuseppe
Panza di Biumo, Varese, Italy

Robert Irwin
Museum of Contemporary Art, Chicago
November 8, 1975–January 4, 1976

This modest eight-work, mid-career survey provided the first opportunity for an art audience east of the Rockies to examine the progression of Irwin's work. Included in the exhibition were early and late line paintings, a dot painting, a painted aluminum disc, a painted acrylic disc, an acrylic column, *Black-Line Volume,* and *Scrim V Volume. Black-Line Volume,* an altered-room environment, was one of the strongest and most difficult that Irwin had done since his first piece at the San Francisco Museum of Modern Art. Here an ostensibly empty three-sided room was subtly altered by the addition of a line of black tape that visually drew in the fourth side of the space.

Because Irwin's work requires a willing suspension of disbelief, it is difficult for many viewers. With the San Francisco piece some assumed the string to be the work. With the first show at Pace, some saw only a wall. And the Chicago piece? Thomas Albright commented:

Robert Irwin
Black-Line Volume
Installation,
Museum of Contemporary Art,
Chicago, 1975–76

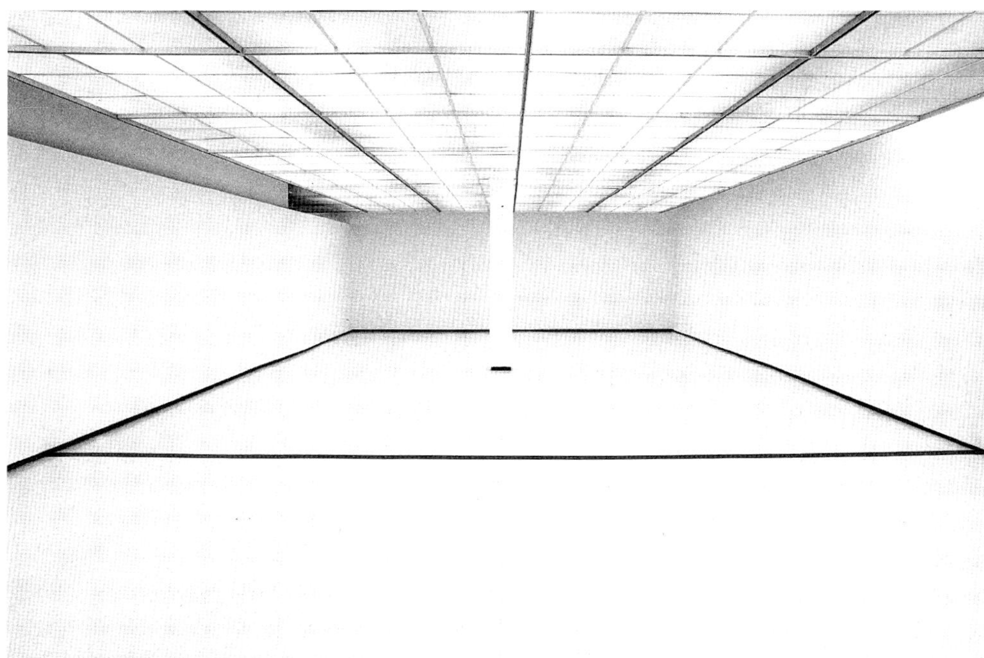

Irwin considers it one of his more successful pieces. On entering the gallery, which had been emptied for his use, Irwin noticed the standard black kickboard edge around the wall just above the floor, and a curiously positioned column in a cul-de-sac that extended from the larger room. By laying a strip of black paper across the floor, he was able to throw these existing architectural features into sharp perceptual relief; at least "four out of ten people who had been working there for years asked if I had built the column. The beauty was, there was nothing there—no art, no hand, no identity."[27]

Roberta Smith saw the same exhibition entirely differently:

Irwin ran a single strip of 4 1/2 inch wide black tape across the floor of a large, empty gallery which had bland, grey-beige linoleum floors and a square column at its center. The tape connected with black molding recesses at the bottom of the room's three walls; it provided the fourth line in a rectangle. The resultant black rectangle was not what you "looked at"—there was actually nothing to focus on—but soon it brought the space into focus with a distinct visual snap. From inside, the light in the area seemed different, more substantial, and the wall color began to shift ambiguously. From outside the area, the tape seemed to lift the plane off the floor upward in your field of vision, and it also made the room seem wider and shallower than it really was.... The area was transformed into a separate volume; it seemed to lift out of the museum and become so exclusively visual that it could have been almost any size.[28]

As if to atone for the difficulty of this work, Irwin presented *Scrim V Volume* for his second installation in Chicago. For many, this work was much easier to see. Diaphanous fabric was used to create a seemingly solid wedge or light trap, as Smith noted:

The scrim piece...is one of Irwin's largest, and like the Walker's [*Slant Light Volume*], it functions somewhat like an enormous white volume cutting into space. It is essentially a closed-off wedge-shaped corridor, the sides of which start at two pillars near the museum's entrance and meet at a far wall, some 80 feet away.... The two panels of scrim were always a different distance from each other and from the wall they generally paralleled. As you moved, whole chunks of architecture and space were constantly dropping in and out of view.[29]

These two installations, like Irwin's other early nonobject works shown in museums, ceased to exist after the exhibition ended. As the artist has noted:

The pieces are given to the place of execution and so far they don't seem to know what to do with them. It's strange, but when you don't place a material worth on things, it's difficult for many to weigh just the aesthetic worth, which raises some interesting questions about our assumptions of permanence and the degrees to which our commitment to it constructs our consciousness.[30]

Robert Irwin
Whitney Museum of American Art, New York
April 16–May 29, 1977

In 1977 Irwin took on what was initially intended to be a twenty-year retrospective at the Whitney Museum of American Art in New York. Instead, he used the opportunity offered by the museum "to exhibit transitions from earlier work, and to ground an extended inquiry of the last vestiges of classical thought."

On a large wall at the entrance to the Whitney was installed a group of plans and photographs related to Irwin's *New York Projections.*

NEW YORK PROJECTIONS

This Whitney Museum project is intended to act out *(in on-site installations), illustrate (in aerial photographs of New York), and* develop the argumentation *(in catalog essay)* for perception as the essential subject of art. *Assuming that content is not only the bond of knowledge, but the basis for perception/conception, this exhibition has been developed contextually. By holding the most essential contextual threads (those elements taken from perception and used in "art," i.e., line, shape, form, color, etc.) and removing in turn each of the additional contextual threads (imagery, permanence, method, painting, sculpture, etc.) which have come to be thought of as givens in the recognition of what is art, we arrive at the essential subject of art. In effect, this is accomplished by a principal change in the relationship of the indicator (object of art) and what it is that is indicated (subject of art) from their acting as one in the object to their being one in the aesthetic perception of the observer/individual.*

Robert Irwin
Scrim Veil—Black Rectangle—Natural Light
Installation, Whitney Museum of American Art, New York, 1977

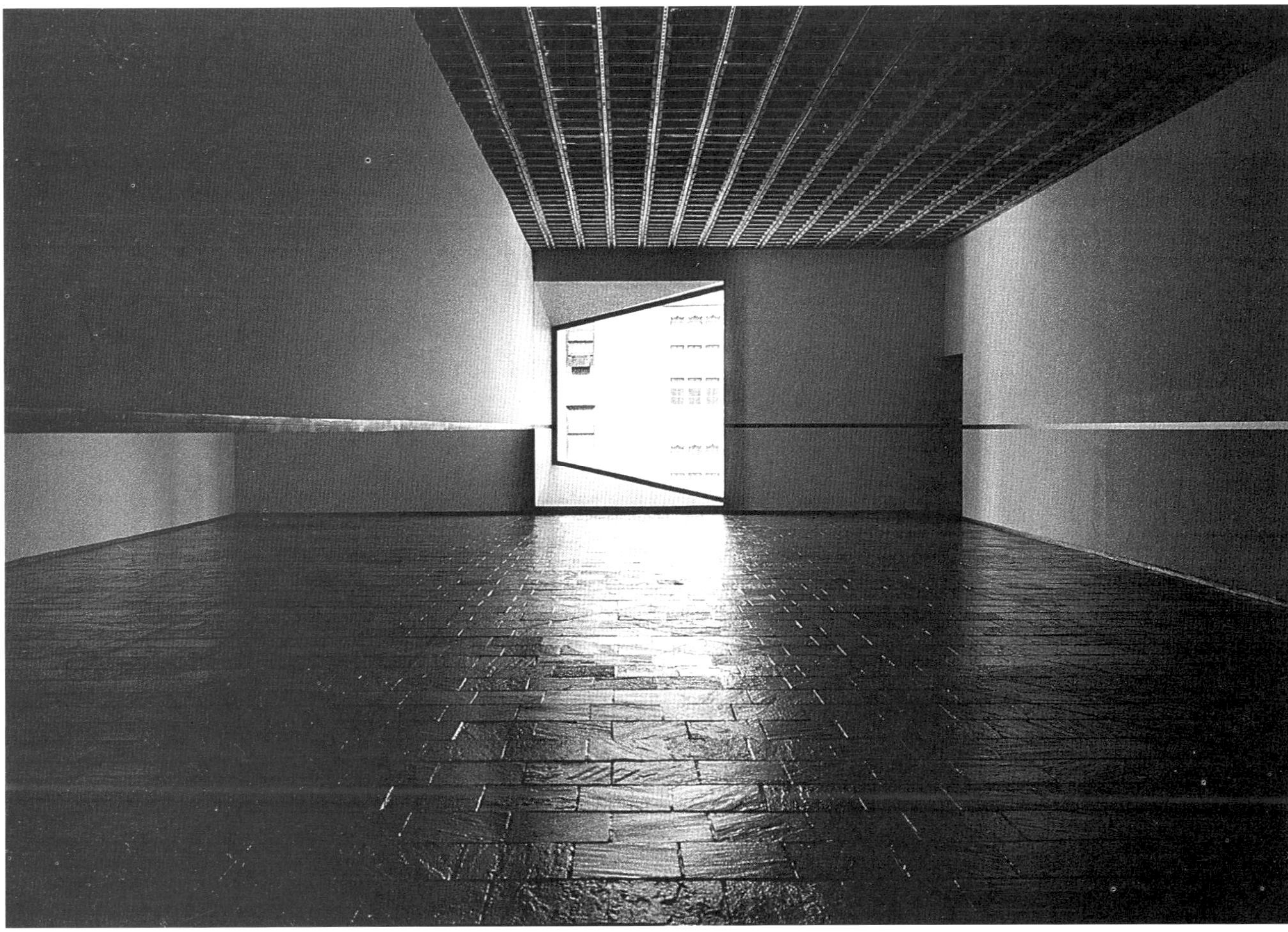

Continuing the questioning begun with his late paintings (which had challenged the boundaries of the frame and object as a "given" in art), Irwin created a large-scale, nonobject installation for the fourth floor of the Whitney Museum. This work, *Scrim Veil—Black Rectangle—Natural Light,* was the most imposing aspect of the exhibition. The entire fourth floor of the museum was given over to the piece. The black slate floor, gridded ceiling, and exterior window all became harmoniously unified elements. The room was bisected by a scrim that began at ceiling height and terminated in a hard, black bar at eye level, leaving the space empty between the bar and the floor. The hardness/softness of the veil met the hardness of the wall at each end of the room. The ceiling and floor were visually united by a black line that ran horizontally around the room near eye level, meeting the black bar of the scrim at each end wall.

All lights were removed from the ceiling, and the only source of illumination was the forced-perspective window that looked out on the brick facade of a building across Madison Avenue. The room was brightest near the window and became quite dark at the far end. During the day sun spilled through the curious geometry of the Whitney's window, misting the scrim and veiling the room in an atmosphere similar to that seen when a heavy fog enshrouds buildings, both intensifying their shape and obscuring their reality. Irwin placed a floodlight so that after dark it beamed in from across the street, transforming the window into a trapezoid of light. This hard spill of artificial moonlight was thrown across the flinty blackness of the floor, linking its gridlike configurations to the equally stark grid of the ceiling. The light also poured along the edges of the scrim and was diffused through the mesh of the fabric. The floodlight illuminated the exterior as well, defining the brutal geometry of the building and uniting outside with inside.

Day or night, one could not look *at* the work; one had to let go of logical seeing. The scrim might initially seem solid, and then suddenly the focus would shift and reality would become the heavy rectangle of nothingness below it. Seldom before had nothingness been so palpable. Mark Stevens noted, "Walking into that room, an observer knew right away that something had changed; it was like being in a forest when things go suddenly quiet."[31]

Irwin said of this room:

> *This was a large space for New York... and I wanted to leave it as "empty" as possible.... I especially liked the qualities of the large black slate floor plane and I left it completely open.... I then took all of the light fixtures off the ceiling, leaving the visual texture of the bee-hive grid.... I used the large "forced perspective" window on Madison Avenue as the sole source of light—which made a dramatic graded transition of shading down the full length of the room which became approximately 50% gray at the far end.... I then painted the facing wall (which of course was lighter) a matching 50% gray... a subliminal move that most challenged our perceptual security, leaving the individual viewer perceptually acute....*
>
> *The effect was a moment of disorientation... a breakdown of our perceptual habituation... followed by the necessity for a kind of first-hand perceiving, capable of revealing the subtle qualities of light and space.*

Irwin also developed three "interventions" outside the museum. First he painted a black plane at the intersection of Forty-second Street and Fifth Avenue. He next inscribed a space at the World Trade Towers by stretching a cable between the two lower buildings. Then he proposed to draw a grid with lasers at the fourth level between Fifty-seventh Street and the Pan Am Building on Park Avenue. (Regrettably, this portion was not executed because of a lack of funds.)

Irwin followed up by "indicating" (and here there was no art per se) "three *existing* visual phenomena.... Each of these was far more interesting and more beautiful than anything I had made," Irwin states. One of these was the pattern of black shadows that march up and down Park Avenue virtually every afternoon. Another was the beauty of a line of newly installed pink mercury-vapor lights circumscribing the dark green rectangle of Central Park. The third was the changing city grid—irregular in Lower Manhattan and becoming more formal as the city moved uptown and as city planners responded less to the cues of the natural environment and more to the abstractions of a logical geometry.

These works brilliantly underscored Irwin's theories. As he wrote in the Whitney catalog for his show:

> *Art as an aesthetic inquiry is a non-thing. Which is to say that, like time and space, it has no actual physical properties, or infinite physical qualities. There are in aesthetic experience potentially as many "arts" as there are encounters with its incidences in the world. In confusing the art/object of "art" with the subject of art, we objectively tried to hold to the idea of one transcending art. While there is no one transcending "art," there is one infinite subject: The subject of art is aesthetic perception.*[32]

These New York Projections and the fourth-floor installation were conceived by Irwin as "one inter-connecting work, a *metacontext,* held together and recognizable in its extremes by the shared graphic elements."[33]

Just as modern art questioned the ideas of pictorial imagery, content, and meaning, so Irwin, as a painter, questioned the idea of pictorial space and finally the frame of painting itself. In the Whitney project he extended this inquiry by questioning the concepts of permanence, of the art object as art, of the art place as a necessary frame of reference, and finally even the concept that the act of making art objects is essential to an art experience.[34]

Pictorial Art	Modern Art	Contemporary Art	Interventions	Indications
		4th floor installation Whitney Museum	4th floor installation Whitney Museum	Park Ave Central Park City Grid
Imagery	Visual Vocabulary**	———	———	Visual Vocabulary**
Content	Pure Feelings**	———	———	Pure Feelings**
Meaning	Experiential Knowing**	———	———	Experiential Knowing**
Composition	Composition*	Particularness**	Determined Relations**	Determined Relations**
Pictorial Space	Pictorial Space*	Site Specific Space**	Space**	Space**
Permanence	Permanence*	Impermanence**	Conditionalness**	Conditionalness**
Frame/Object	Frame/Object*	Frame/Object*		Particularness**
Artplace	Artplace	Artplace*	Place**	Place**
Artmaking	Artmaking	Artmaking	Artmaking*	↓
				Phenomenal Perceptions**
Elements	Elements	Elements	Elements	Elements
Intention (Art)	Intention	Intention	Intention	Intention

Note: "Elements" is the essential contextual thread—"Intention" is the ultimate ground

*Concepts being questioned **Concepts being developed

■ **Robert Irwin**

> *The question I wanted to put to the intelligentsia of the art world was: If we take the words* perceptions, aesthetics, *and* feelings *as bearing directly on what we mean by the term "Art" can we hold the dialogue for art to be the equal of* "making"*?*

> *The point of this exercise is to distinguish the pure subject from the more obvious practices of art, to question just what is it that art uniquely contributes to the overall scheme of human activities—that justifies its exalted position in our society.*

A key aspect of Irwin's theories is his belief that the meaning of modern art lies in its responsibility for eliminating the hierarchical structures that had informed classical art and thought: "What we have witnessed in this history of modern art is the destructuring of meaning as ordered by either a transcendent belief, or singular concepts of truth or social good, by which all subsequent things and action will be measured and judged." Irwin laments that this key change—embodied as merging of figure and ground—has been trivialized by a pseudo-formalist argument that carried it to its lowest common denominator, "physical flatness," when, he says, "the real issue is far more interesting in its complexity and consequences."

> *The phenomenological reduction that was the feature of the nineteenth century brought us, at the end of the century, to a beginning place where we could ask: "How might it be otherwise?" Now, as a consequence late in this century our questions are: "What would a non-hierarchical structure look like? How would it underwrite the questions of understanding, judgment, and practice?"*

Irwin maintains that the meaning of the art of our time lies in how we answer these questions: "Such fundamental questions will necessarily result in a change in our individual consciousness, and how we perceptually/conceptually form our world view *is* the model for all our subsequent social actions and institutions."

In March 1979 Irwin executed three works of major importance in three separate areas of the country: on the West Coast, on the East Coast, and dead center. The implementation of these pieces marked the end of what had amounted to a two-year pause in making tangible work after the artist's exhibition at the Whitney. These three pieces form a trilogy representing three different aspects of Irwin's work. The one at Berkeley was so large and complex in its gestalt that it was overwhelming. The Kansas piece was small, soft, misted, and romantic; the upstate New York piece was hard, formal, and elegant yet brutalist.

Suddenly there seemed to be a troubling divergence in the work of this artist whose hallmarks had always been dazzlingly clear logic and consistency. This seeming incongruity was not only in the feel of each work, which differed considerably from piece to piece, but in the materials. In retrospect, however, these works can all be seen as exemplifying the same attitude toward art: it was clearly the context that determined the materials and the gestures of each piece. As Irwin brought context to the fore as the critical issue, the game opened up and once again all the rules were new.

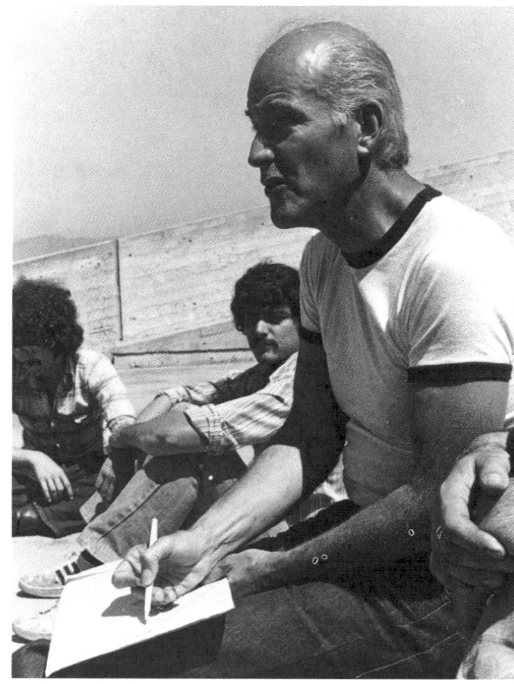

Robert Irwin: Untitled (Three Triangulated Light Planes) in *Andre, Buren, Irwin, Nordman: Space as Support* University Art Museum, University of California, Berkeley March 4–April 29, 1979

Space as Support provided an opportunity for four artists—Irwin, Carl Andre, Daniel Buren, and Maria Nordman—with four different approaches to create installations in the same space at different times. The University Art Museum is a difficult space. A series of wedge-shaped segments fans out to create multistoried open galleries connected by ramps. The bottom floor—a large open area bordered on one side by zigzagging glass walls—often presents a virtually impossible setting for art (the gray cement surface of its walls detracts from paintings, and its scale tends to swallow sculpture). For a situational artist it is a uniquely challenging space.

Irwin took on the architecture with light. Not the gentle, softened, natural light that he had utilized to great advantage over the years, but fluorescent light, glaring and strident. Working with Peerless Lighting, a local manufacturer, Irwin designed a metal-cased fluorescent fixture that was so simple, elegant, and beautifully finished that it was a classic example of good design. Devising his schema from blueprints of the building, Irwin installed these lighting fixtures by the hundreds, using laser beams as a tool to fix installation points from one balcony ceiling to another or from one wedge-shaped gallery to its opposite across the way. He flung his lines of fluorescent light back and forth across the full length and breadth of the building like *Star Wars* swordplay.

If, in its stridency (the exhibition's curator, Mark Rosenthal, called it a "perceptual shock"), this was not the most beautiful of Irwin's pieces, if the acid green tinge of the light was too hard, too bright, too unwavering in its intensity, the work nevertheless underscored his thesis. By responding to the site rather than ignoring it, the artist emerged the victor in what had seemed to be an extremely uneven battle.

Robert Irwin as artist-in-residence at the San Francisco Art Institute, 1977

Robert Irwin
Untitled (Three Triangulated Light Planes)
Installation, University Art Museum, Berkeley, California, 1979

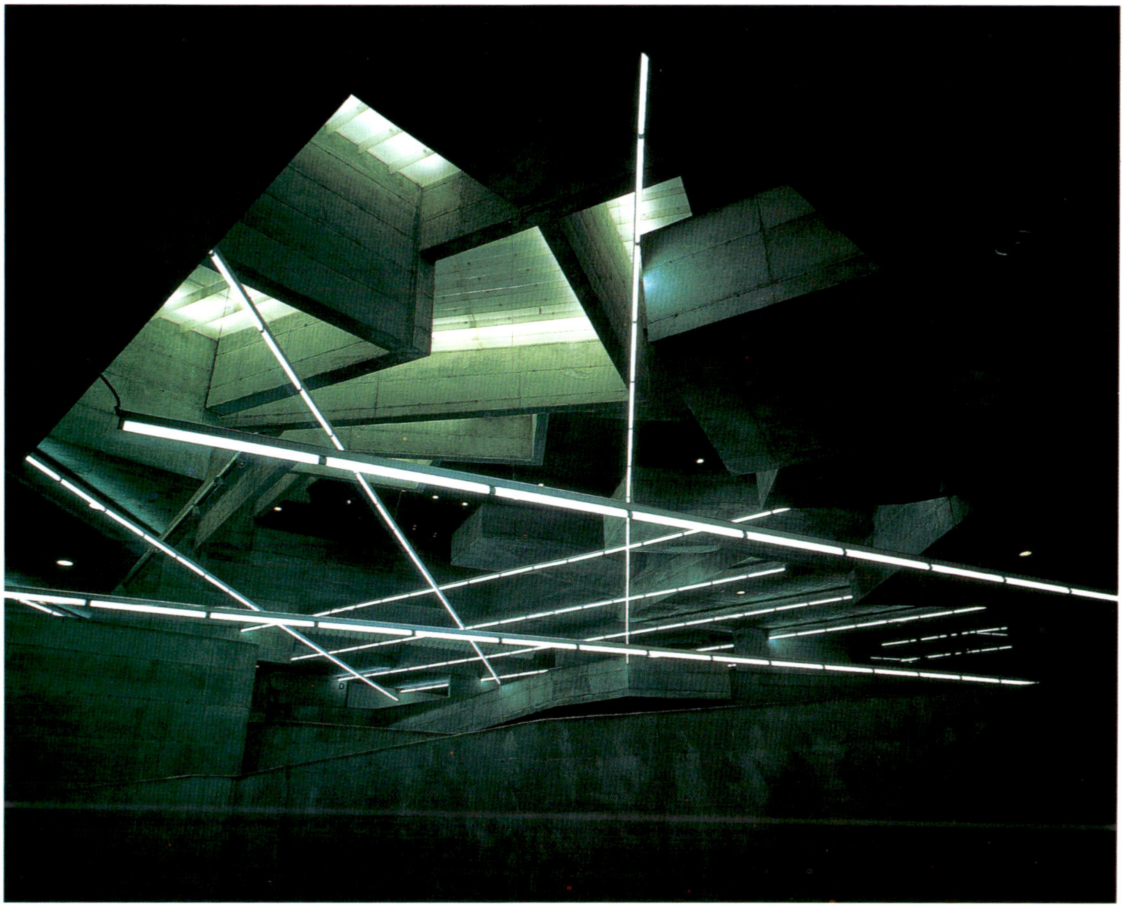

Installation
Helen Foresman Spencer Gallery, University of Kansas, Lawrence
May 1–July 15, 1979

Halfway across the country, two golden scrims cocooned the second-floor galleries of a Kansas museum. The scrims ran the length of two corridors that led to the galleries and overlooked the atrium below. As a result, one viewed the African collection and the Pre-Columbian collection through the veil—almost as if through a mist of time. So, too, with the Spanish gallery below. As at Count Panza's, Irwin worked with tongue in cheek; here he forced the participant to view art history through a kind of veil of time.

Since Irwin has seldom had the opportunity to execute a piece in a museum with a collection primarily of earlier art, the Spencer installation offered an opportunity to see him work with great sensitivity in an unusual context. His installation—warm, rounded, buttery—echoed the Mediterranean quality of the building and was enhanced by the golden light from large Spanish-style chandeliers in the atrium. The participant became acutely sensitive to this warm, softened atmosphere for viewing the great artifacts from past centuries. Irwin had created a work that was all of a piece, and one slid from the past to the present without any sense of rupture.

Installation
in *Christo, Di Suvero, Irwin, Segal*
Roy M. Neuberger Gallery, State University
of New York, Purchase
April 2–May 21, 1979

In the chill of upstate New York, surrounded by the stark trees of late winter and the last patches of melting snow, the dark, cold buildings of the State University of New York at Purchase stand out harshly against the landscape. The harshness continues into the gallery, where the gridded structure of the black brick interior walls made such an impossible environment for contemporary art that white walls have been installed to provide a clean, white frame in which to hang work. Through the central window of the gallery one can see an ancient cemetery, its starkness heightened by a few jagged trees. On the darkest side of the gallery is a small courtyard where a single George Rickey sculpture moves morosely in the still, iced air.

On this site Irwin created the coldest, toughest, and most brutal of his pieces to date. Focusing on the false walls, he painted them pure white, filling in all the scrapes and nail holes so they formed a continuous whole rather than remaining individual parts. On the courtyard side of the gallery he covered the floor-to-ceiling windows with a smoky blue-gray gelatinous material, generally used to tint shop windows or automobiles to prevent glare. To intensify the contrast Irwin affixed white Con-tact paper to the floor on the lighter side and black Con-tact paper on the darker side. Spotlights were aimed to get maximum vibrancy from the white walls. The opposite side was equally intense in its density. The two sides reversed and echoed each other, an effect enhanced by the mirrorlike coating on the windows of the dark side, which picked up the image of the opposite walls and held it like an apparition. There was an intellectual elegance and clarity to this work, a sense not of beauty but of rightness.

Room with Twin Skylights, Facing Wall Removed
Malinda Wyatt Gallery, Venice, California, May 1980

At eight o'clock in the morning, the street was deserted. White brick arches formed a colonnade at 76 Market Street, where the gallery was located. Raking sunlight outlined the symmetry of the arches, and dark shadows hovered under the roof, forming a hard line where the edges of the building met the light.

Irwin had removed the front wall of the gallery and altered its interior. There appeared to be no solid architecture behind the arches. The front wall of the gallery had been replaced by a scrim stretched tightly across the building—the wall's former impenetrability exchanged for a diaphanous plane that was at times transparent, at times opaque. In the slant of streaming morning light, it appeared to be a clear, iridescent white. As clouds moved across the sun, the white changed to a diffused gray.

Looking past the scrim, I sensed or felt the space rather than saw it. The room was empty—yet it was also full. Midway between the scrim and the back of the room, a single line of shadow traveled over the ceiling, down the side walls, and out across the floor. The line defined the volumetric depth behind the scrim. The space was white, yet the shadows exuded a muted range of blue, lavender, and steel gray. My mind knew that the colors didn't exist, yet my eyes perceived them. The sun still had some way to travel before it broke through the two rectangular skylights and streamed across the walls and floor. For a moment the work was silent, hushed.

By two o'clock the light was brilliant as it poured through the skylights and shone brightly on the right wall and adjacent floor. The glow made the back wall into an illuminated plane. It was almost as if that mundane and very ordinary structure were lit from within. The sunlight carried in its rays minute golden particles of dust

Name all the events (facts) in a moment of perceptual experience. Do we have enough words to adequately reflect such a moment's complexity? . . . A cloud passes over the sun, trailing its shadow over the landscape, and a chill wind passes. A surface that a moment ago appeared rough, is now smooth; something in profile is now lost in its environment. How do we picture such a phenomenon, the weave of its texture? Is it enough to say (picture) that a cloud has passed over the sun? and if it (white, curved, rough) was real before, is it
(continued on p. 47)

Robert Irwin
Room with Twin Skylights, Facing Wall Removed
Installation, Malinda Wyatt Gallery, Venice, California, 1980
Photographed at 2:30 p.m.

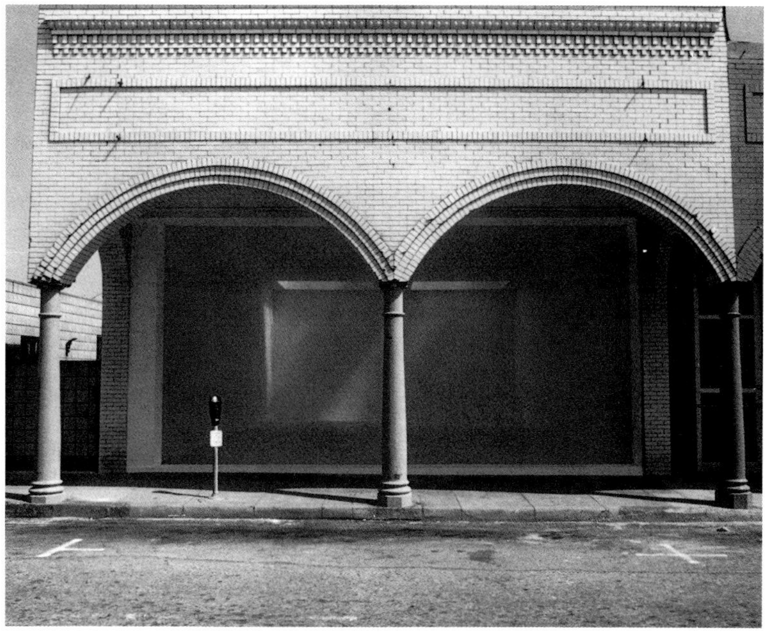

that shone faintly as they fell. The work had an ethereal beauty and an indefinable power.

As dusk came, the residual light provided only an evanescent visibility. The shadows became palpable, the color intense. The scrim, now opaque, was a deep blue violet with a subtly phosphorescent halation. As the light died, so did the color. Finally, when I could no longer see, the work ceased to exist but left an indescribable sensation of beauty.

It was difficult for me then, and it remains difficult now, to describe the impact of that piece. It was not the physical reality of the work but its presence that was so moving, and the experience was entirely subjective.[35] The work was in constant flux. It had the quality that the Japanese call *utsuroi*—the interplay of light and shadow that takes place in a certain locale over a certain period.

Irwin's response to any given phenomenon is as literate or verbal as it is sensate. In preparation for a work he may spend countless hours watching the play of light and shadow in a certain place, but he will spend an equal amount of time recording his intellectual responses to a certain situation. He maintains an ongoing dialogue with contemporary philosophers in the margins of his many books, "weighing this against that and that against this," until in his judgment he has come to grips not with any answer but with the quality of the puzzle he has undertaken to grapple with at the moment.

(continued from p. 46)

(violet, flat, smooth) equally real now? Then what do we mean by reality? Is neither or both the case? Can we disregard these perceptual changes as merely incidental, somehow less than real? While I might walk up to touch the surface, to know its roughness in its objectness, what am I to do about the phenomenon of (white) to violet? Certainly we can say (picture) that a nameable object—clouds—has passed over another nameable object—sun. But how do we account for all the phenomena we experience in such an event? If we say that the cause and effect of the shadows and wind are the clouds and the sun, does such a logical explanation now do away with all the perceptual ambiguities?

On the other hand, if one cannot be compelled to accept anything, we abandon logic and requiredness since something "concrete" like 2+2=4 means nothing to a mind which has negated or relinquished all claims to such a universality. But what kind of a claim for reality does logic stake here? What is universal about a logic that cannot account for even a moment in perceptual experience? In the world of lived perception is not the logic of 2+2=4 something of an impertinence?

■ Robert Irwin, "Some Notes on the Nature of Abstraction," in *Perception and Pictorial Representation*, ed. Calvin Nodino and Dennis Fisher (New York: Praeger, 1979), n.p.

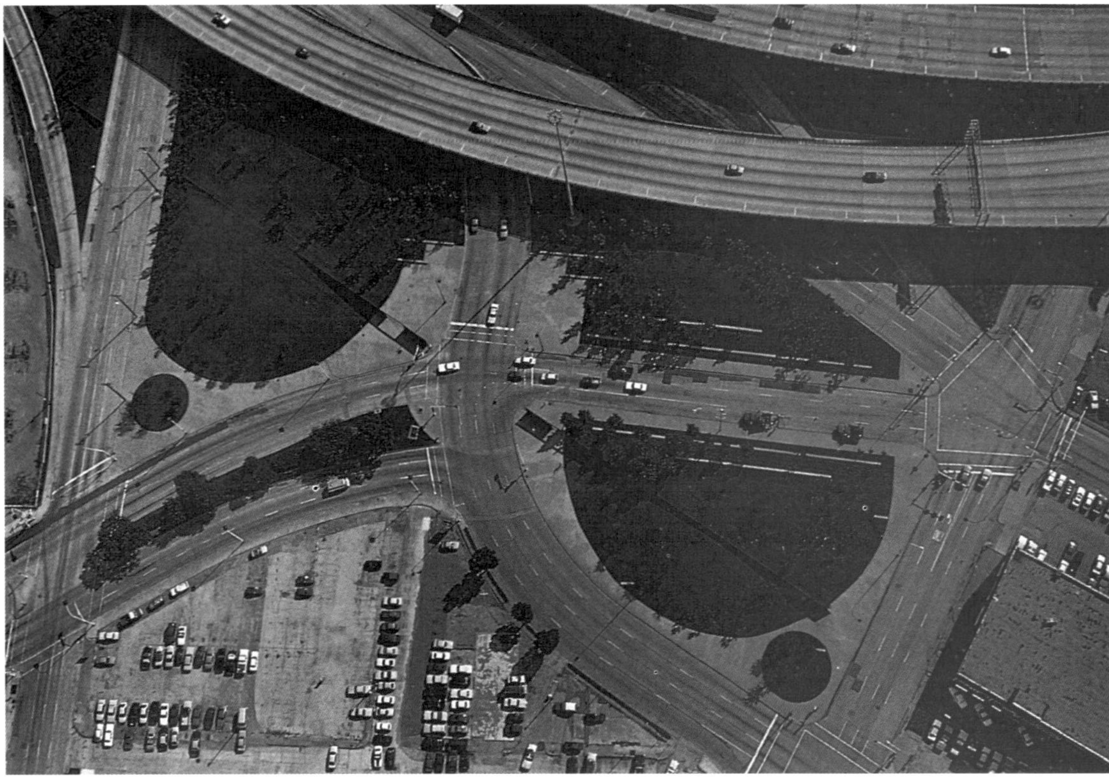

Portal Park Slice
East Portal Park, Carpenter Plaza, Dallas
installed 1980

Carpenter Plaza, located just east of downtown Dallas, is a modest ecological gesture made by the city fathers: a jigsaw puzzle of land scraps framed by a freeway on one side and high-rise buildings on the other. A sculpture was intended for that site from the beginning, even though those who planned the project must have known early on that just about any work put there would virtually disappear in the hubbub of visual noise.[36] Irwin's sculpture made of Cor-ten steel now cuts through this land like a "rusty knife,"[37] pulling the fragments together and providing a strong visual accent in an otherwise lackluster cityscape.

I do the same thing every time, but since all the circumstances are critically different, the *response* needs to be different. In this way, I have total plasticity in terms of all those secondary concerns. The materials, gestures, etc., have *never* really been important to or are crucial to art; they are all simply developed out of necessity, along with the necessary skills to accomplish what it is you want or need to do.

■ Robert Irwin, in Jan Butterfield with Robert Irwin, "Robert Irwin: The Name of the Game Is Context," *University Art Museum Bulletin* (Berkeley, Calif.) (1979), p. I.

After Irwin walked every inch of the parkland, studying the horizontal sweep of the freeway with its hard, clean edges and the relentless verticality, the site eventually began to demand a specific shape and material. The sculpture rises from a deep slot in the earth, traverses three sections of parkland, and then slips into another deep niche in a hillside at the opposite end of the site. Throughout its course, the top is always level—it is the ground that undulates. Although it runs for some seven hundred feet and rises to some twelve feet in height, the wall is only seven-eighths of an inch thick. Thus, in spite of its forceful, thrusting quality, the work has a delicacy when viewed from its side. The color is rich and strong, the surface sensuous. In its maturity the patina of the Cor-ten steel has taken on the texture of suede. Because the sculpture traverses city streets, it is broken by portals to let the traffic through. These portals also frame various aspects of the city as the viewer moves around and through the site.

This work is clearly not a nonobject piece. In fact, it seems to proclaim its sculptural materiality. For those not familiar with Irwin's attitude toward site-determined works, it seemed to signal a sudden interest in producing a grand object. There was the question of materials as well: Cor-ten was clearly "Richard Serra's material"—why would Irwin appropriate it? At the time of the 1979 exhibition in Berkeley (when the Dallas commission

Opposite
Robert Irwin
Portal Park Slice, 1980
Cor-ten steel, 12 x 700 ft.
(3.65 x 213.4 m.)
Permanent installation,
East Portal Park, Carpenter
Plaza, Dallas

was already underway), Irwin was criticized for using fluorescent lights—"Dan Flavin's material." In an interview published that year Irwin stated:

> *The thing that is most important about what I am doing now is the degree to which I have come to let the circumstances of the site condition the response. The most exciting part right now is the latitude I have gained in terms of complexity in aesthetic areas, the character of the gesture, and even the materials I can use. I am ceasing to allow the work to be preconditioned by some assumption of what Art is, what it can be made of, or what it should look like. Its legitimacy lies strictly in its appropriateness.*[38]

Filigree/Line/Plane
Wellesley College, Wellesley, Massachusetts
installed May 1980

This remains one of the most sensuous and lyrical of all Irwin's pieces. Initially it looks so unlike his crisp, knife-edged works that it seems an anomaly, yet it too is a knifelike plane. The piece is situated between two sprawling buildings on a wooded site that slants almost imperceptibly down to a lake. To reach it, one walks along the well-worn paths that lead to the shore of the lake, through piles of oak leaves, and up a slight incline, where the work comes suddenly into view. It rises out of the ground—never more than two feet tall—and continues like a band of foil for some one hundred twenty feet, then disappears into the ground on the other end of the glen. As with the Dallas piece, the piece is level and the terrain undulates.

Taking its cues from the site itself, *Filigree/Line/Plane* is cut through with a pattern of lacy shapes that refer to the leaves of the surrounding trees. Delicate, almost insubstantial, it nearly

Robert Irwin
Filigree/Line/Plane, 1979–80
3/8-in. (1-cm) stainless steel
in concrete footing, length:
120 ft. (36.6 m.)
Permanent installation,
Wellesley College,
Wellesley, Massachusetts

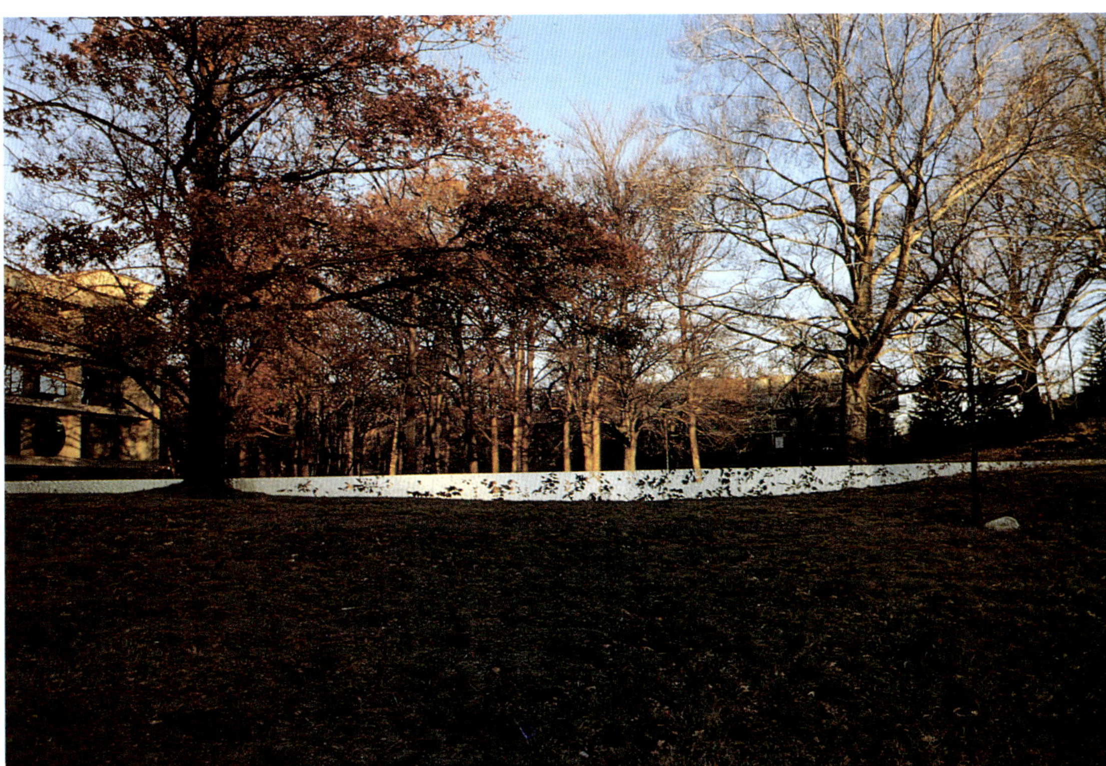

disappears at sunset, when the last rays glance off its burnished surface. Then its silver band merges with the shining line of light that is the sparkling lake below, and it appears to sink into the water just as the sun disappears behind the mountains. It is this quality of change that makes this work so rich.

> *I'm becoming convinced that [change is] obviously the most basic dynamic or physic of our universe. Kant talks about time and space as pre-existing categories, as it were—how they must pre-exist any human perception—and I'd consider change in the same light. That's obvious.... The ambition remains the same; only the scale has changed.... I'm still trying to draw your attention, my attention, to the sheer wonder of all the rich perceptual drama that is taking place all the time just beyond the periphery of our everyday awareness. The gesture is still minimal—only, now it's* spread out.[39]

One of the most unabashedly beautiful works that Irwin has yet created, the Wellesley piece does not shout its authorship even to the initiated; instead, it is a thing of beauty born of a particular place. Hidden among the trees, it waits silently for the occasional viewer.

Having taken permission to use any material, Irwin freed himself from self-imposed restrictions that had been based in part on his need in his late reductive paintings for absolute physical control (such control in the face of the complexities and transience of nature is an anomaly). He proceeded to create a series of works in many different locations—indoors and out—using an astonishing variety of materials, ranging from rusted Cor-ten steel to chain-link security fencing to fluorescent lighting to the now-iconic scrim. Light and Space—with an emphasis on space—had come of age.

> *With my work of the last decade [the 1980s] presented cheek-to-jowl in this manner [in the book* Being and Circumstance*], I would seem from any formal, historical, or oeuvre perspective to be careening out of control in some irrational, even eclectic, manner—one time spare, then again rococo, formal and now romantic, architectural and then sculptural, and so forth. But on the contrary, all of this variety only serves to further establish my point—something more fundamental is at stake here: a new and different dynamic is serving as the grounds for my decision-making, for my art.*[40]

Irwin has proposed four categories for works of art that fall outside the usual definitions of painting or sculpture:

> 1. Site dominant. *This work embodies the classical tenets of permanence, transcendent and historical content, meaning, purpose; the art-object either rises out of, or is the occasion for, its "ordinary" circumstances—monuments, historical figures, murals, etc. These "works of art" are recognized, understood, and evaluated by referencing their content, purpose, placement, familiar form, materials, techniques, skills, etc. A Henry Moore would be an example of site dominant art.*
>
> 2. Site adjusted. *Such work compensates for the modern development of the levels of meaning-content having been reduced to terrestrial dimensions (even abstraction). Here consideration is given to adjustments of scale, appropriateness, placement, etc. But the "work of art" is still either made or conceived in the studio and transported to, or assembled on, the site. These works are, sometimes, still referenced by the familiarity of "content and placement" (centered, or on a pedestal, etc.), but there is now a developing emphasis on referencing the oeuvre of the individual artist. Here, a Mark di Suvero would be an example.*
>
> 3. Site specific. *Here the "sculpture" is conceived with the site in mind; the site sets the parameters and is, in part, the reason for the sculpture. This process takes the initial step towards sculpture's being integrated into its surroundings. But our process of recognition and understanding of the "work of art" is still keyed (referenced) to the oeuvre of the artist. Familiarity with his or*

her history, lineage, art intent, style, materials, techniques, etc., are presupposed; thus, for example, a Richard Serra is always recognizable as, first and foremost, a Richard Serra.

4. Site conditioned/determined. *Here the sculptural response draws all of its cues (reasons for being) from its surroundings. This requires the process to begin with an intimate, hands-on reading of the site. This means sitting, watching, and walking through the site, the surrounding areas (where you will enter from and exit to), the city at large or the countryside. Here there are numerous things to consider: What is the site's relation to applied and implied schemes of organization and systems of order, relation, architecture, uses, distances, sense of scale? For example, are we dealing with New York verticals or big sky Montana? What kinds of natural events affect the site—snow, wind, sun angles, sunrise, water, etc.? What is the physical and people density? the sound and visual density (quiet, next-to-quiet, or busy)? What are the qualities of surface, sound, movement, light, etc.? What are the qualities of detail, levels of finish, craft? What are the histories of prior and current uses, present desires, etc.? A quiet distillation of all of this—while directly experiencing the site—determines all the facets of the "sculptural response": aesthetic sensibility, levels and kinds of physicality, gesture, dimensions, materials, kind and level of finish, details, etc.; whether the response should be monumental or ephemeral, aggressive or gentle, useful or useless, sculptural, architectural, or simply the planting of a tree, or maybe even doing nothing at all.*[41]

Security Stairwell
in _West/East: First-Generation Environmental Sculpture_
P.S. 1, Institute for Art and Urban Resources, Long Island City, New York
exhibition proposed for 1981 but never realized

There is a feeling to schools and playgrounds that recalls basketballs, locked equipment cupboards, the smell of asphalt, and chain-link fencing. Irwin's piece for the P.S. 1 school-building-turned-alternative-space taps into those memories. Utilizing commercial fencing with an emerald green plastic coating, he fenced off various areas of the four-story school building in a way that not only made it more beautiful but also, in this troubled section of Queens, added appreciably to its security. (Irwin's use of chain-link fencing—a relatively inexpensive material that would become a favored medium of his in the 1980s—extended his capacity to produce works outdoors and dramatically expanded his scale.)

Beginning with a green wire cage built around the street entrance, Irwin moved inside, constructing transparent walls of the same green mesh. These floor-to-ceiling planes contained doors to admit or keep out traffic along the corridors that traverse the length of the building. Next he installed glass brick in place of the usual windows in the stairwell. The light that poured in was now dense and murky, aquariumlike. With the light softened and gentled, the improbable green of the wire walls shimmered and rippled in moiré patterns. Gradually one's eyes became adjusted to the work, and once more, as with the scrim pieces, focus slipped in and out. The seedy, peeling walls of the building dropped out of the visual field, and only the throbbing presence of the curious green planes had any reality.

If this work initially seemed more built than created, if its locale seemed to indicate an architectural construction rather than a sculptural one, one's initial doubts were soon assuaged by the visual power of the piece. Once again, Irwin was asking important questions: What are the boundaries between architecture and art? What is the function of art? What is it that I see?

An Exercise in Placement and Relation in Five Parts
in *The Museum as Site: Sixteen Projects,* Los Angeles County Museum of Art
July 21–October 4, 1981

This five-part work represented a considerable departure from Irwin's previous pieces. Three elements—a tall, thin steel plate (13 1/2 feet by 2 feet by 1 inch), a steel bar painted black (4 1/2 feet by 6 inches by 6 inches), and a stainless-steel bar (13 1/2 feet by 1 1/4 inches by 1 1/4 inches)—were used to make five different sculptures in five different locations around the museum, four of them outside. At each site the three elements—plane, bar, and pole—seemed to be placed in random configurations. Closer observation, however, revealed that the relationship between the parts and the relationship of the parts to the whole changed in each situation. Since the beginning of his career Irwin has been concerned with the relationship of figure to ground, and this installation gave him an opportunity to examine these relationships using a traditional sculptural format—it was the repetition and the materials-oriented sculpture that were new for him.

The fifth sculpture was installed inside, in its own room on the third floor of the Ahmanson Gallery. Resonant in its controlled surroundings, it had clear parallels with El Lissitzky's *Proun Space* (see page 11). Its upright, totemic elements, powerfully lit, were balanced in a way that was both formal and dramatic. It was by far the most important, and most successful, of all Irwin's sites in the exhibition. A large part of its impact had to do with context. We have become so accustomed to the way a specific context (a museum, a gallery, etc.) validates a work that we tend to ignore the impact that context can have.

As with Irwin's pieces in Berkeley and Dallas, this work aroused a great deal of speculation, resulting as much from the choice of materials as from the image itself. Had Irwin, having struggled with the problems of the ephemeral, the elusive, found himself at a dead end? Had he decided to execute a "real" work? A cursory examination of the exhibition seemed to indicate that was so, yet nothing could have been further from the truth. As is often the case with Irwin's pieces, there were internal clues, and one was so obvious that it was difficult to miss: there were clearly not five separate sculptures, but a single one composed of repetitive elements—each installed differently in a different location.

Irwin pioneered in site-responsive sculpture. In fact, his four categories for such work have infiltrated the art world, and *site specific,* in particular, has become a sculptural byword. The five parts in Irwin's installation for the museum exemplify all of his categories, and the five-part work, in toto, was site specific—it could not be installed anywhere else.

It was not the material but the context and the intent of the work that were crucial. We have been conditioned to look at sculpture in a very specific manner from a very particular point of view, and Irwin was asking us, once again, to probe the root of our understanding. This work was the most overtly didactic and the least sensuous of any of Irwin's pieces to date, yet it brilliantly illustrated his theoretical position.

***48 Shadow Planes,* 1979–83**
Old Post Office Building, Washington, D.C.
installed 1983

The Old Post Office Building, which has been renovated as office and retail space, is a ten-story structure of relentless gray granite, with a glass canopy centered on a huge atrium and topped by a 315-foot clock tower. It is a curious structure in which to place a commission by a contemporary

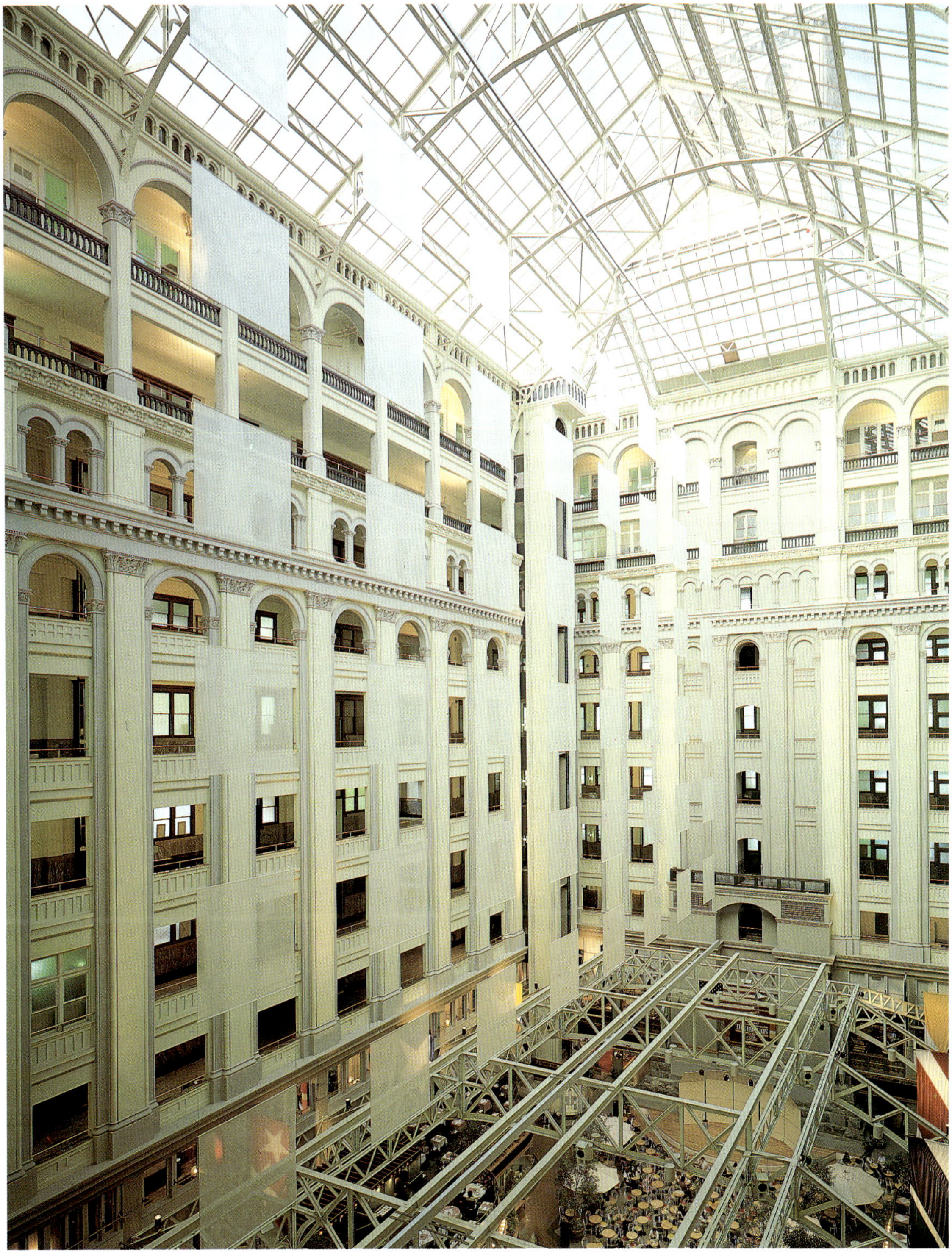

Robert Irwin
48 Shadow Planes, 1979–83
Scrim, natural light
Permanent installation,
Old Post Office Building,
Washington, D.C.

artist. Nevertheless, in 1979 Irwin undertook a proposed project, *56 Shadow Planes.* (The project was later amended to forty-eight planes, eliminating eight panels that would have interfered with day-to-day activity on the first three floors.)

The atrium, with its "crystal-palace" roof, offered endless possibilities for using natural light. Scale, however, presented a very real problem: anything resembling ordinary sculpture would be diminished to virtual invisibility by the building. Irwin's solution: bannerlike pieces of scrim, hung square upon square upon square from the roof. In the early morning the planes of scrim turn butter yellow, taking on the color of the sunlight as it bounces off the creamy walls. In the afternoon, when the sun is no longer overhead, the shadows of the archways and colonnades cast a softened purple haze over the building and the planes of scrim. Viewed head on, each of the planes lines up with an arch. Viewed from the side, they disappear. Only when viewed at an angle do they take on any kind of sculptural form.

Irwin responded not only to the quality of light but also to the building itself:

The Old Post Office Building is a really nice structure with an incredible interior. The key to the architectural interior lies in the some eight hundred window forms facing on to the center atrium. It is all windows. My proposal was to suspend fifty-six window panes of scrim material in the void of the space...floating shadow planes, that keep your eye on the edge. The result was that your read of the qualities of the architectural space was radically enhanced. The floating planes also provided a means to trap and reflect the light differently at different times of day. It also was respectful of the space—and everyone was concerned about what I was going to do. That was just possibly the only solution to the space that would have worked.

As it turned out, the Old Post Office piece is one of the strongest sited works Irwin has done—and one of the most beautiful.

***9 Spaces, 9 Trees,* 1979–83**
Public Safety Building Plaza, Seattle
installed 1983

Downtown Seattle is damp and gray. There is virtually no color, no greenery, nothing to relieve the monotonous grid of stone government buildings. Having received a National Endowment for the Arts commission for an outdoor sculpture, Irwin decided to bring color to the site by introducing blue chain-link fencing into his sculptural vocabulary. For the first time he also introduced color into his work not only in the fencing but also in the form of pink and purple plum trees and a magenta ground cover.

The interesting challenge of the Seattle piece was that it had to work from three very different perspectives. Most people will see it looking down from one of the tall buildings surrounding the site. That means it had to have a very strong graphic read. But, on the other hand, it had to be experienced close up and intimately by people passing through it to pay a parking fine.... And since the plaza on which it is installed is virtually hidden to the casual passer-by, it had to announce itself and invite them in. My solution was a grid.

The classic grid is ordered into nine spaces by the blue fence material—each with a violet-leafed plum tree, created the strong graphic read. At the ground level, the collection of spaces and trees becomes a layered, visually tactile maze...and in passing, the whole thing seems to dance as the fencing creates a moving moiré pattern.

The use of color in the Seattle piece vastly expanded Irwin's visual vocabulary:

People have asked me if I was aware of or conscious of the shift to color when I first began to think about the Seattle piece in 1979. The thing that they have to understand is that it had nothing to do with a shift to color. The thing about my beginning to use color goes back to my beginnings as a painter. You have to remember in all the paintings, the all-white dot paintings, the discs, and all of the white-room scrim pieces, the reason for undertaking that whole process over that long period of time was that it was a period of severe reduction. The reduction was not one of imagery, or of color or of any of those things—it was a reduction of the values that underwrote my putting any of those things in in the beginning. Why *should you make something red?* Why *do you make something filigreed?* Why *should you decorate something? In other words, what is the justification for putting all these things in?*

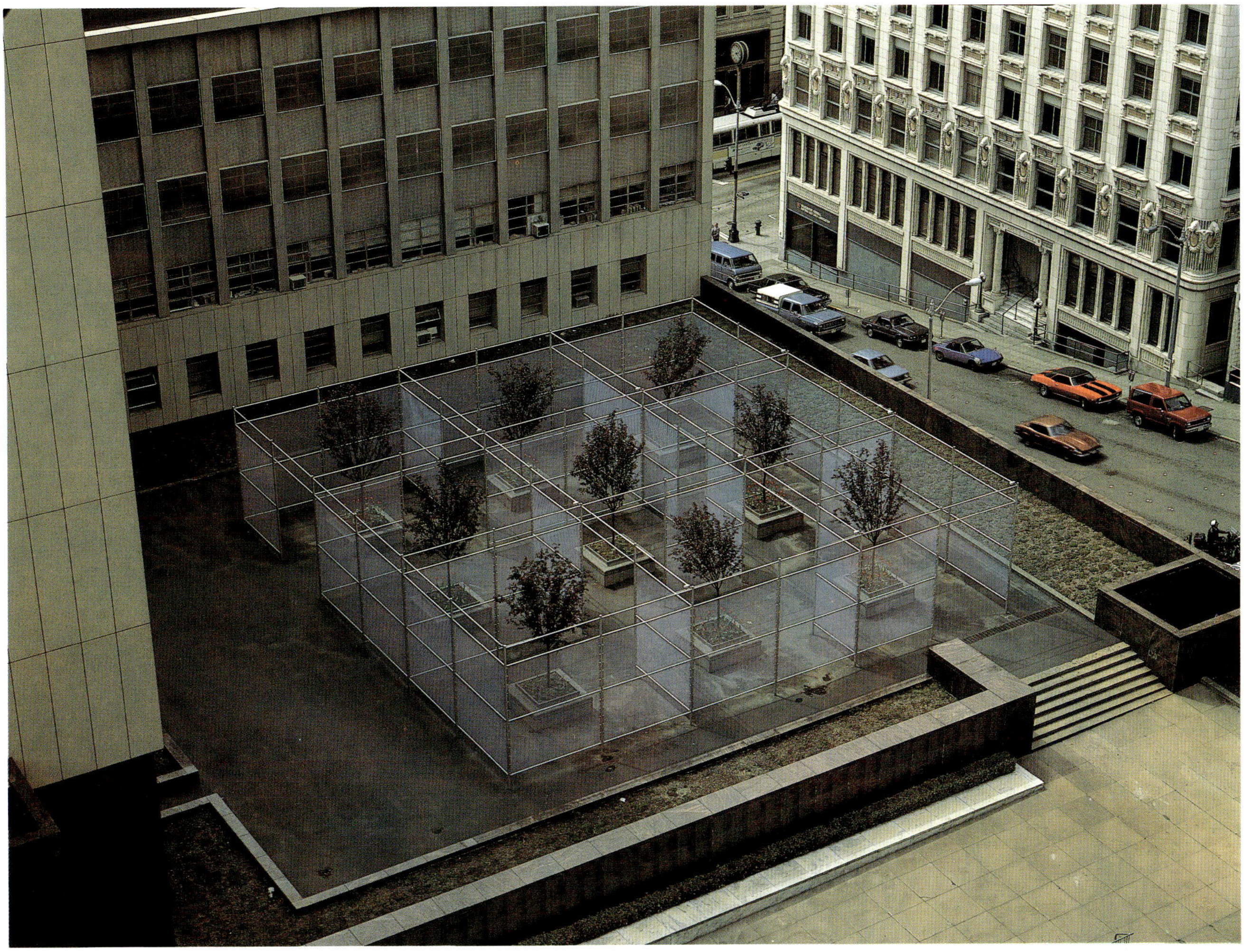

Robert Irwin
9 Spaces, 9 Trees, 1979–83
Plastic-coated stainless-steel wire and plum trees
Permanent installation, Public Safety Building Plaza, Seattle

In a sense my history has been about getting rid of all those things, because I objected to the reasons why those things were done, not to the things themselves. I really like color, I have always liked color. After having begun as a painter, I hated losing it, hated getting it out of my work. It was a major loss not to have color. There were times when I would stand in one of my white scrim rooms and I would look through a window at the trees outside, and think: "Man, there's something really wrong here. What I really want is all those trees. I want those leaves and I want those shadows. I want all that richness, so why am I doing these things?"

I finally realized that for me, those things had become self-distracting because they became self-identified. So in terms of what I was doing, all of those things had to come out of the work first. I'd love to have brought color into the earlier work, but there was no way under the circumstances. I would like to have had the phenomenon of color, but in most situations you could never separate the phenomenon from the color. In other words, if I painted a wall red, it would simply have been a red wall.

Now, what has happened in the last few years is that I have found the grounds, the premise *for why I should do these things—I know* exactly *why and how I can bring back color at a particular point. I have a real* reason *for bringing these things in now. They are no longer arbitrary—because the color is no longer a decoration but an integral part of the whole.*

The hypothesis is simple. We can either organize human beings and human activities to fit our existing need (concepts) for pragmatic order, or, where questions for human potential, mind, and perception are our concern, we can approach and entertain them in their greatest complexity. The former is a true posture of social need; the latter a true posture of open inquiry.

■ Robert Irwin

Two Running Violet V Forms, 1981–83
University of California, San Diego, at La Jolla
installed 1983

On the campus at UCSD, La Jolla, stands a grove of eucalyptus trees planted, curiously, in a grid. The trees flicker in the bright California sun, their silvery leaves and dappled bark providing an ever-changing pattern of light and shadow. They affect the viewer on another level as well, for the pungent smell of eucalyptus permeates the air.

The grove and its neighboring grassy lawn are a part of the Stuart Foundation Sculpture Collection. Commissioned by the foundation to do a site work anywhere on campus, Irwin headed straight for the trees. Fascinated with their light-shot qualities, he conceived a piece that would work in concert with them. He again utilized colored chain-link fencing, as in Seattle

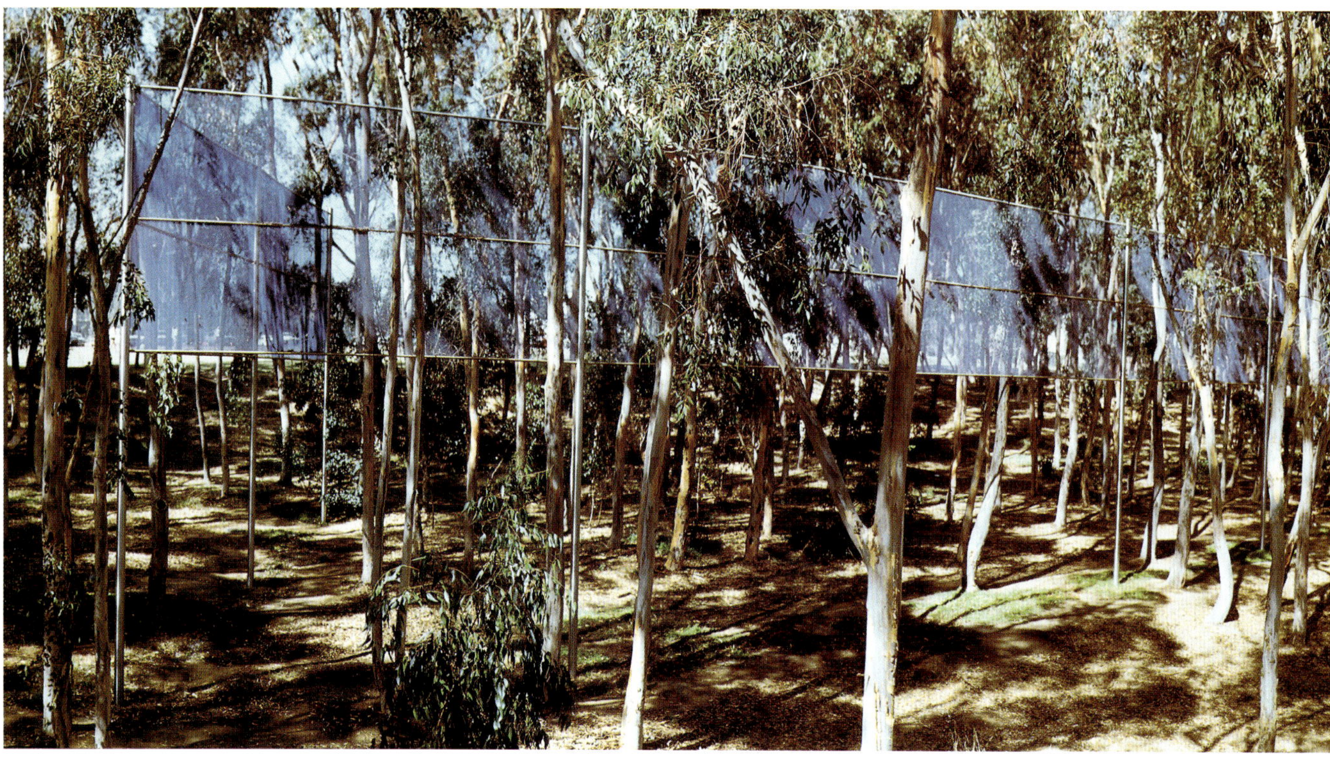

and Long Island City. Here he again used a blue-violet color and wove it through the trees, zigzagging in and out of their grid formation. He also added a ground cover of magenta ice plant, which provided a perfect foil for the colored screening. In some lights the fencing is a diaphanous blue violet, then suddenly it may appear to be a virtually impenetrable wall of Yves Klein blue. In the rain the work is enshrouded by foggy mists tinted with its color, and it shimmers with the raindrops that catch on its weave.

> *I went direct to those stands of eucalyptus trees.... I felt they were the one unique and distinctive element on the UCSD campus. They are not only beautiful, but they cast a special spell over the whole campus. It's nice that everyone passes through the groves every day... allowing the unique opportunity to create an art of natural interface. I have always been uncomfortable with ritual and ceremony and with the idea of having to make a trek-to-Mecca to find "Art." I like the fact that this work is both a piece of art and part of the everyday campus experience at the same time.*

Robert Irwin
Two Running Violet V Forms,
1981–83
Plastic-coated stainless-steel
fencing, 30 x 144 ft. (9.1 x 43.9 m.)
Permanent installation, University
of California, San Diego, at La Jolla;
Stuart Collection

Robert Irwin
Pace Gallery, New York
September–October 1985

A Single Plane: 324 Parts
San Francisco Museum of Modern Art
September 29–November 24, 1985

Having spent several years refining his philosophy and laying out his site-specific works, Irwin presented (in both New York and San Francisco) some of his most evanescent works to date, as well as some of his most tangible.

In San Francisco he filled the museum's rotunda with 324 rectangular boxes. Similar to sculpture pedestals, they were, in fact, specifically designed to echo the light-enhanced grid of the museum's glass ceiling and focus one's attention on the light trapped between the ceiling and the pedestals. That this installation had to be entered through a quiet, darkened space, in which sixteen steel columns recalled a peristyle hall, made the octagonal rotunda seem all the more grand

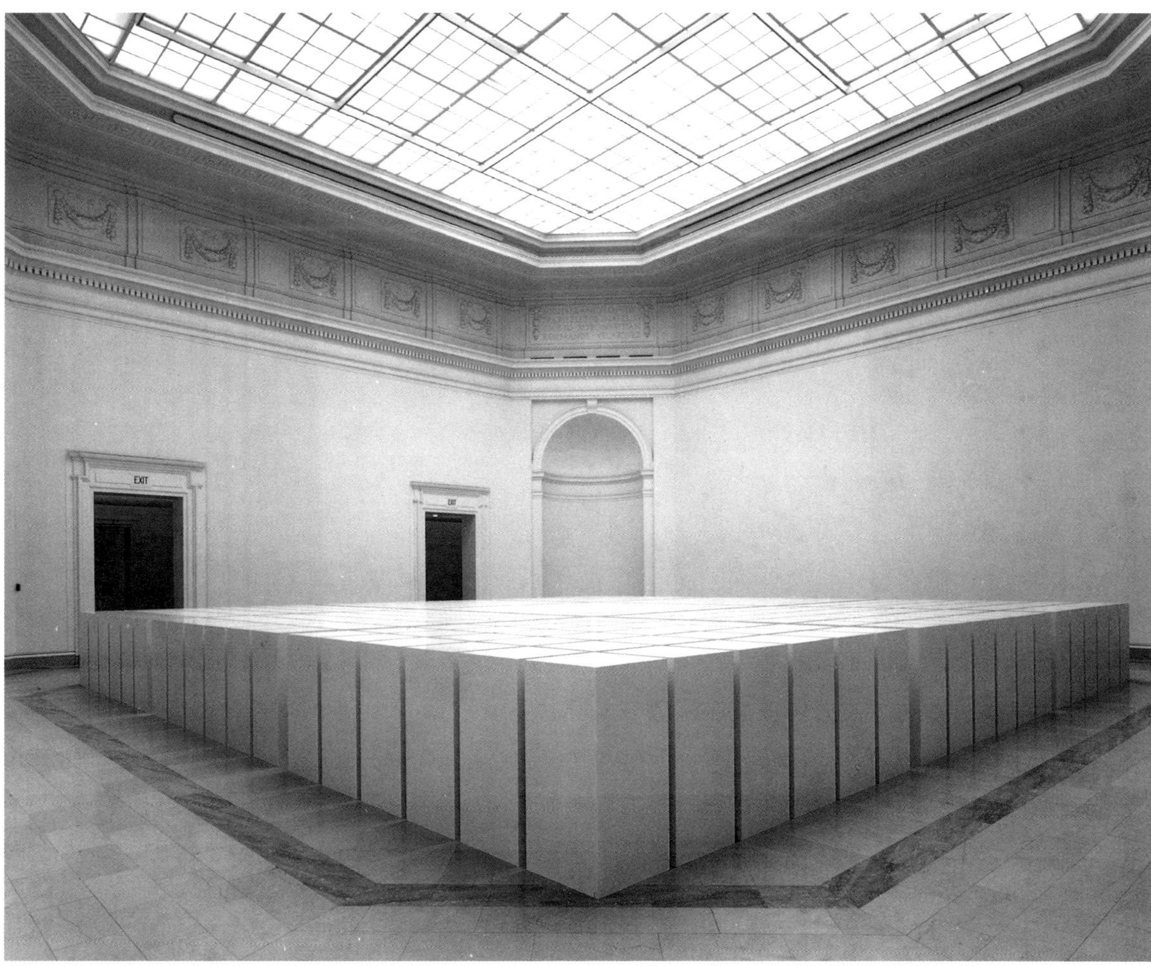

Robert Irwin
A Single Plane: 324 Parts
Painted wood, natural light
Installation, San Francisco
Museum of Modern Art, 1985

and vast. At the same time Irwin wrapped rooms, halls, and corridors with scrim, providing an ethereal respite from the intellectual and visual rigor of the rotunda piece.

Kenneth Baker, critic for the *San Francisco Chronicle,* discussed the scrim pieces:

> The corridors flanking the rotunda show that Irwin does at times have a knack for getting the most from very simple means. To either side of the rotunda, he has blocked off the corridor with white theatrical scrim. In one corridor, he has used a single scrim; in the other two, two scrims with an interval of inaccessible space between them. He has also treated the fluorescent lights in the corridors with theatrical gels, giving the light that reflects against the ceiling soft overtones of pink and green.
>
> Looking down either corridor is like looking through a fog that seems suddenly to turn into a fogged mirror. With the grip of perception loosened by the scrim, your imagination toys freely with the ambiguous information that reaches the eye, which seems more like the stuff of hallucination the longer you dwell on it. The differences between one corridor installation and another are hard to size up, because they can be compared only in memory.[42]

At Pace Gallery, Irwin exhibited for the first time the plans, models, and photographs of the proposals and completed projects for his public pieces spanning the period 1978 to 1985. To give the exhibition a sense of the actual experiences, Irwin made two new gallery installations. The first was a vibrant hot orange cagelike structure built around the elevators and the spiral staircase. It included a small carpet of violet flowers illuminated by the glow of violet "grow-lights." Along the front of the gallery Irwin installed a double wall of scrim with a small window cut through it to correspond with another, larger window he opened to let in the sounds and air from Fifty-seventh Street below.

> *To the degree that the art world represents an active forum for determining what is art at any given time, the problem with public works is that they are spread out all over the world... not to mention that many of the best proposals often never get built. In my case the early works are still in the position of fueling the new work, yet without seeing at least four or five of the works first-hand the viewer cannot comprehend the development. For these reasons, this exhibition was conceived to bridge that gap.*

Central Avenue Meridian
in *Individuals: A Selected History of Contemporary Art, 1945–1986*
Temporary Contemporary, Museum of Contemporary Art, Los Angeles
installed December 10, 1986; accidentally destroyed January 1991

Bisecting the wide street that provides access to the Temporary Contemporary building, Irwin placed two long screens of bamboo and green wire fencing. This curiously Japanese work not only was particularly apt for the Japan Town area in which the building is located, but it also gave an aura of mystery to the locale. Clouds of fog emanated from hidden nozzles, swirled around the green fence, then gradually dissipated as they floated to the top of the bamboo. The work had a strong yet gentle presence; it was also functional in that it masked some of the surrounding parking lots and rather dilapidated older buildings.

Perceiving the Garden
in *Robert Irwin at Wave Hill,* New York
May 18–September 27, 1987

A grand estate overlooking the Hudson River and beyond to the Palisades of New Jersey, Wave Hill is a short hour's drive from Manhattan. Composed of two large manor houses and twenty-eight acres of lawns, woodlands, and formal gardens, it was donated to the City of New York in 1960 for horticultural, cultural, and educational purposes.

In 1986 Irwin was invited to create an exhibition of new works at Wave Hill, "because of his commitment to a particular self-proclaimed philosophy. Through this process, the artist 'seeks to discover and value the potential for experiencing beauty in everything.'"[43] Irwin visited Wave Hill in winter, in the snow; in spring; and again in summer, when the trees and flowers were in full bloom. He then made a number of proposals—all starting with the premise that he would approach the garden in its entirety. Undaunted by the fact that twenty-eight acres is a virtually impossible area for any one artist to cover, Irwin achieved his goal, as Jean Feinberg noted, "on an analogous rather than a physical level."

> The visitor to Wave Hill visually and physically experiences Irwin's work in the same manner as he or she enjoys the garden itself. And what one *learns* through this process is in sympathy with what you would learn during any garden visit, but hopefully you *learn* in a manner that augments your appreciation of the place and makes you just a bit self-conscious about this process of perceiving, so that you will carry it over to other situations and opportunities.[44]

Wave Hill Wood

A nature trail begins at the lower edge of a sloping green lawn and curves down into a wooded path so overgrown that one cannot see the sky. At the start of the trail Irwin placed three stone markers several yards apart in the earth. The first was a large, flat step of plain granite set flush with the ground; the second was slightly raised; and the third bore the legend

WAVE H WOOD cut deeply into it.
I
L
L

Inside the woods, far along the path, was a fourth marker, also deeply incised, which read:

EVER PRESENT
NEVER TWICE
THE SAME

The nature trail takes about half an hour to walk. Alerted that this trail had been designated as a work of art, the hiker proceeded differently, *perceived* differently. Birds twittered, small animals rustled in the underbrush, and the wind made its own quiet sound. The damp, pungent path was lit with bits of sunlight that intermittently broke through the dense trees. The trail gently aroused the senses. Intuitively, the participant became, for a brief time at least, an acutely perceiving human being.

One of my key proposals was to bring in a "master artist" for each of the seven concourses—seven distinct worlds keyed by the unique sensibilities of each artist—each developing a kind of permanent/impermanent installation, where each artist was free to bring in other artists, artisans, and craftspeople of like sensibility, to give each concourse a scale and cohesiveness—rather than simply scattering a lot of art objects around. Airports are dynamic and always changing places, and each artist would have the ongoing responsibility to continually weave the new into the old. Among the artists I chose to work with were Alice Aycock, John Baldessari, Charles Garabedian, Richard Fleischner, Alexis Smith, Terry Allen, and Siah Armajani.

We came very close to creating something unique—but at the critical moment, Dick Judy quit the airport over a fiscal crunch of accountability with the city and county.

This story of bureaucratic dead ends is one with which Irwin has become all too familiar: he has been awarded commissions in twenty-five competitions during the last ten years, yet he has seen only one of them come to fruition. What is amazing is that Irwin never seems to lose his optimism or his enthusiasm. About his three years spent on the Miami Airport project, he said: "I got my Ph.D. in public arts in Miami. I did my homework and I am now prepared to take on a project of this scale again!" This Miami experience seems to have heralded another transition in Irwin's continuing inquiry into the implications of, as he puts it, "modern thought." The information he gained from the project seems to have indicated to him the possibility of a whole new role for the artist in society.

Sentinel Plaza
New Police Building, Pasadena, California
dedicated January 1991

In the course of his complex career Irwin's work has moved full circle, from painting and sculpture through a process of dematerialization and then back to employing a full range of materials. Now, for the first time, he has gone beyond the reintroduction of materials to full-scale exterior embellishment.

The 1980s saw a great development in Irwin's work:

In the studio, you may reference nature but you also reference all art. The big shift now is that my art is not historically referenced, but circumstantially referenced. When I reference a space I do so by taking all of the circumstantial aspects into account. If you arrive at a work of mine from the New York subway or you arrive at it directly after spending time in the Montana desert—it is very different. I try to take all of those things into account.

Robert Irwin is widely regarded as the theoretical godfather of California Light and Space art, arguably Los Angeles' most original contribution to the lexicon of contemporary styles. No conversation ranking local artists gets very far before Irwin is nominated for the imaginary "most important artist of his generation" award. He's already received the real and much coveted MacArthur fellowship, the so-called genius grant. Yet for all the respect he commands, his informal ranking was once greeted by a disgruntled former gallery mate with the jeer: "That's pretty good for a guy who never makes any art."

■ William Wilson, "Pasadena Police Nab Robert Irwin," *Los Angeles Times*, July 22, 1991.

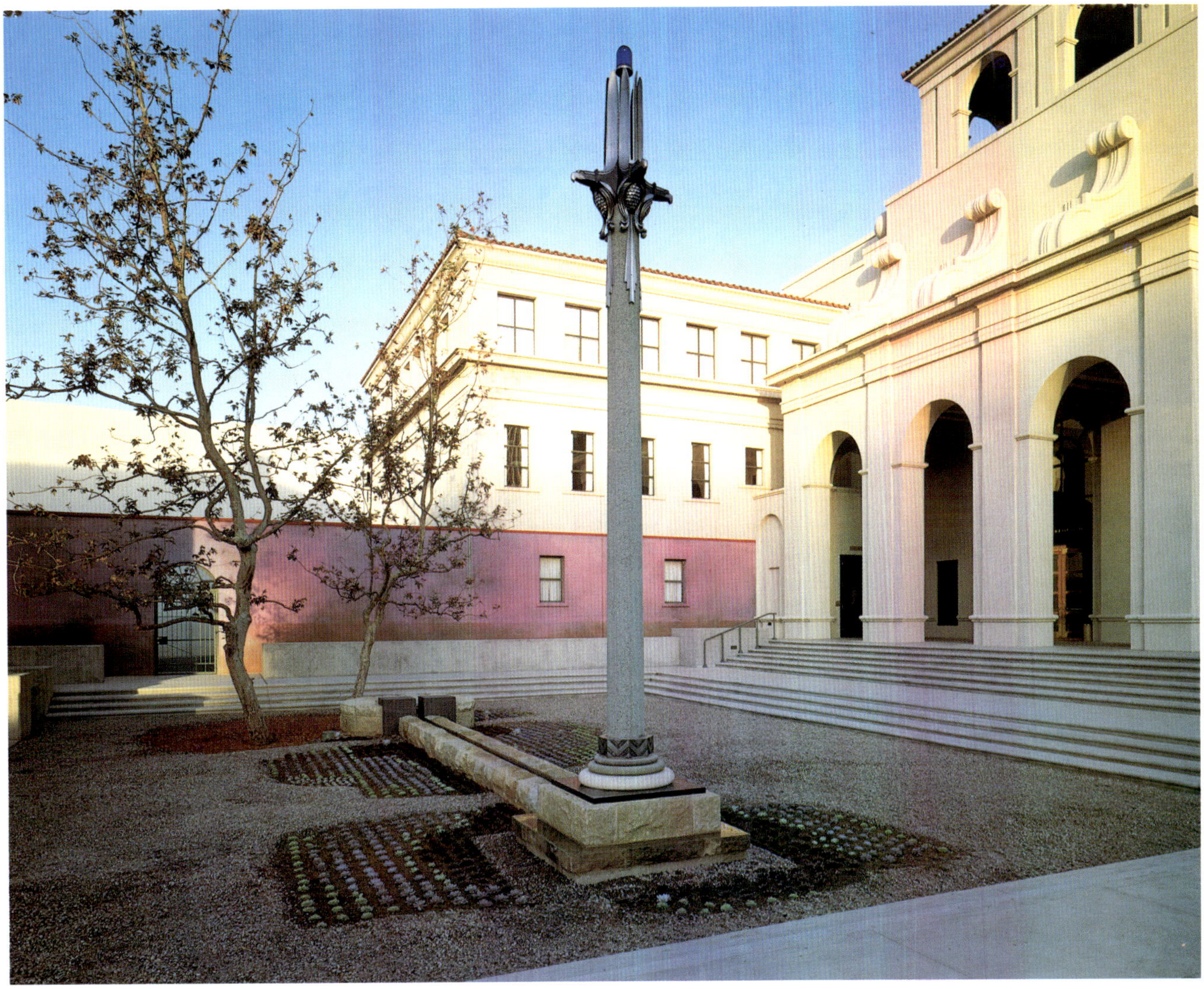

Robert Irwin
Sentinel Plaza, 1991
Permanent installation,
New Police Building, Pasadena,
California

Now, in the 1990s, having finessed his concerns with light and space and color, Irwin is clearly moving into another arena. His work with the landscape firm Campbell & Campbell for the New Police Building (Robert Stern, architect) seems to be his first step toward a new body of work that has been conceived and refined in the purest of laboratories but that functions very well in the real world.

Irwin often refuses to discuss a work with me ahead of time or to tell me precisely where it is, and he sent me off to see the New Police Building with only a general location but no description, street number, or name. Having repeatedly driven around a square-block area several times without seeing the work, I became concerned that the light would soon be absorbed by dusk. I passed the same corner, driving back and forth past a handsome plaza with a dappled, orchid-tinted wall until I finally realized that *was* the work. The wonder of it is that for twenty-five years now I have been looking at Irwin's art—art that has gestures as personal as brush strokes—and this piece was *still* a surprise.

I stopped the car and got out. The late afternoon light intensified the colors and turned the entire plaza into a kind of set for an Italian opera. With sensitivity to the Beaux-Arts architecture of the old building and its echo in the new one, Irwin had filled the plaza, linking them in a way that unified the entire block. The master of restraint had flamboyantly painted the back wall of the courtyard a vibrant violet, then installed in front of it a slender column some thirty-six feet tall, topped with four "federal" eagles and the police station's emblematic blue light. The wall is punctuated by a wrought-iron gate painted the softest of greens, through which can be seen a moiré pattern of an acid green screen somewhere just behind the wall. In the center of the plaza water flows down a long incision—its length reiterating the height of the column. On either side of the fountain are planted succulents in pinkish purples and bluish lavenders that echo the hue of the back wall. The new building ripples toward the plaza down two levels of steps gently descending to a courtyard of soft earth tones and multicolored pebbles. Perhaps the strongest elements in the entire piece are two sycamore trees, which provide a symbolic link with the days when sycamores were Pasadena's only inhabitants.

Both Irwin's art and his theories have had relatively slow acceptance. A body of work concerned with "the obscure questions of doubt and curiosity," as Irwin terms his investigations, cannot readily be absorbed into the existing art-world structure. And when such a body of work does begin to be accepted, you can be sure that the artist is no longer working on what Irwin has termed "the periphery of knowing." It will be highly interesting to see whether his concepts will continue to infiltrate the art world at large (as in the case of his concept of "site-specific" sculpture), or if they will simply be dismissed as an obscure and arcane game.

Two highly regarded contemporary writers have summed up the importance of Irwin's contribution. Writing at the time of the publication of Irwin's book *Being and Circumstance,* Calvin Tomkins said: "Irwin has set forth the thinking behind his recent work in a remarkable essay.... As a rationale for going beyond art it ranks right up there with Kandinsky and Mondrian."[45] At about the same time, in a special section of the *Chicago Tribune* entitled "Who Will Last?—Our Critics' Pick of the Artists Who Will Survive the Next Century," Alan Artner commented: "Robert Irwin is an artist whose thinking is so advanced that it will take a century to unravel all the implications (and applications). The comparatively few objects he produces will achieve a stature beyond their actual achievement, for he is our best candidate for secular saint."[46]

James Turrell

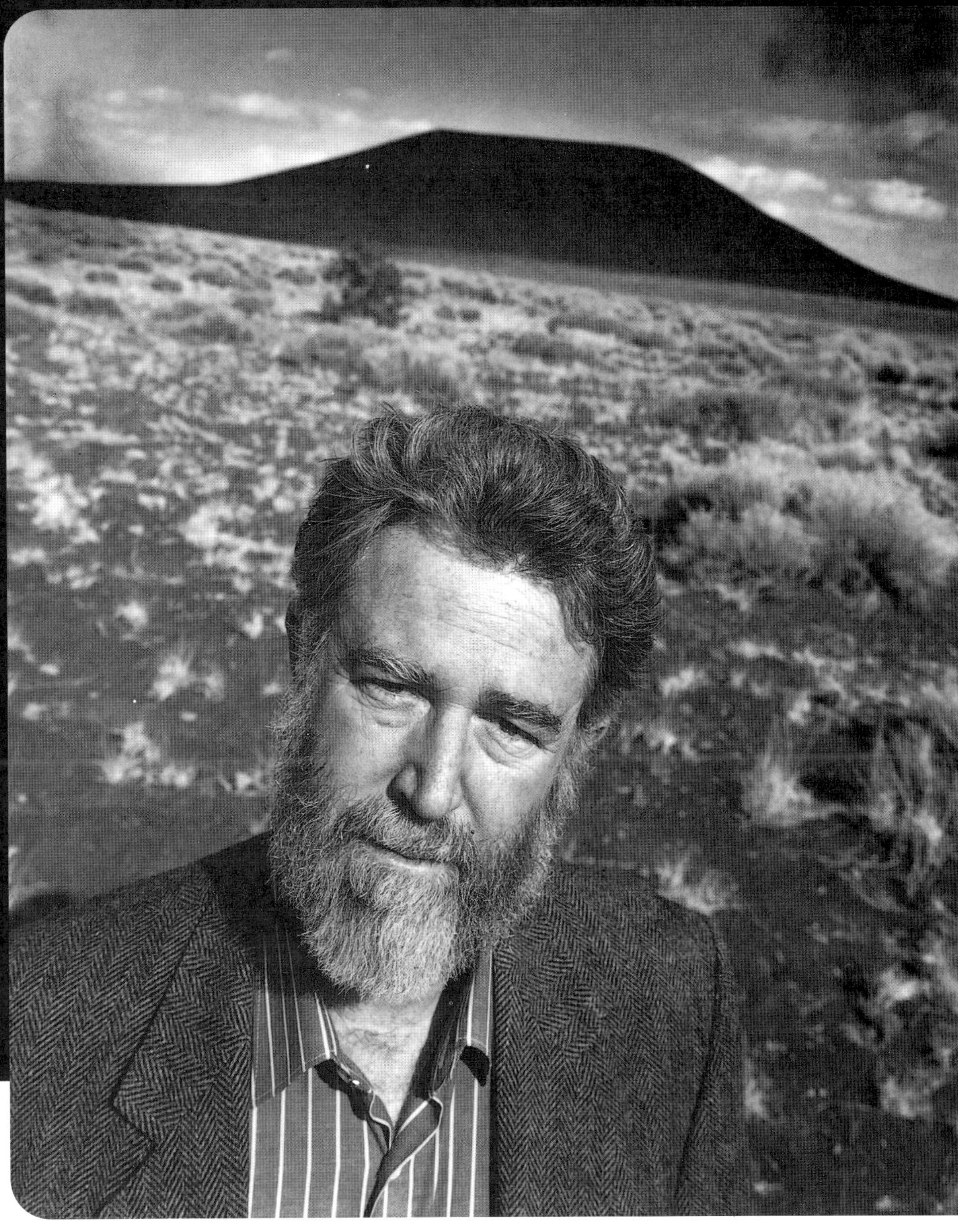

The best magic of all is the magic that is real. I am interested in working straight with that power.

James Turrell

James Turrell

Irwin's work examines perception. Turrell's work also examines perception—but with a difference. Irwin begins with material and dissolves it into light. Turrell takes the light itself and makes it material. "There is no object in my work," Turrell states firmly. "There never was. There is no image within it. I have:

—no object
—no image
—no point of focus.

"My interest is in plumbing the space."

Irwin began as a painter and worked his way through to an attitude of Light and Space. Turrell began as an artist of Light and Space, having come to it in his earliest days as an artist. As a result, Turrell had no preconceptions to overcome. Early on Irwin and Turrell came to not dissimilar solutions to their investigations, but in maturity their interests and concerns have become radically different. Turrell's sensibilities have been conditioned by being a pilot as well as an artist; his art plumbs space just as he plumbs it in his plane. His monumentally important *Roden Crater Project,* currently being created within a dormant volcano in the Arizona desert, is enormous both in its scale and in its implications.

Turrell's earliest works, made with gas light, were quite the opposite. They were modest, simple, and it is doubtful that more than two or three of the people invited to view them fully understood the importance of what they saw. "My first attempts to use light as space were in 1965 and 1966...during which time I worked with gas," Turrell recalls. "The flow of gas that I achieved was quite flat and laminar (divided into plates), and the speeds were the same in the center as they were out toward the edges. The friction was similar across the entire flow of gas, so I was able to achieve very flat flames."[1]

The Mendota Hotel Stoppages
Santa Monica, California
Light Projections, summer 1968–summer 1969 (xenon as light source)
Light Spaces, 1970 (existing outside light as source)

In the late 1960s Turrell lived in the old Mendota Hotel, a building that still stands at the corner of Hill and Main streets. It was there that he began the investigations and experiments that have formed the basis of all his work.

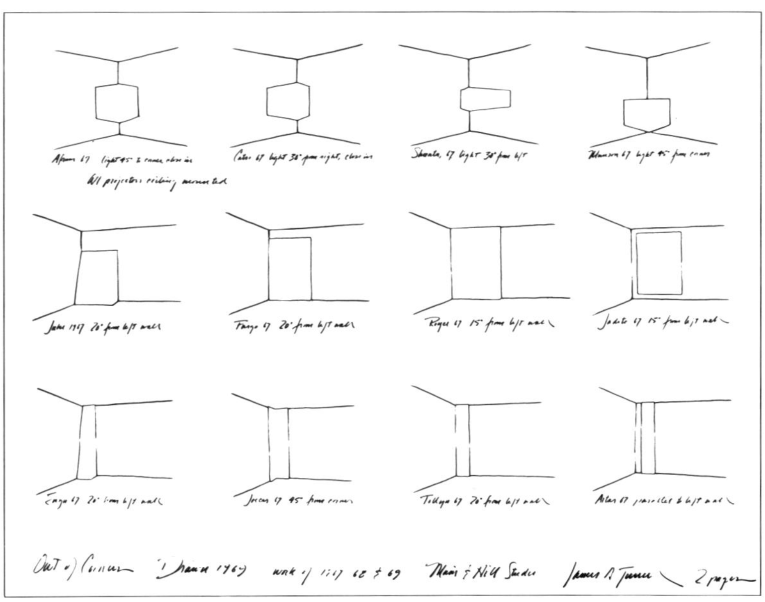

James Turrell (b. 1943)
Drawing for "The Mendota Hotel Stoppages: Out of Corners," 1969
Melinda Wortz

The Stoppages were created by controlling natural phenomena. In his studio, with its pristine white ceiling, floors, and coved walls, Turrell created a laboratory of sorts in which preexisting conditions could be manipulated to produce highly interesting results. The windows that faced the street were blocked, and a series of small square apertures were created through which light could pass. Walls were erected to block the light in some cases and

I had this piece that worked exclusively off things which took place at 2:00 A.M., when the bars closed. At that time of night, the cars would begin to come in strange and erratic patterns. What I had was this: I knew that cars were basically going to stop behind the crosswalk, and what happened was that if they stopped behind the crosswalk *nothing happened.* Now, if somebody crept into the crosswalk in a car, that changed everything. What I had then was an angle from the crosswalk into the Main and Hill studio. I actually had to make spaces to allow the light to flood in at one spot and have ambient light in another. So I had an antechamber.

What happened was this: if a car pulled up in the outside lane, I had a window or an aperture at one point and a window or an aperture at another. The *headlights* would *not* beam into those small apertures, only the red *taillights* would. The whole thing was made to plan. There was a space outside, and there were activities which took place out there, which were totally ordered. Some were bizarre. For example, some cars would turn at one point and sit there while the rest of the traffic cleared, with their left turn indicator blinking. Also, at a point, red light would pour through one of the windows because of the rear taillights, and it would make *another* window "work." I could actually count on it, and it would happen three or four times a night.

■ James Turrell

let it through in others. The light level was very low and required a kind of stepping-down process to be seen. The pieces, which could be viewed only at night, derived their color and light from stoplights, headlights, and traffic signals, and were perceived at first as a series of colored abstract shapes. The color would then begin to spread, and the effect was of a diffused area of color with a distinct grain.

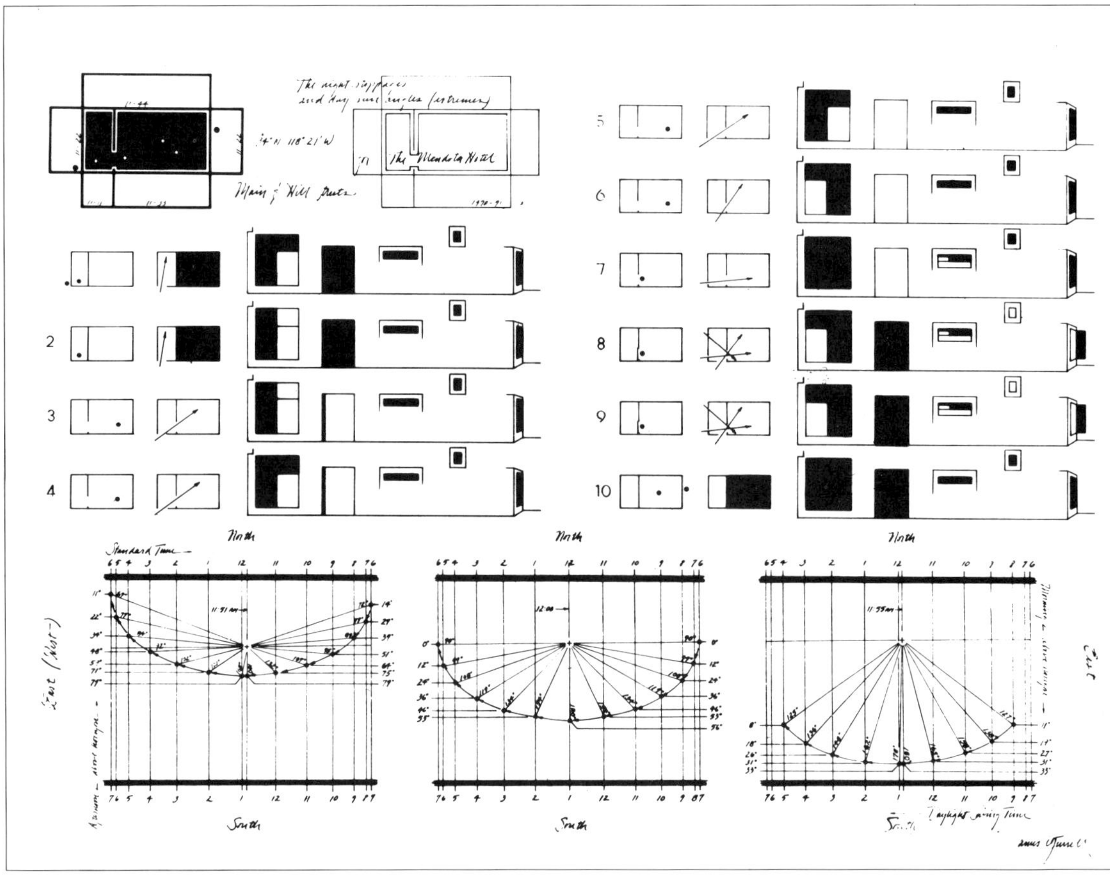

From the beginning Turrell has been interested in color created not by the artist but by the percipient, under specially controlled circumstances that cause the surroundings to appear flooded with an intensely colored light. It is important to note that there is never any applied color in his work; no color is ever added to the walls themselves. The closest he comes is to use titanium white to paint his walls and ceilings, because its tone tends toward blue (as opposed to zinc white, for example, which is slightly yellow). But this is a subtle point, since to all but the most sophisticated viewer both of these paints appear to be pure white. Turrell commented:

> *If the color is in the paint on the wall, then in making a structure and allowing light to enter it, the color will tend to ride on the walls. But if the color of the wall is white, which in one way is noncolor, then the light is allowed to enter the space riding on the light, and that color has the possibility of inhabiting the space and holding that volume rather than being on the wall. This is true in pieces like* Laar *and* Avar *from the Prado series.*

The Mendota Hotel Stoppages, like all of Turrell's pieces except those using projected light, derived part of their essence from a space outside the one occupied by the viewer. Throughout his career Turrell has talked about the importance of a "space looking at another space and deriving its characteristics from that space." Of the Mendota Hotel pieces he said:

> *They came from outside the space. There was an intersection at Main and Hall, and there was nighttime activity that took place within that space... shop lights would come on, and I knew*

James Turrell
Drawing for "The Mendota Hotel Stoppages: Music for the Mendota," 1967–74
Collection of the artist

exactly what time they would do so. I also knew what time they would go off. Traffic signals would work—and they had a set time. Cars would go up and down, and they would always stay within the lines of the street and crosswalks.... I knew the taillights would be going in one direction and that the headlights would be in a line someplace else.

So I had this universe—outside this space, and there were activities which happened within it, and light energy. Then I had a space inside, within that room. A physical confine. It looked out into that space outside through the apertures I had made. Now, I could make openings to accept *light in that space or walls to occlude it.... Some of the pieces were quite complicated in that they received light from many different directions.... Then I could shape the walls where they joined. I could control how close they were, so that if I had a wall at one angle, the light coming in on a slant would fall on that wall. If I moved the wall back, the light would fall on* another *wall.*

Although matter-of-fact in their structure, *The Mendota Hotel Stoppages* were nevertheless somewhat obscure. For one thing, their most powerful aspects could be seen only at night, and this, coupled with Turrell's relative reclusiveness during this period, meant that few people had the opportunity to experience these early works.[2] That did not prevent their becoming known, however. *Time* and *Newsweek* chose to review them, and *Life* and the art magazines covered them as well, thus dramatically expanding their sphere of influence. In retrospect, the Mendota Hotel can be seen as a laboratory in which Turrell, who was originally trained in psychology, continued his work with Light and Space, the most rudimentary aspects of which had taken place in 1965. At the hotel he began the trial-and-error processes that became finished pieces and that eventually led to his highly sophisticated ability to control light within a contained environment, as well as to track the sun, moon, and stars, as he will eventually do in the *Roden Crater Project.*

Light Projections
Pasadena Art Museum, Pasadena, California
October 9–November 9, 1967

Turrell's first truly public works, exhibited while he was still in school, were the Projection Pieces he showed at the Pasadena Art Museum. Projections of intense light, they appeared to have curious properties that they did not physically possess. A now-iconic work, *Afrum,* seemed to be a three-dimensional cube of light hanging in the corner of a darkened room, without any physical means of support. Mysterious and enigmatic, it seemed to possess density and weight. In fact, however, it took its reality solely from an intense light beamed from a xenon projector through a plate masked off to create its specific shape. That it was perceived as cubed rather than flat was a function of the viewer's psychological and perceptual need to pull that known form, a cube, up into three-dimensional solidity. These works existed in a *virtual reality*—that is, a hypothetical reality that appears to have as much reality as "real" reality.

Turrell began his studies at Pomona College in Southern California, where he received a B.A. in psychology in 1965. He went from there to study art for a semester at the University of California, Irvine, and then received a master's degree in art from the Claremont Graduate School in 1973. It was in art school that Turrell began to be fascinated with the power of light, and he started to make works formed not in paint, marble, or clay, but by the intellect. While in school he was particularly intrigued with paintings by Mark Rothko, but it wasn't until much later that he

realized that their luminosity was a function of the light shining through a 35mm slide onto the screen:

> *What happened then is that I got more interested in the plumbing of hypothetical space and the idea of the presence or quality of light.* Afrum... *was more of a painting in the sense that you have painting on a two-dimensional surface that alludes to perhaps three dimensions or unsolvable three-dimensional things. This work was about taking three-dimensional space and making the same kind of allusions to the space beyond that—you don't need to call it fourth dimension but just one that does not solve up in three. So in that way, my work does have a lot more to do with painting than it does with sculptural or architectural senses, because the first thing that is important is that the light is used as material, and that it has a physical presence as such, and that space is solid and filled and never empty.... Let's call painting our concept of three-dimensional space... then from that, create paintings that don't solve up in that space—rather they* are *that space. They become like little "holes in reality."*

With hindsight it is clear that these early works were neither painting nor sculpture but something new that was to break down the distinctions between the two. Turrell was one of several West Coast artists to head in this direction. It was perplexing territory, and many of the artists exploring it, Turrell included, found themselves in a kind of critical limbo. As Turrell notes: "There is a critical vocabulary attached to painting and sculpture, but there has been no vocabulary attached to works of Light and Space—which further complicates the issue." Many writers refused even to acknowl-

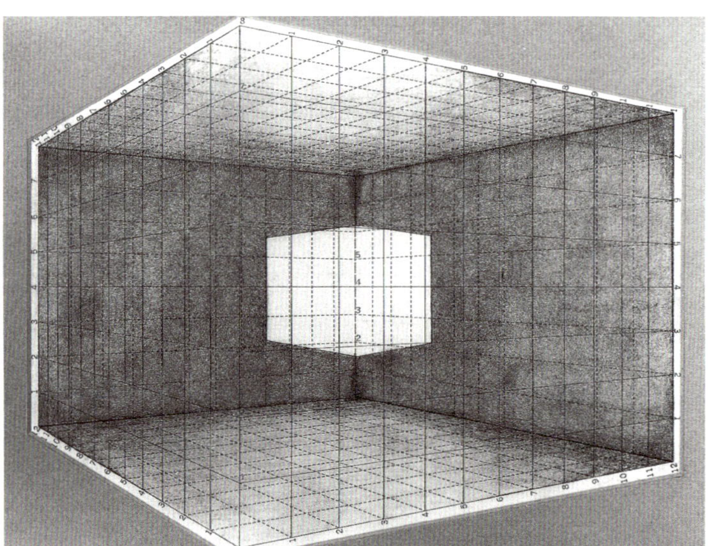

Above, top
James Turrell
Afrum, 1967
Xenon-light Projection Piece, 16 7/8 x 19 5/8 in. (43 x 50 cm)
Installation, Stedelijk Museum, Amsterdam, 1976

Above, bottom
James Turrell
Drawing for "Afrum," 1967
Collection of the artist

edge the new work as art, though many of the artists who were later to be defined as Light and Space artists had no doubts, even from the beginning. Reared in the comparatively history-free environment of Southern California, they pursued their own courses independent of accepted opinion. "One of the advantages of growing up in California is that you're not under pressure to repeat the past," Turrell told the *New Yorker* at the time of his retrospective at the Whitney Museum in 1980. "I never even had a *thought* that what I was doing wasn't art."[3]

Irwin-Turrell collaboration, in process 1969–70
on view at the U.S. Pavilion, Expo 70, Osaka, Japan
March 15–September 13, 1970
and at *Art and Technology,* Los Angeles County Museum of Art
May 11–August 29, 1971

Irwin invited Turrell to participate with him in the Art and Technology Project (see pages 25–28), the psychological and perceptual research for which began in January 1969. Flush with the success of his one-man exhibition at the Pasadena Museum (immediately followed by Irwin's exhibition in the same locale) and already conducting experiments of a phenomenal sort in his Mendota Hotel works, Turrell readily accepted Irwin's invitation.

Difficulties began almost immediately, and by August 1969 Turrell had abdicated his role and resigned from the project, terminating his relationship with Irwin. Turrell's problems with the project seem to have stemmed from a number of sources. One suspects that the colleagueship was satisfying to him but that he found *collaboration* with the two older men (Irwin and Edward Wortz) exceedingly difficult. The greatest area of concern seemed to be the method of the search itself. Turrell later discussed what he derogatorily called "taking a Pavlovian approach to spirituality":

> *Our culture is going through a strange time—looking at Eastern thought—their work with meditation, their sense of the body and mind and soul.* We're approaching it through psychology. *We're very physical. When we want to go into the universe, we can't look at a rock, like the Japanese. We have to actually go to the moon. We're so literal. We totally ignore the Eastern way. There are actually meditative sciences or sciences of the soul. We have devices, sensors, alpha conditioning machines. The machines are just manifested thought. Technology isn't anything outside us.... We just go about it very clumsily and wastefully. Because we have to actually* make *all these devices, we have to* go to *the moon. We can't see the cosmos in a rock and we can't meditate without having this thing strapped on us.*[4]

It is extremely difficult to say whether this statement is an indication of what Turrell considered to be a general metaphysical malaise—with which he was also afflicted—or an indication of a deeper spiritual need. The facts are that in the early years Turrell would refer to his work only in technical or scientific terms, and his work and his discussions of it are among the most technological and scientific of all those considered in this volume. Since the late 1980s, however, Turrell seems to have shouldered the mystical mantle with which many initially attempted to cloak Irwin—but that Irwin resolutely shrugged off.

Lunette, 1974, and *Skyspace,* 1972
Giuseppe Panza di Biumo, Varese, Italy
installed 1974

Count Panza visited Turrell in 1972, then purchased six works from him in 1972–73—three years before their first public showing. Panza's purchase was based largely on faith: none of the room-environment work had yet been executed, and they could be examined only in sketch form.

Many artists, including Friedrich, Turner, and the American Luminists in the nineteenth century and Kandinsky, Malevich, Rothko, and Newman in the twentieth century, attempted to use the painted surface as an opening into a world of metaphysical light. Turrell follows in this tradition but carries it one step further. By releasing light and color from the painted surface, he makes it possible at last for the viewer literally to enter, through vision, into the metaphysical space itself.

■ **Charles Miedzinski, "Affirmations of Perception and Spirit,"** ***Artweek,*** **January 25, 1986, p. 1.**

Some of Turrell's works in Panza's collection seem to take their vocabulary partially from Italian sources, such as the Roman arch that makes up so much Italian architecture. *Lunette* serves primarily as an architectural amplifier, rather than as an independent light-work. It traverses one half of the second-story corridor in the pristine remodeled stable where Panza's Light and Space works are installed. As I moved down this slender hallway (painted pure white, with an impeccable surface), my eye perceived an airy, softened haze that was thickest closest to me, brilliant and light-filled at the far end of the corridor. This longitudinal bar of soft light runs the length of the corridor's ceiling, terminating in a perfect lunette. As I progressed toward the lunette, it opened slowly to reveal a cloud-filled sky of deep robin's egg blue. (At least that was what I saw; at times there must be gray skies as well.) The effect was so overwhelming that I was reminded of divine light.

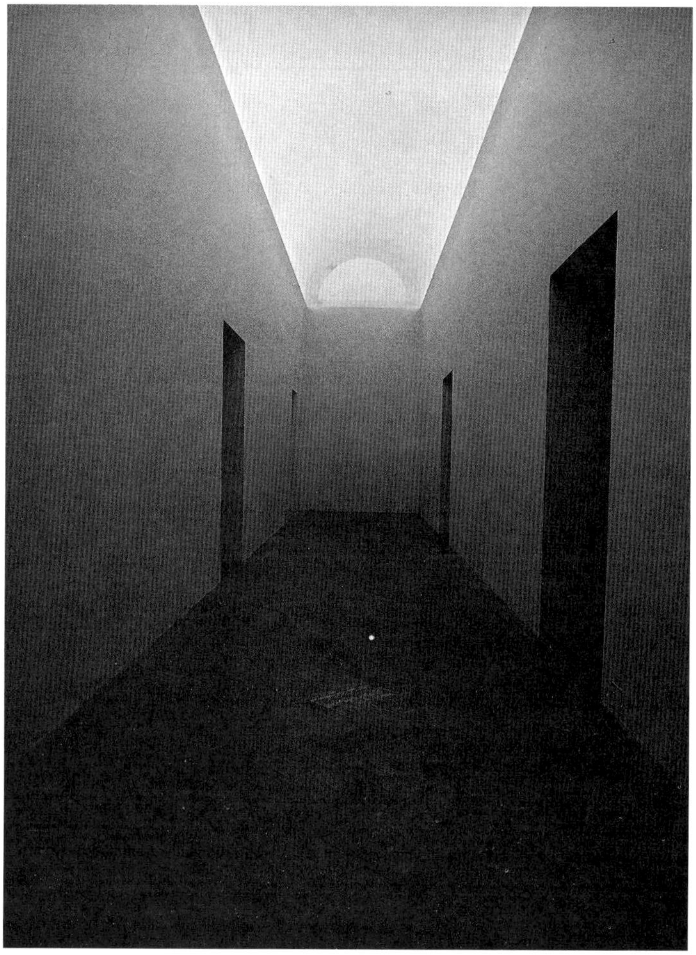

Turrell's *Skyspace* in the Panza collection is equally impressive, and for somewhat the same reasons, although its effect is quite different. This work consists solely of a small room with pure white walls and a square cut through the center of the roof to reveal the sky. The intensity of the Italian light is almost blinding. Lying on the floor—the only way to see the piece properly—I saw a shimmering cube of sky that was an improbable shade of ultramarine blue. As time passed, the sun cooled, the sky grew paler, and the view featured a cloud-filled sky that Tiepolo would have been proud to frame. Eventually that sky changed, too, and began to pull tight and flat over the ceiling, until nothing was left of its former color and shape. Later in the day it became a pale membrane that capped the ceiling like a flat silver scrim.

My art deals with light itself. It's not the bearer of revelation—it is the revelation.

■ **James Turrell,** ***Long Green*** **(Zurich: Turske and Turske, 1991), p. 89.**

James Turrell
Lunette, 1974
Natural-and-artificial-light installation
Permanent installation, Giuseppe Panza di Biumo, Varese, Italy

Light Projections* and *Light Spaces
Stedelijk Museum, Amsterdam
April 9–June 23, 1976

Turrell's modest exhibition at the Pasadena Art Museum, which was seen by relatively few people in the art world, was precociously early in the history of the art of Light and Space. Nonetheless, that exhibition represented the sole basis for Turrell's then totally underground reputation. Some nine years elapsed between it and his Stedelijk retrospective of ten pieces, which included the Projection Pieces, the Shallow Space Constructions, and models and plans for the *Roden Crater Project.* The foresightedness of Edward De Wilde, who curated the Amsterdam show, should be underscored: the exhibition, which proved to be a success, was a high-risk venture since it was mounted before anything other than Turrell's Projection Pieces had been on public view.

The most remarkable aspect of the Stedelijk show was the installation of *Arhirit,* a Shallow Space Construction with four chambers. *Arhirit* appeared to be nonexistent—its four rooms seemed empty and the walls bare. In fact, however, these were each Ganzfeld rooms, filled with sensory information. Each room resonated with a different color manufactured in the viewer's eye, and those colors changed or deepened as the percipient passed from room to room. The piece consisted partially of one solid wall, with small apertures cut through to the outside and canted to receive light from different sources. A passageway ran the length of the wall, separating it from the four chambers, each of which appeared to be a hazy cube of softened color. The exhibition catalog provided some of the piece's specifications:

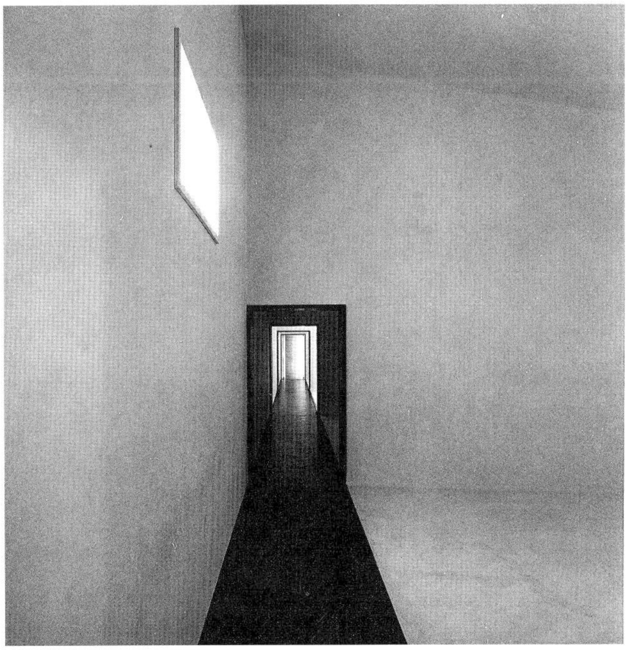

James Turrell
Arhirit, 1975–76
Ganzfeld room
Installation, Stedelijk Museum, Amsterdam, 1976

> The window in each cabinet is covered with a sheet of black Wilene plastic in which square perforations have been cut in order to regulate the incoming light in such a way that the entire space is filled with the same kind of light. A screen wall (painted white) has been erected in front of the window, with an aperture of 13.2 x 48.8 centimeters which is, in turn, covered with the layers of coloured and plain transparent paper, giving the suspended light a specific colour. The intensity of the coloured light depends on the time of day, the time of year, the clouds, in short, the weather. Each cabinet is subject to constant change: a space of ever-changing dimensions, immeasurable, a space where the light seems to hang as some kind of mass.[5]

The viewer progressed through the chambers, or "cabinets," in inverse order: number five was first, then four, three, and two (there was no number one). Number five was tinged by the turquoise paper in its windows, number four by red paper, number three by purple paper, and number two by violet paper.

Turrell later explained the piece as follows:

> *What happened with that series of pieces is that the color was essentially manufactured perceptually. In the first room, room five, the color tone...had the quality of lunar moonlight green. In all of those pieces the walls were completely white. You never saw color in paint. Any color was always picked up by light coming in. That is where it began. It was reflected off surfaces that were the outside space. So you never saw the material. In none of those works do you ever look through a material nor does light pass through a material. The screen wall had boxes inset, so that light entered in a certain manner after it was reflected off surfaces and off of certain portions of the sky.*
>
> *The first room, number five, takes the color and light off the grass; the next room, room number four, is an afternoon-looking piece; number three is a morning-looking piece, and the last room, room number two, takes the light off the surface of a [red brick] wall on the outside.... None of these pieces was strongly colored—but they were more colored than you think. Here is what happened: in room number five...you are looking at this pale moon green space, and as you are looking at it it is always that color. It is a Ganzfeld. What happens is that when you first*

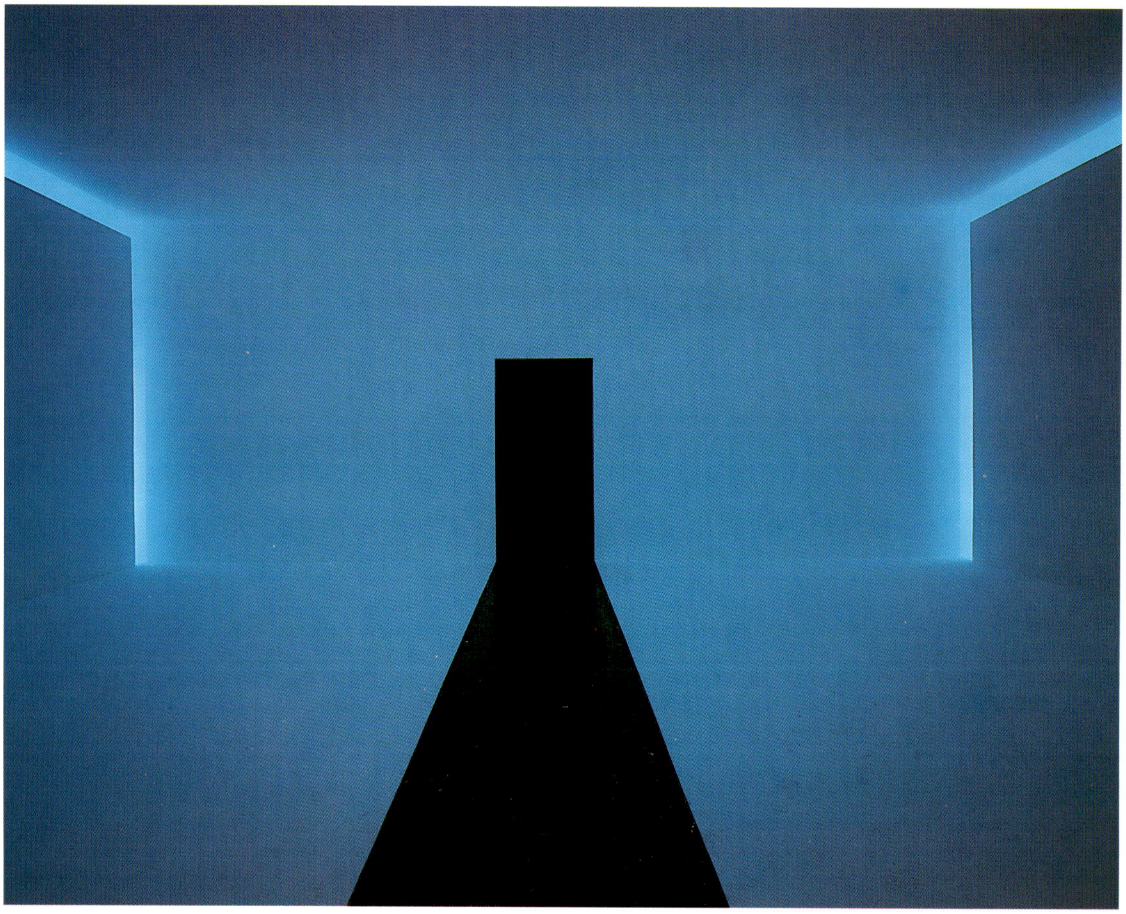

James Turrell
Rondo, 1969
Fluorescent-light installation
Newport Harbor
Art Museum, Newport Beach,
California, 1989

come in, that color has strength. Now, first of all, because there is no definition there, and there is no possibility of seeing a surface unless you are eighteen inches from it—the color fades, and you can't hold the color.... You then went into the next room, room number four.... As you go into that room, you carry an afterimage of the green—even though it is not so strong to you at that moment. So here is what happens: you have a very pale moon green, and after you leave the first room with this very pale green, the afterimage is a sort of very pale pink. So you go into the second room,... which is already a very pale reddish color from the outside brick in Amsterdam... and it is overlaid on top of this very warm pale red [enhanced by the red transparent paper], and color bouncing off the brick, and it makes a very rich color.... So now you are holding onto a pale green (which is the afterimage from the red room), and it comes in and mixes in room number three, which has a little red in it from the [purple] paper and blue from the sky. It is very light, but there is a touch of red in it because of all the brick.

There is another level to the piece, as Turrell went on to explain:

Now, if you are in the second room, room four, and you decide, "Wait a minute—what's happening?" and you go back to room number five—that room now doesn't look anything like it did before—because you are going the other way on the spectrum. What you have now is the fact that in the second chamber you have been looking at red and you return to the first room with a green afterimage. Now the green in the first room is darker and richer even than it was initially.... So no matter which way you move back and forth they become like chords.

The intense yet diffused color of Turrell's pieces affects the senses like a colored fog. You see it, think you could touch it, even inhale it, yet in reality it isn't there.

Turrell also installed *Raemar* and *Rondo* in the Stedelijk exhibition. *Raemar* was a large room-environment work composed of a light-edged plane that appeared to be free-floating. Perceived at first as a flat wall, *Raemar* gradually took shape as a full room-size piece, as the field of blue fluorescent light that emanated from behind the plane gradually permeated the viewer's vision. The blue was intense. It resonated in the eyes and gradually surrounded the participant in a bath of color. The piece took time, but eventually the white walls, floor, and ceiling pulled into shape, and the percipient was a lone observer in a vast field of blueness and light for which there was no visual precedent.

The structured presentation of this work was crucial to its apprehension. As in most of Turrell's pieces, there was a defined walkway and a line of demarcation (the white flooring that came out to the correct viewing position). The vast majority of viewers consciously or unconsciously honored these nearly invisible boundaries.[6]

In *Rondo* a false wall was erected directly in front of the existing walls on either side of a wide corridor. A false floor was laid down, with a walkway cut down to the original floor. Except for the portion of the wall closest to the floor, the piece was lit similarly to *Raemar*, the difference being that here the light illuminated and highlighted the architectural space rather than serving to cut a wall loose from its visual moorings.

Perhaps the most spectacular of all Turrell's pieces to date is *Wedgework*. An iridescent, transparent plane of pink and blue and lavender angled across a room on a shimmering diagonal, *Wedgework* was so corporeal it seemed to be solid and so powerfully hued it seemed to be in Kodachrome. The light was a vivid blue at the edges and suffused with baby pink in some nether

I want to create an atmosphere... one that can be consciously plumbed with seeing, like the wordless thought that comes from looking into the fire.

■ James Turrell

space behind. The work's heady beauty recalled Claude Monet's misted views of Venice and the visions of Charles Baudelaire:

> A room that is like a dream, a truly *spiritual* room, where the stagnant atmosphere is nebulously tinted pink and blue.
>
> Here the soul takes a bath of indolence, scented with all the aromatic perfumes of desire and regret. There is about it something crepuscular, bluish shot with rose; a voluptuous dream in an eclipse.... There are no more minutes, there are no more seconds! Time has disappeared; it is Eternity that reigns.[7]

To analyze how Turrell's pieces are made is akin to revealing how the magician saws a woman in half: it explains the phenomenon but not the magic. Turrell's works raise more questions than answers, as Ross Wetzsteon has noted:

> As we look at Turrell's light works, the questions familiar to us from even the briefest brush with philosophy—what does the mind do with the information it receives from the senses? What structure does it impose on our perceptions? To what extent do we create the external world by the order we give it?—become both disorienting metaphysical enigmas and wordlessly ecstatic experiences.[8]

James Turrell: Light and Space
Whitney Museum of American Art, New York
October 22, 1980–January 1, 1981

City of Arhirit, which Turrell realized for his Whitney exhibition, was a Ganzfeld piece that stemmed from the same principles as the multichambered *Arhirit,* seen at the Stedelijk. The primary difference was that the Whitney installation was a single-room piece and thus did not provide the full scale of color chords seen at the Stedelijk.

A lavender, light-defined room, *City of Arhirit* throbbed with a curious intensity. In this piece there was again a prescribed walkway, but the viewer could walk into the space. The room, which was coved and painted white, had a frontal plane defined by what seemed to be layers of lavender-tinted net or scrim. On closer observation the participant realized that there was no scrim at all, only color, which hung somewhere in front of the viewer's eyes. A wall with a small aperture designed to admit the specific amount of light had been built in front of an existing window. Into the aperture was inserted a translucent, aquariumlike construction, some three inches thick, filled with argon gas that was excited by sunlight in the daytime and by an electrical charge at night. The light through this aperture flooded the white room and mixed with the ambient light to create the richly colored atmosphere.

The Ganzfeld effect was so pronounced that a few people who chose to ignore the prescribed position in front of the plane of color found themselves dizzy and disoriented. Some slipped and fell. To ground the illusion the Whitney installed a bench in front of the piece. Each day museum employees would dutifully put the bench in place, and each day it would mysteriously disappear again, leaving the work pure.

Laar, also executed for the Whitney show, was created with ambient tungsten light that reflected off the walls of the museum. Here, according to Turrell, "the space that you looked at was looking at the space you were in." Upon entering the gallery the viewer saw what appeared to be a painting hung flat against the wall—a painting with a waxy blue-green-gray surface that looked like encaustic or softly painted silk. Knife-sharp at its edges, it was first perceived as flat, with a strong sense of surface. Then slowly, as the participant felt compelled to approach it, the space began to open up, revealing the outlines of a room behind it, filled with a misty fog. It was so uncanny that participants would tentatively reach through the flat frontal plane to determine whether it was a surface or a space.

James Turrell
Wedgework III
Fluorescent-light installation
Whitney Museum
of American Art, New York,
1980–81

James Turrell
Leo Castelli Gallery, New York
November 29, 1980–January 15, 1981

Turrell's Space Division Constructions are the most cool and cerebral of his pieces. Their forte is not beauty but being, pure and simple. A number of these have been exhibited in the United States since 1976, with slight variations in intensity of color and thickness of atmosphere.

Phaedo, made for Leo Castelli Gallery in November 1980, was similar to *Laar* in the Whitney show, with one important addition, which Turrell described:

Turrell is not simply working with a sublimity that comes ready-made. He makes sure that, by watching ourselves see, we compound the sublimity.

■ John Russell, "An Earthwork Looks to the Sky," *New York Times,* January 5, 1986.

> *In this case the space that you were looking into not only looked at the space that you were in but also looked at the sky above it. There was a skylight directly above it so it took information from those two spaces, and mixed it. The piece would change as clouds went by, and so*

I, too, in this flight, am renouncing things. I am giving up the broad golden surfaces that would befriend me if my engines were to fail. I am giving up the landmarks by which I might be taking my bearings. I am giving up the profiles of mountains against the sky that would warn me of pitfalls. I am plunging into the night. I am navigating. I have on my side only the stars. . . .

Earth and sky begin to merge into each other. The earth rises and seems to spread like a mist. The first stars tremble as if shimmering in green water. Hours must pass before their glimmer hardens into the frozen glitter of diamonds.

■ **Antoine de Saint-Exupéry, *Wind, Sand and Stars*, trans. Lewis Galantière (New York: Harcourt, Brace, Jovanovich, 1967), p. 139.**

bowl [of the volcano] with the original vegetation, which will come as a shock to the tumbleweeds. The finished project will have none of the clues that identify works of art institutions: there will be no labels on the walls, no information booth. . . .

Roden will be swept clean of references not only to the artist, art object, and art institution but also, aside from a few concessions to safety, to post-Renaissance Western civilization. There are no lenses at Roden, no track lighting, no loudspeakers. . . . Someone left to poke around the project on his own, knowing nothing of the actual history, might guess that it was a temple built thousands of years ago by a sect of Native American skyworshippers and long since abandoned. As much as possible, only local minerals are being used: desert sand, volcanic obsidian for the resonating bathtub, and shale from the bottom of a nearby Jurassic lagoon for the outside walkways, which will give the construction the look of having been built by a people without trucks. (One chamber escapes from the present era in the other direction: a shaft pointed to the North Star is intended to monitor the procession of the earth's pole from Polaris to Vega, which will become the new North Star in 12,000 years).[10]

In conversation Turrell seeks to clarify an important point: Earth is simply his *material*, not his statement. It is, in a sense, his canvas and his stretcher bars:

I am not an "earthwork" artist. I am totally involved in the sky. Let me make this very clear: The main thing is that I am totally interested *in space and* not *in form.*

If you go out on a very clear day and look up into the sky, it is not an infinite shape. It has a shape, a definite shape. The shape is generally more spherical or rounded right above you, and then it tapers off pretty quickly into this wedge that goes to the horizon. It does not rise up completely as a sphere.

Turrell has also spoken about his sense of time and space:

Roden Crater is a volcanic crater located in an area of exposed geology, the Painted Desert, an area where you feel geologic time. You have a strong feeling of standing on the surface of the planet. Within that setting, I am making spaces that will engage celestial events. Several spaces will be sensitive to starlight and will be literally empowered by the light of stars millions of light-years away. The gathered starlight will inhabit that space, and you will be able to feel the physical presence of that light.[11]

Once the project is completed, visitors will begin their involvement with it by spending a night in a comfortable space on the fumarole alongside the crater. This overnight stay is part of the letting-go process, which is an important preparation for the piece. No more than two people will be allowed to participate at one time, and Turrell prefers that the piece itself be experienced alone. With Turrell, the participant's own experience is paramount: "I don't want to take a photograph of Roden Crater and bring it back to you—nor do I wish to do a painting of the crater's effects and bring it back to you, I want you to experience the effect yourself."

The visitor will ascend to the outbuilding from the desert floor by way of a long series of steps made of rippled Moencope red stone, constructed in a style perfected by the Hopi and

James Turrell
Roden Crater: Ground Plan of Site,
1975
Collection of the artist

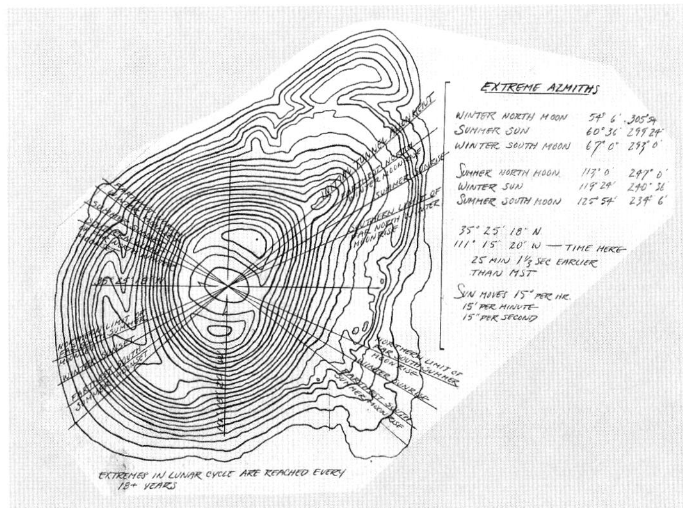

Zuni Indians. At the bottom of the crater is the floor of an ancient lagoon, and the ripples made by the wind blowing over shallow water have been there for 150 million years. Turrell notes: "The Hopis are a sky culture. When thunderstorms shriek across the sky and over the mesas, we are *literally* in the sky. They were very deeply involved with that intimate relationship."

The crater space will be a multiroom structure housing several sun and moon pieces, as well as Skyspaces similar to the one in Panza's collection. In all the pieces the participant feels that light is inhabiting the space. The artist's work with astronomers has yielded charts of all the celestial and astronomical events to take place in the area during the next two thousand years. Experiencing these events will be an important aspect of the work: every 18.6 years, for example, the moon will appear dead center in the tunnel of the crater—a spectacle that should be virtually overwhelming. At the same time, visitors will see a moon-cast image on the back wall of the tunnel—upside down and backwards, as if in a camera obscura. At the time of the summer solstice an image of the sun in its furthermost sunrise will appear on the opposite wall.

Some rooms will be oriented east to the sunrise, some north to the sunset, others south to the moon. Turrell even plans a lunar bathing chamber. He will use solar and lunar tracking devices to create some of the works; others will be created from natural light and atmospheric conditions alone. In every sense Turrell is, as he puts it, "playing the music of the spheres."

When ready to participate in the crater, the visitor will enter a room that opens into a tunnel about a quarter of a mile long, lit only by sunlight or moonlight. The tunnel leads to what Turrell calls a "kiva-like circular chamber." From there the visitor will see only sky and star patterns, even in the daytime.

Turrell has been a pilot for many years, and the experience of flying has greatly affected his work and his way of seeing:

> *For astronauts the sky is black. Then it becomes a deep purple when you are in a fighter plane at about seventy thousand feet. In a jet, at thirty thousand feet, you get a rich, deep blue. Down lower you get a bright, hazy pale blue. So, consequently, if you go to the Rocky Mountains, to a high altitude where it is cold, you see sky that is such a crisp blue you feel that you could cut it and put it in cubes! That is the kind of sky I want, and I have been able to get it by selecting the altitude. There are gradations near the horizon where the blue is lighter, and then gradually, toward the zenith, it gets deep. With Roden Crater I have taken out the first fifteen degrees of height by aiming the tunnel sight lines above that level. At that point you see thirty degrees less than one hundred eighty degrees. That is how you get that incredible color—by eliminating all of the white at the horizon.*

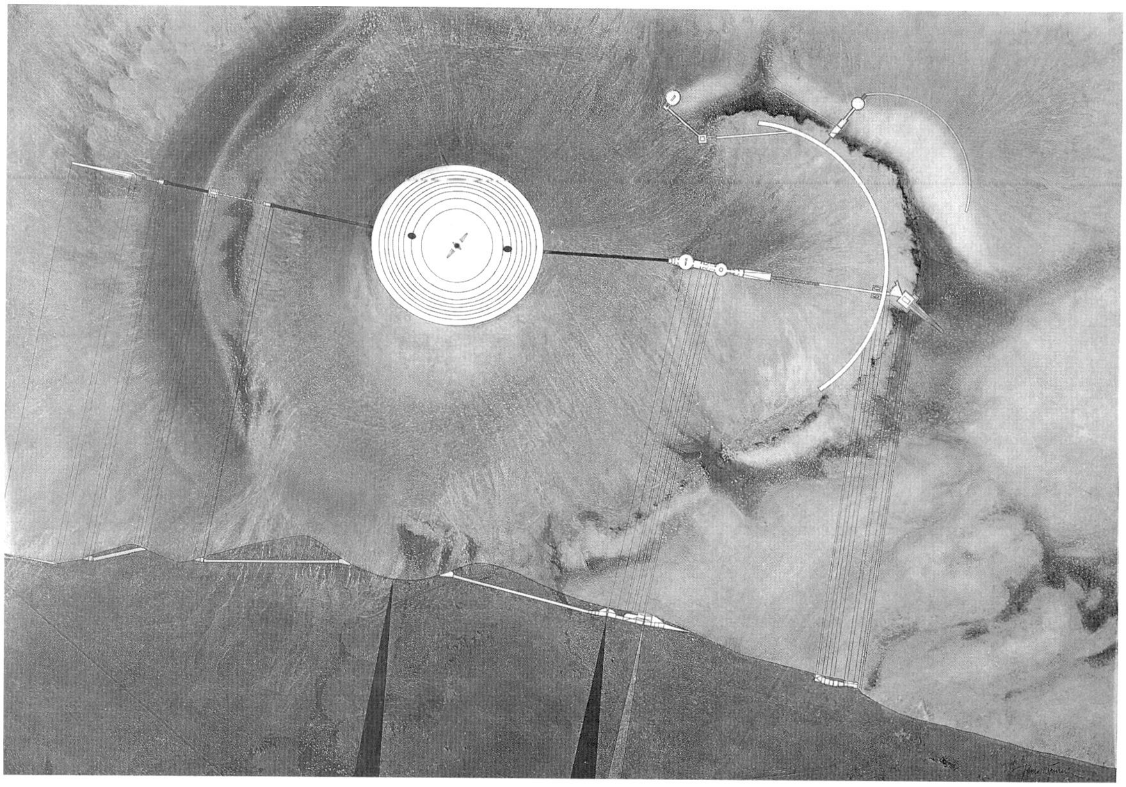

Perhaps it is the Italian patron and collector Giuseppe Panza di Biumo who put the matter best when he said that "the Roden Crater project is one of the few things that must be made, to prove that the light in the human mind is not gone." Flying above the crater in a tiny aircraft... we feel as the ancient Greeks might have felt, had they been able to fly over the unfinished Acropolis.... Coming home, we realize that what we have just seen is not a privileged playpen, but an attempt by a greatly gifted and still young man to come to terms with the universe in a way, and on a scale, of which Walt Whitman would have approved. In no other century, and at no other time, would such an adventure have been undertaken.

■ John Russell, "An Earthwork Looks to the Sky," *New York Times*, January 5, 1986.

The "celestial vaulting" effect at Roden Crater will likely be the most extraordinary aspect of the work, with the east and west spaces the most incandescent. As the viewer progresses through the tunnel and into the chamber, the sky will loom larger and larger, until suddenly the whole dome of heaven will appear overhead like a giant glass bubble, and the celestial vaulting seen in William Blake's etchings and in Renaissance paintings will become a vivid reality. "When you come from the enclosed space of the tunnel into the crater area, there is an opening up, *and you can hold onto it*. It's like blowing a bubble on a bubble-pipe slowly and gradually having it get bigger and bigger. If you just blew it out gradually it would burst. The same thing happens here with the celestial vaulting of the sky."[12]

Fully contained in one's own curved earth, one will have a sense of hovering below a curved dome of vibrantly intense turquoise. This dome, deep and resonant at its highest point, will gradually pull down and become a softer blue where it meets the rim of the crater.

The *Roden Crater Project* is complex and highly ambitious. If it succeeds—and it is far from being completed or even fully funded—it may become one of the great icons of our time. The power potentially inherent in it is perhaps best expressed in the "Parable of Geocentrism," which Jacob Needleman retold in *A Sense of the Cosmos:* "Your experience of illusion is enough to make you careful. What matters to Earth's inhabitants is that they should know of their vital connections with the sky. As to the movement of the stars, it is better to note what you see than to imagine what may deflect you from the real meaning. Then we will place ourselves at the center of the sky we are watching where all star-movement is seen by reference to ourselves."[13]

Above
James Turrell
Roden Crater: Third-Stage Site Plan with Segmented Cross Section, 1985
Collection of the artist

In the 1980s Turrell (whose MacArthur grant, with its very substantial stipend, came in 1984) was able to concentrate much of his time and energy on the *Roden Crater Project.* At the same time, he was still able to have a number of key exhibitions, and they made it evident that his work on the crater was radically reshaping his vision. (Turrell had exhibited widely in Europe but had not had a major museum show in the United States in the fourteen years between his Pasadena exhibition in 1967 and his Whitney exhibition in 1980–81). Finally, as the 1980s progressed he had a number of important venues at his disposal in which he could fine tune his perceptual concepts. In addition to those shows, mentioned earlier, at the Whitney, Castelli, and MoCA, he had exhibitions in Seattle, Los Angeles, and San Francisco.

In his 1980s exhibitions Turrell tested *Razor* and *Wedgework* (the Whitney); *Afrum Blue* (MoCA); *Sensing Spaces* (Center on Contemporary Art, Seattle); and *House of Wax, Iltar, Amba,* and *Razor* (Capp Street Project, San Francisco). Interestingly, the MoCA, CoCA, and Capp Street venues were all alternative or nontraditional spaces. Elegant they may be, but they are all clearly avant-garde.

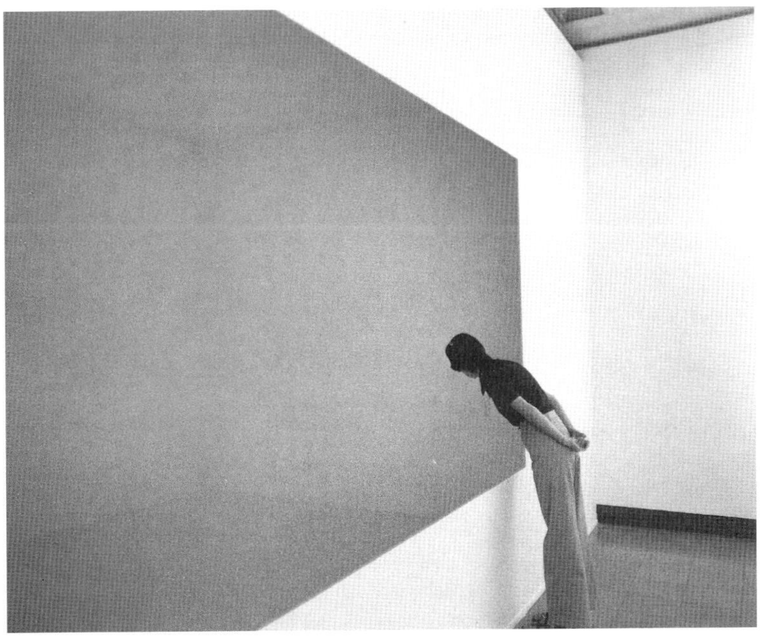

James Turrell
Iltar
Installation, University of Arizona Museum of Art, Tucson, 1980

Turrell is more shaman than magician. An artist who likes space to "yield to vision," who says "light is not so much something that reveals, as it is itself the revelation," who wants, in short, to make light manifest—this is an artist with a spiritual turn of mind.

Turrell himself rarely uses a word like spiritual. He would not want to trap his art in sentimental rhetoric or risk being taken for a warmed-over hippie. This careful reticence (also felt in his art) is partly why the Roden Crater project seems convincingly contemporary. It evokes the star-struck religions of the ancients, yet is confined to no particular religion; it hints at magical geometries, yet is plainly respectful of the contemporary sciences of psychology, aeronautics and astrophysics. Most of all, perhaps, its whole vast crazy precision, its marvelous remoteness, seem appropriate. Not because Turrell is a holy fool, but because a spiritual light, in this society, is best seen from the corner of the eye.

■ **Mark Stevens, "Turrell's 'Celestial Vault,'" *Newsweek*, February 10, 1986, p. 70.**

Having shaped his works with these exhibitions and many others during his very active period of the 1980s, Turrell began to radically expand his visual vocabulary. The works of the 1970s and '80s seemed to some to be repetitive, but that was only the case for those who did not grasp the larger picture. The works that Turrell has undertaken so far in the 1990s have expanded his concepts even further. With *Irish Sky Garden,* for example, he has responded innovatively to an exquisite site while still using his familiar visual vocabulary.

Irish Sky Garden
West Cork, Ireland
Commissioned by Veith Turske, 1990; in process

Irish Sky Garden is located in southwestern Ireland, where Turrell found a different type of sky than he had previously worked with. "It's a much more dramatic, cloudy and brooding sky.... All through the walk, and especially at the very end of it, visitors will get different perceptions of the Irish sky." This damp and lushly green garden, which seems to go on forever, is "a little bit of heaven." As Turrell notes: "In many ways it is just like the Crater, in the sense that the shape determines the inside space. The difference is that [with the Crater] I am more involved with

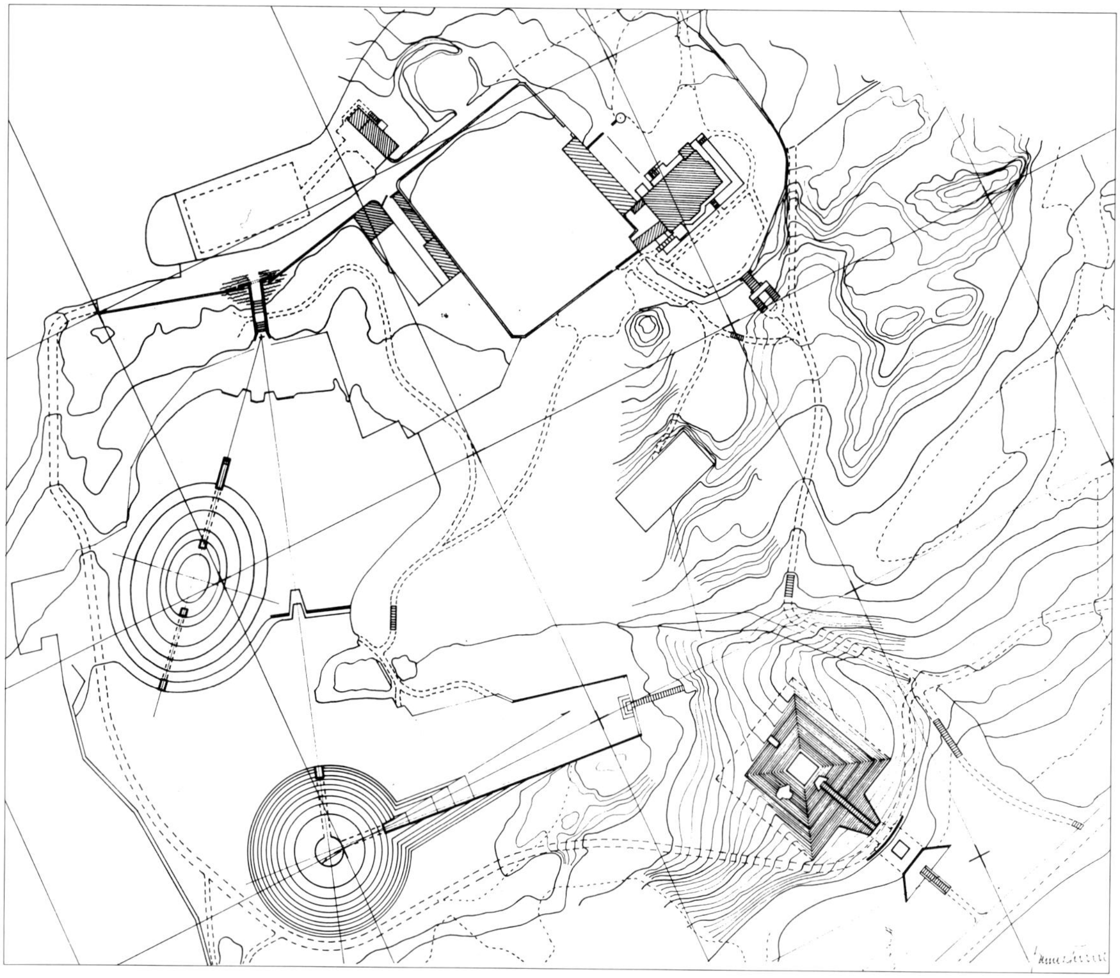

In the end what we are doing is gardening or tending the sky.

■ **James Turrell, *Long Green* (Zurich: Turske and Turske, 1991), p. 120.**

James Turrell
Irish Sky Garden: Third Overall Site Plan, 1990
Ink on Velin d'Arches paper,
22 7/16 x 30 5/16 in. (57 x 77 cm)
Hess Collection, Napa,
California

James Turrell
Irish Sky Garden: Space 3, the Pyramid, 1990
Ink on Velin d'Arches paper,
$22^{7}/_{16}$ x $17^{1}/_{2}$ in. (57 x 44.5 cm)

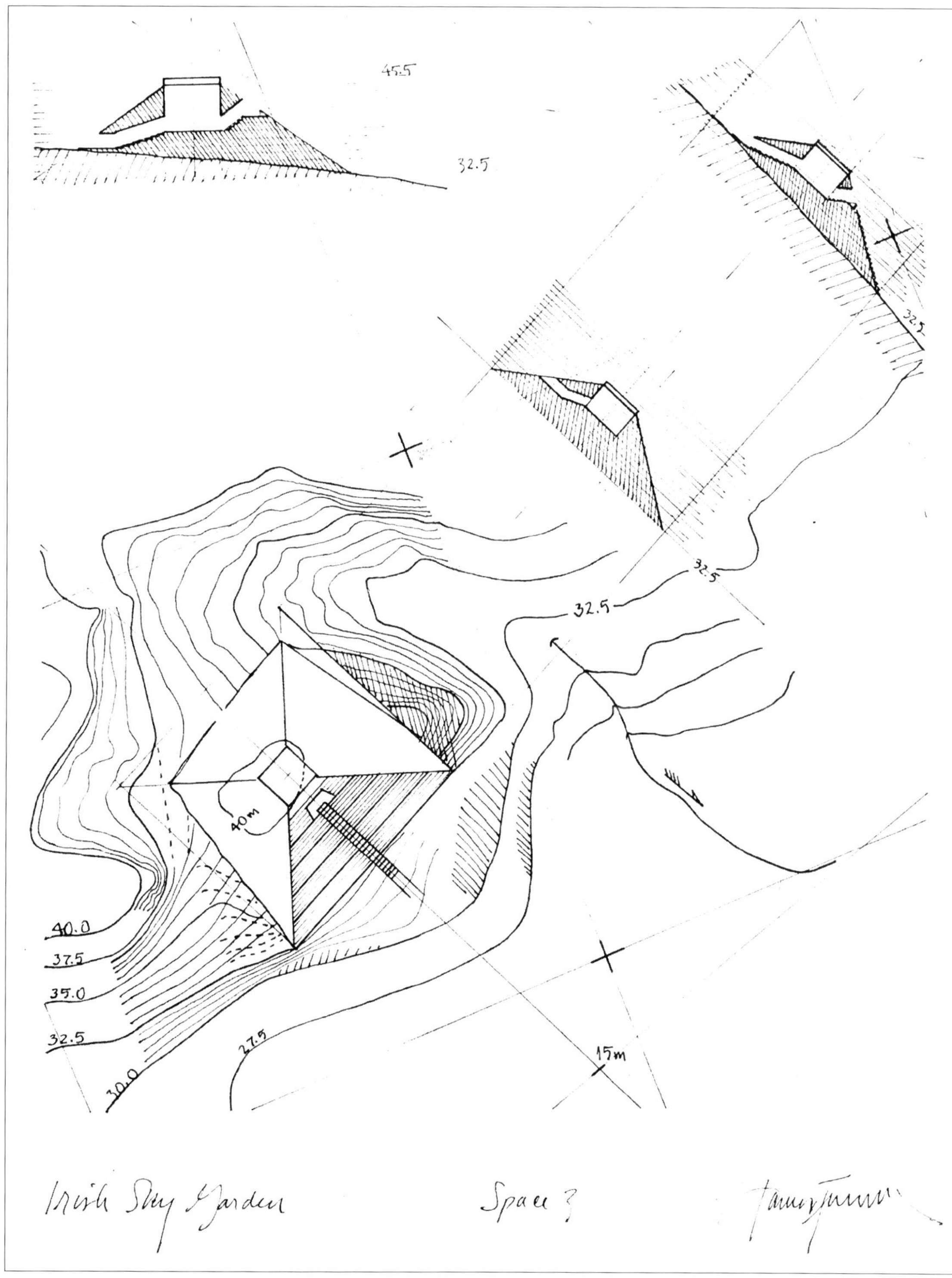

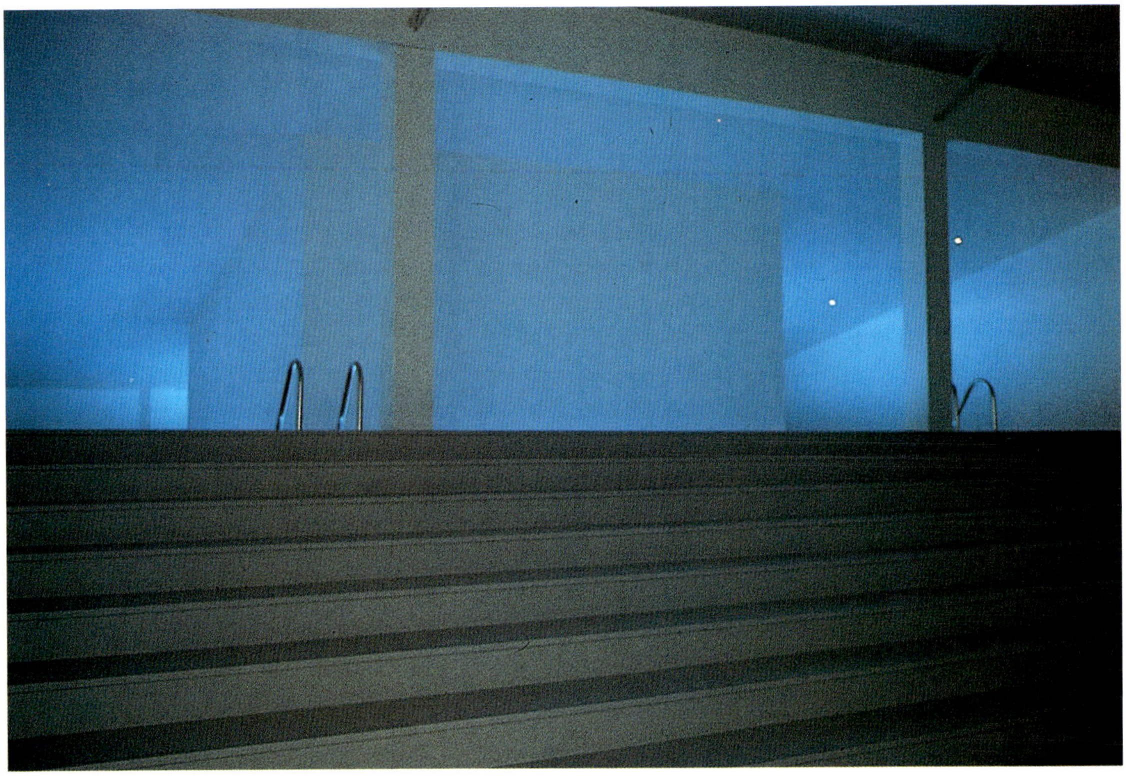

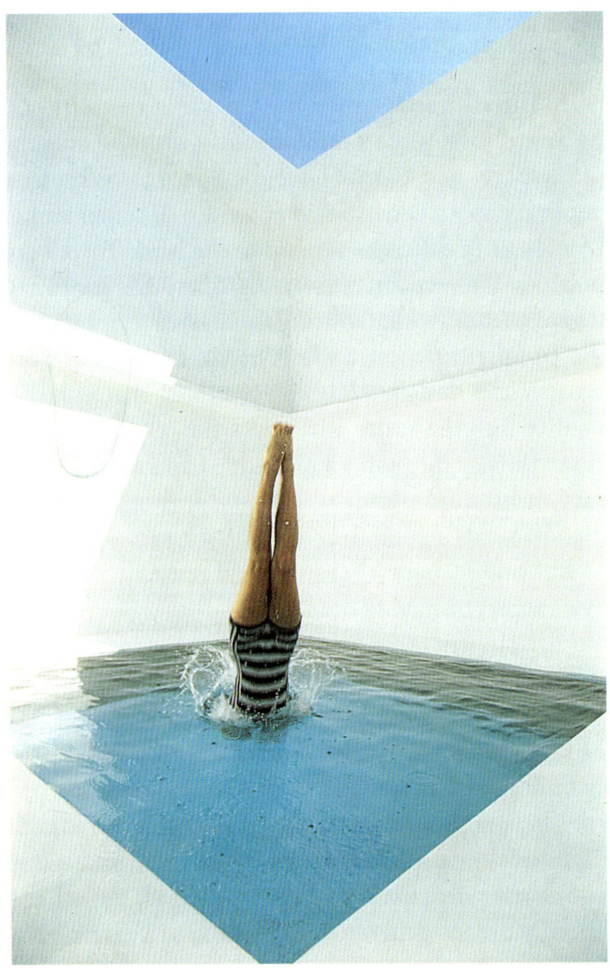

Opposite and right
James Turrell
Heavy Water
Installation, Confort Moderne,
Poitiers, France, 1991

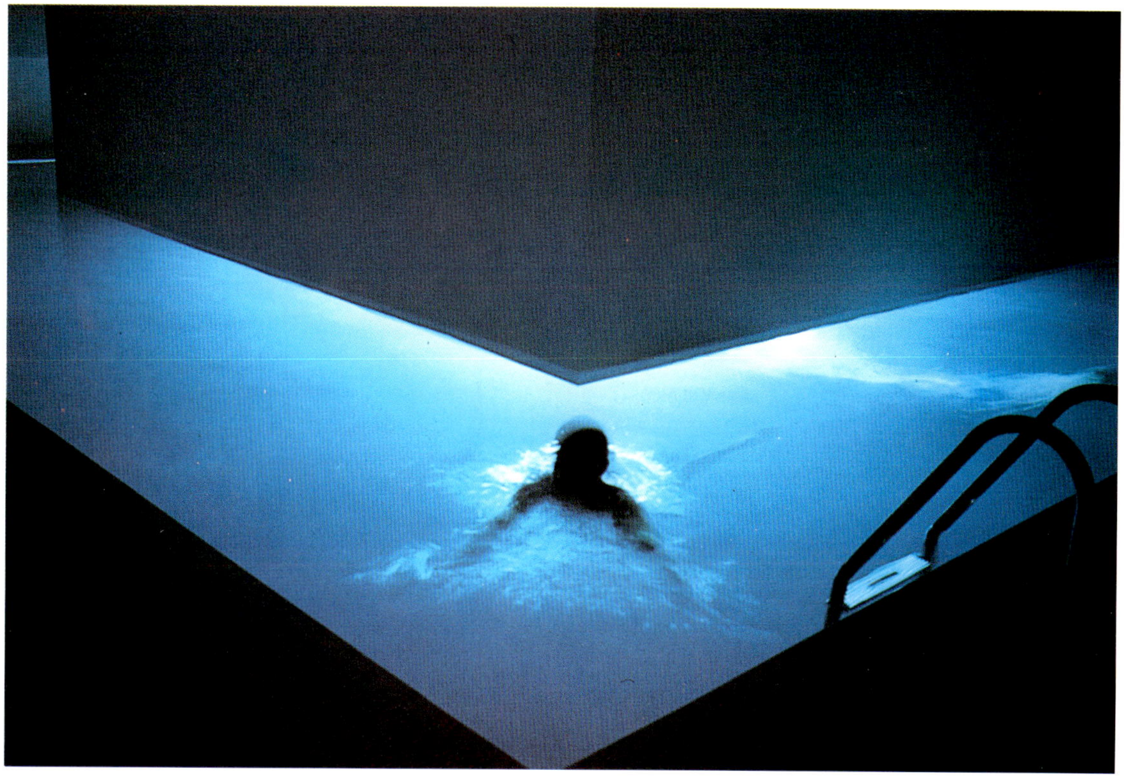

Right
James Turrell
Earth Shadow
Installation, Confort Moderne,
Poitiers, France, 1991

emerge. The emergence comes through self-generated seeing, like in a dream, not through physical entry as in *Heavy Water.*"

With *Earth Shadow,* the initial event takes place behind the eyeballs. In a velvety dark room a strange red sensation slowly floods the space until a red/purple/blue rectangle begins to take shape.

> When I saw [Turrell's] almost indescribable light installations at SteinGladstone last summer, they made me think of the late paintings of Mark Rothko and Barnett Newman. Turrell's light seems to have the same kind of glow that comes from those mystical canvases. In Turrell's case, though, there is no surface, there is nothing but the light itself. After the SteinGladstone show, I felt an urge to touch what appeared to be a luminous purple rectangle on the wall of the darkened room. It turned out to be a rectangular hole in a false wall with a fluorescent light behind it playing off low-watt incandescent bulbs.[14]

Describing the physical aspects of the piece, Turrell said:

> Earth Shadow *is a piece using black light, ultraviolet, and red light, as opposed to tungsten light [as in the SteinGladstone exhibition]. The work isn't revealed until your eyes adapt to the dark. You enter it from daylight and over time your pupils begin to open; and then you see the work. Both pieces* [Heavy Water *and* Earth Shadow] *deal with emergence; in one it's the physical act of the self entering the space, and the other it's the emergence of color from the dark. In one the piece changes; in the other, you do.*

Maria Nordman

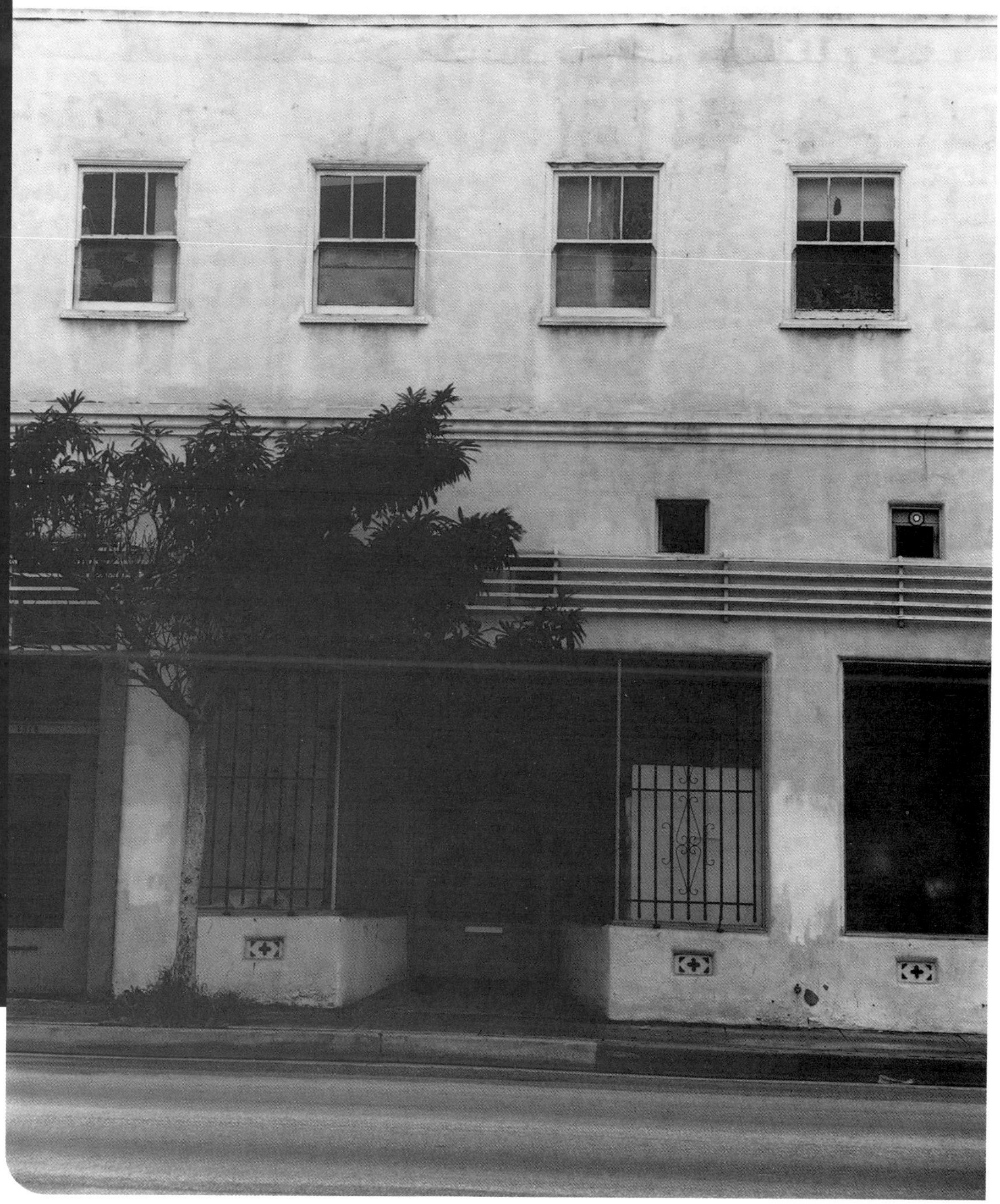

For we feel
We evaporate
Oh we
Breathe ourselves out
and away
emberglow to emberglow
We give off a fainter smell.
It's true that someone may say to us
"You're in my blood
this room
the spring
is filling with you."

Rainer Maria Rilke

Maria Nordman

Maria Nordman wants her work to be experienced through the senses—to be seen, to be talked about. Her inclusion in this book—or in any other not of her own making—does not meet with her approval. If an aura of mystery surrounds Nordman's work, it is because she has contributed to it. Unlike Irwin, whose acute articulateness illuminates his work, Nordman remains virtually mute, refusing to give interviews and continuing to request that her work not be written about or photographed. (Even without her opposition it would be impossible to photograph the incessant changes of light, shadow, and natural sound that take place within her pieces, or to capture the alterations made by the entry of each participant.)

Nordman is open as a friend, totally closed as a colleague. About life she is effusive, penetratingly intelligent, warm, fey. About her work she is cold, firm, obsessive. Attempt to interview Nordman, and she will end up interviewing you. Invite her to teach about her work, and she will accept—then take the students out of the dark lecture hall into the sunlight. Ask her if she meditates, and she will ask if it isn't true that we all meditate in one way or another. Ask her what or who has influenced her, and she will say it was the ocean or ask what "influences" means. A question is answered with another question again and again, until the questioner is forced to contemplate his or her own response—to search there for meaning. Nordman deflects all "why" questions as metaphysical—and unanswerable.

Of all the people dealt with in this book, Nordman is the most elusive and the most difficult. That difficulty lies with the beholder, however, for the artist is clear: she simply wants to be left alone and to have her work experienced on its own terms. By attempting to thwart the critical process, Nordman raises important questions about its validity and morality. Because we have so little information from her, there is always the danger of overinterpreting or underinterpreting her work. Yet there are clues planted here and there, and by paying attention to them we can begin to understand.

Nordman's work did not begin to filter into the art community until 1970. Although she had been living in Santa Monica for many years, she did not participate in Southern California's community of artists during the 1960s. However, she was quietly pursuing her own investigations during that period and creating a solid body of mature work (or, more accurately, an immaterial body of mature work). That work was first exhibited in her studio in 1970 and 1971 and then to a larger public in exhibitions at the Pasadena Art Museum in 1972 and at the Newport Harbor Art Museum and the University of California, Irvine, in 1973.

Studio Pieces
1014 Pico Boulevard, Santa Monica, California, 1967–70

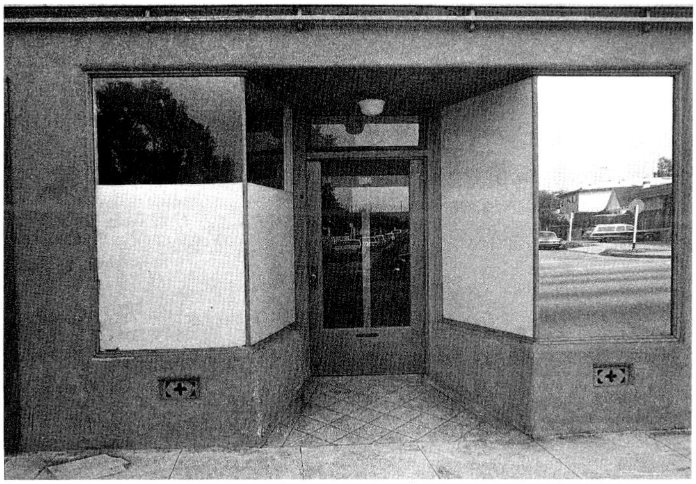

Maria Nordman (b. 1943) Exterior of studio installation at 1014 Pico Boulevard, Santa Monica, California, 1971

Between 1967 and 1970 Nordman executed in her studio at 1014 Pico a number of works that few people in the art world saw. These pieces were conceived not for the usual viewing public but for the random passerby, untutored and uninitiated. This reaching out to the accidental participant remains a crucial aspect of her work, as is the transmittal of information about it solely by word of mouth. In her own private laboratory she sets up a kind of controlled experiment through which she determines how long it takes a work to become known and how that awareness happens. This is a principle she will not discuss, but it is clearly part of her art. Nordman's near-fanatic insistence that her work exist on its own terms—without media attention or critical overlay—is essential to the work's power. By the time Nordman's first major studio work, *1014 Pico*, was done in 1971, however, many art-world people participated in it, having heard about it gradually. It represented the first semipublic presentation of her investigations.

About this room, which was plunged into utter darkness, I knew everything. I knew everything, I had entered into it, I bore it within me, I made it live, with a life that is not life, but which is stronger than life, and which no force in the world can vanquish.

■ Maurice Blanchot, in Gaston Bachelard, *The Poetics of Space*, trans. Maria Jolas (Boston: Beacon, 1969), pp. 228–29.

I entered her storefront studio—a sparse, clean space totally devoid of furniture or any other of the usual accoutrements of a living-working area. Tatami mats were the room's only embellishment. There was clearly no place to sit except on the mats, either facing or beside the artist. A nervous cat jumped back and forth across the small room, punctuating the curious tension. This was clearly a private space, and the participant was an intruder. The piece was nowhere to be seen.

At a given point some decision was reached, and Nordman moved slightly to one side, revealing a small door behind her. "You may go in now," she said, leaving me no other choice. Having passed through the tiny portal, I heard the door click softly and was instantly cast into inky darkness. The ceiling of what appeared to be an entrance tunnel seemed only four to five feet high, and like the approach to a formal Japanese tea house, it necessitated my stooping for a short distance before I could enter the central chamber.

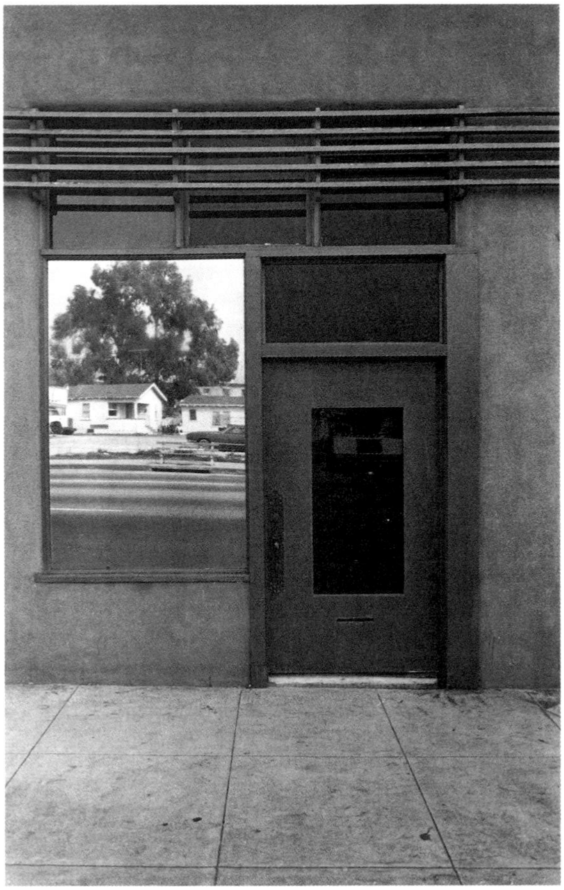

The darkness was total—a rich, palpable darkness that was the darkness of night or sleep, the darkness inside the mind's eye. Its effect on me was overwhelming, but it was *my* response. The space itself was neutral. I found the initial impact of the work overpoweringly claustrophobic; for others it was warm and enfolding. If initially there was anxiety, it was because the sensation was so intense, the presence so strong. There was obviously no immediate danger, and it was clear that whatever fears were raised were of a psychic not a physical threat.

Gradually, as my pupils adjusted and my breathing slowed, the room lightened. A tiny pinhole admitted enough outside light to soften the room. It was no longer dark, yet it was not light. The space had a presence so pungent that it was surprising there was not some smell like the mossiness of medieval churches.

As the room became lighter, walls and corners began to define themselves almost imperceptibly. What appeared to be a scrim veiling a deep void became a thin wall of light with all the corporeality of a real wall, but far more luminous. Suddenly the passages in space where the corners met became critical to my focus. The end of the room appeared to drop off into nothingness. The room seemed to pulsate—yet it was not the room that throbbed but the flow of blood through the veins of my eyes, controlled by the regular beat of my heart. I became fully aware of perceiving myself perceiving the room.

This work made clear that Nordman's early involvement with anechoic chambers had profoundly affected her. She noted in 1973: "I used to go into an anechoic chamber a few years back, where I discovered that I was emitting everything myself into a black and soundless space. My eyes were projecting white onto the void; my ears were playing my body sounds."[1]

After spending some time in the space, my experience of the room became compounded, polymorphous. There was a sense of precognition, of having known about this place before. Yet sorting through known sensations, my rational mind grasped in vain for a shape; there was no frame of reference to check the experience against. Having initially responded to the piece with extreme anxiety, I now found it to be seductive, embracing, even hypnotic. The experience was deeply moving and meditative, and now, finally, there was a desire to stay. Time, which had

Opposite
Maria Nordman
Exterior of studio installation at 1014 Pico Boulevard, Santa Monica, California, 1972
A mirror coating on the window created a one-way viewing situation.

Right
Maria Nordman
Exterior of studio installation at 1014 Pico Boulevard, Santa Monica, California, 1972

seemed to pass so slowly at first, was long since forgotten. Time and space had become one, and I had become a part of that whole.

There was another piece in Nordman's studio, a workroom piece entitled *Window Frame Rectangle* that was realized first in 1971 and then again in 1973 in a slightly different version. This "place," as Nordman terms it, consisted of a bare room from which all light fixtures, furniture, and floor coverings had been removed. The walls were white; the floors were stripped down to the bare wood. The studio had only a door, a window, and several steps leading up to a platform that was level with the bottom of the large window facing the street. The window had a deep frame. The surface of its glass had a mirrored coating, which let in only 20 percent of the existing light. The piece was conceived so that any person passing by or any other change in the outside conditions became a part of the work. It was never written about or publicized; it was participated in only by accident.

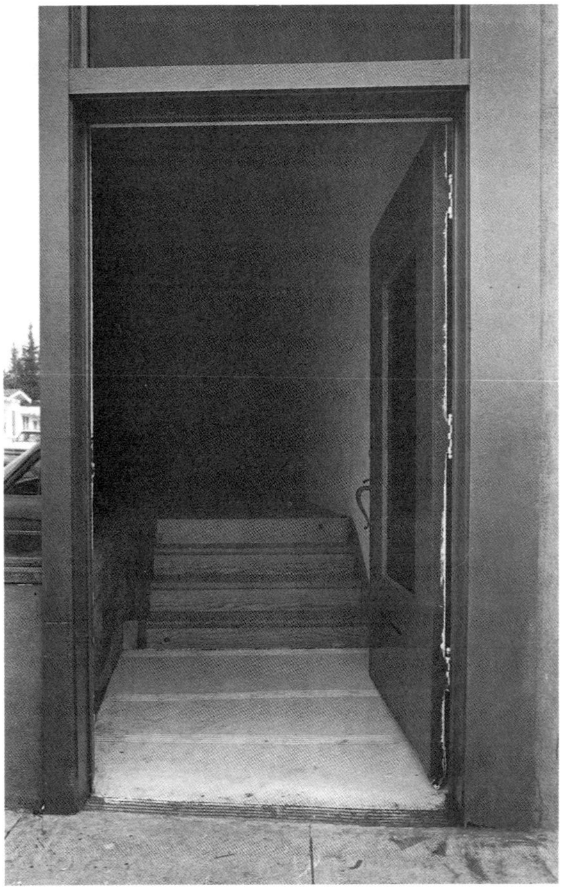

Nordman wrote of this piece:

The rectangle is in a constant position and
I take a constant position with it.
Two fixed positions and a frame of constant change.

The frame is still with each change that fills it with the attention.
The attention is still with the frame that fills it with each change.
Each change is still with the attention that fills it with the frame.[2]

Sitting on the platform in front of the window in the daytime, the participant could see out but the chance passerby could not see in. At night the situation was reversed; when a single work-light was turned on in the back of the studio, the interior was visible to the outside world. On many occasions the interior was left dark, and then it was only the periodic flash of an automobile headlight that penetrated the darkness and momentarily

Looking from outside into an open window one never sees as much as when one looks through a closed window. There is nothing more profound, more mysterious, more pregnant, more insidious, more dazzling than a window lighted by a single candle. What one can see out in the sunlight is always less interesting than what goes on behind a windowpane. In that black or luminous square life lives, dreams, life suffers.

■ Charles Baudelaire, *Paris Spleen*, trans. Louise Varèse (New York: New Directions, 1970), p. 77.

a place open to any person
a place open to any person
and any condition of light
and sound
a place open to any person
and any condition of light
and sound for 24
hours dawn to dawn on an
unused
(unnamed) ground

■ **Maria Nordman, "Fragments from Directions of Approach,"** ***Saman*** **(March–April 1979).**

defined part of the room. This piece was reciprocal: it took during the daytime and gave away at night.

There is virtually no vocabulary for describing Nordman's work, and those who have participated in the pieces are often unable to discuss them easily—even with each other. So unprecedented are these works within Western art that one turns to the Orient for illumination. A Japanese magazine, for example, described Nordman's 1979 piece for Documenta 6 as "The Room That Has Nothing."[3] Nothing. Nothing and everything. Light and dark. Empty and full. Nordman describes that same piece simply as "a chance entry place for any two persons and the light and sound from two doors." Certain Japanese words help define concepts that have no counterparts in English. *Ma* is a term used to describe the overlapping of time and space in the same space at the same time. *Utsuroi* refers to "the perception of things—things fading and growing, shadows shifting with the light, space as a moment in the continual process of change."[4] These two words come far closer to capturing the phenomena of Nordman's pieces than do any art-historical or critical terms in our own language.

Nordman puts great importance on the meaning of words. She terms her pieces "places" rather than "spaces" (a space, she feels, is empty). Her places are designed to be used—by persons unknown. They encompass constantly changing qualities of light, shadow, and sound, which differ with the time of day and the response of each participant. In these pieces, clock time stops and internal time begins.[5]

Negative Light Extensions or "There Are No Ocean Streets"
Newport Harbor Art Museum, Newport Beach, California, 1973

Newport Beach has bright, dry light and air kept clean by sea breezes. In *Negative Light Extensions,* Nordman's first documented public work outside her studio, she used the clarity of this light and the intensity of the sun to superb advantage. Pursuing her concerns with public/private spaces, in the alley behind the museum she constructed, in white plaster, an architectural piece in the shape of a large door, which could not be entered. An unexplained, undifferentiated white space, it was moderately deep, coved, and rectilinear. It bore no label, and as a result many participants came upon it unawares. Others sought it out deliberately. The work was totally dependent on the sun, which first rose slowly up its face, then, moving overhead and reaching its optimum intensity at high noon, spilled downward, giving the rectangular volume shape and the blinding intensity of the light on Greek islands.

On a working drawing of the Newport piece Nordman made the following notations:

> A DOOR *(rectangular shape into building facade)* OPENING *(from a public walkway or street from south into north)* AND THE PROJECTION *(strikes the frame and carries its edge to the ground)* OF SUNLIGHT INSIDE *(Plan suggests a given moment and place)* A CONSTRUCTION *(Raw materials plaster board and frame structure) enter room from the street. The surface is precisely surfaced and painted white.*
>
> *The piece is called* Negative Light Extensions *with the given daylight and the given sound in a city.*[6]

Writing about this piece in *Artforum,* Peter Plagens said:

> Although Maria Nordman is clearly related to friends, Irwin (the senior theorist), and contemporaries like Michael Asher, Jim Turrell, Eric Orr and (perhaps) Barbara Munger, she is very much her own artist. Perhaps in the long run, such is the contribution of a West Coast art which began with the latent electricity in Larry Bell's boxes: an art which, without quoting scripture, without wearing its own dialectic as a badge of style, *will get us out of history.* Because, you see,

an art like Nordman's is not the history of the demolished piece, but of those who've been there, and gone on.[7]

What Plagens says is important—but he makes a crucial error in suggesting a relationship between Nordman's art and Irwin's. The fact that she is younger than Irwin and that her first public exhibition dates are slightly later than his has tended to obscure the originality of her contributions. Nordman never studied with Irwin, nor was he ever her mentor in any way. They cannot even be considered friends. The paths they have taken have, on occasion, crossed and have produced reactions of an uncanny similarity—but that is only because each responds so intensely to the feeling of a space and what might occur within it.

Germano Celant summed up the distinguishing characteristics of Nordman's art:

> Unlike her colleagues, Nordman has never used artificial illumination in her works, relying instead on natural light and its permutations: Light—direct and indirect, baffled or translucent, in minute color gradations from local reflections—and most emphatically private spaces (clean, contemplative, tailored, and sparse) that open onto public places (lively, circumstantial, unpredictable) are central to her art. She creates spaces in dualities: open and closed, in and out, fabricated and natural, Eastern and Western. If her constructions, which have included a stone wall built across the German landscape and a reconstructed freight barge in which she plied European rivers, suggest a Western heritage, her manipulation of light seems both Eastern and intuitive. Gone are the specifics of psychological investigation found in the work of Irwin or Turrell. Nordman's spaces often feel like sacred precincts, buffered from the outside world and yet made available through the illumination she admits.[8]

The clearest examples of how differently Irwin and Nordman work are their individual installations in the *Space as Support* exhibition at the University Art Museum, Berkeley (see pages 44–45 and 107–9). Irwin's approach was bold, aggressive, even strident. His installation, which was up for a month and a half, utilized fluorescent lights that zigzagged across the levels of the museum, clarifying the logic of its brutalist architecture. In precisely the same space Nordman executed a piece for one day only, using only the day's light to illuminate a space made white by the addition of pure white flooring.

Saddleback Mountain
Fine Art Gallery, University of California, Irvine
September 25–October 28, 1973

Saddleback Mountain was a room environment entered via a hallway. In the opening between the hallway and the room, Nordman placed a sixteen-by-eleven-foot mirror, which reflected Saddleback Mountain through the door and outside the entryway behind the viewer. The outside light bounced off the mirror, slipped across the floor, up the corner, and back across the ceiling to its point of instigation, its beam dividing the room into dark and light.

Doors that open on the countryside seem to confer freedom behind the world's back.

■ **Gaston Bachelard, *The Poetics of Space*, trans. Maria Jolas (Boston: Beacon, 1969), p. 224.**

Nordman's notations on a working drawing for the piece describe it as "an existing room with a concurrent entry made for the person, the light, the sound. Entering at ground level with 51-foot entrance beginning 22 inches wide, opening to 5 feet with a floor to ceiling mirror (second image of entry) dividing the room in two. Diagonal light touching a dark room."[9] On either side of the line of light, the room (which was painted white but appeared hazy, gray, and molecular) took on varying degrees of darkness or intensity as the percipient's pupils dilated and he or she began to see differently.

The information is not coming in only visually. I am interested in a range of experience that happens with one's whole body sensing and conversing over a period of time.

■ **Maria Nordman, in Hal Glicksman and Barbara Haskell, *Saddleback Mountain* (Irvine: University of California, 1973).**

Saddleback Mountain was an inside/outside room. Personal, meditative, and serene, it was also infused with daily "real world" noises such as bird sounds that found their way in from the trees at the base of the mountains. Many of Nordman's pieces are partially open to the outside in order to incorporate various external sounds. Often the Ganzfeld effect in her works is disorienting, and the participant, trying to ground himself, finds that it cannot be done visually but it can be done aurally—a reassuring discovery.

Only after having spent a long time at a site does Nordman determine what kind of work should take place there. She then roughs out simple floor-plans. Her pieces arise directly from the experience of the site itself, and they are neither interchangeable nor transportable.

I usually will tend to sit still with a place for a while before I decide. Then it's just a matter of the floor plan and everything is finished. When I came out to Irvine to draw up the floor-plan—I just walked around a lot. After a while the buildings seemed to recede and I began to see new animals, plants, the unspoiled parts of the landscape and the Saddleback Mountain.[10]

4th and Howard Streets, San Francisco, 1975
San Francisco, 1975

Nordman created a work in the Yerba Buena section of San Francisco just before that tattered area was razed to make way for a new convention center. Abandoned, derelict, out of the way, the neighborhood was populated by a constantly changing cross-section of office workers, blue-collar laborers, and transients.

Nordman's exquisite piece, perhaps her most poetic up to that date, was created "for the occasional passerby." She asked that the piece not be publicized or discussed in any way except by word of mouth (indeed, she considered forbidding that it be written about—which she later realized was impossible). She wanted the percipient's response to be uncontaminated by any prior conceptualizing. Initially this seemed not only regrettable (the work was so profoundly impressive that one found it difficult to comply with her wishes, because of the desire to have others see it too) but also naive, since it was difficult to believe that information about the work would get out. In retrospect, the artist was clearly right, for an essential aspect of the piece was its dissemination by osmosis.

By the end of the roughly two and a half months of its existence, a remarkable number of people had seen the work, including Count Panza (who later commissioned work from Nordman) and Alfred Frankenstein, the art critic from the *San Francisco Chronicle*, who, as a general rule, never ventured south of Market to participate in San Francisco's underground art activities. He wrote a sensitive article entitled "Nordman's Hidden Work of Magic," respecting her wish that he not reveal its location.[11]

Walking down Howard Street looking for Nordman's piece, I noticed a recently repainted storefront that was brighter and cleaner than its surroundings. On closer observation, I discovered that the door was ajar. For me, as for many others, the curiosity about what lay behind that open door proved compelling, and I entered. A short corridor led from the entryway into the interior (masking, I later realized, the spill of light from the door). There I encountered a space of curious intensity. Neither light nor dark, white nor gray, it had a feeling rather than a look, a presence rather than a shape. Being inside it was like being in a sauna or a fog bank. I was surrounded, enveloped, suspended. For some undefinable reason, the experience was profoundly moving, sublime, a feeling akin to a state of religious ecstasy. My body felt clumsy and intrusive, and I had an overwhelming desire to experience purely—with the psyche rather than with flesh and bone and synapses. The pull between the need to define the experience and the need to let go and be swept up in it was agonizing, but eventually the piece took over.

This work was much like the permanent piece in Nordman's studio. The room appeared to be divided into two sections by a pale gray scrim that shimmered softly, beckoning. On closer observation, it became apparent that there was no scrim at all—only a mysterious wall of light. Gradually, as my pupils dilated, the room began to lighten and firm up, and its corners appeared. Rationally, it was clearly empty, yet perceptually it was full. It is difficult, even impossible, to detail how Nordman constructed the piece, and it almost seems wrong to do so. Suffice it to say that a floor-to-ceiling slit, no more than one inch wide, was cut through the exterior wall so that outside light drifted into the room and formed what at first appeared to be a scrim, then gradually mingled with the dark to create the evocative atmosphere.

The presence of the work lingered long after the immediate experience, and it proved no less powerful on successive visits. Many years later its imprint is still strong, and I can return to it in memory.

Installation
Giuseppe Panza di Biumo
Varese, Italy
installed November 1975

Installation
in *Arte ambiente*
Venice Biennale
June 18–October 16, 1976

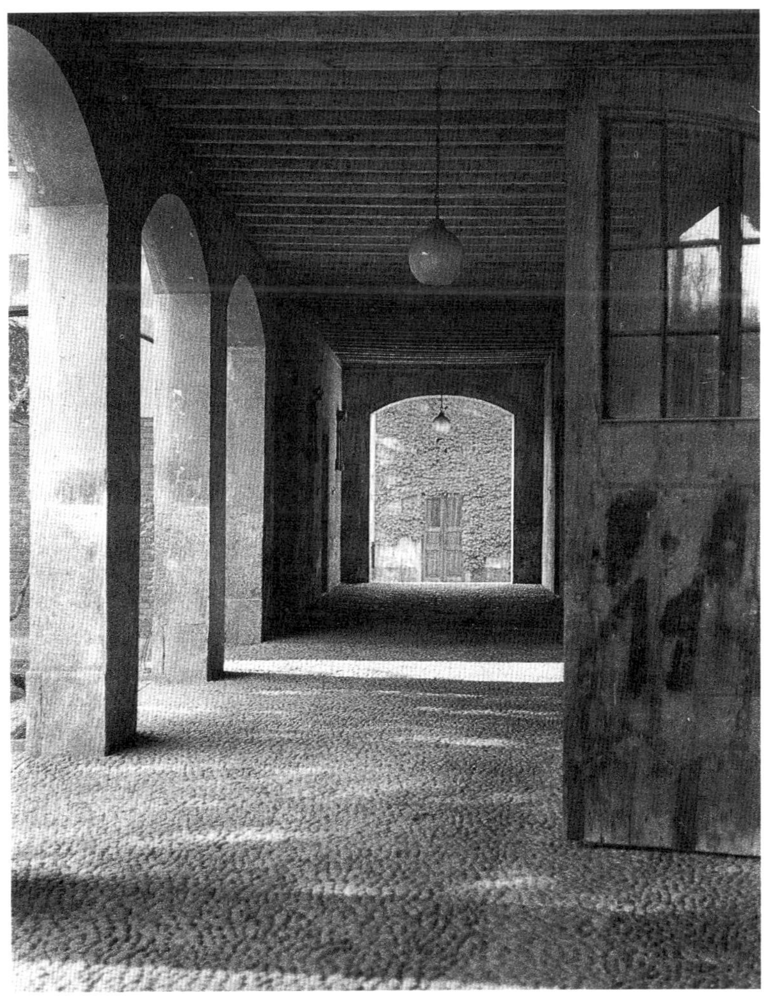

Maria Nordman
Exterior of permanent installation,
Giuseppe Panza di Biumo,
Varese, Italy, 1976

Nordman's work in the Panza collection is similar to her San Francisco piece, with the same power and intensity. As one enters through the great wooden doors in the stable area, there is an abrupt shift that is acutely metaphysical. The experience of this space is rich, dark, and serene. Two walls of light curtain off areas of inky blackness that appear to drop off into nothingness. There are narrow, light-admitting slits that are opened to the outside. For the duration of one's stay in this grainy, misted room, one senses the pulsing of the blood through the eyeballs, feels the pounding of the heart and the exhaling of breath, hears the dozens of twittering birds in the garden, and even seems to smell the nearby roses and lemon trees. Nordman could mask off outside sound as she does the light, but

The effect is of extreme peace, coolness and tranquility so as to induce an intensely calm meditational state in the spectator. The room is indeed a temple, In the line of those planned but never realized by, among others, Epstein, Modigliani, and Brancusi. Its use of light makes it specifically reminiscent of Brancusi's temple for an Indian Maharajah.

■ Simon Wilson, *Burlington Magazine*, October 1976.

instead she chooses to incorporate it. As a result, the impact of these multisensory experiences is even stronger.

The effect is of having returned to some preconscious place, and finding one's way out again is like waking from a dream. One has come so far from the logical, reasoning self that the door seems to have disappeared, and finding a way out requires struggling back through many layers of sensing.

Nordman's installation was one of the triumphs of the 1976 Venice Biennale. It had the now-familiar molecular grayness and almost mystical quality seen in her earlier works, but this space was even more powerful and perceptually rounder than those previously created. Nordman used the intensity of the Italian light and the octagonal shape of the room to full advantage. Because the corners of the octagon shape curved gently rather than meeting at hard angles, the space appeared to be far more undifferentiated than her others, and the effect was of great beauty and serenity.

Five Public Proposals for an Open Space
Rosamund Felsen Gallery, Los Angeles
October–November 1978

Ground Owl, Ground Squirrel Park
California State College, Bakersfield
installed September 1978

Further clues to Nordman's concern with timelessness are evident in her later work, including the proposals she showed at Rosamund Felsen Gallery in 1978. These proposals dealt with definitions of public spaces. Each project, called *Public Proposal for an Open Space,* was concerned with the specific planting of particular trees. One of the proposals, which I saw sometime after the show came down, involved interspersing pines with California fan palms, "on Public Land surrounding park lands or streets." The drawing for it stated that the site-specific piece would comprise "levelled ground / covered with grass / light and sound" and would provide "right of passage from every direction through the walls of trees."

The trees were to be planted twenty feet apart to form two rectangles—one of pines, one of palms. Watering was to be controlled so the trees in each rectangle would all reach the same height. Both species grow tall: the palms as high as sixty feet, the pines eventually some two hundred feet. Both the pine and the fan palm are native to North America and so familiar that they are taken for granted, yet Nordman decided to use them to create a kind of "power spot," a public/private forest for contemplation. (Trees are important for Nordman. When she disappears and one locates her again, more often than not she will say, "Ah, I have been in the woods.")

In the summer of 1978 Nordman was given the opportunity to realize one of her proposals on the Bakersfield campus. There she created a mysterious work from 150 redwood and ginkgo trees. The trees form a three-part piece, comprising a large circle, a large rectangle, and the space between them. One assumes that these configurations were not chosen lightly. Writing in *Man and His Symbols,* Aniela Jaffe observed, "The circle is the symbol of the psyche, and the square (and often the rectangle) is a symbol of earthbound matter, of the body and reality." Further, she states: "The frequency with which the square and the circle appear must not be overlooked. There seems to be an uninterrupted psychic urge to bring into consciousness the basic factors of life that they symbolize."[12]

There are curious relationships between the redwood and the ginkgo: both were originally native to China and both are among the most ancient of trees. Ancestors of the present-day redwood originated in Jurassic times, and flying reptiles may have rested in their branches. Ginkgoes originated in Permian times, and by the Jurassic period they were worldwide in distribution. In maturity both trees are gigantic. The redwood, the world's tallest tree, can grow to more than three hundred feet; the ginkgo can reach more than one hundred.

About this piece, Nordman wrote:

> *The information of a public park which is situated in front of a California State College: The land made available for use by the school was until this point uncultivated. The park results from a cultivation of part of the land. Another part is to remain untouched by the gardeners during the whole year, leaving open to chance the arrival of seeds and any animals that burrow into the ground.*[1]
>
> *Deambulatoria:*
>
> *1. The oval planting of a double row of sequoias around a dirt walkway that is ca. 6 meters wide, leaves open a constantly changing series of images between the trees. In the center is the oval area that is to remain open to local flora and fauna. The Sequoiadendron Giganteum is planted at the time that it has the height of people. It has the capacity of living three thousand years as it is found in California.*
>
> *2. Adjacent is a cultivated lawn of ca. 30 by 30 meters which surrounds the square of Ginkgo Biloba trees, planted also at the height of people, in pairs around a walkway of compacted local earth. In time, this walkway will be covered by the shade of trees, which have reached the age of one thousand years in their native China. The Ginkgo is a constant in the plant world, in that it has not changed or adapted its form in ca. 270 million years.*
>
> *The center of the Ginkgo planting is open, and functions as an atrium as it is planted with a cultivated lawn.*
>
> *The Ginkgo and the sequoia structures are oriented to the geographic north and to the axis of the equinox.*
>
> *It is open for anyone of the college, and for whomever might pass from the city, during night or day.*[2]
>
> 1. *One of the proposals of the park to the gardeners, botanists and students is to construct a form of maintenance which could be predicted to allow the trees to grow in size one relative to the other, and to allow the trees to reach their potential age in an area to which each is new, using the present context as a base.*
>
> 2. *Sponsored by the National Endowment for the Arts. Also by Elyse and Stanley Grinstein. Planted and maintained by gardeners of California State College, Bakersfield.*[13]

Nordman's concerns with the psyche and with time and space are more visible here than in previous works. Yet even though this piece initially seems to be radically different from her others, it still relies on the phenomenal to achieve meaning.

12839 Washington Boulevard (at Beethoven), Los Angeles, California
Venice, California
installation for the Los Angeles Institute of Contemporary Art
May 1–July 22, 1979

This work, located near the intersection of Washington Boulevard and Beethoven Street on the outskirts of Venice, was in a modest storefront between an apartment house and awning shop. Walking by, one noticed only the building's newly painted surface, the mirrored-glass windows and doors, and the white cement entryway. As with so many of Nordman's pieces, this work was created for the chance pedestrian. A passerby whose curiosity was aroused by the shiny white entryway and the open door could proceed up the walk and go inside.

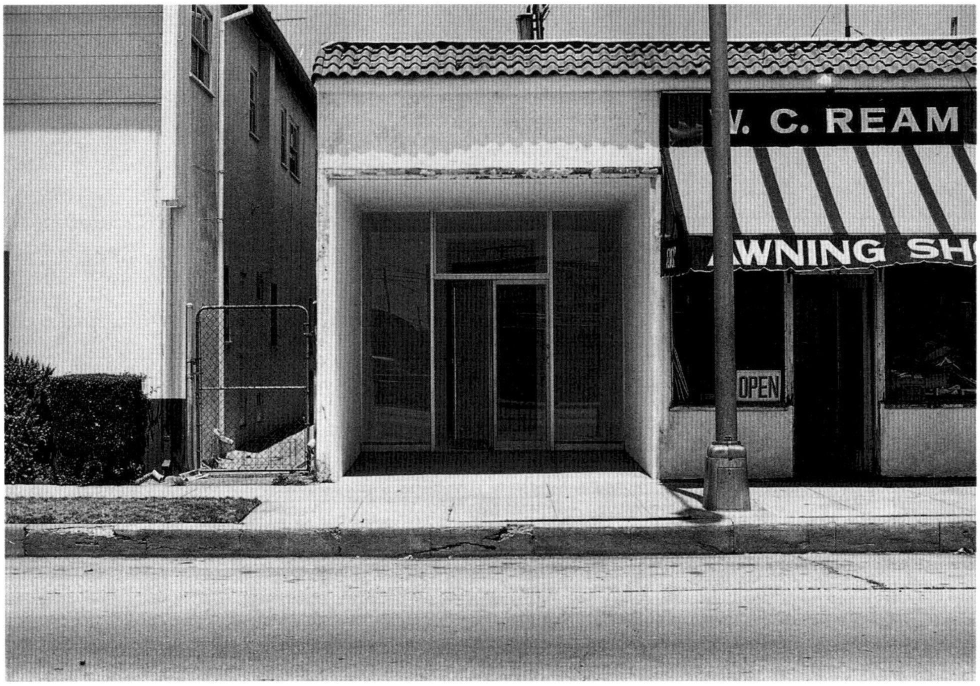

During the middle of the day no key was necessary; the piece was left open and a caretaker sat unobtrusively in a car outside. To participate in the work at an off-hour, one had to get a key from the German delicatessen across the street. Nordman rolls words around, enjoying their implications. Here she played with *delicatessen*—a word from the Latin *delicatus* (pleasing to the senses, voluptuous) and popularly believed to be from *essen* (to eat), thus putatively meaning "to feast delicately"—and also with the notion of creating the piece at a point where Washington and Beethoven (American and European cultures) meet.

The coating on the windows and doors prevented those outside from easily seeing in. Upon entering the work, the participant was suddenly immersed in a whiteness of such blinding intensity that it was like the reflection of sunlight on snow. There was no preparation for this response and no hiding from it. The whiteness pulsated in the eyes and seemed to fill the ears and nostrils. It was so intense that it seemed difficult to hear clearly.

The entire piece consisted of just two rooms and the beckoning entryway. Behind a wide portal in the central room lay a second room—a small coved space, which was equally white though slightly shadowed. It became, suddenly, a kind of temple. Entering it, the participant became an initiate in an inexplicable ritual that was intriguing but not understood. There was no precedent for the specificity of the sensate response—not even in past experiences with Nordman's work. The piece was powerful, mysterious, and timeless.

Maria Nordman
Exterior of *12839 Washington Boulevard (at Beethoven), Los Angeles, California*
Installation for the Los Angeles Institute of Contemporary Art, 1979

6/21/79, One Day Only, Dawn to Dusk
in *Andre, Buren, Irwin, Nordman: Space as Support*
University Art Museum, University of California, Berkeley
June 21, 1979

Nordman has a consuming interest in the summer solstice, June 21. Her first visit to the site of her Irvine piece took place on that day. And in 1977 she published an article dealing with the time and the position of the sun in Los Angeles and in Milan on the summer solstice. At the bottom of the piece is the statement "Calculated Geocentric altitude and azimuth of the sun, uncorrected for atmospheric refraction, recorded to the nearest 1°."[14]

The intensity of Nordman's *6/21/79, One Day Only, Dawn to Dusk* was derived from the magic of the summer solstice and the quality of its light. Unlike her previous works, there was no directed light, no single space; the multiple levels of the museum provided her structure. To prepare an arena in which the solstice could be celebrated, Nordman covered the museum's large ground floor with a pure white adhesive-backed paper and applied transparent theatrical gels in red, yellow, and blue to the upper- and lower-level floor-to-ceiling glass doors. All artificial light was turned off.

Maria Nordman
6/21/79, One Day Only, Dawn to Dusk,
Installation, University Art Museum, University of California, Berkeley, June 21, 1979
These photographs (see also pages 108–9) taken during the course of *6/21/79* are the work of Craig Vista Svare, an artist-photographer. They represent his own meditative experience of the site and do not, in any sense, constitute a documentation of it.

Participants arrived at the museum at 4:30 A.M., in the undefined darkness of predawn. To be there that early, many had camped out or spent the night in nearby hotels, thus preparing for the piece by transporting themselves to another place. The elements of planning, of expectation, of readiness for a celebration were there.

6/21/79
On making a record[1] of the instance[2] of a work.[3]
(having taken place 6/21/79 Berkeley)
I propose to give the unknown speaker the first word
The work could be for any person who is present
Any person in the presence of any other person
(The possible presence of one or more unknown persons is a public instance.)
Record of realization:
The day chosen is the one in which the location has the longest orientation to the sun. (in 1979: June 21)
The time is 5 A.M. to 9 P.M.

The room is the exhibition area of the museum in Berkeley, which has two ground floors and various levels of rooms facing into the main area. These sub-rooms—open to entry—with works from various times and places on walls and floors are a part of the larger room and have the same conditions of the ground floor.

The materials placed into the building became temporarily a part of its surfaces: the colored filters were removable from the frames of glass doors. The ground paint was a white removable (vinyl) coating.
The realization of the work was carried out together with persons named by the museum "preparators."

—No title was given to the work by the artist. It is identified as *6/21/79* Berkeley.

(continued on p. 108)

Tjoba, A Ship
Amsterdam; Düsseldorf; Bonn; Strasbourg, France;
Basel, Switzerland; Cologne, West Germany;
Rotterdam, the Netherlands; Groningen, the Netherlands;
Winschoten, the Netherlands
December 21, 1981–January 21, 1982

In 1981 Nordman acquired a small "work ship," once used to carry sailors and their families. She cleaned, scraped, and painted the old ship with white fish-oil and oil of linseed to protect its metal parts from rust. As she worked to make the vessel fit for her rituals, the dark belly of the ship gradually took shape from spills of light that poured in through the door. Once the piece was completed, a large brazier in the center of the bow provided warmth; it was filled with burning coal, which would eventually change into a mound of white ash. The only color in the work was introduced by a large red, green, and blue cloth, woven by Maria Janssen from one of Nordman's drawings. It hung against the wall of the barge like a ship's flag—or an altar cloth—its squared shape symbolic of the Jungian quarternity. Its colors, along with the (yellow) light from the sun that beamed on it, were those that make up *Prima Materia,* or Prime Matter (what C. G. Jung termed the most elemental material in the universe).

The ship sailed the Rhine, docking at various cities: Amsterdam, Düsseldorf, Bonn, Strasbourg, Basel, Cologne, Rotterdam, Groningen, and Winschoten.[17] As Nordman explained: "All parts of the ship interior were open to whomever arrived by chance. The galley, the cabin, the pilothouse, the room at the bow, the sleeping and eating area of the sailors, were all readied for the same changing conditions as the large hold."[18]

Nordman's choice of a ship was a fit metaphor for the journey of life—yet the work was more than passive sculptural poetics. Rather it encouraged, *demanded* that the viewer become a participant.

Works in the City of the Angels—and the Waves, Yang Na,
315 N. Alameda 166 N. Central, June 8, 5:41 A.M.–8:30 P.M.
Museum of Contemporary Art, Los Angeles
June 8, 1983

***165 North Central, Los Angeles,* November 1983**
in *The First Show: Painting and Sculpture from Eight Collections, 1940–1980*
Museum of Contemporary Art, Los Angeles
November 20, 1983–February 14, 1984

In 1983 and 1984 Nordman created two key works under the aegis of the Museum of Contemporary Art. The museum's director, Richard Koshalek, offered her the opportunity to use virtually any space in the complex of MoCA's Temporary Contemporary buildings. For her first work she chose Building 6, which has since been destroyed. The vacated building was large and airy. Its industrial doors provided access from both the addresses cited in her title. Daylight and the workaday sounds from the surrounding area flooded the space, filling it with intentional and unintentional content.

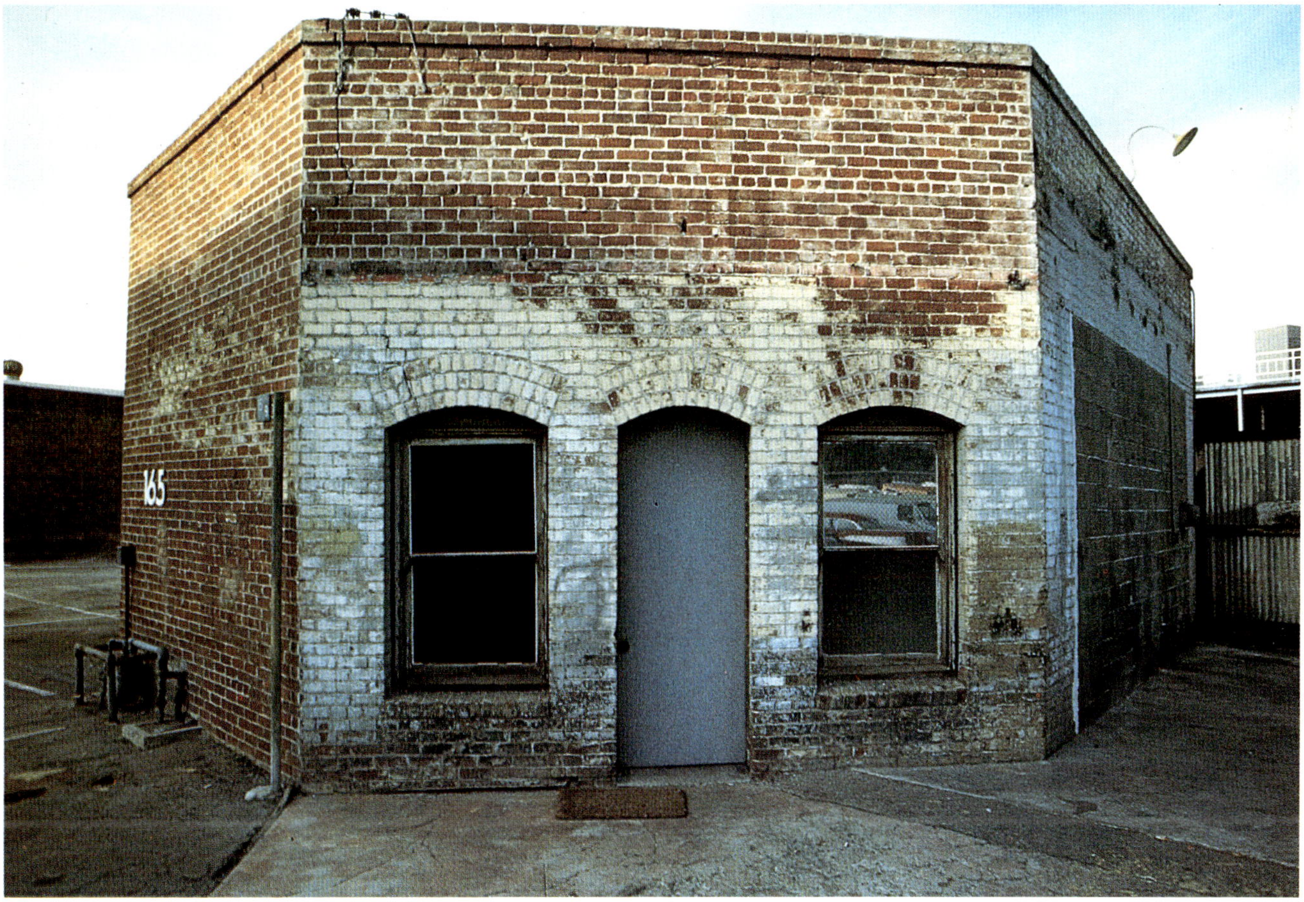

Maria Nordman
Exterior of
165 N. Central, Los Angeles
Installation, Museum of
Contemporary Art,
Los Angeles, 1983

Nordman made full use of the warehouse. By flooding the dark cement floor with water, she created a black reflecting pool in which the old building and its structural beams were seen as if through a glass, darkly. Floating in this phantasmagoric black sea were a painted chair and a constructed fragment that was less clearly definable but that looked something like a frame. With its eerie darkness and lurking sense of foreboding, this one-day work provided a fascinating counterpoint to her ethereal all-white earlier rooms.

About this work the critic Melinda Wortz wrote:

> The building that Nordman opened has a large square door on either end of a 260-foot long corridorlike space supported by two rows of square columns. From the Alameda side visitors passed through a freestanding handmade frame that stood like a gate to the space. Nordman's beautifully polished and stained plywood frame, fitted together without nails, was the only handmade element in the installation, a reference to craft and tradition framing the passage into a space exemplifying urban neglect, decay, and destruction.
>
> Inside, the building was dark, and the floor was flooded with water which reflected the bright doors, dissolving the barriers between inside and out, up and down. The depth of the water was visually indeterminable because of the reflection. As one walked through the space, one's feet

> became soaked; as one sat on carefully placed, brightly painted wooden chairs, one's clothes got wet. The dark dankness in the setting of industrial decay had an ominous beauty, like the sets in the movie *Blade Runner.*
>
> In contrast to the dim interior, however, the doorways to the street at either end were brilliant beacons to light and air.... They were framing devices, framing views of the world outside. Traditionally the frame has been essential to the definition of the artwork, establishing its territory and sharpening one's focus on it, but in Nordman's work the same scene that one saw framed was also reflected at one's feet.
>
> What does all this fusion/confusion of outside and in, here and there, up and down, art and the world, immediate and universal suggest? Perhaps that the dualistic oppositions we use to separate concepts are more inherent in the structure of language than in actual experience, which in any specific moment can yield a more holistic, relativistic understanding of the nature of things.[19]

Nordman's other piece for MoCA was created for a structure that was unofficially dubbed the Old Gas Station. Although it had actually served as a gas station at one point, the curious shape of this small structure was more reminiscent of the fifth-century tomb of Galla Placidia than of the twentieth-century structures that house Chevron, Texaco, Exxon, and the like. Totally out of sync with its own time and space, this isolated building provided the perfect setting for Nordman's work. The external door set into the red brick was painted an almost luminous gray. Entering, one saw in the foyer a small gray-painted table and two chairs, which were an inseparable part of the work. Having passed through a second door, one encountered a shadowy blue-grayness, as light from slits in the ceiling flooded the back wall with an otherworldly brilliance and brought a plane of light down from the ceiling to the floor. My memory paints the side wall a brushy midnight blue; others who saw the piece remember it differently. Some have a clear sense of the wall and ceiling as dark gray; others remember it as a shadowy black.

Writing about this work in MoCA's newspaper, the *Contemporary,* Gabriella Mills encapsulated Nordman's attitudes toward her work:

> Nordman does not use the word "installation," an art term denoting temporary art works constructed in interior or exterior spaces. "Car widows are installed," she says, implying that this word indicates something permanently placed. She sees her work as a continuing process, an ongoing investigation that can change and does so constantly. She prefers the word "work" because she is working with what is there rather than creating a monument, temporary or otherwise.
>
> "Dialogue" is another word Nordman uses frequently. The summer work she created for MoCA last June 1984 was, she says, "in dialogue with two different groups of people." The first piece [June 1983] between two dramatically different streets, Central and Alameda, allowed the sounds, lights and inhabitants of each environment to pass through it and to establish a "dialogue."[20]

Describing the second piece, Mills continued:

> Both rooms at 165 N. Central were illuminated so that the light effect was different at different times of the day. The first room, with a window directly on the street, was arranged to be significantly darker than the street. The inside room was painted black, and a band of natural light was visible. The contradiction between the two spaces formed another dialogue. She reminds us of the contrasts of urban spaces: that it is artificial and unnatural, yet at the same time connected to nature. It changes over time and from every presence. To quote from her "Poiema": *"And this flow of light which could produce a place, this flow of air which could produce a sound, all of it remaining unpredictable—this incidence could have a moment of hesitation in the case that at least two people are there."*[21]

Trabajos en la ciudad de ondas (Work in the City of Waves)
La Jolla Museum of Contemporary Art, La Jolla, California
February 12–March 17, 1985

Sam Francis once wrote about his work: "There is a place for you in these paintings."[22] In much the same way, there is a place for you in Nordman's art. Her works are never simply to be looked at. They are to be walked in, stood in, sat in—to be experienced. The work derives its meaning as much from the response of the participant as it does from the artist's intent.

The La Jolla museum is built on bluffs above the sea, overlooking water that is vivid turquoise, sand that is brilliant white. The smell of the salt water, the feel of the sea breezes, and the sound of the surf all pervade the site. In *Trabajos en la ciudad de ondas,* Nordman used these givens with great sensitivity and understatement. The simplicity of her work drew attention away from its "thingness" and toward its function as a stimulant of experience—"a machine for the senses," in the phrase of the curator, Ronald Onorato.

The tangible portions of Nordman's work were frames of fragrant cedar—beautifully crafted using traditional Japanese techniques of joinery—and artist's linen, which were used to cover the museum's eight doors to the outside. Linen was also used to cover benches in the gallery and outside. Some of these were located halfway down the stairs to the garden, where the roof threw a shadow across the stairway for part of the day. The benches, covered in red and blue and green, were simply to sit on. Light was everywhere, inside and out. It flooded one of the rooms in particular, in which Nordman had installed a cedar-and-linen, multidoored structure that led to a door opening to the outside.

Marga Bijvoet, a perceptive writer, has noted that Nordman studied at the Max Planck Institute in Stuttgart, and that Nordman "must be familiar with these notions [of quantum physics, which Planck discovered], in particular, those concerning light, one of the most important constants in her work....Eric Bohm writes about light: 'Light and action are the undivided whole from which other things descend,...matter and time are derived from light, and...light is the fundamental activity and potential for everything.'"[23]

For Whomever May Arrive, Carried by the Ruhr, Carried by the Rhine
Museum Folkwang, Essen, West Germany, 1985

Nordman lived in Essen for some six months and while there she contemplated the idea of working in a coal mine. However, she then discovered a small island in the Ruhr, on the outskirts of Werden, where she created a piece instead. It comprised simply two freestanding arches—one white and Minimal in feeling, the other dark, rough, and seemingly in a state of romantic decay. Both served as entryways. Writing about these enigmatic structures, Stephan Schmidt-Wulffen said:

> Two gates await the newcomer, though it's impossible to determine what kind of traveler the romantic type tumbledown rubble gate is meant for and what type the smooth, geometrical sandstone gate is intended for. Their proportions are so reduced that they appear as visions, more than as structures. Although they are placed far apart, they converse with one another along a north-south axis that traverses their exact center points.[24]

After I had been meeting with Nordman for several years, there was a rupture in my relationship with her. I did not fully understand the magnitude of it at the time, but with the exception of one final encounter, our meetings were to cease, making my profound involvement with her work extremely difficult. This difficulty was compounded by the fact that many of her exhibitions have taken place in Europe and by her penchant for privacy and secrecy. Further, she has refrained from disseminating written material such as press releases to describe her work, and she has discouraged critical writing as well. As a result, it has become virtually impossible to participate in all of her pieces, let alone communicate, even by word of mouth, the importance of them to others.

My final encounter with Nordman is worth telling because it sheds light on how she functions. The choice of a meeting place was always Nordman's—on a beach, in a seemingly empty studio, in a restaurant in the clouds. This time it was at an outdoor café in New York, during a light snowstorm. Nordman was dressed entirely in white. Seating herself outside as if it were summer, she tucked her long skirt under her and sat quietly. She looked at me for a long time. Finally she said, "I must ask you not to write about me. That is my right as an artist." With equal intensity I replied that I felt I must, because that was my role—to write about those works I felt made a difference. "But you cannot write about me," she said. "We have an agreement." It was true; we did.

Many years before, in 1971 or 1972, I had seen early work in Nordman's studio. It was among the most powerful nonobject work I had yet seen. Nothing had yet been written about her. I discussed with her the possibility of doing the first written piece. Not yet ready, she nevertheless agreed tentatively to talk about her work with me on tape, to show some of it to me, but only under the most stringent conditions: I must promise not to publish until she agreed it was time, and she was to maintain control over the tape and any transcript derived from it. I respected her work and her concept that it is for the "occasional passerby"—to be communicated by word of mouth only—and so I agreed, never guessing that after some ten years had elapsed she would still hold me to that promise. (I have not violated that agreement. The taped interviews have never been published.)

By the time of our New York meeting it was 1981. Nordman's work had appeared on the cover of *Artforum* in 1979, the Italian critic Germano Celant had written an extensive article for the same magazine about her piece at the University Art Museum in Berkeley that year, and I had written the brochure for that exhibition, with Nordman's full approval. Her work had now become public, and I felt it was time to write more extensively about her, in a book.

Light stands for an ongoing
fire
light from the sun.

■ **Maria Nordman, *De Sculptura: Works in the CIty,* (Munich: Schirmer/Mosel, 1986), p. 13.**

The snow was beginning to fall in earnest. "I've written you a letter," Maria said, "explaining why you must not include me in your book. But I didn't want to mail it—I wanted to read it to you in person." She began to read the letter, which was many pages long, and which, after so many years, I can only paraphrase. Essentially she wrote: "I am not part of any school or movement. I did not study under, or with, nor was I influenced by any other artist who might be construed to be working in the same arena. I am not an artist of Light and Space. I am exactly who I am."

As an art critic, art historian, and art journalist, I feel equally strongly about the singleness of what I do. I attempted to explain that I was free to do exactly what my art demanded, too, but my explanation seemed long-winded and off the point.

It was snowing hard now. Nothing had been accomplished. There were tears. Nordman finished the letter, folded it up, and thrust it at me. I started to put it in my bag. Then the solution became obvious: The letter represented the core of Nordman's beliefs—the crux of her philosophy. I asked for the right to publish it as her chapter in this book. She looked at me penetratingly for a long time. "I guess that would be all right," she said, "but there are personal things in the letter. Let me rewrite it, and I will give it back to you."

I never saw the letter or Maria again.

SOME CHOSEN WORK CONTEXTS 1967–

—In a room on a sidewalk near apartments and a laundry (1970–).
—In wild-growing meadows, near a stadium; near railway tracks (1984–).
—In the passage from a street to a garden (1977).
—On open land near a small town (1968, 1969).
—Before a college: the planting of trees to form a park (1978–).
—On a small meadow where foreign ships dock at the Rhine (1979–).
—In the shadow of old chestnut trees by the Düssel (1979–).
—In the upper rooms of a villa Medicea built by Bernardo Bountalenti (1976).
—By the Dommel (1980–).
—In midst of a courtyard surrounded by apartments (1974).
—On a walkway near the birthplace of Christopher Columbus (1976).
—In various buildings with exhibitions by contemporary artists.
—In a room with works from the Gabon, from Roman antiquity, of Arp and Maillol (1980).
—In concurrent open places of two cities opposite on the earth (1976).
—Near a winter wheat field on one side, and apartments on another (1984).
—In a public park by a music school (1984).

—On the grass center of a mid-city street (1984).
—In a harbor (1984).
—In what was once built as a stable (1976–).
—In an unused workroom loaned to me by an artist (1972).
—In conjunction with the historical collection of a university (1979).
—On the street where Gian Lorenzo Bernini was born and also buried (1984).
—In conjunction with a mountain and a tree (1973).
—Across from an ongoing rodeo (1980).
—On an island in the Ruhr (1984–).
—In the basement of a university building (1967).
—By a parking lot in view of the state capitol of Texas (1980).
—On the whole ground floor of a Mies van der Rohe house (1984).
—By the Mars Hotel, where people live in abandoned buildings (1975).
—On a medieval marketplace (1983).
—In an emptied street level building (1977).
—In one of a row of shops where people work and also live (1979).
—On unused land near Sant Agostino and Salita Tre Re Magi (1977).
—In what was once a three-room, street-level apartment (1977).
—In an alley between the Pacific Ocean and the highway (1973).
—Where Chinese, Japanese, English, and Spanish speaking neighborhoods meet (1984).
—Under a grove of trees in an open park of Lac Leman (1985).
—In the valley of the Dora and the Po (1985–).
—On a terrace of Filippo Juvarra and the masons of the Piemonte (1985–).

■ Maria Nordman, *De Sculptura: Works in the City* (Munich: Schirmer/Mosel, 1986), pp. 11–12.

Douglas Wheeler

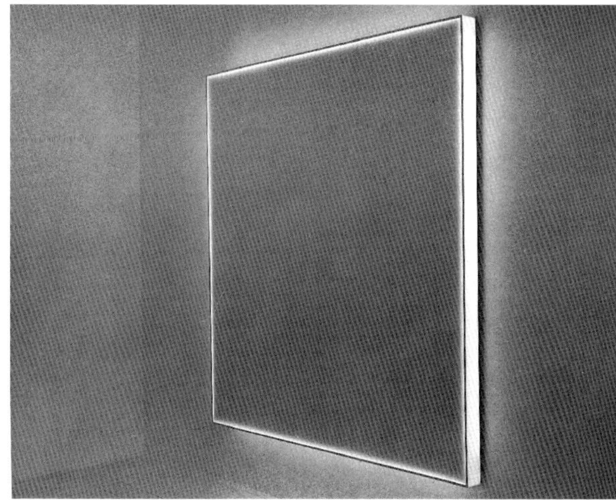

The effect of these illuminated works is difficult to define—they were rigid and eerie, seductive and awe-inspiring. William Wilson of the *Los Angeles Times* was one of the first to perceive them not as paintings but as environments: "The whole light-suffused room is a work of art. Suspended like electronic icons on facing walls of the divided room...they feel like Mark Rothkos spilled from their frames, as coldly exciting as beautiful sexless angels, as jarringly attractive as a virgin princess in an ice palace."[4] Curiously emotional statements, those, but they were representative of the response this new kind of work was beginning to evoke.[5]

It is a little-known fact that the all-important 1967–68 Pasadena exhibitions (one-man shows by Irwin, Turrell, and Wheeler) were originally intended to be one three-man show, but it soon became apparent that there simply was not enough room for all of them to exhibit at the same time. Had the one show taken place as originally planned, the "who did what first" battle over dates would have been avoided.

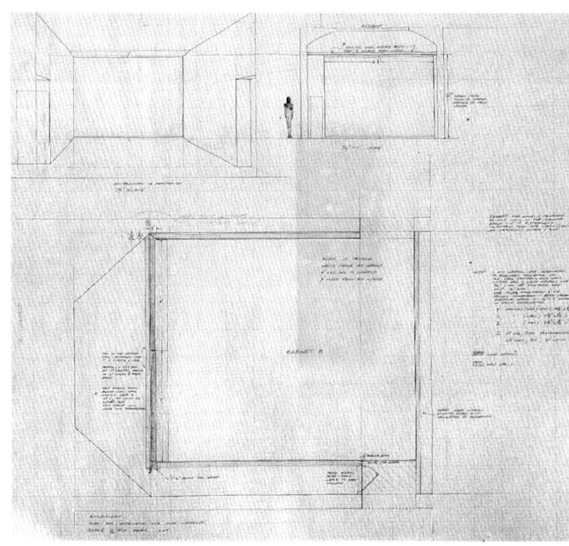

Within two years of his show in Pasadena, Wheeler had two one-man exhibitions at Ace Gallery in Los Angeles and another at the Ace in Vancouver, British Columbia. He was a participant in significant exhibitions at the Fort Worth Art Museum in Texas (with Irwin); the Stedelijk Museum in Amsterdam (also with Irwin); and the Tate Gallery in London (with Irwin and Larry Bell). He was also included in Prospectus '69, at the Städtische Kunsthalle Düsseldorf, and in Kompass 4, at the Van Abbemuseum, Eindhoven. His contributions to all of these exhibitions were installation pieces. Wheeler had moved far beyond the early encasements.

Light Wall

Ace Gallery, Los Angeles, January 1970

Wheeler's first show at Ace Gallery was a gigantic work, fifteen feet tall and twenty-nine and a half feet long. It was presented in a carefully prepared all-white environment, which included, for the first time in Wheeler's work, a white scrim ceiling and a white linoleum floor. Every effort had been made to reduce any unnecessary elements, so that nothing marred the visual field and detracted from the effect of its Ganzfeld. As Peter Plagens observed in *Artforum*:

Opposite, top
Douglas Wheeler
Untitled, 1966
Canvas "encasement," with adapted neon and plastic, 88 1/2 x 83 in. (224.8 x 210.8 cm)
Installation, Pasadena Art Museum, Pasadena, California, 1968

Opposite, bottom
Douglas Wheeler
Plan for "Untitled"
For installation at Van Abbemuseum, Eindhoven, the Netherlands, 1969–70

Right and below
Douglas Wheeler
Untitled, 1967–70
Neon tubes encased in wall, room size: 15 x 29 x 33 1/2 ft. (4.6 x 8.8 x 10.2 m.)
Installation, Ace Gallery, Los Angeles

> The room has been altered at the ceiling and floor; a few feet before the light wall the floor rises, slightly but unnoticeably and the ceiling has been "lowered" by stretching fine, polyester gauze over the room several feet below the permanent ceiling. The room "is" white ("is" only because white material—flooring, paint, etc., has been used); the color of the room during the Wheeler installation is something else, but "white" is enough to acknowledge its starting point.[6]

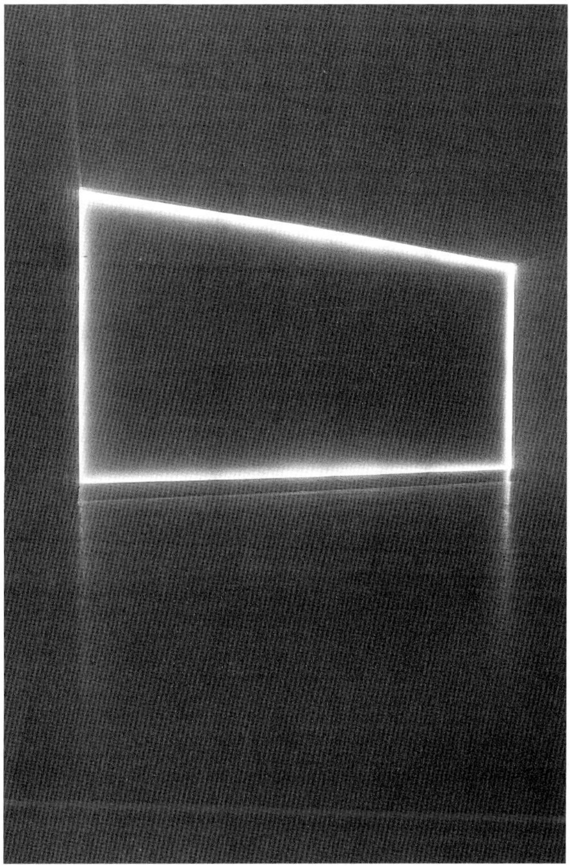

As Plagens noted, the ceiling, walls, and floors were substantially altered, clearly making this a room-environment work rather than a large light painting. Plagens's review also documents—but does not discuss—this early public use of scrim.

Created after the 1969 show in Amsterdam, *Light Wall* was a unique work, made specifically for the Ace Gallery space. It was different from the works that followed in that viewers could not walk into it, yet even here Wheeler created a transitional hallway space so that the viewer could be perceptually cleansed before entering the main portion of the work. Lights projected onto the wall about twelve to sixteen inches away from it, but the real focus of the piece was the complete dematerialization of the scrim. "I wanted to effect a dematerialization so that I could deal with the dynamics of the particular space," Wheeler says. "It was a *real* space—not illusory—it was a cloud of light in constant flux. That molecular mist is the most important thing I do. It comes out of my way of seeing from living in Arizona—and the constant awareness of the landscape and the clouds."[7]

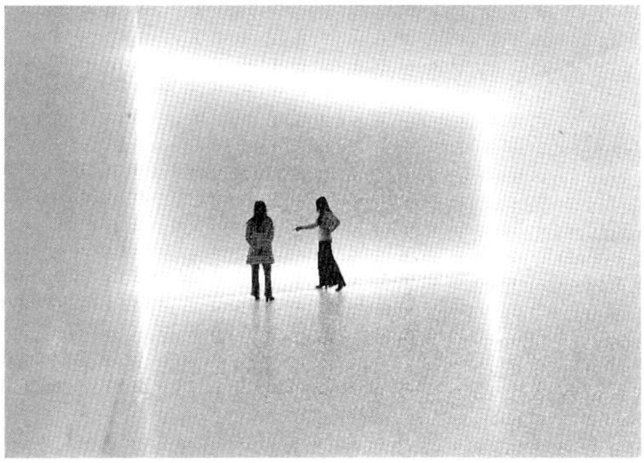

Light Wall was as intense as a neon sign, and it left an afterimage of color that looked different each time you saw it, yet the colors one saw were all variations of white. One could merge with the piece or choose to stay grounded as an observer, on the white floor, looking at the throbbing white room as if it were an object like any painting or sculpture. Haunting, seductive, the work played on the eye and mind. Viewers who were willing to spend some time with it found that normal depth perception no longer seemed to apply: the work seemed remote at first, then eventually seemed to open and receive them. Many felt that its enigmatic void had profound metaphysical implications.

Installation
in *Larry Bell, Robert Irwin, Douglas Wheeler*
Tate Gallery, London
May 5–31, 1970

The Tate show marked a major change in Wheeler's work from the curved, emptiness-focused space of his Ace Gallery show of January 1970. Presented just four months later (though there was probably a longer period between the conception of the pieces than their exhibition dates seem to indicate), Wheeler's Tate piece was far more complex and efficacious. The large scale and the expense of room-environment works limit the opportunities to exhibit them. As a result, many of the changes in a body of work take place in conceptual form, often embodied in plans or drawings. The Tate Gallery work no doubt benefited from Wheeler's experience in making pieces for Ace as well as from his presentation of a coved-space piece in his Venice, California, studio—also in 1970. The latter comprised angled spaces made round at their corners by the use of concave molding. Having physically executed these works, which were more resonant in three-dimensional reality than on paper, Wheeler could make refinements that were based on experience rather than intuition or speculation.

For his installation at the Tate, Wheeler was given three contiguous rooms. His light paintings were installed in the chambers at each end. The room in the middle contained a separate environment, which was described by the exhibition's curator, Michael Compton, as "a fan-shaped, all-white room in which the sloping floor drew one almost imperceptively down to a curved wall some 40 feet wide and distant. This was illuminated from the edges all round by a hidden faintly purplish light-source diffusing across the surface and dissolving it to give a sensation of deep space, calm and peace, as if one was approaching the edge of the world."[8]

Two new factors are notable here: the piece was considerably larger than the one at Ace, and the wall was literally rather than apparently curved.

> *What I was trying to deal with was that I wanted you to end up in a certain place in the space, to get from this place to that place and to have that transition be unconscious. To do that I had to de-accelerate you, so I made this entrance where you perspectively distort, where physically going through it made you start to move faster.... Slanting the floors was part of that. The floor had to be slanted subtly so that you were unconscious that that was happening, and that's where you would get pulled right into the space.*

This physical "torquing," subtle but very real, was to be an important aspect of Wheeler's later pieces as well.

The Ace piece had measured twenty-nine and a half feet long; the Tate piece was forty. Ten and a half feet is a considerable change in a work of this sort. The expanded size and the curved walls at the Tate meant that viewers no longer looked at the work, they were immersed in it. The use of white carpeting instead of the white linoleum used previously not only softened the work acoustically, as did the overhead scrim, but also eliminated the jarring reflections that the white linoleum floor had given off from some angles. Wheeler had succeeded in creating what Compton termed "a still, but fathomless space":

> His presentations involve the substitution of light for pigmental colour and the dissolution of the wall surface (which becomes the picture) by the light and by optical effects like retinal bleaching. But his aim is to provide an experience as simple and universal as that of gazing at the stars on a clear night, and to leave the viewer to deal with it in his own way. The simplicity of the experience, which involved the design of the physical approaches to the work, tends to minimize the most superficial of cultural responses.[9]

The metaphysical experience provided by the piece was decidedly not the usual art experience, and most viewing it found parallels not with art but with phenomenology, psychology, or religion. Like Compton, the writer Robert Melville saw cosmological implications:

> [The] back wall is curved and framed on all sides by a bluish white strip of lighting. There is nothing else; not even shadows or reflections. The light is the exhibit, but the invading spectator acquires an intensified presence. People standing close to the curved wall to inspect its unblemished surface look as if they have reached the edge of the world. If they could take one step further, they would fall into the void because the wall has forsaken its substances and turned into white space.[10]

An anonymous critic in *Punch* spoke of "the illusory space of Wheeler's neon temple," and continued: "While each participant's response to and sense of the piece was different—a portion of that experience seemed common to all of them—an experience not only of a limitless void, but the limbo-like presence of it."[11] This experience triggered many curious interpretations. Wheeler tells the story of a writer who approached him during the exhibition and insisted that all three of the artists—Wheeler, Irwin, and Bell—were in cahoots in presenting a show with three themes: "Heaven and Purgatory and Hell." Wheeler's interpretation of the factors that led to this fanciful reading of the exhibition are worth recounting:

> *Irwin's space was real nice. It was pleasant, beautiful. There is no way around it... [his piece] was sanity, it was reality, it was clarity, and then you walked into mine. You actually walked up a ramp into this white-carpeted, white-walled, sound-dampened space (it was soft visually because there weren't any shadows); then you walked into the space and it got bigger and bigger and the walls fell away because of the way the lights were hitting them. It was a real illusion, because people were afraid of falling over the edge—as if there really were an edge to fall over! The light that I used there was the white UV light, which was sort of violet-bluish. What happens is that you'd go from whiteness to gray in the areas where there isn't much reflection and so you'd have the wall itself where the light was spreading, and as you'd get away from that gradation, it got pretty dark and deep. I wanted you to end up at a point where your whole peripheral vision was encompassed by this.*
>
> *What... I was after was a Ganzfeld effect in which you couldn't trust your own vision.... Everybody is always looking at things from the standpoint of an anchor, and they're always anchored in one place... and if there isn't anything hard-edged around, then they start becoming conscious of things they've always overlooked before, so that it's also a kind of insecure feeling because there is this feeling of being drawn into the void. Then they would walk into Larry Bell's piece and it was sweaty and black and there was this roar of ventilation equipment in it.*

Heaven, Purgatory, and Hell aside, there were vast differences in the ways each artist utilized his space. It is exactly at this point that Wheeler reached his first impasse. His work had achieved perfection, but that perfection could not be maintained in a public setting: the carpet and the walls became scuffed and dirty despite frequent cleanings, and the marks detracted from the purity of the experience.

Something happened to Wheeler after this point, and he did not show large-scale works again until 1975, at the Galleria Salvatore Ala in Milan. Virtually all of the core Light and Space artists have dropped out of public sight for prolonged periods. Turrell's, the longest period, lasted nine years; Irwin had at least two—the last one at least three years long. For Nordman, the period of invisibility was at the beginning. Wheeler's was the most poignant, for he underwent a severe personal crisis. Lacking the financial resources to execute major works, he saw older artists who could move faster and explain better take the spotlight—often using materials whose use he had pioneered. In spite of his success in Europe, Wheeler did not have a track record in the United States that would lead to public exhibition and support for the execution of large works.

Wheeler's situation was unfortunate but not unique. All of the artists discussed here have had to grapple with the unusual difficulties presented by this new way of working. Environmental art is problematic because unlike object works—which can be reworked in the studio until they are right—environmental installations must be refined on the spot, on schedule. Even after the most detailed calculations—often involving sensory information not available until the installation is nearly complete—a piece may not work within a given space. And unlike painting or sculpture, these pieces cannot be painted over or melted down if they don't work out right. "Each time you go some place it is a new thing," Wheeler has said, "and you are like a producer or a stage manager. Doing work of this kind is very much like producing a stage play, because you are not producing objects or commodities."

Douglas Wheeler
Mizuno Gallery, Los Angeles, 1974

Wheeler's complex drawings and plans often represent personal visions and fantasies as well as specific proposals. Though rarely exhibited, they provide important clues to works that he hopes to build someday. They also convey information that fills the gaps between what one knows about his work from actually having experienced it and what one suspects that he is, has been, or will be about.

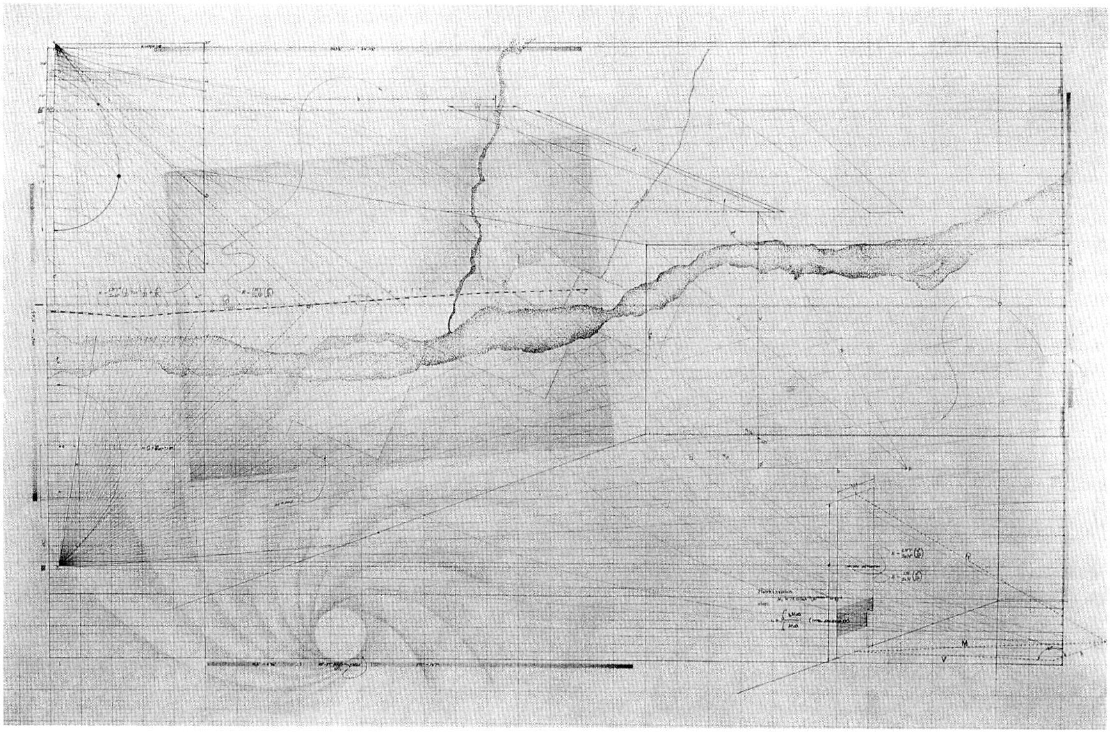

Douglas Wheeler
Untitled, 1973
Ink and graphite drawing on paper,
24 x 36 in. (61 x 91.4 cm)
Collection of the artist

Douglas Wheeler
Synthetic Desert III, 1974
Drawing for an anechoic space with neon
Giuseppe Panza di Biumo, Varese, Italy

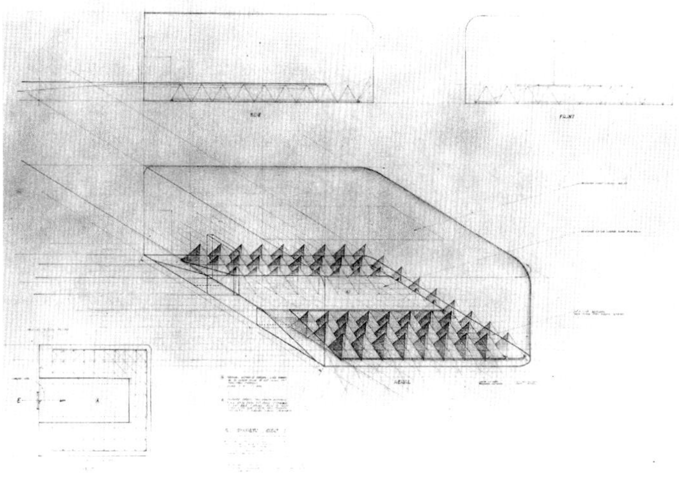

Douglas Wheeler
Suspended Volume in Reflected Spectrum, 1975
Giuseppe Panza di Biumo, Varese, Italy

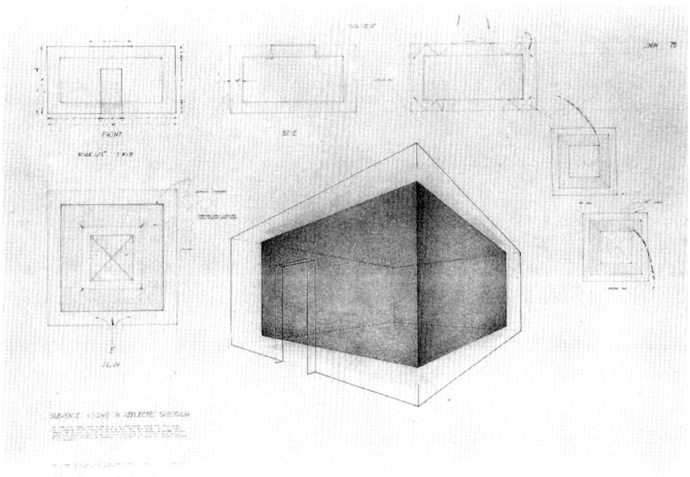

One proposal in particular intrigues: *Synthetic Desert,* now in the Panza collection. As envisioned, this large-scale work would be a light-and-sound piece (or rather, a light-and-the-absence-of-sound piece) in an anechoic space. A drawing for it, shown in Wheeler's drawing exhibition at Mizuno Gallery, includes a description of the piece: "A soft white featureless ambience—polyester scrim material stretched over microwave absorbers creating low luminous atmosphere—infinite boundary, anechoic quiet space, no visual or sound reflections—a 'mobius manifold.'"

Another drawing in this exhibition provides evidence of Wheeler's interest in natural as well as artificial light. This work, *Skylight Tracing Piece,* is intended to last fifty-two weeks, beginning and ending on the winter solstice. The central axis is a skylight in a room approximately twenty-four feet square. The constantly shifting position of the sun would create a series of softened geometric shapes, which would slip down through the skylight and across the walls and floor in innumerable mutations over a year's time.

In the absence of physically executed pieces, these well-conceived and gently magical works provided continued evidence of Wheeler's power.

Douglas Wheeler
Galleria Salvatore Ala, Milan, 1975

"Recently, in a show in Italy," Tom Marioni wrote regarding this exhibition: "Wheeler built a room, rounding all edges and corners, making a seamless white space. The indirect lighting was controlled with an automatic rheostat gradually turning the lights up to full brightness over a six-minute period."[12]

Installation
in *West/East: First-Generation Environmental Sculpture*
P.S. 1, Institute for Art and Urban Resources, Long Island City, New York
exhibition proposed for 1981 but never realized

The same room was available to Wheeler for his second installation at P.S. 1—a rare opportunity for a site-specific artist to rework a major piece in the same location.[13] The second P.S. 1 piece was scheduled to be on view in the fall of 1981. As Wheeler described it prior to completion, the piece involved the following:

> *I am refacing the entire room interior—walls, ceiling, and floor—so that it is tilted from the entry wall up six inches at the window wall, and yet all the angles will plumb off that tilted floor, so that there is nothing* visual *to show you that that has happened. The door will be hung with a tilt, also, so that to open the door will require a slight effort, and to walk into the room will also require a slight effort, because you will be going up that incline. The windows will be hung with the tilt as well.*
>
> *Downstairs the room as you see it is the same room you've seen before, except that I'll reframe it and resurface it and make sure that all of the angles are plumb off the new incline. You won't have any visual information that will tell you that it is just the floor that is doing that.... The windows will be made out of a coated glass—a very clear optical glass that they use in skyscrapers, which will be silvered—and the room cavity will be painted a light gray, a cool gray. The entry wall and baseboard area will have indirect placement of white ultraviolet light, so that at night the cavity will reflect itself. Because of the coating on the windows, it will be difficult to see the skyline at night—you'll see it, but it will be much easier to see the interior of the room. The area outside the room is going to have a natural hardwood floor; the door will be natural wood, and solid. I will build a spiral staircase up to the roof.*
>
> *On the roof there will be a door which opens in the same position as the one below, except that it is hung on a tilt that is the* reverse *of the floor below. The floor we're building above that wall goes around that space up there, so that it will appear as you open the door that the floor just goes off into space and there is nothing to stop you.*
>
> *Downstairs you'll feel this resistance to walking in, and upstairs it will be just the opposite. You'll feel you are being pulled out, and the floor and what is left of the wall around it—which is basically two sides—have a step-away wall that will be painted bright white. Around the insides where the windows* would have been *(like down below), I'll have high-intensity fluorescent lights, which you won't be able to see, but they'll be right over the edge so that at night, if there is any moisture in the air, there will be condensation. There will be a light-conversion coming up and creating a wall that I feel will be seductive and will draw you out even more.*

Immediately one can imagine the compounding in this piece. Instead of simply working with the windows, Wheeler restructured the entire room, so that both visual and tactile sensations would be askew. The room upstairs would be built in a mirror image of the room below—further questioning the process of perception. And there would be an element of real danger added—participants ran the risk of stepping off the roof and literally into eternity. Wheeler felt strongly about this aspect of the work: "In our society and civilization now we are so insulated from things, and that takes our responsibility away from us, whereas in nature you come up to a cliff edge and it is up to you to know better than to go over the edge—so that is all a part of this piece." Not surprisingly, Wheeler's piece was deemed uninsurable because it was too dangerous, and he ultimately was not allowed to finish it.

During his periods of art-world invisibility Wheeler gave extended and serious thought to his role as an artist and to the questions asked by his work.

> *I just want to do whatever I feel like doing in my work. I would like to be vulnerable enough to do that—no matter what people say.... I am an artist for the rest of my life—not just for three or four years. I can't help it. I just am, and even if I never do a show in a gallery or museum again, that's how I see things, and that is what I have to deal with.*
>
> *You know what it is in a nutshell? You start as if you were on a train, and you are in a particular car on the train and you gradually get to know everybody on the car, and this is the world you move in—your company. Eventually you become conscious of and semi-used to the landscape that is whizzing by outside, and you get sort of apathetic about it. But then you move from that car to the next car, and you realize quicker than you had before that the landscape hasn't really changed from before, and that the people don't even seem that much different,* because the container is the same, *and the direction and momentum are the same, as you keep moving through more cars. It is very much like what it was for me in the art world for a while. Then, when you get to the observation car or you go outside the car and you go up on top, for the first time you can look back to where you've been, you can see where you are now, and you can look ahead to where you are going. At that point, you don't go back down into the car again—you could go back down, but you can't be the same person anymore, because they're in there looking out the windows and talking to each other and you can't deal with it anymore, because you've seen what's coming, and where you've been, and what's on this side, and what's on that side, and it really changes you.*
>
> *Those kinds of things really affected me; I felt I wasn't going anywhere because the track was controlled, and so I got off the train. Once you get off the train, it becomes a very small thing in the distance way down the track, and it is impossible to catch.*

Eventually Wheeler became frustrated and angry both at himself (he felt aspects of his work were getting too precious) and at the art world, which seemed to be bypassing him. For a variety of reasons he was unable to get major new work executed. (Panza, however, bought drawings and proposals for a large number of significant pieces but did not have room to install them.) At this point Wheeler, as he put it, "got off the train."

In 1981 Wheeler received an award from the Marie-Louise Jeanneret International Center for Artistic Experimentation, in Geneva, which involved a year's residency at Boissano, Italy. He returned to the United States in 1982.

SA MI DW SM 2 75 TC LA, 1975
in *The First Show: Painting and Sculpture from Eight Collections, 1940–1980,* Temporary Contemporary, Museum of Contemporary Art, Los Angeles
November 20, 1983–February 14, 1984

RM 619, 1967
in *Individuals: A Selected History of Contemporary Art, 1945–1986,* Temporary Contemporary, Museum of Contemporary Art, Los Angeles
December 10, 1986–January 10, 1988

Originally Wheeler was to be represented in *The First Show* by *SA MI DW SM 75, 1975,* which was in the collection of Count Panza. For various reasons, however, that work did not arrive, and it was necessary for Wheeler to create another one, *SA MI DW SM 2 75 TC LA, 1975.* This work consisted of two rooms—one chamber was twenty-four feet square, the other, forty feet square—with eight-kilowatt quartz-halogen lights, black ultraviolet lights, and an automatic dimmer. Radically different from the work in Panza's collection, it added new elements to the artist's visual vocabulary. Whereas the light sequences of the Panza work were controlled by a simple mechanical cam system, the light sequence of the new piece was timed to relate to the beat of the human heart. In addition, the wave lengths of the ultraviolet were of a different intensity, and the new piece always stayed at least as light as dusk, whereas the earlier one had gradually turned completely dark. Most viewers remained blissfully unaware of such technical changes in this decidedly spiritual work.

Wheeler was also represented in the inaugural exhibition of the Museum of Contemporary Art's new building, with a luminous encasement from the museum's own collection. This early work is a ninety-six-inch-square, vacuum-formed-Plexiglas work that utilizes both white ultraviolet light and neon light.

Wheeler's construction of *SA MI DW SM 2 75 TC LA, 1975* was the first indication of renewed interest in phenomenal art that he had evinced in some time, and it can be seen as a rekindling of his desire to create works of Light and Space. Nearly a decade later this has just begun to happen, and one waits in eager expectation for new works from the superb and highly private artist.

Bruce Nauman

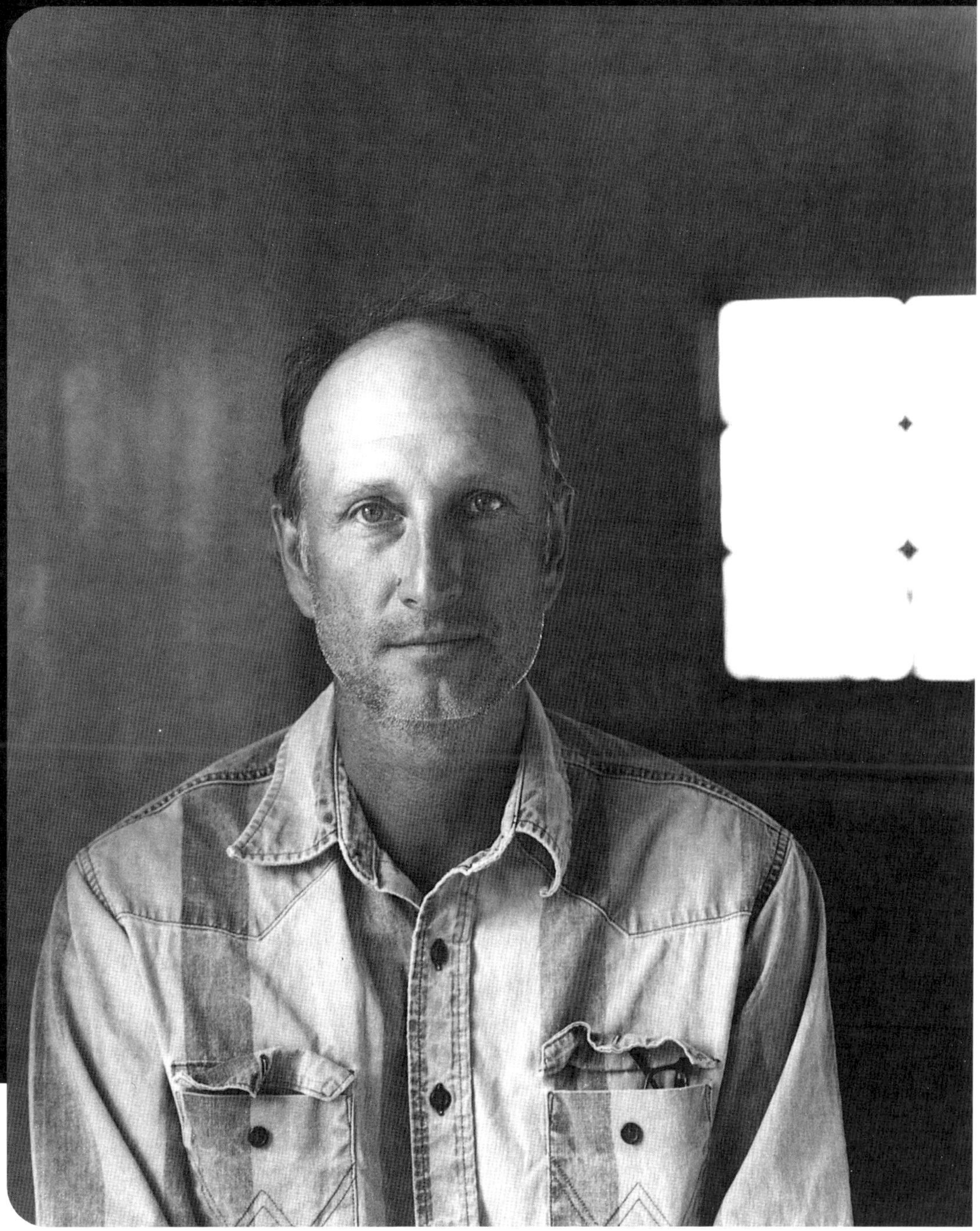

This is the BRUCE NAUMAN STORY. I AM THE BRUCE NAUMAN STORY. The true artist helps the world by remaining. I don't like feathers and I don't like butterflies.
With neon glance and hands that shape
He is the student's favorite.
His nimble fingers trip and thrill
And sing his praises high we will
Bruce Ding Man
Dong Nau Man
Bruce Nauman
Far from his home in Indiana
Folks seem to wonder, can you
Take this fellow seriously
Who answers so mysteriously
Bruce Dong Man
Sing Dong Man
Bruce Nauman
His name is heard on every tongue
Across the land his feathers hum
Cast off your wool and sing along
And join in praise of old Ding Dong
Bruce Ding Man
Dong Nau Man
Ding Dong Man
You know we love you no
matter what you do
No matter what you do.
Plunk, plink, plunk.
plunk, plunk, plunk.
plink, plank, plunk

Shelby "Hindu" Kennedy
and Don Whitaker

Bruce Nauman

Bruce Nauman's work is so diverse that it has variously been classified as Body art, Conceptual art, Eccentric Abstraction, Funk art, Light art, Minimal art, Process art, and Situational art. His use of materials runs the gamut as well: video, film, still photography, holography, latex, neon, concrete, plaster, wood, wax, foil. Nauman is clearly not a Light and Space artist exclusively, yet when he functions within that framework, he is one of the toughest of them all. His phenomenological work is clean and spare, with no unnecessary gestures. Perhaps the primary quality that separates his pieces from those by the other artists in this book is the degree of control he exerts. Distrusting the wide-open situation, Nauman sets specific conditions for experiencing a work. He takes great pains to ensure that the participant's response to a piece will be similar to his own.

Nauman has been considered an artist of international reputation for more than fifteen years, but he is younger than many of the other Light and Space artists. His career began in 1966, the year he graduated from the University of California, Davis, with an M.F.A. and began to teach at the San Francisco Art Institute. His first exhibition was that same year, at Nicholas Wilder Gallery in Los Angeles. In addition, he was included in Lucy Lippard's important *Eccentric Abstraction* exhibition, also in 1966, at Fischbach Gallery in New York. Nauman was represented in the latter show by wormlike fiberglass sculptures, made at U.C. Davis, that related to individual body parts—a career-long preoccupation. His works were ragged, raw, unfinished; they melted, flopped, and dangled from the ceiling and walls. By creating them, Nauman gave tacit permission for others to make work that was rough, open, and unrefined.

Nauman had also presented several performance pieces at U.C. Davis, and by the time of his show at Nicholas Wilder Gallery, he had begun to make films of himself. These films, in which he paced around his studio and bounced balls, dealt with the phenomenon of boredom—another career-long preoccupation.

From the very beginning Nauman chose to work as an artist-phenomenologist and artist-conceptualist rather than as an artist-maker. There is often not much to look at in his work—but always a great deal to think about. This became increasingly true in the 1970s. Knowing where to begin and where to end with Nauman is difficult; my discussions will be confined to those works that are clearly relevant to Light and Space art.

Window or Wall Sign, 1967; _Dark_, 1968; and _Lighted Center Piece_, 1967–68 in _Bruce Nauman: Work from 1965 to 1972_
Los Angeles County Museum of Art
December 19, 1972–February 18, 1973
Whitney Museum of American Art, New York
March 29–May 13, 1973

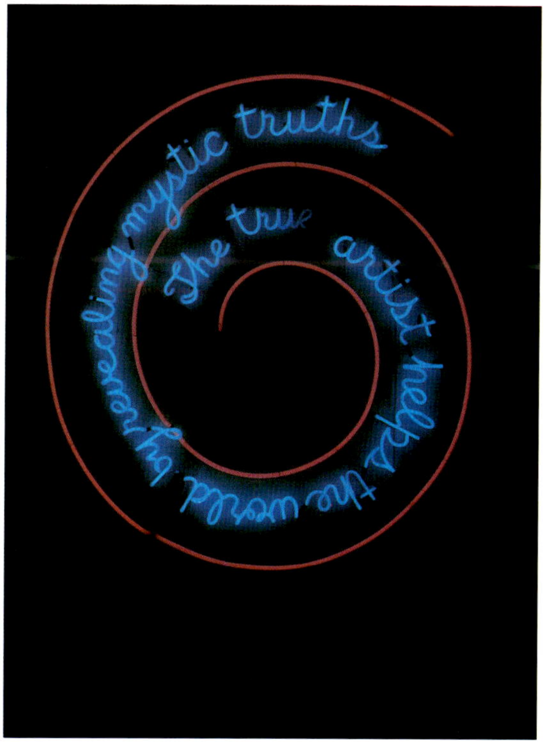

Bruce Nauman (b. 1941)
Window or Wall Sign, 1967
Neon and glass, 59 x 33 in.
(149.9 x 83.82 cm)
Leo Castelli Gallery,
New York

Hanging against the wall in Nauman's retrospective was a large peach-and-blue neon spiral that bore the words THE TRUE ARTIST HELPS THE WORLD BY REVEALING MYSTIC TRUTHS. At first reading this, I was embarrassed for Nauman, then irritated by his ego. There is even a kind of extortion in the work, as Peter Plagens noted: "If this piece is truly art, then there is a mystic truth here somewhere, and we are blackmailed into looking at it and thinking about it until we find that truth. Or we can say the hell with it and move on, but we'll never be sure."[1] Exactly. Nauman has the viewer right where he wants the viewer to be—on an uncomfortable edge between profundity and corniness. He said that his intention was to "put it out there to see if you believe in it; sort of like the thing that everybody would like to believe but can't."[2]

Nauman is alone among the Light and Space artists in his use of light as syntax rather than ambience. In *Window or Wall Sign* his use of neon—strident, garish, commercial—intensified the power of the work. Other of his neon works, such as *My Last Name Exaggerated 14 Times Vertically* and *My Name as Though It Were Written on the Surface of the Moon*, are not only conceptual works made of light; they begin to deal conceptually with space as well. They are not Light and Space works in the usual sense used in this book, but they lay the groundwork for such pieces. The mental extensions required by these pieces (what *would* Nauman's name look like written on the surface of the moon?) were beginning to feel like the conceptual-perceptual jumps soon to come, in which he would ask participants to involve themselves physically, rather than theoretically, in the work.

Dark straddles Nauman's conceptual period and the beginning of his nonobject or room-environment period. The work is four inches high, roughly fifty-eight inches square, and, as Jane Livingston explained: "It consists of a 2,500 pound square slab of steel, planted permanently in an outdoor location. On its underside—irrevocably hidden from view—is inscribed the word 'DARK.'"[3] Nauman said about this ominous work:

> Dark *is one of the first pieces having to do with a leftover feeling. This feeling has been important in my work ever since. It's hard to be more specific. It's partly the idea of "Given this piece of information there's nothing you can do about it." Of course, the obvious thing is establishing a place you can't get into—you have no control over it. It's sort of like trying to think about the universe.*[4]

Dark is damp and close. There is an absence of light, but also an implication of other things—claustrophobia, for example. The piece is ominous, yet it is safe. We can think about it, but there is no way to participate in it. For all of its enigmatic qualities, *Dark* is more specific than Nauman was to be in some later pieces: "I liked the feeling of the weight of the piece. I thought I made a good job of getting the word with the piece, having the word '*Dark*' underneath so you can't see it.... If I did the piece now, I probably wouldn't put the word there. But it seems that having the word there helps you think about that bottom side and what it might be like under there."[5]

Centering is important to Nauman. It first came to the fore in works such as *Lighted Center Piece* (1967–68), an extremely literal work about which Plagens wrote:

> *Lighted Center Piece*...focuses on four very bright floodlights shining down on a piece of metal lying on the floor. It makes my fillings hurt from terror and I want to cry out something. From the collected writings on Nauman, the catalogue, and the rest of the exhibition I can find nothing to indicate he put that anguish there deliberately. The possibilities are: (1) he didn't put it there and it's in my head; (2) he put it there and nobody knows it but me; (3) he didn't put it there, and it's there anyway.[6]

The four floodlights remain fixed on the center of the work, seemingly for eternity. Looking at it, the viewer was supposed to think only about the concept of center—at least that is what the artist told me that he intended. But Plagens experienced only teeth-gritting pain. Therein lies an innate conflict in Nauman's work: no matter how hard he tries, he cannot completely control the spectator's response.

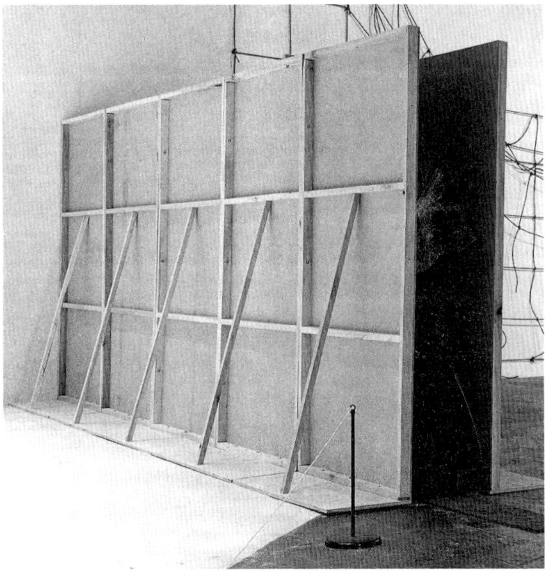

***Performance Corridor,* 1969**
in *Anti-Illusion: Procedures/Materials*
Whitney Museum of American Art, New York
May 19–July 1, 1969
videotape portion of the piece exhibited at
Leo Castelli Gallery, New York
May 19–July 6, 1969

Early in his career Nauman made videotapes that continued his investigations of the human body as a sculptural medium. One of those tapes is relevant here because it consists of images of the artist walking up and down a corridor. Nauman had built the twenty-eight-inch-wide corridor in his studio, creating two parallel walls, each eight feet tall and about twenty feet

Opposite
Bruce Nauman
Exterior of *Performance Area*
Wood and Homosote,
8 x 20 ft. (2.4 x 6.1 m.)
Installation, Van Abbemuseum,
Eindhoven, the Netherlands,
1969–70

Right
Bruce Nauman
Interior of *Performance Area*
Installation, Van Abbemuseum,
Eindhoven, the Netherlands,
1969–70

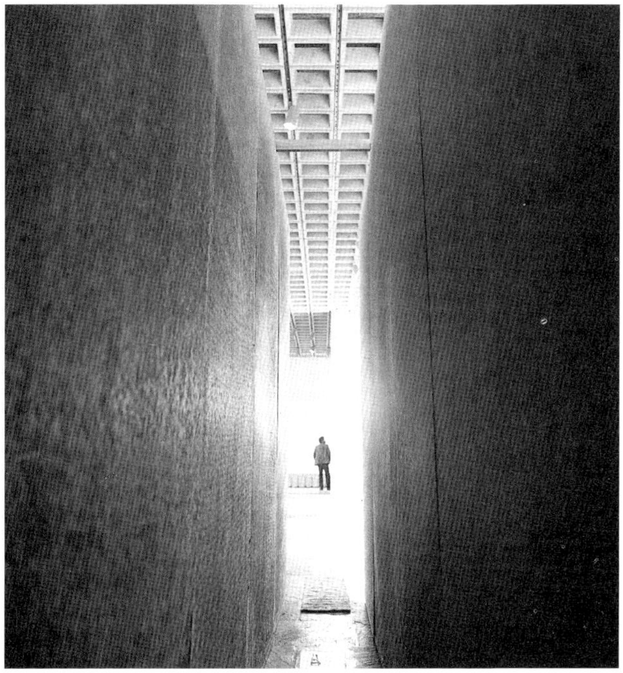

long. The original purpose of this confined hallway was solely as a prop for the tape. Then, realizing the power of the enigmatic structure, Nauman decided to exhibit it at the Whitney. Viewers not yet used to Nauman's work were understandably confused:

> Willoughby Sharp: I don't think people realized that they were supposed to enter it.
>
> Nauman: *Well, that was difficult. I didn't want to write it down, or have an arrow, so it was left open. That piece is important because it gave me the idea that you could make a participation piece without the participant being able to alter your work.*
>
> Sharp: Was it only possible to get in from one end?
>
> Nauman: *Yes, it ran directly into the wall, like a channel.... [In the tape] I walked very slowly toward and away from the camera, one step at a time. My hands were clasped behind my neck, and I used a very exaggerated contrapposto motion.... The way you saw it, the camera was placed so that the walls came in at either side of the screen. You couldn't see the rest of the studio, and my head was cut off most of the time. The light was shining down the length of the corridor and made shadows at each side of me.*[7]

The space in this corridor was narrow (twenty-eight inches barely permits passage of the human body), yet the effect was of serenity, not claustrophobia. The twenty-foot length somehow provided breathing space, and the shadowy gray neutrality of the walls added to the sense of respite.

L- or V-Shaped Corridor
Galerie Sonnabend, Paris, 1969

Acoustic Piece for Konrad Fischer (also called _Acoustic Wall_), 1969
Galerie Konrad Fischer, Düsseldorf
February 5–March 3, 1970

No longer content with the body as sculpture, Nauman began to create environments in which that body could be placed—still controlling the situation so that the participant would have an experience as close as possible to the artist's own original experience of the piece. These environments were crude structures, finished inside but rough and unfinished on the outside. This lack of interest in refined surface and materials separates Nauman from the other Light and Space artists. His structures are functional enough to provide an experience but not so well built that they call attention to themselves. It is not the structures that constitute the piece, but the experience.

The acoustic works at Sonnabend and Fischer were odd. They were either padded and muffled, to shut out sound and deaden the space, or they combined human sounds with room environments to create a highly charged audio atmosphere. The materials were simple: acoustical padding covered two nine-foot walls, in which flat speakers were hidden. The two walls, which were installed at an angle across the gallery, converged at the back corner. The visual effect was somewhat like walking between two large mattresses. Nauman described the Sonnabend piece as "a large L- or V-shaped wall covering two walls of her Paris gallery. It was flush with the wall, with very thin speakers in it. For that work there were two different tapes: one was of exhaling sounds, and the other of pounding and laughing alternately. You couldn't quite locate the sound. That was quite a threatening piece—especially the exhaling sound."[8]

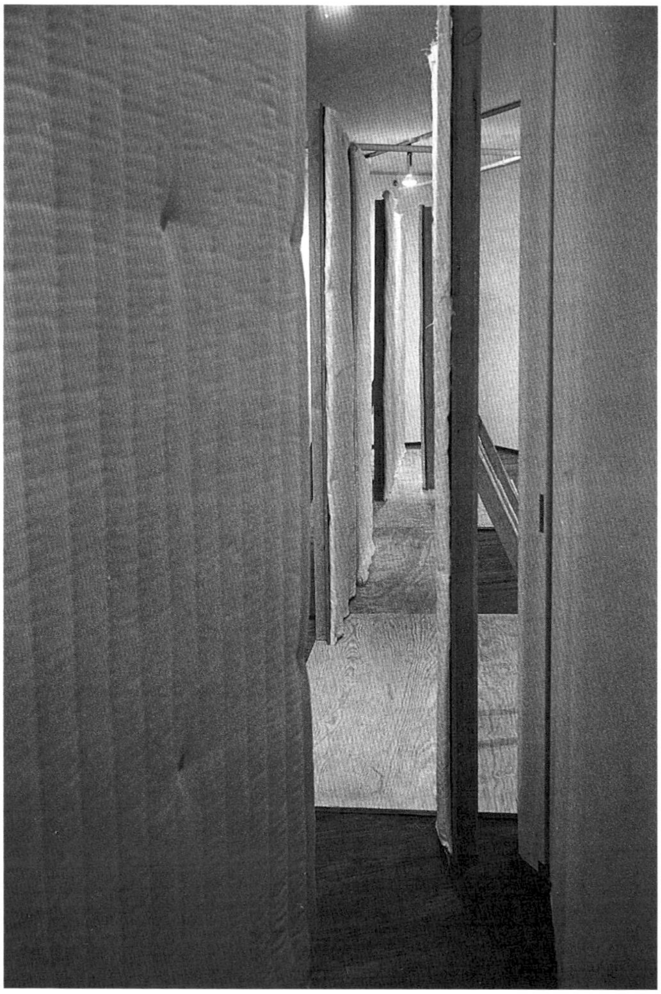

Willoughby Sharp: Do you think you are deliberately perverse?

Bruce Nauman: It's an attitude I adopt sometimes to find things out—like turning things inside-out to see what they look like. It has to do with doing things that you don't particularly want to do, with putting yourself in unfamiliar situations, following resistance to find out why you're resisting, like therapy.

Sharp: So you try to go against your own nature, and to go against what people expect: exhibiting things from the back or that you can't see.

Nauman: Yes, but I tend to look at these things in a positive way and I've often been surprised when people take them in the opposite way and think I am being perverse.

■ **Bruce Nauman, in Willoughby Sharp, "Nauman Interview," *Arts Magazine* 44 (March 1970): 26.**

Entering this work one sensed, or rather heard, someone else in the room—perhaps in a back portion of the gallery. Whoever it was was pounding, apparently trying desperately to escape. One heard the pounding, then maniacal laughter, then pounding again, and eventually heart-rending sighs. The effect was not so much threatening as terrifying. Marcia Tucker has talked about the "kinds of tension resulting from the psychological effect of changes of pressure on the auditory system used by Nauman." And she continued:

> Nauman has pointed out an analogous situation existing in nature, when certain winds or approaching storms can create even minute pressure changes in the atmosphere, which are said to account for widespread emotional instability and increased suicide rates in a given area.
>
> The "emotional overload" that he is interested in can be partly accounted for in these kinds of terms, but is also due, in a less definable way, to how much of his own ideas and feelings he has been able to incorporate into the work—to how personal it is. For him, this quality is essential, even if it is impossible to measure and evaluate.[9]

Bruce Nauman
Acoustic Pressure Piece
Wallboard and acoustical material, approximately 8 x 50 x 4 ft. (2.4 x 15.2 x 1.2 m.)
Installation, Leo Castelli Gallery, New York, 1970

It is interesting that Nauman, in recognizing the tension triggered by the positive ions prevalent in sirocco-like winds, chose to emulate the uneasy atmosphere they generate. Eric Orr, by contrast, has chosen to harness the negative ions that encourage calm and serenity. Nauman did not actually charge the gallery with ions, as Orr would do, but he psychologically charged it. This quality of perversity is an undercurrent in many of his pieces.

Two Rooms: Empty, Sealed, and Private, **1970**
and *Green Light Corridor,* 1970
Giuseppe Panza di Biumo, Varese, Italy
installed 1970

Entering the space that contained *Two Rooms,* the viewer saw on a monitor an image of another room—a sealed room that could not be entered. A camera surveyed the viewer's room, transmitting that information to the sealed room, to nobody. Nauman has invited us in and then shut us out with a piece that relates to his frequent reference to the problems of telling too much, of exposing himself too much, and of needing to keep a part of himself hidden.

Green Light Corridor is the icon of Nauman's room-environment pieces. Its intensity, its threatening quality, its economy of means combine to make it one of the most important pieces he has done. *Green Light Corridor* is very tall, very thin, and very long. Entering the room that contains it, the participant sees a narrow, freestanding hallway that goes nowhere. Its interior is flooded with a blinding yellow-green light, as vivid as Day-Glo. There is nothing to indicate that the participant cannot enter the work, but one is reluctant to do so because it is so aggressively uninviting. Yet the work is clearly intended to be participated in, and so some make an attempt to do so. The going immediately becomes difficult. For one thing, the corridor is so narrow that one must shuffle sideways like a crab to move down its full forty-foot length. Once inside, the intensity of the green light is overwhelming. It pulls the color from the skin, deadening it to gray. It bombards the eyes, making them hum and sting. Sidling slowly down the corridor, one at last reaches the end and escapes. Then it happens. The entire room and all of its contents have turned a brilliant, vibrating magenta, the result of retinal bleach.

In Italy, where a version of *Green Light Corridor* has been built for Panza, one emerges to see the top of an arched window suddenly fill with magenta sky. This Technicolor effect is made all the more unreal by a sudden burst of song from the hundreds of birds that nest in the trees outside. The sensory deprivation/sensory overload inside the work is so profound that one is unable even to hear, and this abrupt intensity of the chirping birds is unnervingly intense.

Some of the pieces have to do with setting up a situation and then not completing it, or in taking away a little of the information, so that somebody can only go so far and then can't go any farther. It attempts to set up a kind of tension situation. I think it has to do with a personal fear of exposing myself. I can only give so much. If I go further, it would take away something, or do something that would throw me off the track. We all go so far that we have the fear of exposing ourselves. We really want to expose the information, but, on the other hand, we are afraid to let people in.

■ Bruce Nauman, in Jan Butterfield, "Bruce Nauman: 'The Center of Yourself,'" *Arts Magazine* 49 (February 1975): 54.

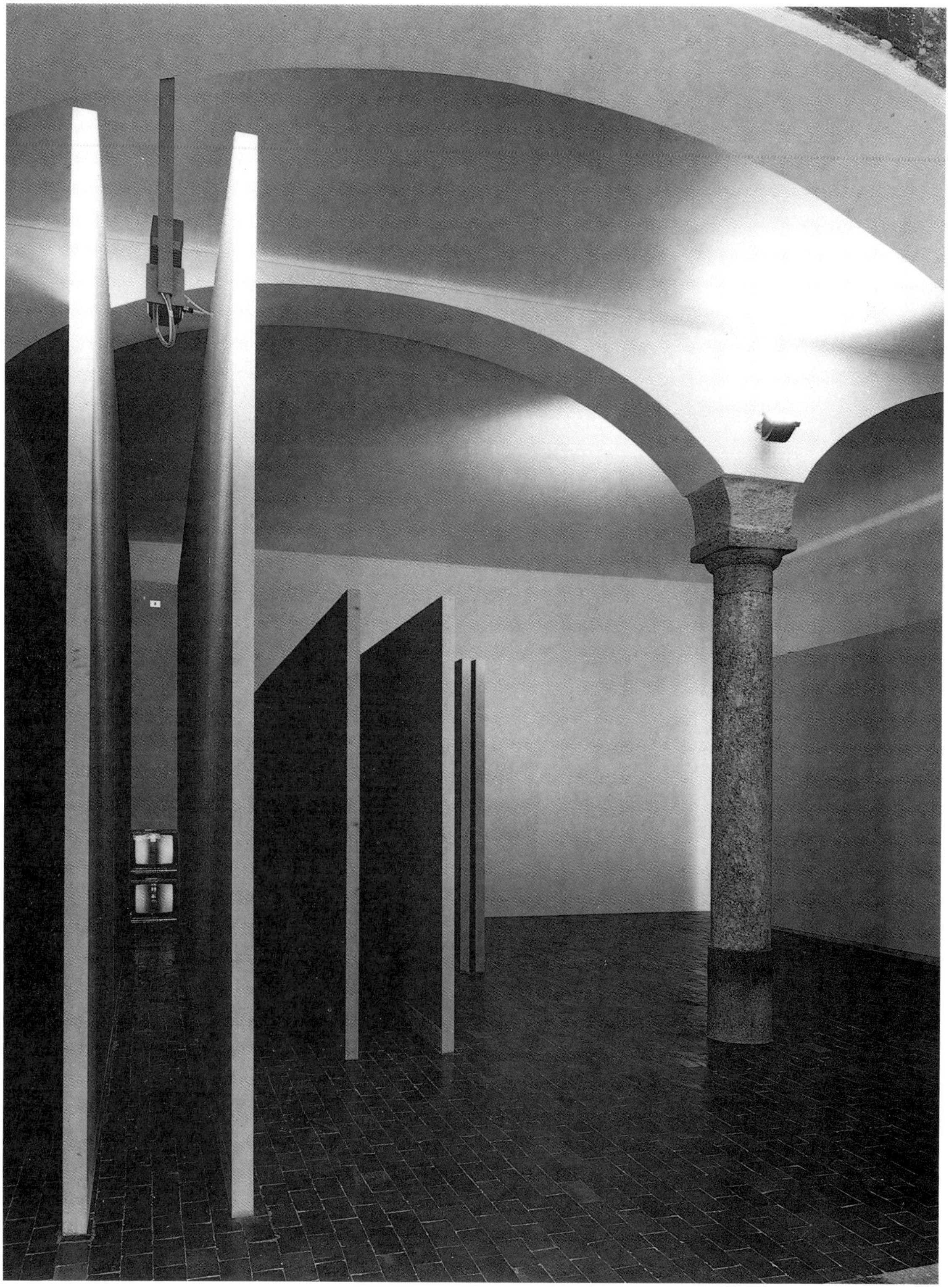

Opposite
Bruce Nauman
Corridors, 1969–70
Plywood, dimensions variable
Giuseppe Panza di Biumo,
Varese, Italy

Right
Bruce Nauman
Green Light Corridor, 1970–71
Wallboard and fluorescent light,
dimensions variable
Giuseppe Panza di Biumo, Varese,
Italy; promised gift to the
Guggenheim Museum,
New York

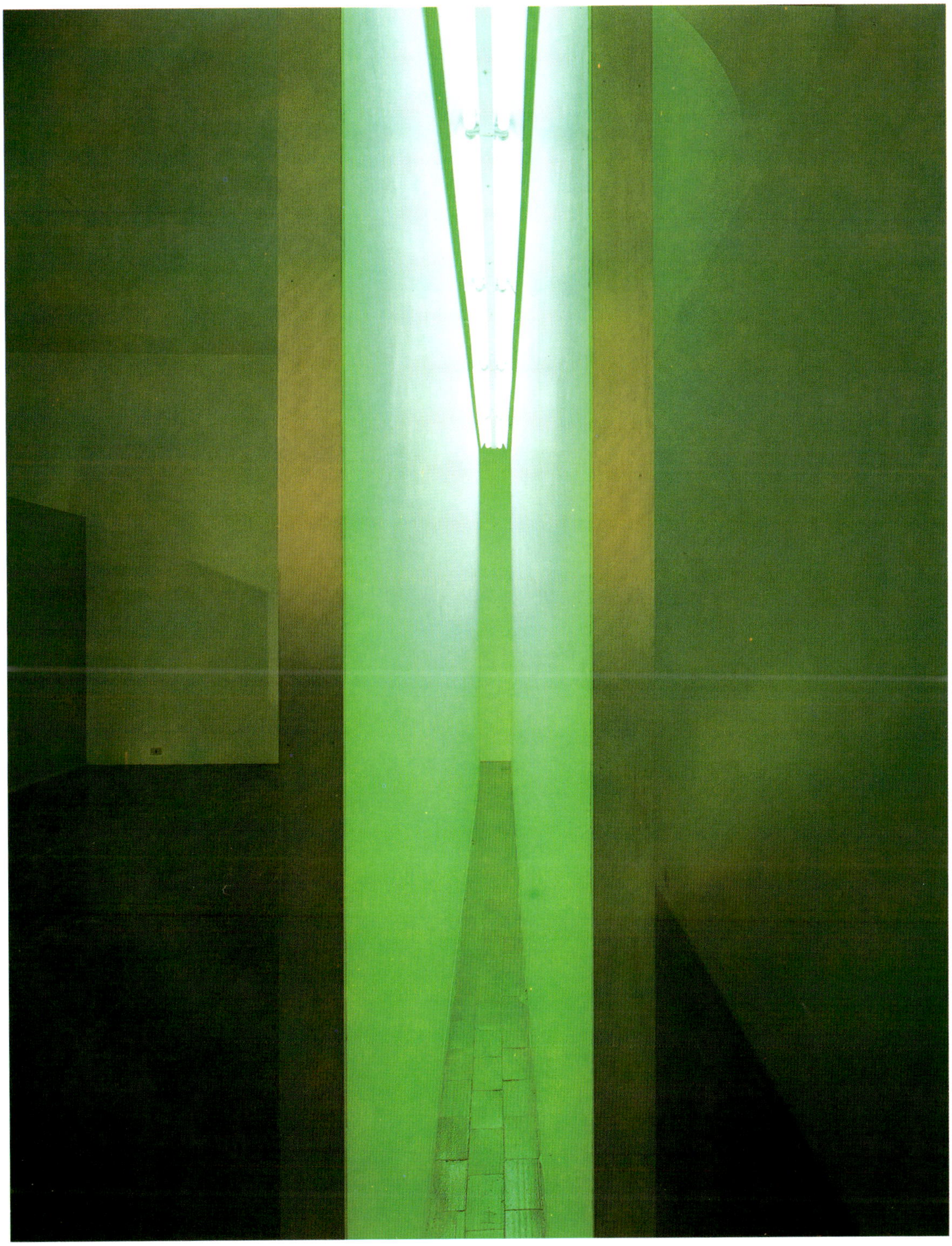

***Soundtape: Get Out of My Mind, Get Out of This Room,* 1972**
in *Bruce Nauman: Work from 1965 to 1972*
and in *Bruce Nauman, 1971–1981*
Rijksmuseum Kröller-Müller, Otterlo, the Netherlands
Aprll 5–May 25, 1981

Soundtape was one of Nauman's most conceptual and most unnerving room-environment pieces. One entered the white, dimly lit room only to discover there was nothing in it. Frustrated, one looked around, making every attempt to discover where the art was. Then, softly, without warning, came the whispered admonition: "Get out of my mind, Get out of this room, Get out of my mind, Get out of this room, Get out of my mind, Get out of this room," repeated over and over. Resembling *Acoustic Wall* with its laughter, pounding, and long, breathy sighs, this work had a chilling aspect, hovering between reality and abstraction. One knew that no human being was trapped inside, yet it seemed one could not be sure. Then, without warning, the voice stopped and the work reverted to being simply an abstract sculpture.

***Floating Room,* 1972**
Fine Art Gallery, University of California, Irvine, February 1973
Leo Castelli Gallery, New York, March 1973

Upon entering the space one faced a second room—a room within a room. It was large, measuring about twelve feet square. It seemed almost to fill the first space, and it floated a few inches off the floor, suspended by cables. A single door led to the violet-hued interior of this room. Pairs of blue and white fluorescent lights lent a lavender color to the walls, but there were also places where the splays of light met and arched, and a softened butter-yellow eased in. Despite all of this color, it was darker inside than out, and once in it, the participant could see a band of light around the outside.

When sitting centered on the floor inside the room, the experience was pleasant, contemplative, meditative. There was, briefly, a euphoric sense of "being"—out of time, out of space, out of this place. Yet even this relatively benign space had a psychological edge to it, related to Nauman's own sense of space:

> *I think in terms of the psychological aspects, how we locate ourselves in a room, how we fill a space and are comfortable in it. I am also interested in how we control a space. For example: when you're a kid and you have to go down the stairs to the basement and there are dark corners and only one light bulb, you make a lot of noise, or you whistle. When you are grown up, you do the same thing. You fill the space up with yourself somehow by making noises. That is how you control space. I think those are very real feelings, and adults have them, too. You do try to make yourself comfortable in a space. You try and know the space in some sense. You at least try to look around the room you're in, to see how you fit in. By providing that strip of light or dark around the bottom (as in the* Floating Room*), you're suddenly not able to control the environment or fill it up with yourself, because you're blocked up in this much of it and there is stuff outside—the rest of the world is always out there and you can't make a connection somehow. I found that especially if the room was light inside, if you went in there and stayed for any length of time—ten minutes or so—it got harder and harder to break the barrier and go over and open the door and step out. The longer you were inside, the less you knew about what might be going on on the outside, even if you know perfectly well that it's just your studio, and the door is closed.*

This is the kind of edge I am dealing with. What that grew into was a sense of public space and private space. How you relate to those two different kinds of spaces and what the difference is.

We are trying to get to the center of some place: that is, exactly halfway between each pair of parts.

We want to move our center (some measurable center) to coincide with such a point.

We want to superimpose our center of gravity on this point.

Save enough energy and concentration to reverse.

(The center of most places is above eye level.)

■ **Bruce Nauman, *Floating Room* (New York: Leo Castelli Gallery, 1973), exhibition mailer.**

Yellow Triangular Room (Installation with Yellow Lights)
Leo Castelli Gallery (downtown), New York
November 20–December 11, 1973
Santa Ana College, Santa Ana, California
February 10–March 6, 1975

Left or Standing
His precision and accuracy
suggesting clean cuts, leaving
a vacancy, a slight physical
depression as though I had been
in a vaguely uncomfortable place
for a not long but undeterminable
period; not waiting.
Standing or Left Standing
His preciseness and acuity left
small cuts on the tips of my
fingers or across the backs of
my hands without any need to
sit or otherwise withdraw.[10]

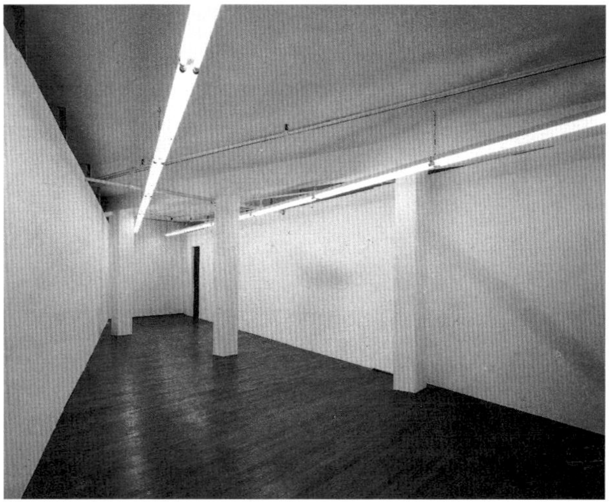

Bruce Nauman
Yellow Triangular Room
(Installation with Yellow Lights)
Partitions and fluorescent light, dimensions variable
Installation, Leo Castelli Gallery, New York, 1973

In *Yellow Triangular Room (Installation with Yellow Lights)* at Santa Ana, the participant entered the traditional well-lighted white gallery space (which measured thirty-five by twenty-three feet) to find that a triangular room had been built inside it. The outside of the triangular space (measuring ten feet tall, with sixteen-foot-long walls) was roughly finished and unpainted. It looked like an exhibition under construction. As with many of Nauman's installations the lack of outside finish served to "make the thing less important to look at"[11]—and it also focused the percipient's attention on the fact that it was not the room but the sensate experience that was the art.

At Castelli Gallery the effect had been similar. The participant entered the triangular room through an exaggeratedly small door, whose threshold was several inches off the floor. The strangeness had already begun. Having entered this curious space, the percipient closed the door and suddenly was very much alone. The space was conceived to house only one person at a time. The triangular shape made the room feel tight, constricting, because the three points took up so much of the space.

In contrast to the outside, the interior of the room was perfectly finished and painted white. Yellow emanated from eight-foot-long fluorescent tubes installed on the ceiling and along the walls. The color was so strong that its intensity obliterated everything visual except the yellow itself. The participant saw no objects, no shadows, no other colors. Like the green of *Green Light Corridor,* it was eerie, disorienting. There was a feeling of dizziness and a sense of not being able to hear well—both a result of sensory deprivation.

For some the space in *Yellow Triangular Room (Installation with Yellow Lights)* was too forced, the color too hostile. For others the work did not constitute art as they understood art to be. Still others felt the work was unclear in relation to its art historical roots. Robert Pincus-Witten, for one, found fault with Nauman because, in his view, the work no longer related to Marcel Duchamp's:

> Nauman has exchanged elitism for populism and, devoid of the verbal flourish that his work once possessed, only gives us sensitivity boxes which he imagines turn his observer on to the fresh experience of color and sound. In proselytizing for the "Wow" experience—"Wow" soundproofing, "Wow" yellow fluorescent light, "Wow" the room is built on a diagonal axis—he has now abandoned Duchamp and, in leaving Duchamp, has abandoned his claim to being interesting, at least for the moment.[12]

The shape of *Yellow Triangular Room (Installation with Yellow Lights)* and the volume it encased accounted for a part of the experience, which some participants reacted to strongly, among them Michael Auping:

> By defining a space within a defined space, Nauman sets up an interrelated series of volumes that allude to our perception of exterior and interior spaces—the volume outside the gallery, the volume between the gallery walls and the walls of the triangle, and the volume within the triangle. While the space inside the triangular room would appear to be the focal point of the piece, the viewer becomes intrigued with the space between the gallery walls and the exterior of the triangular room and the degree to which this space can be perceived as exterior or interior. Further, a volume within a volume creates a sense of compression that makes space seem more dense and results in alerting viewers to their perceptions of atmosphere.[13]

Flayed Earth/Flayed Self (Skin/Sink)
Nicholas Wilder Gallery, Los Angeles
December 17, 1973–January 11, 1974

There was a profound sense of forceful movement in this piece: of spiraling, of twisting. The piece was created out of tape that began in the center of the room and then splayed out, so it encompassed the entire space. Two or three inches wide at its point of origin at the core, the tape gradually narrowed to no more than an inch wide as it was flung against the walls. This tapering of the curving arms established a kind of perspective and gave the sensation of moving away.

Having first read the small book of Nauman's poems that was conceived as part of the exhibition, I sensed a muffled terror in the piece: a terror of force and power. It was a work that affected my stasis: I was, in the psychic sense, out of control. This rollercoaster-ride kind of fear was very much a part of the work. An excerpt from Nauman's book of poems published with the exhibition graphically conveys this frightening sense of confrontation:

> *Spiraling twisting ascent descent screwing in*
> *screwing out screwing driving diving*
> *invest invert convert relent relax control*
> *release, give in, given. Twisting driving down.*
> *Spiraling up screwing up screwed up screwed*
> *Twisted mind, twist and turn, twist and shout.*
> *Squirm into my mind so I can get into*
> *your mind your body our body*
> *arcing ache, circling warily then*
> *pressed together, pressing together*
> *forced.*[14]

False Silences
Los Angeles Institute of Contemporary Art
September 16–October 24, 1974

As with many of Nauman's pieces, the physical construction of *False Silences* was simple: it consisted primarily of a drywall corridor, painted white. Yet in this cramped space, alternately dark then harshly lit, I experienced a deeply successful merging of the poetic and the literal. Entering the work and proceeding down the narrow corridor, which was deeply shot with shadow, I perceived only grayed darkness at the end and a wedge of intense white light midway down on either side, which only partially relieved the tension of the space. Made anxious by the constriction of the walls, I was further disturbed when a voice within the space began to chant:

I don't sweat
I have no odor
I inhale, don't exhale
No urine
I don't defecate: no excretions of any kind
I consume only
Oxygen, all foods, any form
I see, hear
I don't speak, make no other sounds. You can't hear
my heart,
my footsteps
No expression, no communication of any kind
An observer, a consumer, a user only
My body absorbs all communications, emotions,
sucks up heat and cold
Super reptilian soaking up all knowledge,
compactor of all information
No growing
I feel don't touch . . .

Initially the words could not be made out, but gradually they took on a kind of cadence:

I have no control over the kinds and qualities
of thoughts
I collect, I can't process
I can't react to or act on sensation
No emotional response to situations
There is no reaction of instinct to physical
or mental threats
You can't reach me, you can't hurt me
I can suck you dry

And then the chanting voice became very loud:

You can't hurt me
You can't help me
Shuffle the pages
Find me a line
Arapaho
Arapaho
Where did you go
I blink my eyes to keep the time.[15]

Now desperately needing space to breathe, I reached the center of the work, where triangular rooms, brightly lit and painted white, opened off the claustrophobic hallway, momentarily freeing the spectator. After remaining in the rooms long enough to shake off my qualms, I then reentered the corridor, proceeding down the rest of the sixty-foot length into increasing darkness, where I was stopped dead by the back wall of the piece. At this point, I could only turn around and go back.

Forced Perspective
Galerie Konrad Fischer, Düsseldorf
December 16, 1974–January 24, 1975

Enforced Perspective, Allegory and Symbolism
Ace Gallery, Venice, California
October 9–November 13, 1976

The year 1974 marked the beginning of Nauman's involvement with an entirely different kind of work. On first consideration, the new work was confusing. The room-environment pieces were left behind, replaced by work that utilized traditional sculptural materials. From 1974 to 1977 Nauman had a series of key exhibitions that presented various aspects of this work.

Enforced Perspective, Allegory and Symbolism evolved from *Forced Perspective,* a more complex piece shown at Galerie Konrad Fischer. Accompanying the exhibition at Ace Gallery was a statement that read:

OPEN MIND
CLOSED MIND
EQUAL MIND
PARALLEL MIND

At first the exhibition appeared to be one of Minimal work. Steel ingots (six inches high by two feet by about two feet) presented themselves initially as squares, then suddenly appeared not to be true squares at all but squares that had been distorted, forced. These curious units were clustered here and there on the floor in groups of three or four or five, and each group was out of line, askew, so that the whole feeling was one of irrationality, of imbalance (yet later it became clear that there was an underlying grid). The viewer was further confused by the terms *allegory* and *symbolism* in the title—terms that are poetic and conceptual and that seem to have no real connection with what seemed to be a Minimal piece. Writing about the work, Melinda Wortz suggested, "Nauman's subverted geometry might be seen (with the mind or with the eye?) as an allegory for the irrationality of the system of perspective."[16] And that, one suspects, is as close as one can get.

There is something else to the work as well: the curious melding of linguistic and visual elements. Beginning in the early 1970s—especially with *Flayed Earth/Flayed Self (Skin/Sink); The Consummate Mask of Rock; Enforced Perspective, Allegory and Symbolism; False Silences;* and others—Nauman has coined poetic and descriptive titles for his works and published extensive notes related to them. But his enigmatic writings do not solve any puzzle, they only compound it. They are part of the work, not an explanation of it.

As we have seen with Irwin, it is sometimes assumed that certain artists have claims on certain materials—Cor-ten steel, plastic, neon, and so on. The following statement appeared in a brief, unsigned entry in the *Los Angeles Times*: "Bruce Nauman's 'Enforced Perspective' makes simple arrangements of parallelogram-shaped steel ingots that create spatial illusions in an exhibition that attempts to attach mystical and poetic ideas to techniques associated with the work of other artists."[17] Yet to a careful observer, *Enforced Perspective* did not look like the work of any artist outside the Light and Space arena. First, it was a room-environment work in the sense that it utilized the four right-angle walls to frame its elements as well as to reinforce their irregularity. Second, the work was clearly not three-dimensional sculpture in the traditional sense, because its thrust was largely conceptual.

The Consummate Mask of Rock
Atholl McBean Gallery, San Francisco Art Institute
January 9–February 22, 1975
Albright-Knox Art Gallery, Buffalo, New York
September 26–November 9, 1975
Sonnabend Gallery, New York, November 1976
Nicholas Wilder Gallery, Los Angeles
May 31–July 1, 1977

The Consummate Mask of Rock was made of fourteen- and fifteen-inch cubes of limestone, scattered around the floor in irregular groupings. The poignancy of the accompanying text, mounted on the gallery wall, infused the work. That text, also titled *The Consummate Mask of Rock,* is extensive; two of the six sections bear repeating here.

Section 2

1. *This is my mask of fidelity to truth and life.*
2. *This is to cover the mask of pain and desire.*
3. *This is to mask the cover of need for human companionship.*
4. *This is to mask the cover.*
5. *This is to cover the mask.*
6. *This is the need of cover.*
7. *This is the need of the mask.*
8. *This is the mask of cover of need.*
9. *No thing and no mask can cover the lack, alas.*
10. *Lack after nothing before cover revoked.*
11. *Lack before cover*
    paper covers rock
    rock breaks mask
    alas, alack.

12. *Nothing to cover.*
13. *This is the mask to cover my infidelity to truth.*
(This is my cover.)
14. *This is the need for pain that contorts my mask*
conveying the message of truth and fidelity to
life.
15. *This is the truth that distorts my need for human*
companionship.
16. *This is the distortion of truth masked by my*
painful need.
17. *This is the mask of my painful need distressed by*
truth and human companionship.
18. *This is my painless mask that fails to touch my*
face but floats before the surface of my skin my
eye my teeth my tongue.
19. *Desire is my mask.*
(Musk of desire.)
20. *Rescind desire*
cover revoked
desire revoked
cover rescinded.
21. *PEOPLE DIE OF EXPOSURE.*

Section 7

1. *(This young man, taken to task so often, now finds*
it his only sexual relief.)
2. *(This young man, so often taken to task, now finds*
it his only sexual fulfillment.)
3. *(This man, so often taken to task as a child . . .)*
4. *(This man, often taken to task, now finds it*
satisfies his sexual desires.)
arouses *needs*
5. *This man, so often taken as a child, now wears the*
consummate mask of rock and uses it to drive his
wedge of desire into the ever squeezing gap
between truth and falsity.
6. *This man, so often taken as a child, now uses his*
consummate mask of his rock to drive his wedge of
his desire into his ever squeezing (his) gap
between his truth, his falsity.
7. *(This) man, (so often) taken as (a) child, finding*
his consummate mask of rock covered by paper, he
finding his wedge being squeezed (from) between
his desired truth (truth desired) and his desireless
falsity (falsity desireless), he unable to
arouse his satisfaction, he unable to desire his
needs, he proceeds into the gap of his fulfillment
his relief lacking the task of human companionship.

Moral

Paper cut from rock, releases rock to crush scissors.
Rock freed from restrictions of paper/scissors/rock,
lacking context proceeds.[18]

The Consummate Mask of Rock is a fascinating document within the plastic arts, and it seems far more difficult to deal with it than if the author were a writer. We generally mask our insecurities and our desires, along with our truths and falsehoods. Now Nauman comes along and exposes himself—and we are at a loss as to how to deal with it.

Diamond Mind II
Sperone Westwater Fischer, New York
October 30–November 27, 1976

In *Diamond Mind II,* an exhibition conceived to run concurrently with *The Consummate Mask of Rock* in New York, Nauman presented another, far shorter poem:

Diamond Mind II

Plaster for stone
Diamond Mind
Circle of tears
Fallen all around me
Fallen mind
Mindless tears
Cut like a diamond.[19]

In this exhibition twelve white *faux-marbre* blocks were scattered on the floor around a large steel-mesh cage with mazelike corridors and an empty center. The cage was of human scale and could be entered, though it was oppressive and claustrophobic. The references to Duchamp's *Why Not Sneeze Rrose Sélavy?* (a wire birdcage filled with marble blocks, among other things) were clearly intended, as several perceptive critics noted at the time.[20] But this was not only an homage to Duchamp, it was a primal cord-cutting, for Nauman released the cubes from their imprisonment in Duchamp's cage, and, as he wrote, they now made a "Circle of tears / Fallen all around me."

Untitled, 1980
in *Architectural Sculpture*
organized by Los Angeles Institute of Contemporary Art
installed at Baxter Art Gallery, California Institute of Technology, Pasadena
October 1–November 30, 1980

Building on knowledge derived from various installations of *Yellow Triangular Room (Installation with Yellow Lights),* Nauman created another, even more impressive version of that work for the *Architectural Sculpture* exhibition. Installed outdoors, this work was altogether different from any of Nauman's interior pieces. It also appeared initially to exert less control over the participant than previous works—an impression that proved fallacious.

Expecting to encounter the work inside the gallery, as had been the case with Nauman's other environments, the viewer was initially confused not to find it there. A scanning of the grounds and entrance area did not reveal it either. Then the work was encountered—at the back of the building, just off the parking lot.

The work appeared initially to be a gigantic black Minimal cube some sixteen feet tall. Yet as the participant moved closer to the doorway, the structure revealed itself as clearly not a cube but an equilateral triangle, which was approached toward one of its flat sides. This deliberate distortion was achieved by positioning the piece at a point where several cement paths converged—forcing the viewer to perceive it from its flat side (assuming one always used the proper paths). This spot was located on the path that led to the parking lot. Since no one uses the front door at Baxter Art Gallery—most people enter from the parking lot—this location, initially perceived as obscure, was actually at the gallery's front door.

It was a strong work. The doorways were exaggeratedly small, causing the spectator to stoop to enter. Walking in was like entering a small house rather than a room, yet the ceiling was open to the sky. Looking outward through the truncated doorways on each side, it became clear that each vista was carefully framed.

There was a disturbing aspect of the piece that resulted not only from the exaggeration and manipulation of the space but also from the intensity of the sodium-vapor lamps installed above each doorway. These lights appeared invisible in the daytime, yet they subtly altered the light inside the space. Gradually, as the day wore on, they appeared more and more pronounced, until they reached their zenith in full darkness, beaming out their acidic yellow light into the night through the doors and windows of what now looked like a lunatic's playhouse.

Nauman's simple, riveting works clearly established the primacy of the private experience. There is an inherent rightness in the works, yet it is a rightness that cannot be put into words. Nauman once commented: "When I do something that is a powerful piece—I know that it's right. I couldn't tell you why, though. At one point I said to somebody that as the pieces become simpler, they become more difficult to describe, or the experience is more complex. I think that's true still. There is less to talk about as the visceral impact becomes stronger." This visceral impact is crucial. The body, which has been so important to Nauman from the beginning, continues to be the receptive instrument—rather than the mind.

Vices and Virtues
Stuart Collection, University of California, San Diego, at La Jolla
installed October 28, 1988

Perhaps Nauman's most important work to date is the impressive *Vices and Virtues,* commissioned for the Stuart Collection at the University of California, San Diego, and installed all the way around the top of the Charles Lee Powell Structural Systems Laboratory Building.

Nauman's enormous outdoor neon piece comprises fourteen seven-foot-high words, with the seven vices superimposed over the seven virtues. The total of eighty-eight letters that make up the work incorporate more than a mile of neon and require eighty-eight electrical transformers. Clicking on and off, the words ANGER/FORTITUDE, GLUTTONY/TEMPERANCE, AVARICE/JUSTICE, PRIDE/PRUDENCE, SLOTH/CHARITY, ENVY/HOPE, LUST/FAITH flash in sequence around the building until they reach their starting point, and then the sequence starts over. The words are made from pairs of brilliant neon colors: emerald, turquoise, pink, peach, coral, yellow, red, sky blue, fuchsia, orange, and light green.

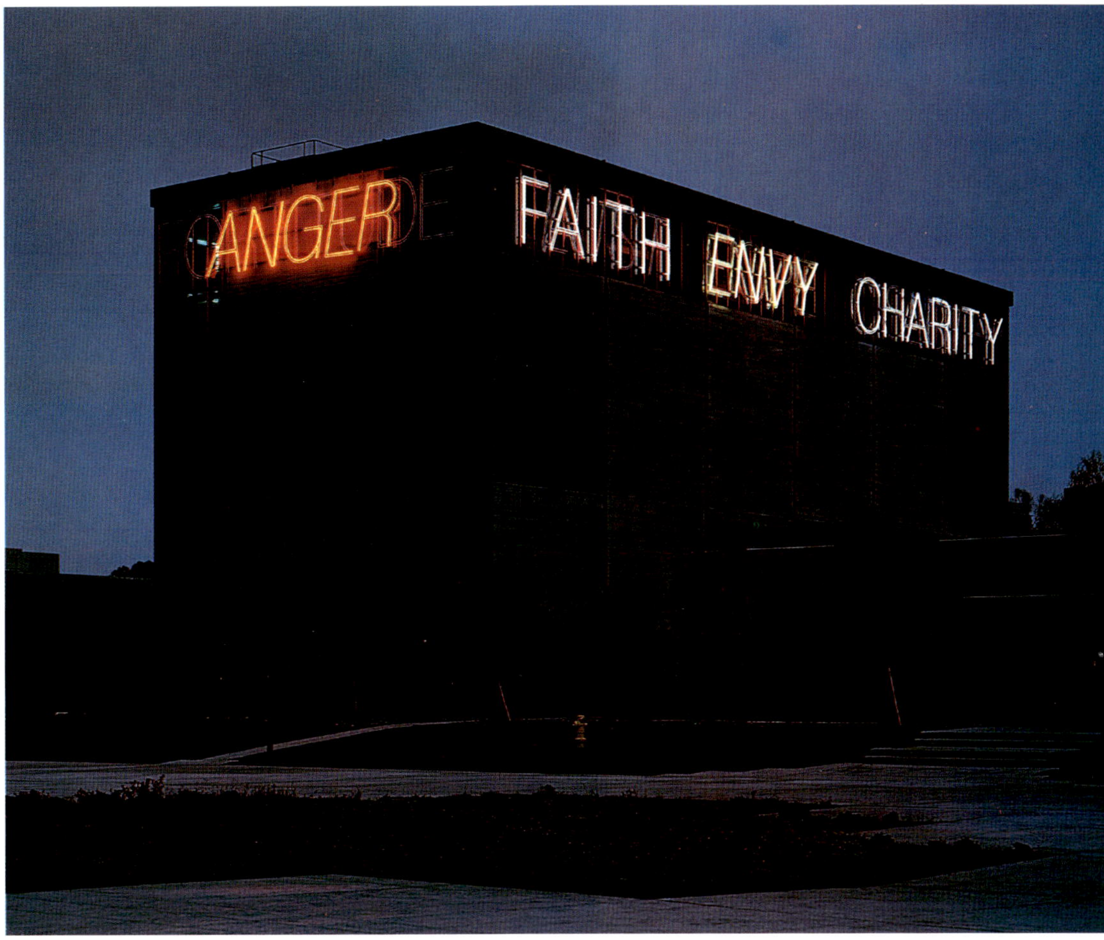

Bruce Nauman
Vices and Virtues, 1988
Neon
Permanent installation,
University of California, San Diego,
at La Jolla; Stuart Collection

The virtues flash sequentially right to left around the building, with each word illuminated for three seconds (3 x 7 = 21 seconds). The virtue cycle restarts every seven seconds. At two-and-a-half-minute intervals, all seven virtues flash on simultaneously for ten seconds. The vices flash in sequence, left to right, at a slightly faster rate of two-and-a-half seconds per word (2.5 x 7 = 17.5 seconds). The vice cycle restarts every 5.83 seconds. All the vices flash together for ten seconds every two minutes. The interplay of the two cycles allows every possible combination of the words to appear and includes the occasional display of all the words simultaneously. The work is illuminated daily, from dusk until 11:00 P.M., and it is frequently lighted for special events as well.

Vices and Virtues asks the viewer to ponder eternal truths and higher values, thus continuing in the same tradition as *Window or Wall Sign* (The True Artist Helps the World by Revealing Mystical Truths). *Vices and Virtues* also subtly embarrasses the viewer by asking him to contemplate truths that flash on and off seven feet high and are therefore unavoidable.

Center of the Universe
University of New Mexico, Albuquerque, installed 1988

Bruce Nauman has pinpointed the center of the universe: it is located in Albuquerque, New Mexico, where Yale Boulevard, N.E., dead ends near the duck pond on the University of New Mexico campus. *Center of the Universe* is an environmental sculpture, created for the campus. If ever there was a Nauman work that epitomizes the merger of the artist's Light and Space sensibilities with his more tangible sculptural work, this is it. As Nauman noted: "I didn't think of the title until I started working on it. Nobody knows where the center of the universe is, anyway. This piece takes you *out* of *this* place and puts you where the center might be. It puts you . . . into the huge scale of the universe, which is, after all, an interior space—you can only imagine it."[21]

Nauman's UNM work has been controversial since the very beginning—amusingly enough, because it has, for some, too little content, as opposed to *Vices and Virtues,* with its eternal refrain of morality. *Center of the Universe* is most simply described as three concrete hallways,

Why is light the rosy path for physics and art?
Why is Space active and object passive?
I use silence the way a painter uses color.
The future of art depends on artists not
copying art but finding it.
I want to make a work of art as simple as
the concept of zero.

Eric Orr

Eric Orr

Of all the artists examined here, Eric Orr is perhaps the most concerned with transformation, in both the literal and the metaphysical sense. His interest in alchemy lies not in the actual transformation of lead into gold but in philosophical secrets that are based on transformative processes. Orr calls himself a "Proto-materialist," which his friend the writer Thomas McEvilley has described as follows:

> A Proto-materialist is put off by the slowness and complexity of heavy things. He is drawn toward the state before matter, and the proto-state of matter in utter simplicity—before the process of differentiation has cluttered up the primal place. He dreams of flying, of leaving the body, of reading minds. Proto-materialism heralds an age of new solutions. It is the primitive art of the twenty-first century.[1]

Orr arrived in Los Angeles in 1966 with a B.A. from the University of Cincinnati and a background in poetry and economics at the New School for Social Research in New York. He had also studied briefly at the University of New Mexico and the Ecole de Pataphysiques in Paris. His journeys had provided him with a matrix of metaphysical questions that would be addressed through his art more intensely and more directly as time went on.

DEFINITIONS FOR THE PROTO-MATERIALIST GUIDE

***Zim-zum*: Hebrew Cabalistic term meaning the contraction of god: i.e., before the universe, god contracts, creates a little space within himself, in which the universe will take form; this space is zim-zum.**

***Paratantra*: in Avatamsaka and Vijnanavada Buddhism, the highest of the three metaphysical levels of the universe: the absolute, beyond form; etc.**

***Tachion*: a metaparticle that is slowing down from a system faster than the speed of light.**

***Arche*: Greek, means Source, Ground, or Basic Substance of universe; the One; the Infinite.**

***Empyrean*: highest point of the sun's daily transit of sky: the point where Horis becomes one with Re.**

***Dharmadhatu*: in Avatamsaka Buddhism again, the field of infinite interpenetration: the metaphysical awareness of all things as parts of one another.**

***Aperion*: Greek: the Unlimited, the Boundless; the Raw Stuff out of which all "things" arise and into which they dissolve again.**

■ **Eric Orr**

PROTO-MATERIALIST GUIDE

Shadow
Breath
Light
Cloud
Human Bone
Time
Blood
Vapor
Iron
Dirt
Gold

Zim-Zum
Paratantra
Tachion
Air
Zero Mass
Prime Matter
Arche
Silence
Fire
Timelessness
mmm

Sound
Prime Matter
Fire
Glass
Sex
Fire
Ash
Dream
Lead
Paratantra
Meteorite

Prime Matter
Zero Mass
Zim-Zum
Void
Infinity
Empyrean
Absolute
Arche
Dharmadhatu
Paratantra
Empyrean

Absolute
Mercury
Infinity
Threshold
Void
Aha
Ions
Number
Infinity
Pigment
Ash

Silence
Radiance
Prime Matter
Aperion
Simplicity
Empyrean
Absolute
Simplicity
Prime Matter
mmm
Luminosity

Bliss
mmm
Whew
Void
Void
Silence
Sublimity
Absolute
Lucidity
Absolute
Prime Matter

Life
Zero Mass
Wisdom
Infinity
Equanimity
Ecstasy
Simplicity
Purity
Telepathy
Silence
Bliss

Ecstasy
Sublimity
Joy
Radiance
Levitation
Bliss
Silence
Tranquility
Delight
Luminosity
Whew

Animated Hogshow
University of California, Los Angeles
Pasadena Art Museum, Pasadena, California, both 1966

After arriving in Los Angeles, Orr achieved his first visibility as an artist with *Animated Hogshow*, which he put together with Joe Byrd. Executed under the aegis of the New Music Workshop, *Animated Hogshow* was a huge, dark environment. Participants climbed up onto a large, open net that was suspended nine feet above the ground. Byrd (who had worked with John Cage) and Orr wired the net so that it emitted various sounds as participants moved on it. The space in which it was located took the shape of a cube, and the walls lit up intermittently. Although the work had overtones of light-show fun and games, the piece provided useful information for Orr:

> *It was interesting because it gave me an idea of how much the spectator or participant's response meant to a work of art. But I didn't want to end up making spaces that were goofy or silly—. . . (that was how people responded to them). . . . So I made a demarcation line in my mind that had to do with what I was really up to. I realized that I had to pay attention to what it was I wanted and that I couldn't be as gross as I had been in whatever I used to achieve my goals.*[2]

Dry Ice and *Sky Lights*
installations in Century City, Los Angeles
sponsored by the Los Angeles Arts Commission, 1967

Orr began to play with ideas that could be used to create an undifferentiated space, which was later to become one of the hallmarks of his work. Among these concepts was one that he discussed with Lloyd Hamrol and Judy Gerowitz (now Judy Chicago): a gigantic soft space, constructed of inflatable material and to be filled with feathers. "That was *really* a silly one," Orr recalled bemusedly. Yet even there his concerns with space and weightlessness were beginning to be examined.

Then, in 1967, Orr participated in a sculpture exhibition at Century City, an office complex adjacent to Beverly Hills. Most of the participating artists contributed large-scale permanent sculptures that were installed in various locations around the complex; Orr, in concert with Gerowitz and Hamrol, produced what can now be seen as one of his first Proto-materialist works. The piece was a gigantic maze of dry ice, which gradually dematerialized, leaving only vapors behind. A day and a half after the installation, the only visible traces left of the work were damp spots on the grass.

For the same exhibition Orr created *Sky Lights*. This work consisted solely of a slit in the ground, some nine feet deep, out of which seeped a glowing xenon light. Orr recalls: "It was a pretty low-profile work. I had envisioned that you could see it from an airplane. It was as if it came from far below the earth and was directed at an airplane."

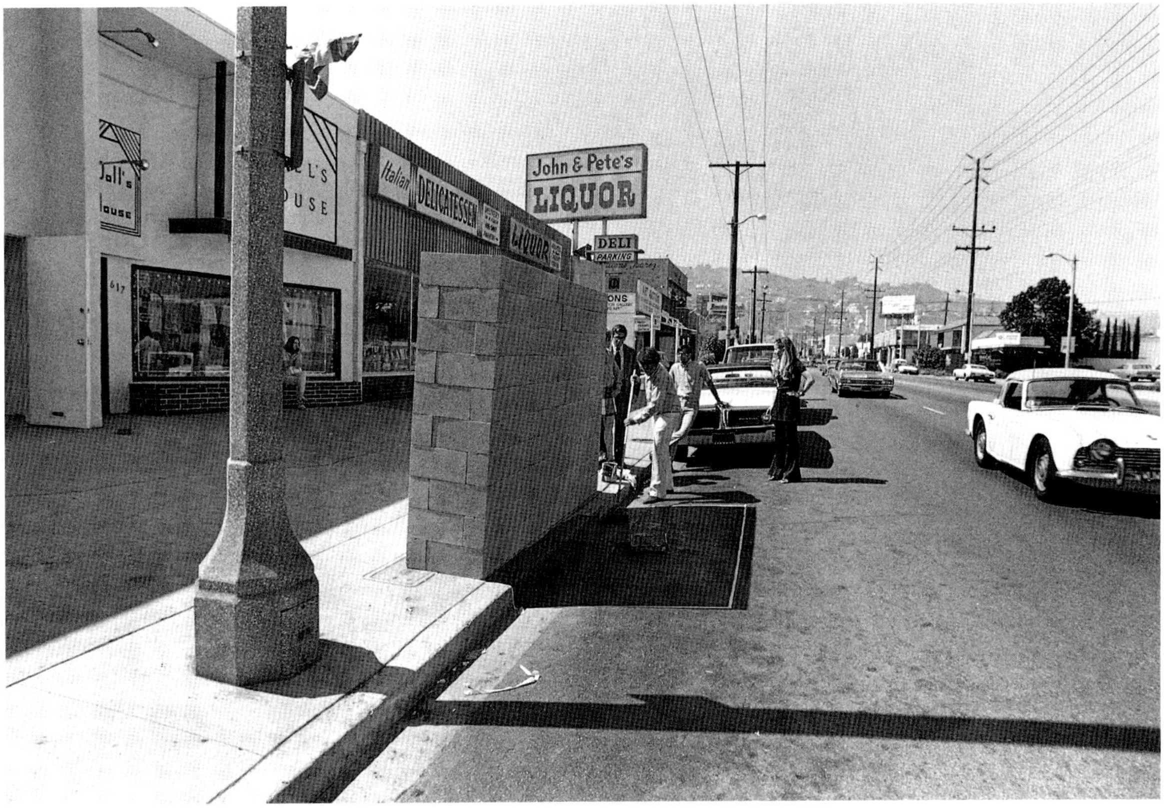

Eric Orr (b. 1939)
Wall Shadow
Cement bricks and shadow
Installation outside Eugenia Butler Gallery, Los Angeles, 1968

Wall Shadow

Eugenia Butler Gallery, Los Angeles, 1968

Outside the gallery, on the busy thoroughfare of La Cienega Boulevard, Orr created a "shadow trap." First he built a wall of ordinary cinder blocks, some seven feet tall. Then, in the afternoon, he traced the wall's shadow on the asphalt and painted it in. He subsequently removed all of the bricks, leaving only the painted shadow behind. Although sparse and a bit clumsy, this piece, along with *Dry Ice* and *Sky Lights*, marked the beginning of Orr's attempts to capture the ephemeral.

Sound Tunnel

Los Angeles Municipal Art Gallery, 1968

University of Southern California, Los Angeles, 1971

In all of Orr's early pieces the means were simple but the concepts were not. Orr was using ice, light, shadow, and air to grapple with those elements that lack the substantiality associated with material things—and with art. (A fairly recent arrival to Los Angeles, he was devastated by the smog, and one of his early works was a performance piece in Pershing Square in downtown Los Angeles, in which he gave away plastic bags filled with fresh air.) There was sound to deal with as well, and sound (or the absence of it) has always been an important element in Orr's metaphysical workshop. As he put it: "I was attracted to sound art, because it was the most vivid and least defined. A freestanding wall of sound in a silent space is realized by the mind's eye."

Orr's *Sound Tunnel* consisted of a forty-foot-long black-walled, lightproof corridor, which housed two hundred hidden speakers. It was conceived as a space where the participant could sense the presence of sound as an object. As the participant moved through the tunnel, the speakers emitted a ghostly litany: "Life—dream—shadow. Life—dream—shadow. Life—dream—shadow." A word would float by and disappear. The sound seemed omnipresent. Orr remembered: "It was also set up so that I could have sound 'shapes.'...I had this corridor, and a wave went down it, and then another one went through that one, and another went through that. It was like a matrix of sound—you could do any number of things with it."

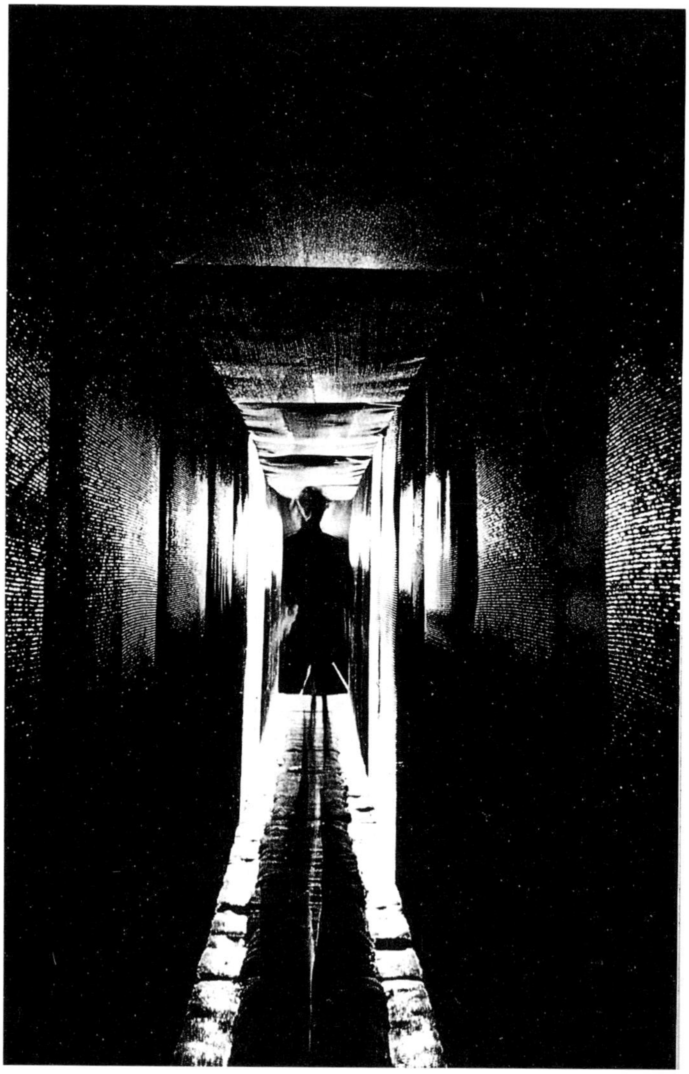

The piece was expensive and complex, and eventually he felt that the trade-off between the hardware and the effect was a poor one. "It drove me nuts, because all the technology just got out of hand. I was always dealing with these engineers with black ties and white socks. That kind of sensibility eventually got into the piece, and I was really burned by it." The piece constituted what Orr called "state-of-the-art technology," which he defined as "being right on the edge of breaking down all the time." After having solved numerous technological problems, executing the work, constantly repairing it, and then finding out that the expensive speakers were being stolen one by one, he decided it was time to retrench: "I backed off sound altogether....I just put the brakes on all of that, and began raking sand with wind....I got some real pretty white sand and a big fan, and I spent days raking that sand, which got those tiny little ripples in it. That changed my whole sensibility. From there I went into making undifferentiated spaces."[3]

***Zero Mass*, 1972–73**
Fine Art Gallery, University of California, Irvine, 1973
Cirrus Gallery, Los Angeles, 1974
Fort Worth Art Museum, 1977
Temporary Contemporary, Museum of Contemporary Art, Los Angeles, 1983

It is a quantum leap from state-of-the-art technology to raking sand with wind (which he began to do in 1969), but Orr made that leap with great finesse. His first major work dealing with undifferentiated space was *Zero Mass.* This piece, which bears a 1972–73 date, was seen in its initial stages in Orr's studio in 1971 by Hal Glicksman, who presented it as the opening show at the University of California, Irvine, gallery in 1973.

Eric Orr
Sound Tunnel
Installation, Los Angeles Municipal
Art Gallery, 1968

The beauty of *Zero Mass* lies partially in its simplicity. There is no complicated hardware, no technology. The dimensions of the final work (it was originally much smaller) are forty by twelve feet. Outside the room is a twelve-by-fifteen-foot rectangle of pure white sand, soft and wind raked. In the center of the sand is a large rock, highlighted by a tiny spotlight.

Before entering the work at Cirrus Gallery, visitors were treated to a traditional Japanese tea ceremony, served by a kimono-clad woman. After relaxing over tea, participants proceeded down a black hallway, which was curtained at both ends, and entered an oval room constructed entirely of paper. It was very dark; the sensation was one of roundness—not of shape, but of atmosphere. There was a wholeness to the work. Ambient light filtered through the seamless paper membrane, causing the room to glow faintly. There was nothing to see. Participants could not ascertain where the wall and floor met, or where the ceiling met the wall. There was no sense of surface. After a while, as the eyes adjusted, vague masses appeared and then other participants gradually began to emerge out of the darkness. Slowly they became more and more defined, and legs, arms, and bodies could be distinguished. But one never saw a face.

Orr said of this piece:

> *I stopped the light level at the face. If somebody was in the space and they walked away from you... they just disappeared into this amorphous place.*
>
> *[When you were in the piece] everything you were seeing was the same. There was no way to tell where you were. It was like another world, THE Void. It was the best example of the void that I know of.... You were in a space that you had never been in before. You could allude to the sensation of being in a cloud, or you could allude to being in a fog, but that's not it. It is The Void.*

This experience of the void seemed a pleasurable phenomenon, even a known one. Viewing a later manifestation of the work, in Forth Worth, the critic Janet Kutner said: "Moving around, one felt as if one were floating. When a person walked away, I felt as if he had disappeared off the face of the earth. The experience was extremely interesting, both sensuous and enveloping, somewhat like a return to the womb."[4]

Orr works with the conscious ambition of creating spaces that will focus the viewer's sensibility on infinity.

■ Thomas McEvilley, "Power Objects in Zero Mass: The Art of Eric Orr," ***Artforum*** **20 (June 1982).**

The work had other implications as well. After having executed *Zero Mass* again in 1983, in the Temporary Contemporary building at the Museum of Contemporary Art, Los Angeles, Orr said:

> Zero Mass *is still wonderful for me. Now I am using cloth to shape it—and that is a much better solution than using paper. In the recent version, I made a bigger space,* much *bigger because it was cloth. I wasn't constrained by the paper size. The piece was twenty feet wide by forty. The MoCA piece was* much *wider than the twelve footer that I first built. Twenty feet's a* lot *wider than twelve. I can also use carpet on the walls if I do a permanent installation, which is much more durable. Now, with the new materials, the power of the undifferentiated space is really heavy. It gets real spooky in there, even for me,* still. *It really* is *a limitless void.*

The first version of *Zero Mass* (begun in 1969) was purchased by Count Panza in 1974, a year after its first public showing, for his collection in Varese.

Orr's art, with its predilection for the esthetics of infinity, is based on the religio-philosophical tendency of space worship, found in Platonism, Hinduism, Taoism, Cabala, and elsewhere. These traditions regard materiality as primarily a limitation and aspire to a state where gravity and spatial boundaries will have been left behind. Within such a horizon, space is not regarded as dead emptiness. The *Chandogya Upanishad,* for example, says (III.8.1), "Space [Sanskrit *akasha*] is to be worshipped as the absolute source [Sanskrit *brahman*]." It is space out of which all these creatures proceed and into which they are again received."

■ ***Zero Mass: The Art of Eric Orr*** **(Lund, Sweden: Anders Tornberg Gallery, 1990), n.p.**

Orr spent much of 1971–73 traveling around the world, looking at spaces and in situ sculpture and seeking out primitive magic. Once he returned, his work increasingly embodied his concerns with ancient mysteries and primal materials. Orr's travels, then and since, have taken him for extended periods to Egypt, India, the New Hebrides, Africa, the Far East, Ceylon, and Europe. One senses in his work of the last decade a familiarity with the secrets of the great pyramids, an understanding of the Tantric use of gold, a pull toward black magic, and an affinity for the Eastern concept of the void. It is not borrowed magic that he uses, but a magic that has become his own. Nor is it yet the magic of a master, for Orr goes about his work as an initiate, respectful and aware. If his experiments are not always successful, they do not need to be, for they are not ends in themselves but way stations on a longer journey.

Thomas McEvilley's important essays on Orr have focused on the roots of what he terms the artist's "reverberantly empty spaces":

> The great point of the piece *Zero Mass* was its creation of a space beyond (or before) boundaries—like Ovidian Chaos, the Egyptian Primal Abyss, or the world-edge realm of Ultima Thule, between mist, liquid and solid. From inside, one could not identify a wall, or limit, anywhere. The boundary-form, and hence limiting, property of space had been dissolved into an indefinite light substance surrounding one with equal density on all sides. The world of forms seemed returned to Prime Matter. The experience of this transcendentally bare plane of light caused the time-space continuum, or one's attention to it, to skip a beat. A certain transmogrification analogous to those described in ancient funerary cults, mystery religions, and in enlightenment texts was briefly glimpsed.[5]

Blood Shadow
Venice, California, and Egypt, January 1971

The bridge between Orr's old work and the new was his mysterious 1971 piece called *Blood Shadow.* This work was not written about for ten years—partially, one suspects, because it was executed for private magical reasons and not for public exhibition. At the time of its creation only two people besides Orr knew the full extent of the piece—a friend and a mysterious Arab. McEvilley first recounted the tale in 1981:

> On a full-moon in January, 1971, Orr and a friend carried a sheet of tempered glass, three by nine feet, out onto the Venice, California, beach. One side of the glass was covered with the artist's blood, which had been blown with a mouth and straw, as paleolithic painters did it. They laid the glass at waveside, where the friend's moonshadow fell life-size upon it. As Orr, using handfuls of wet sand, scraped away the blood outside the silhouette, a strange human shape emerged and glimmered with ambiguous life. The materials: blood, shadow, moonlight, glass, wavesound.
>
> The *Blood Shadow* was crated and shipped to Venice, Italy, where the artist met it and accompanied it by boat to Alexandria.... Its accumulation of oceanic experiences was part of the work, of the return to the beginning.

After it arrived in Egypt:

> *Blood Shadow* rolled to the sandy plain of Giza and was uncrated and leaned, about midnight, against the Mycerinus pyramid. Calculating for moonset, Orr began to dig a pit in the sand. A

silent Arab appeared and pitched in without a word. They laid the glass face up, in a pit three by nine by one foot deep. As the moon approached the horizon, the shadow of the pyramid-apex glided slowly upon the blood-self on the glass; with the last light, the moving shadow tapped the still one's frontal lobe with the lightest of greetings or summonses. When the moon disappeared, the glass was buried.

In that piece, Orr understood for the first time some of the enduring themes of his work: the layering of performance and object art; the questioning of the solidity of the self; the talking of the void inside the object; the artist as primitive transcendentalist, scratching at the door of time, fumbling at the entrances to other worlds.[6]

The Stone Snake
Junior Arts Center, Barnsdall Park, Los Angeles, 1973

This piece, also seemingly simple in concept, linked the shamanistic rituals of other cultures with the matter-of-factness of our own—forcing viewers to confront archetypes long buried. Orr first inscribed the form of a snake on the ground, using a gasoline-soaked rope that meandered for some twenty feet. Ignited in the dark of night, the curving image looked like an apparition as the flames crackled along the length of its sinuous body. After the image had turned to ash, Orr returned to the site each day for several days and placed smoothed, rounded stones over the charcoal tracings, until the piece reached a three-foot height. Nearby, a negative image of the serpent was dug deep into the earth. (In 1991 the outlines of that snake could still be seen in the lawn at Barnsdall Park, in front of the Frank Lloyd Wright colonnade.)

Here, as in a number of later works, Orr used fire to tap into a magic as old as time. He was beginning to understand how to capture such magic without destroying it, how to let it speak for itself. This is a complex and mysterious area, and one not easily entered. Since then, seeking greater power, Orr has occasionally reverted to materials that have grounded his visions too much in this world.

Sunrise
Cirrus Gallery, Los Angeles, and various studio presentations in Venice, California, 1976

The artist's concern with sound, or rather with the absence of it, played an important role in *Sunrise*: "I am engaged in using silence as a color," he has said. Having built a nine-by-twelve-foot room, Orr sheathed its outside entirely with soft gunmetal lead, a surface that spoke of no color, no light, just of silence and darkness. The work had obvious alchemical implications. At the same time, the room became what McEvilley has termed "a cosmic ray void," in which "the absence of cosmic rays was an invisible but physically real material used in the work as color is used in a painting."[7]

The room was about silence. It was also about light. Having entered the solemn, leaded space where footsteps were muffled and no exterior noises could penetrate, one saw a gleaming bar of sunlight pulsating on the back wall; it traveled slowly up that wall until it became a column of light. To trap the sun in this fashion, Orr had placed a solar tracking device on the roof, which guided the sun's rays into the space through a careful arrangement of mirrors. As he described it:

There you have silence and light, and the space drops away. It has the sense of expanding space that you get in the desert. If you go out to the desert, and you are suddenly driving along, and you get out of the car, suddenly ZZZZZZZAAAAAP! the space does that to you. I am trying to trace the conditions under which you begin to pay attention to subtle elements, which, if they are focused on, become much more.

This work, silent, awesome, magical, had echoes that were eerie and nonrational.

The first time I built it I used electrum. Electrum is an amalgam of gold and silver—20 percent silver, 8 percent gold. It's an ancient material. The Egyptians use it on the tops of abas, pyramids, etc., and ceremonial doors. It was the metal for translating the spirit. I decided to use electrodes. The piece had so much religiosity. I couldn't understand it. People entered the room and experienced it. I thought: Oh, God, what have I wrought? So I decided to get rid of the electrode panel and all its overlays and I just put a simple white panel in there. Sunlight hits the white panel and fills the niche gradually during the course of the day.... The niche is forty-four inches high by nine inches wide. It's a nine-foot-tall wall. There's a very tall slot with light coming out of it. Sometimes the light looks like it's totally on the surface. That's one of the more subtle aspects of what it's all about. I think the best work changes in time with nature. The work I like least is work that has a rigidity, and only gives you one hit—which remains a constant.

Viewing *Sunrise,* I was reminded of the extraordinary light that penetrates the inner chamber of Egypt's temple of Abu Simbel just twice a year and of the celebration of the rebirth of the sun-god in a nearby temple, where once a year, on the winter solstice, the sun rises precisely between two upright columns. And I remembered that Orr spent time in Egypt. McEvilley, like Orr, has studied the underworld, and he also clearly understood the Egyptian aspects of this work:

> *Sunrise* was a kind of sacred monster in the space-light tradition. It was also Orr's most Egyptian-influenced space, with its references to the King's Chamber; the flight of the *ba* bird through a small channel in the tomb to the sun; the sunrise of the dead, when Osiris rises into the morning sky as Re; the obelisk as source of sunrise, and sunrise as the primal moment reconstituted each day.
>
> But above all the "lead box," as it came to be called, was a laboratory situation for certain refined avenues of exploration.... Orr's goal of producing spaces that will transform everyday experiences was mildly fulfilled here. Yet no one flew out the door as a bird. Rather, one walked out as one went in, but with a certain mental aura, as of secret ambiences and veiled promises of transcendence.[8]

Silence and the Ion Wind
Los Angeles County Museum of Art
November 12–December 14, 1980

Orr's piece took up a full floor of the museum's Hammer Wing. At the entrance was a wall label written by Orr and McEvilley, which stated, in part:

> *The work proceeds in an axis through the rooms, where sound, (color?) and light intermingle.... The axis begins with a doorway of light and continues through an aperture of lead to a gold accumulator infused with ion wind.*

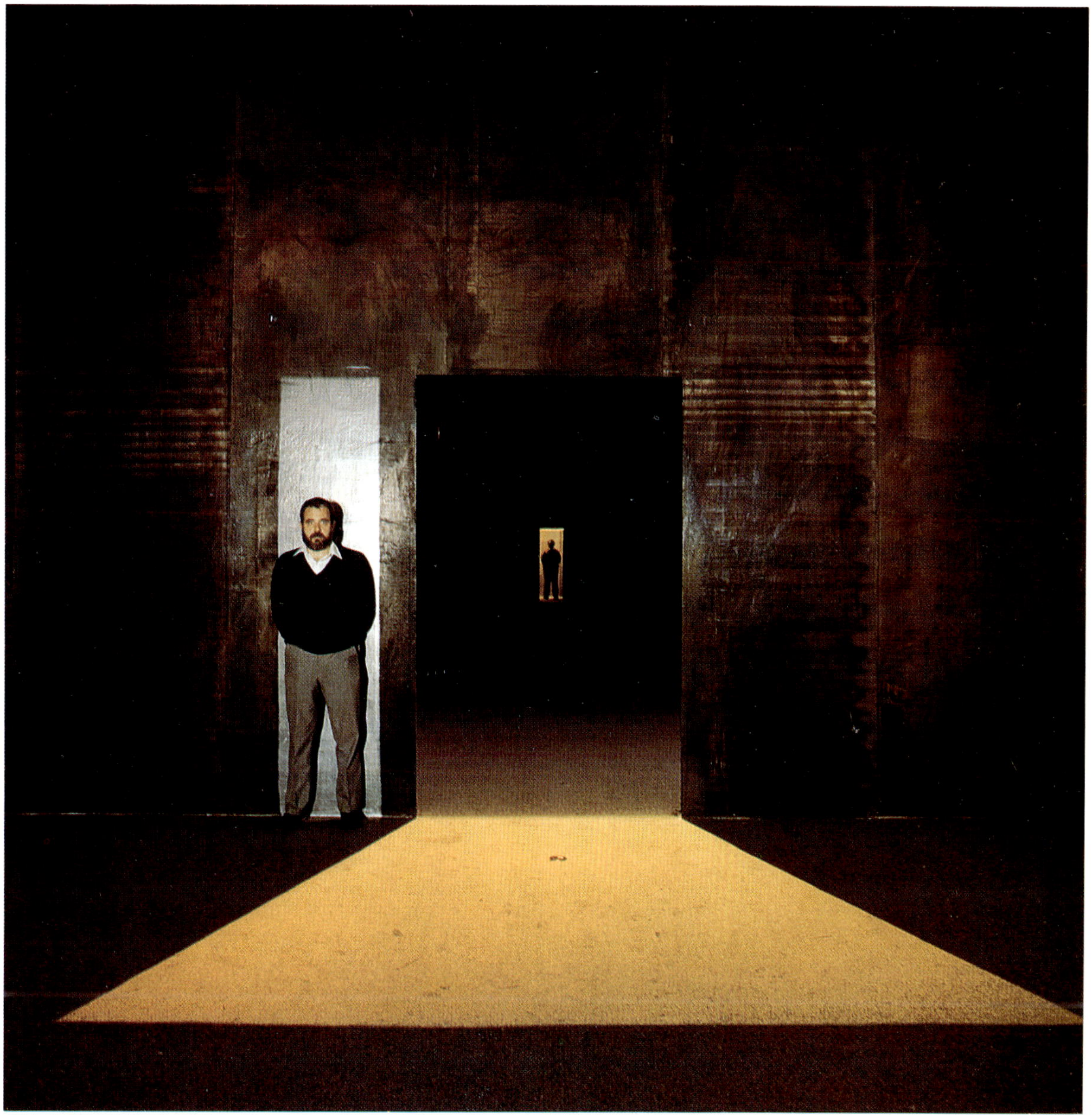

Eric Orr with his installation *Silence and the Ion Wind,* Los Angeles County Museum of Art, 1980

The first room, between the light door and the lead, is an acoustically active or reverberant zone. The leaden portal functions as an acoustical lens to a zone of increasing silence where the Golden Room is approached through an ion wind. In the dark central area, the ion wind increases, till it reaches its greatest intensity in the Golden Room.

The Golden Room is an allusive structure for an elusive experience. Here is the opener of time. As you leave it, this room ties the axis in a circle returning your gaze to the door of light.[9]

This installation was ninety-nine feet long. The first room, painted a soft gray, was totally empty. On its far wall was a shimmering white void that turned out to be an impenetrable portal, with dimensions in the proportion of the golden section. Powerful, mesmerizing, it hovered inexplicably—a plane of light. As I turned around, darkness beckoned through a knife-edged door of lead. Inside it there was a smaller room, also silent, cold, and empty. The two rooms created an atmosphere that was awe-inspiring and somewhat fearsome. It called to mind the beehive tombs at Ceveteri in Italy, where, in addition to the buried dead, built-in chairs still remain to seat the spirits, the guardians of the underworld, and the intrepid visitor.

Orr had infused the second room with negative ions, and so the air was heady, like jungle air after a rainstorm or salt air near the sea. I moved through the silence only subliminally aware of its strangeness.

I wanted to do something that was an undifferentiated space with a gold field behind a wall, where you couldn't ascertain the purpose of the space. . . . I wanted to use gold, because I know damn well that it does a job better than anything else. I have seen enough of it in situ. . . . It makes a connection. I am very interested in making things that are not hard to get hold of. I am interested in making things that are very direct—that go right into you. . . . I want to dump rationality and intellectuality and make everything impact right at the center. . . . I'm very interested in a non-intellectual approach, in the sense that I'm using elements that key in before the left brain takes over from the right—before language and before right-angle mathematics really kick in.

■ **Eric Orr**

At the end of the second room, opposite the entryway, stood another portal—also of golden-section proportions—and beyond it was a third chamber, lined with lead. Above it, a golden slit of radiant light illuminated the ceiling. As I slowly approached through the darkness, the tiny chamber underwent a process of transformation. What was at first only a hint of golden light became a powerful radiance; what appeared to be a cold lead chamber was now transformed into one of gold leaf, which appeared to be flooded with divine light. Somewhere in the silence of these rooms, a transformation took place. Bathed first in a darkness that seemed inky sweet, then in a glorious golden aura, I was drawn into a reality that was quite apart.

Leaving the golden chamber behind, I moved back into real time through the darkened, ion-suffused chamber, conscious that the golden glow from the third space had faded and that that small gold chamber had returned once again to gray. Before me at that moment was the lead doorway that divided the two main chambers, still razor sharp at the entry edge. At that juncture between the known (the first room) and the unknown (the second, ion-filled space), a trapezoidal spill of light extended into the first room, now silvery gray with light. The shining void of the third chamber, once so seductive and beckoning, now looked flat and closed. There was no escape through there. The only visible exit could be found at the far wall, which led to the outside world.

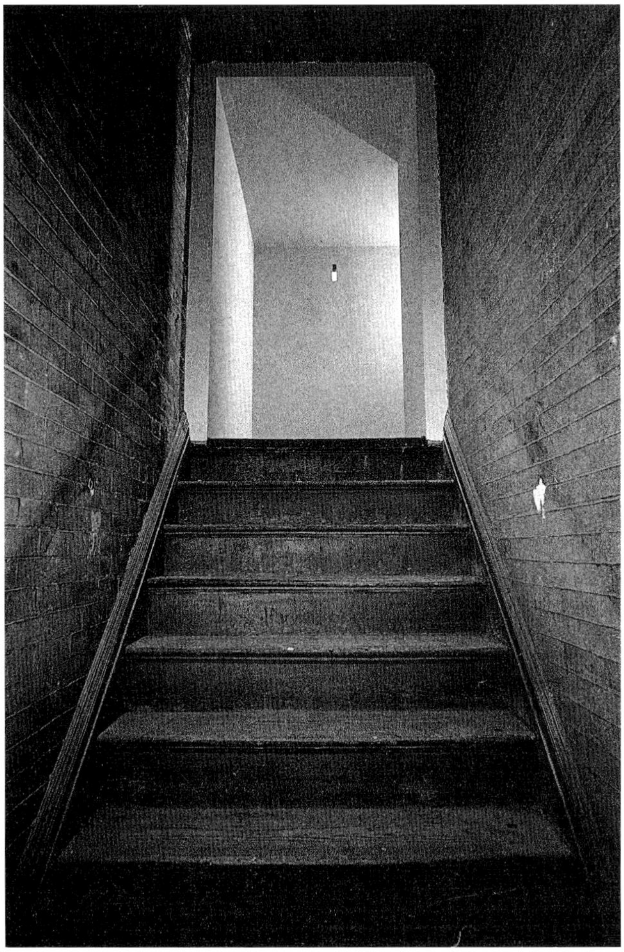

Nothing Special
in *West/East: First-Generation Environmental Sculpture*
P.S. 1, Institute for Art and Urban Resources, Long Island City, New York
exhibition proposed for 1981 but never realized

The entrance to Orr's work was an unmarked, padlocked door, devoid of paint except for multicolored fragments that clung to its pocked surface from previous coats of beige, old rose, and hospital green. When the door was unlocked, a dense black stairwell was revealed, ascending to some undisclosed location. At the top of the first landing, through a narrow vertical slit, a shaft of white light poured in from the outside. As I climbed the stairs toward that tall, thin window, the Empire State Building came into view, framed in the slit as if in miniature. Turning at right angles, I climbed the final set of stairs, which disappeared into the total blackness above. The blackness was alarming, almost brutal, and the ascent was not pleasant. Footing seemed unsure. Fear of the unknown weighed heavily.

At the top of the stairs was a door, which could be felt but not seen. (Maurice Merleau-Ponty once raised the question of whether we see with the eyes only; here I decidedly did not.) Blind, I sensed a configuration that telegraphed "door" to my senses, and hesitantly I opened it. I sensed rather than saw that I was in a room, but the size and the shape of that room were not yet known, nor could I ascertain its function.

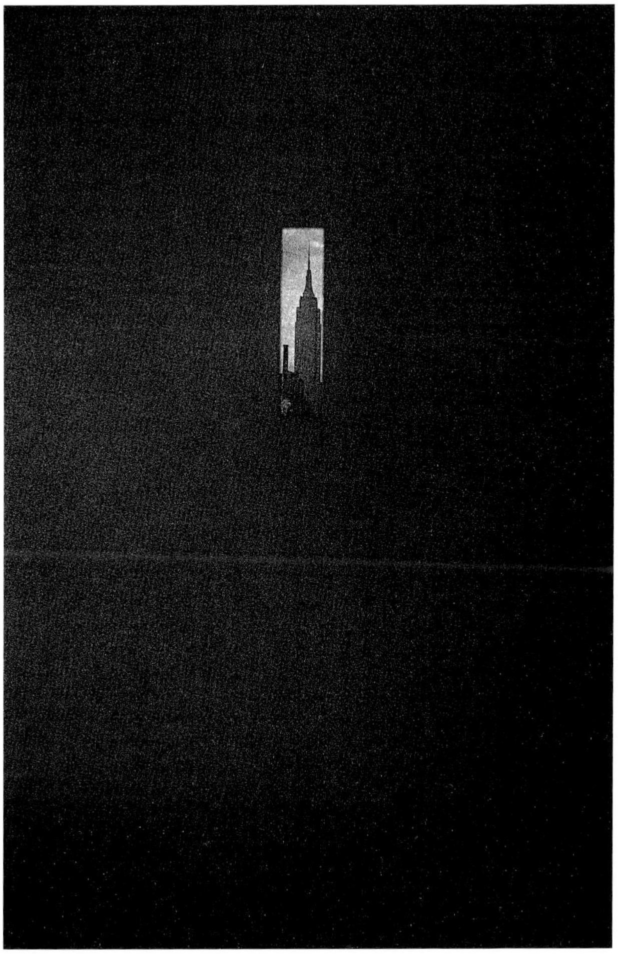

Opposite and right
Eric Orr
Nothing Special
Installation, P.S. 1,
Institute for Art and Urban Resources, Long Island City, New York, 1981

Gradually, almost imperceptibly, the room began to lighten, and so did my fear. The room became charcoal rather than black, then dove gray. The coved corners slowly began to appear. The room shaped up, solidified. Suddenly it was no longer dark, and in a kind of overhead well I could see a muted square of light with a second ceiling below it, which, like a camera shutter, admitted only a select amount of illumination. No sounds broke the seamless fabric of space. Soft scrim fabric stretching over the walls muffled all outside noise, and the thick, shadowed carpet silenced footfalls. The sensation was now altogether pleasurable, meditative, soothing.

Orr said about this work:

> *The sense of space is different now: it is no longer architectural space—it is a case of it being nonfunctional space—the only function being the perceptions that you are dealing with. If my sense of space is a real thing, that has as much solidity as the walls, and changes the way I am, just by my being in it.... different rooms have different resonances. How can I make up a resonance that is going to be close to what I want? In my head, I want a space without definition.... then I go about trying to eliminate all of the possibilities that have definition until I find something that has no definition at all—that is what I want.... just pure space.*

Silence and the Ion Wind marked a major turning point in Orr's work, which led the way to *Nothing Special.* Solid, simple, complete, these two works had a magic available to those who would seek it. With them, Orr came into his maturity as an artist.

Fire as Prime Matter
Dixon Art Gallery, Claremont Graduate School, Pomona, California, 1980

Prime Matter
in *The Museum as Site: Sixteen Projects*
Los Angeles County Museum of Art
July 21–October 4, 1981

Climbing the steps to the Los Angeles County Museum of Art one night, I felt Orr's piece before I saw it. There was a sound like the roar of the ocean and a cloying dampness in the air, like summer humidity. Turning the corner, I was suddenly enveloped in billowing clouds from which—high up—leapt darting, crackling tongues of flame. The clouds, too, rolled upward, releasing their vapor into the atmosphere. It was as if the earth had burst open. The alchemical implications were clear, and the combination of the age-old opposites of fire and water gave the piece a strong presence.

The twenty-foot column that emitted gas for the fire and water for the steam stood in a shallow reflecting pond, which elevated its base to eye level and placed its top somewhere in the clouds—thus increasing the mystery of the piece. But Orr's work was, regrettably, flawed. Both the column and the pond were poorly crafted—warped and badly welded at the seams. Because of the initial impact of the piece, it was hard to forgive Orr for too quickly exposing "the man behind the curtain" and thus diminishing the effect of his wizardry.

A year earlier, at the Dixon Art Gallery, Orr had performed what he called one of the shortest pieces on record, witnessed by only a few invited artists, students, and faculty. In a cleared field, in the dark of night, a gigantic column of flame burst out of the earth, swelled, roared, raced skyward to a height of about twelve feet, and was gone. The entire piece took only a few seconds, but the primal image was resonant and unforgettable.

This work, which required only a single buried gas jet, was infinitely more successful than the one at the Los Angeles County Museum of Art. Orr is the first to scoff at state-of-the-art technology, and the poet-alchemist in him sometimes has trouble using a twentieth-century vocabulary. He constantly works to achieve what he terms "a good trade-off between the materials and the ultimate impact of the work."

Blood Shadow, Blue Void, Time Shadow, Chemical Light
Neil G. Ovsey Gallery, Los Angeles
June–July 1981

In June 1981 Orr presented, for the first time, public documentation of his mysterious *Blood Shadow.* His narrative about the ritual journey of that piece was a missing link that connected many aspects of his curious oeuvre.

Blue Void, in the same exhibition, was a powerful, serene work that spoke of eternity. It was an eight-foot granite panel, installed in a wall; close to the top of the panel, a knife-edged open window framed the sky. Sometimes the square was blue and solid; at other times the sky

For a long time I thought sculpture was moronic. In part I still share that. I think about molten metal that you see in a foundry and what's made out of that, and 99.9 percent of the time the molten metal is going to be a lot more interesting than what's going to come out.

■ Eric Orr

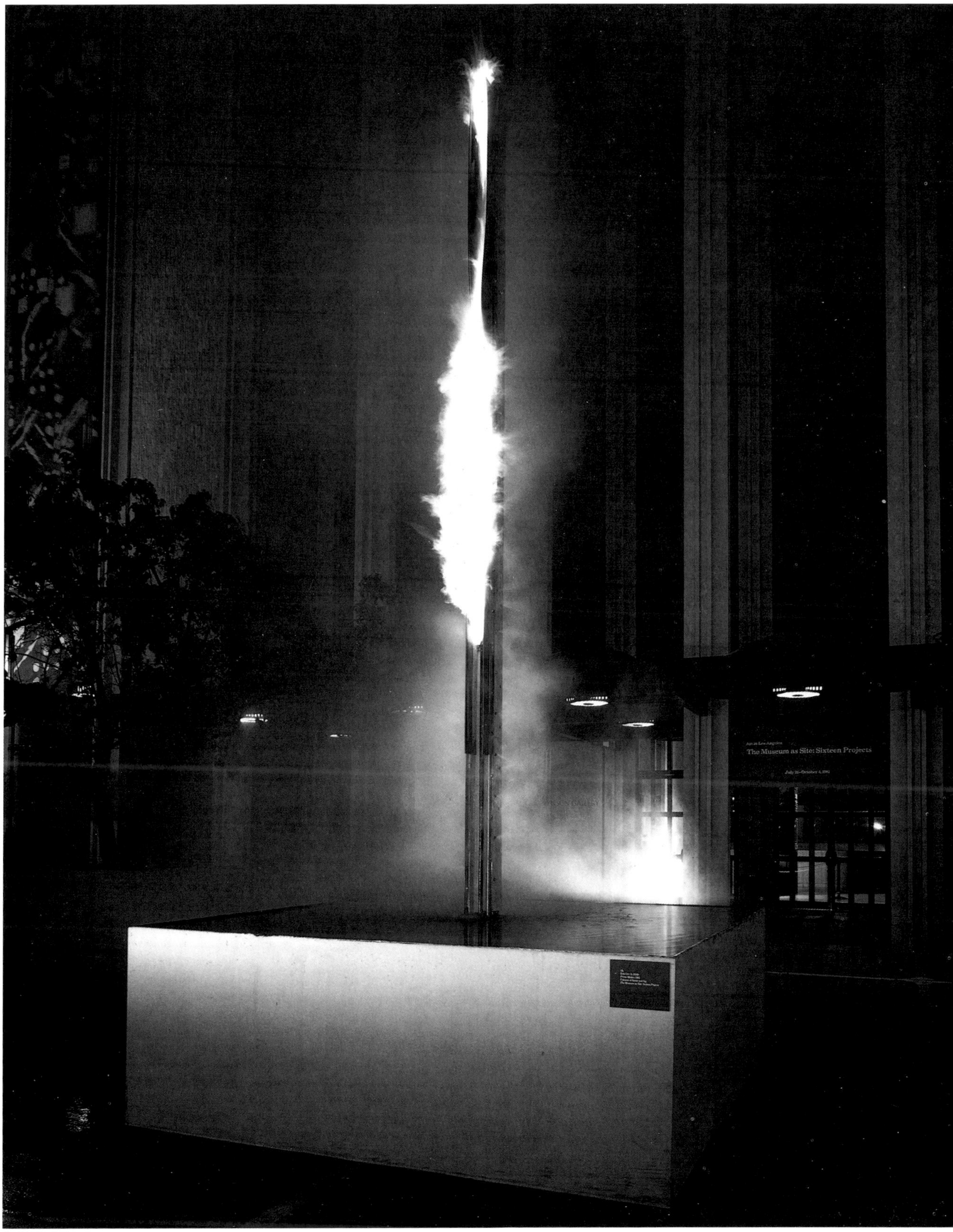

Eric Orr
Prime Matter
Metal column with flame and fog,
height: 20 ft. (6.1 m.)
Installation, Los Angeles County
Museum of Art, 1981

When an artist goes to a store that sells art supplies for his materials, it's a whole lot different from taking a hammer and crushing a skull. The act is incredibly different, the moment is incredibly different. That moment reverberates into the work in a way that acrylic painting never did. You can paint all you want with acrylic and still not tap the essential power. If one is alluding to our temporary position on the planet earth, then one of the best ways to do it is to use materials that directly relate to that. Given the power within the material itself, the mind will give you the rest. I'm using ju-ju on the practitioner, the maker, *me.* It *does* affect you a little bit. I spook myself sometimes. I spook myself a *lot.*

***All* my paintings have my blood in them, by the way. The reason I use my own blood is because when you look at the work, not only is it a representation of my *imagery,* it is also *me.* It is a very primitive system that comes out of shamanic practices, which is where art ultimately begins. I've traced it all the way back to there, and it also can be taken as a possible DNA, which means an advanced culture could take that out and replicate me from my painting.**

■ **Eric Orr**

At one time the artist was more than just the maker of objects. He took care of many other aspects in man as well—and I am very interested in that. He dealt with the use of materials at the level of superstition, where the material had its own innate power. It is the combination of these kinds of materials that will produce that power.[12]

Orr's shift from Light and Space (in his case—darkness and space) to more traditional painting and sculpture has happened gradually, but with the same intensity evidenced in his Light and Space work. He began to paint for the first time in the early 1980s, creating paintings in brilliant blood red or phosphorescent blue. The edges of those paintings have soft halations, like auras. Squares or rectangles visually float within them, reminders of the portals of his earlier work.

I'm the new kid on the block when it comes to painting. In order to definitely use the few moments I have on this earth, I just go right to the edge and say, "Man, this is it." Sometimes you scare the shit out of yourself and just go right into the work. I do that with a lot of paintings. I hate to use this word [whispering] "Ganzfelds." But that is what I'm doing. I do surfaceless paintings which are like sky, and then I combine them with some of the painted elements, so there is a little crossover stuff going on. I try to mix the light so it feels as if you're looking at a sky and there's another light going into that—so there's a blending of light. There's a light that looks like a flat surface. If I can get them thin, then I can take some of the sensibilities that I have developed in the arena of Light and Space and move them into painting. I'd like to try to drop yet another thing into painting. There are no surfaceless paintings, you know.... There are no paintings you can look at and see God.[13]

Orr's lead-lined rooms with golden apertures and knife-cut walls exposing planes of gold led the way to the new work. Somber lead objects began to hang next to curious paintings made with gold leaf and often framed at the edges with a line of blood red.

As Jeff Kelley noted:

It helps to believe that the paintings are not about art, but a ritual approach to the void, and that Orr can use lead, gold, hair, and blood to poke infinity in the eye. But infinity is something we can only approach from the edge. The best we can do is aim sensitive plates at where it seems to be, and see what develops. Perhaps these are Orr's sensitive plates; with them he presses hard against the void. So hard he bleeds.[14]

McEvilley put Orr's new work in context:

Artists all around are returning to painting on canvas in styles recognizably derived from elements of classical Modernism. Most of this activity is called "quoting"—a playing of semiotic games with the time sense by appropriating a classical style or motif into contemporary moment.... Orr's new work is not semiotic playing. It is not a matter of quoting so much as of personal arrival. He did not leap onto the post-Modern opportunity, but was dragged into it by a process of personal development which synchronized with the arc of recent art history.... Orr has arrived, by way of Dada, Egypt, and the Tao, at an expression of classical Modernism without ironic distancing or semiotic indirection.[15]

In the early 1980s Orr also began to make sculpture, which is often composed of golden columns in which fire and water mix. In them tongues of flame dash and flicker at the bottom of the columns, then roar upward against rippled currents of water that cascade down the surface. There are many versions of these works, some of which are "water doors" of transparent mesh, which become invisible as water slowly seeps down them. Orr has mastered his materials now, and the results are spectacular.

Light Space
Haags Gemeentemuseum, The Hague, the Netherlands
installed 1985

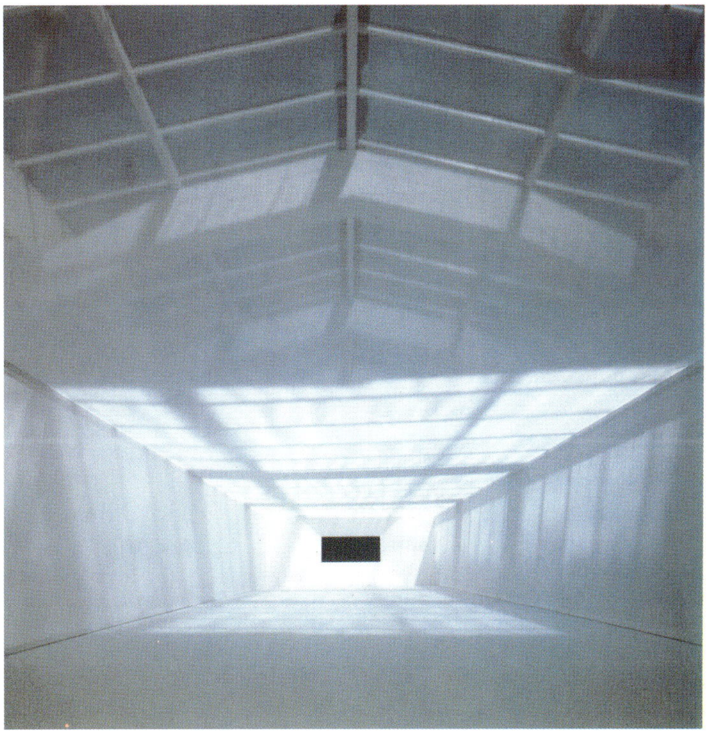

Meanwhile, Orr's consuming involvement with environments has continued. One of his most extraordinary is his fifty-foot-long *Light Space,* made for the Gemeentemuseum. It occupies a space twenty feet wide by about nine feet tall, underneath a skylight. The whole area is lined with scrim. The cloth appears transparent when one looks up, but as one looks down one wall toward the opposite end, it seems to become a skin, an opaque surface. Two knife-edged windows, which appear black, are cut into the short end walls. The result is a tunnel of subdued sunlight. As the day goes on, the space is illuminated in as many different ways as the day outside. Because the room amplifies light, the room seems to breathe, getting larger and smaller before your eyes. When people walk into it, they look oddly flattened. *Light Space* is an ethereal yet powerful work.

Orr explained the structure of the piece:

You cannot walk into the space; rather it is viewed from either end. From the point of view of the camera, the aperture you're looking through in the photograph is four times the size of the one in the back. With this piece, the entrance to the small opening is four galleries back, so gradually you lose track of the work. Then you walk through two doors and onto a little platform. People look at you looking at the space, and since the razor-edge opening flattens the space, the people looking at the space out of the larger opening look like a painting. It's very odd. The work was commissioned for the fiftieth anniversary of the museum, which is dedicated to light. I dedicated it to all the people who work in Light and Space.

Eric Orr
Light Space
Room size: 50 x 20 x 9 ft.
(2.74 x 15.2 x 6.1 m.)
Installation, Haags Gemeentemuseum, The Hague, the Netherlands, 1985

Heat Work, 1987
James Corcoran Gallery, Los Angeles, fall 1987

Orr's installation for the Corcoran Gallery was pure sensation. Orr said of it:

> *I'm doing a work at Jim Corcoran's gallery in the fall. It's akin to the effect that you see if you drive down the highway on a hot day and you look out and see the heat waves rising off the surface. In this piece you have a work which is a freestanding heat wave. The sculpture will be created of heat. It will be real, tangible. I'm not talking about going out to the highway and pointing at a phenomenon—I'm talking about a little black box that sits on the floor and produces heat and waves which roll out. It's an informal thing. Look at the exhaust of a diesel. You see those little heat waves come off. It blends with space. It's a lens for space.*

Vena-Mondt residence, Los Angeles, installed 1986

Perhaps the best embodiment of Orr's concerns on permanent view is the Vena-Mondt studio-residence he created in collaboration with the architect Fred Fisher. Located on the edge of Los Angeles's booming Japan Town, it is also, fittingly, within a virtual stone's throw of the Temporary Contemporary building of the Museum of Contemporary Art.

Artists seldom have sufficient time and space to create installations outside of their own studios. The short preparation time available at most museums and galleries scarcely affords time to build a work, let alone fine tune it, and once a show is over, the piece is removed. The Vena-Mondt commission offered a rare opportunity to create a permanent room environment.

Upon entering the loft, the first experience is of a soft, round, sound-deadened room of inky blackness and a ceiling lit by a strip of golden light. All at once one's voice seems too loud, and movements too rushed. The heart pounds as a result of the climb up the stairs to the space. Then the body slows down and the other senses take over. As blood pulses behind the eyeballs, the room throbs with a dark red—a color not seen, but felt. The room is lined with black scrim overlaid with white, turning the room a shadowy blue-gray, like the translucent color of ice in a crevasse. The golden strip on the ceiling is a solar slit, which allows a controlled amount of sunlight to flow gently into the chamber. Depending on the amount of available light, the room is a study in grisaille, the many aspects blending one into another as light fills the room—or is withdrawn from it. A highly effective version of *Sunrise,* the leaden room originally built in Orr's studio, this anechoic chamber is the entry to the Vena-Mondt studio-residence, which is located on the second floor of the loft building.

The loft is huge, supported by giant concrete columns with postmodern capitals and rough, sandblasted surfaces. The space has great solemnity and presence. In it the blend of art and architecture is so smooth that at first they seem inseparable. Gradually Orr's hand and eye can be seen, as in the series of five knife-edged sky windows cut into the ceiling, which cast brilliant squares of light on the polished hardwood floors.

The multipaned windows along the length of the loft are at once works of art, channels of light, and screens. Having been sandblasted to obscure a blighted urban view, the first set of four windows functions primarily as a work of Light and Space, with opacity drifting across their surfaces like low-lying clouds. The sky, constantly changing from sunrise to sunset, becomes a richly colored panorama. A second set of windows alongside them has been etched to create the effect of a shoji screen—appropriate to this neighborhood. Yet there is a visual twist. Key panes in the window have been left untreated, framing exquisite glimpses of the city, such as the garden of the Buddhist temple directly across the way.

In the living end of the loft is a floor-to-ceiling fireplace; across its golden surface run thousands of tiny numbers that make up the prime number of the owner. A knife-edged aperture surrounding the fireplace frames the fire, as if in a ritual temple ceremony. Elsewhere in the space, another knife-edged aperture is cut in a long horizontal line through an end wall. It visually pulls in two lines of red brick from the building across the way, causing a trompe-l'oeil effect, as the bricks seem to hover on the inside wall of the loft. In that same part of the loft is installed a version of *Raemar,* a wall work by James Turrell. Both works are first-rate examples of Light and Space art in situ.

At the kitchen end, two long, thin windows line up perfectly with the buildings across the way, providing a visual vignette. A handsome old building on the right trails green plants growing from its balcony. On the left, a redbrick building spills its color across the loft's floors. This is an almost breathtaking example of a work of Light and Space achieved, as Orr put it, "through the courtesy of Mother Nature and a great economy of means."

L.A. Prime Matter
Mitsui Fudosan Building, Figueroa Street and Wilshire Boulevard, Los Angeles
installed October 1991

Landmark Lumière
Landmark Square, Ocean Boulevard and Pine Avenue, Long Beach, California
installed October 1991

The year 1991 was a stellar one for Orr, who had two magnificent large-scale sculptures installed that year. *L.A. Prime Matter* is breathtaking: located on the plaza of the Mitsui Fudosan Building, this thirty-five-foot construction of water and fire sends a column of flame shooting upward every half an hour. A highly sophisticated response to a corporate commission, it is a superb refinement of Orr's *Prime Matter* made for the Los Angeles County Museum of Art in 1981. The success of the new work, which received a 1991 L.A. City Beautiful award, should please Orr, who has traveled a long way in his attempts to resolve and refine the technical aspects of his work.

Landmark Lumière was commissioned for the new Landmark Square Office Building in Long Beach. Here Orr has lit the entire building: white lights are installed all the way around the base of the work, and blue lights illuminate the serrated glass sides of the building. The pièce de résistance is created from four xenon lasers that are set on the roof of the building, creating a tall, slender pyramid of light. Orr received permission from the Federal Aviation Administration to make the pyramid, which will serve as a beacon for pilots.

These most recent commissions mark a major advance in the maturation of this Light and Space artist, who at last is clearly comfortable with both his scale and his materials.

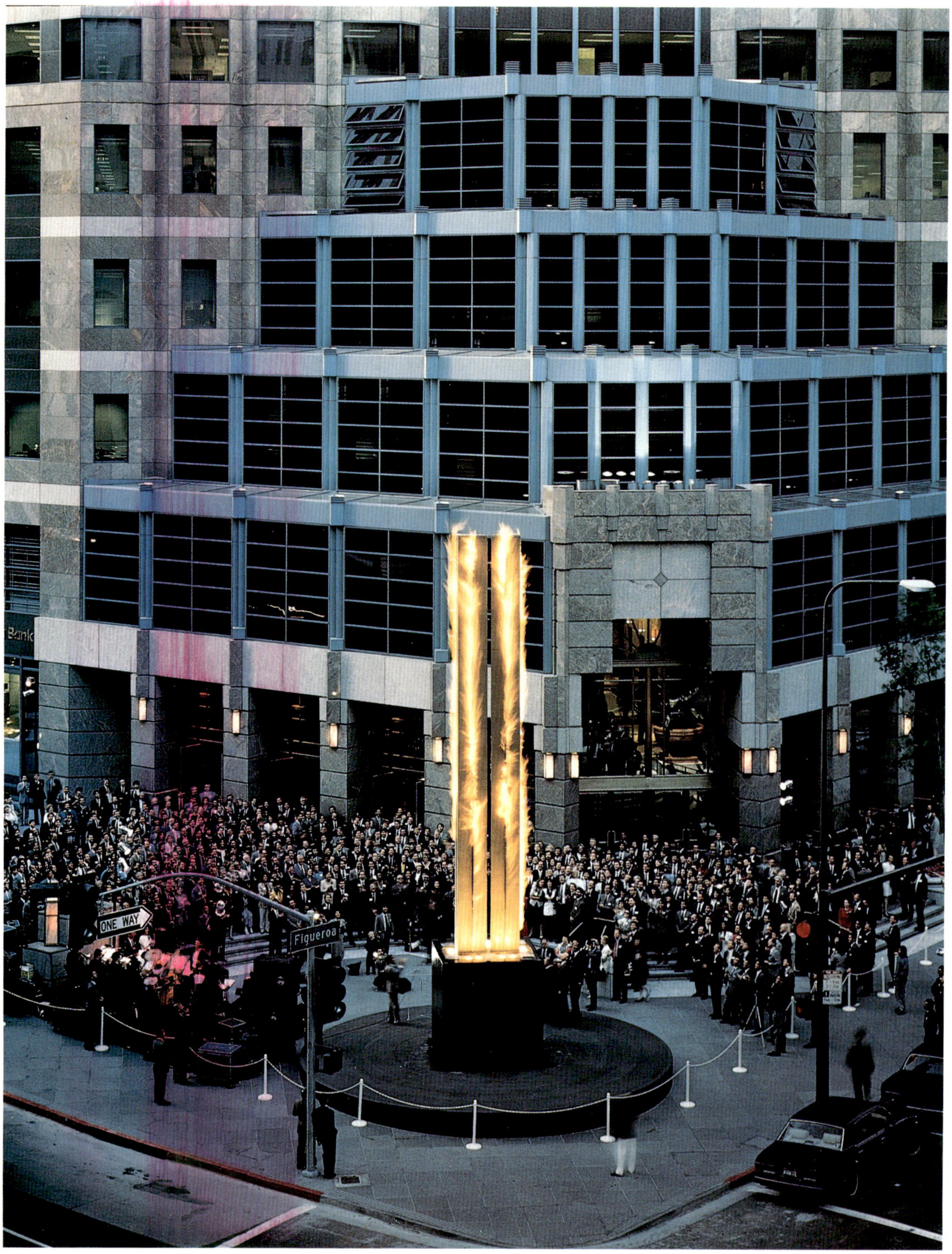

Eric Orr
L.A. Prime Matter, 1991
Brass column with fire and water,
height: 35 ft. (10.7 m.)
Permanent installation,
Mitsui Fudosan Building,
Los Angeles

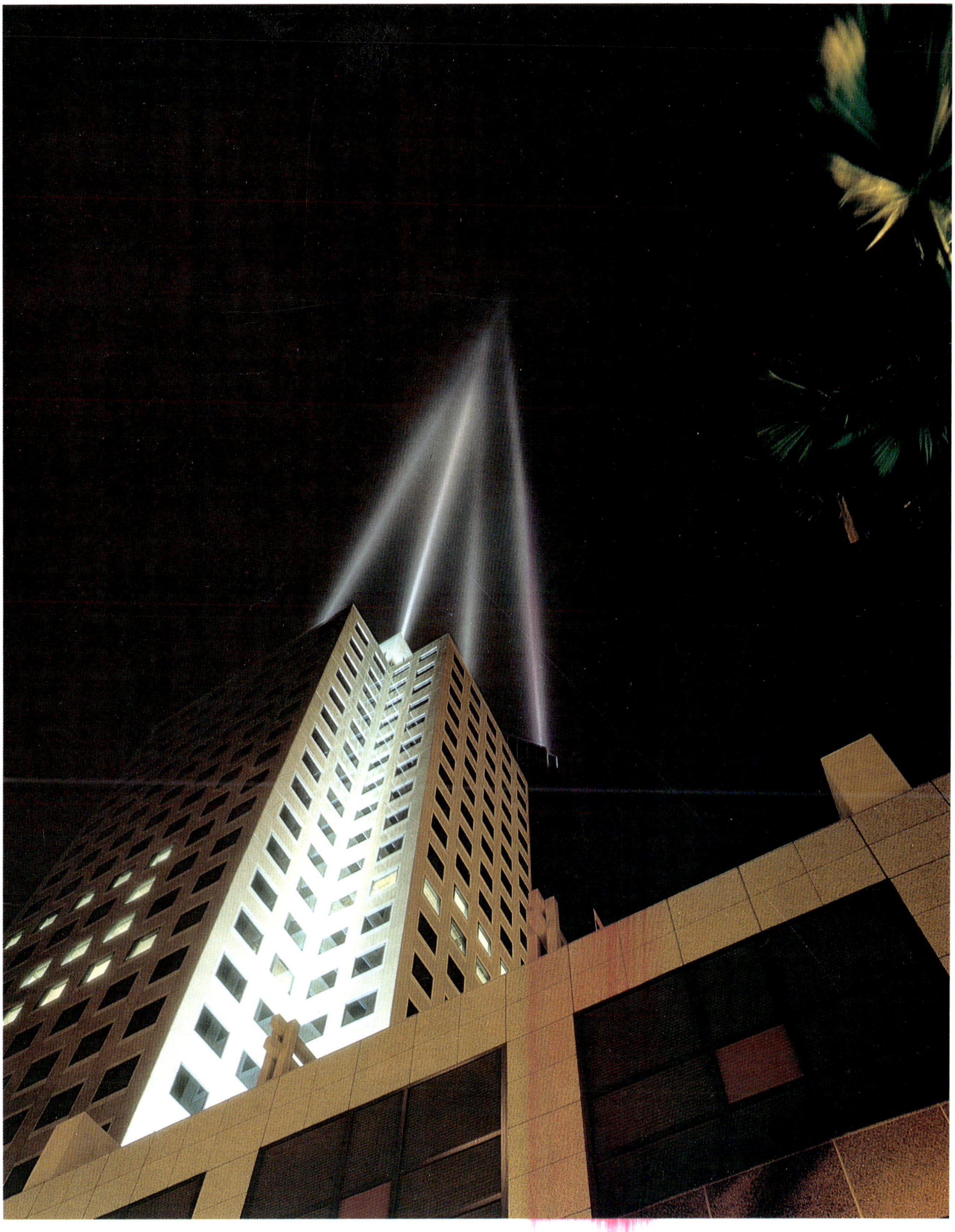

Eric Orr
Landmark Lumière, 1991
4 xenon lasers
Permanent installation,
Landmark Square, Long Beach,
California

There have been many changes in Orr's art during the last five years. "The future of art depends on artists' not copying art, but finding it," he has said. Long a seeker, Orr has at last begun to find. A list of those things he is on the trail of appeared in my mailbox one day, with no explanation. It is reprinted here, just as it arrived:

Futures

To make a room/space that is a silent, gold, luminous atmosphere that has no definition.

Déjà Vu

A simple comfortable room. Art viewer arrives and is asked to sit down and relax. Then by use of guided imagery (soft-core hypnosis), live or recorded, the viewer is taken to the mental space of déjà vu. *Upon leaving, the viewer has the feeling that he has been there before.*

Quaking Trees

Sometimes the space between two buildings is a man-made wind lens. The lens causes the wind to channel between the two buildings and flow in a certain direction. A line of trees are planted along the axis of the wind so that the wind's flow is indicated in the leaves quaking from the tree to tree.

Sky and Fire Space

A room 18' x 29' x 10' high is constructed on dirt with two doors on the long axis. The walls made of screen emerge from the earth. The sky is the ceiling. The screen walls allow for a uniform surface of fire. The image is a room with the walls made of fire open to the sky.

Walls of Fire and Ice

Wall to be constructed using heat-exchange principle. One side of wall is a sheet of fire, other side is wall of ice. Between fire and ice is space for heat exchange. The wall is 9' high and 6" wide and 14'8" long.

Larry Bell

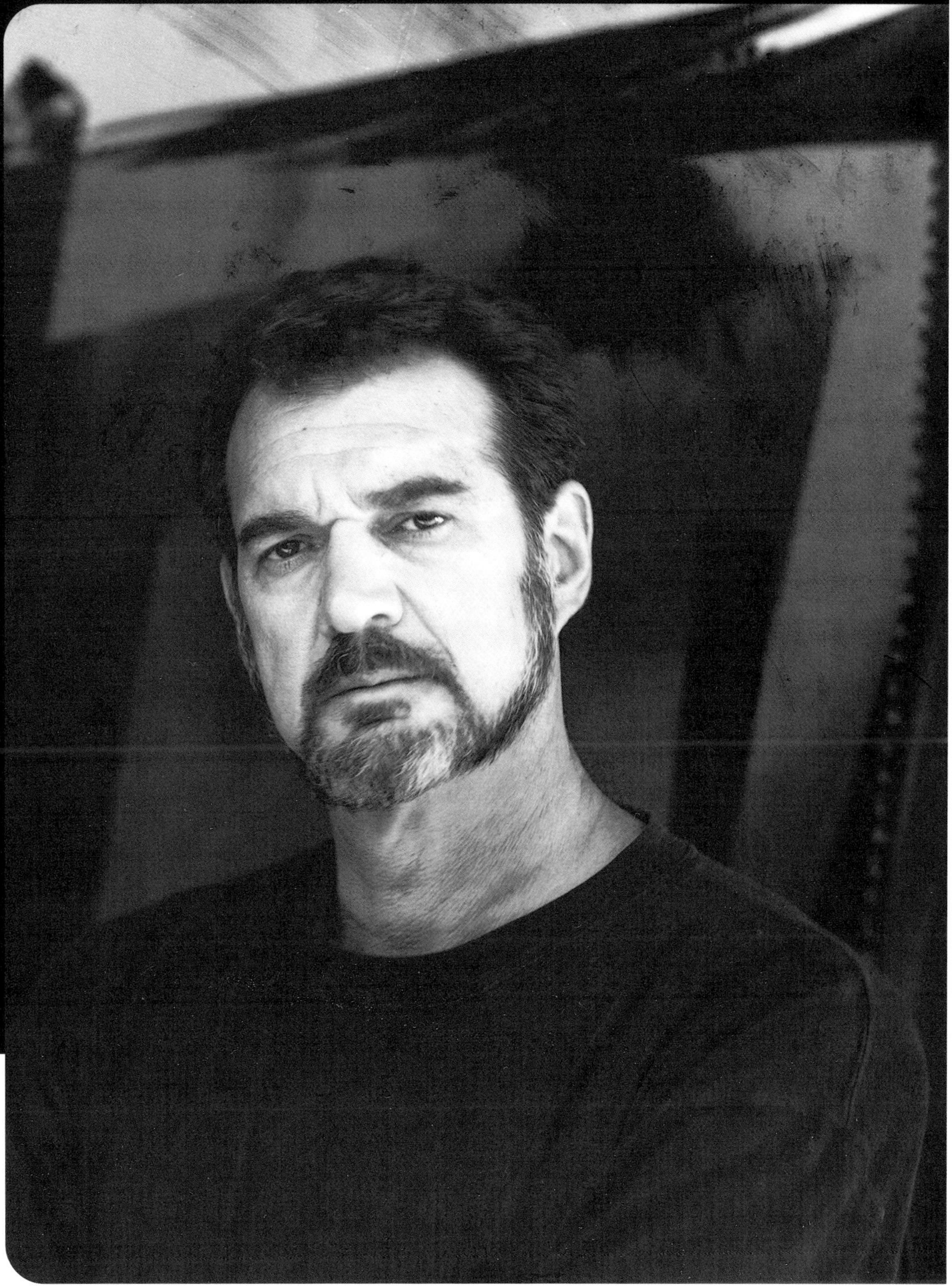

The object in madame's drawing room is a black mirror. It is seven inches tall and six inches wide. It is framed within a worn black leather case that is shaped like a book.... But there is nothing there to be read or seen—except the mystery of one's own image projected by the black mirror's surface before it recedes into its endless depths, its corridors of darkness.

"It belonged," she is explaining, "to Gauguin.... that was his black mirror. They were quite a common artifact among the artists of the last century. Van Gogh used one. As did Renoir."

"I don't quite understand. What did they use them for?"

"To refresh their vision. Renew their reaction to color, the tonal variations. After a spell of work, their eyes fatigued, they rested themselves by gazing into these dark mirrors."

...soothing, and also disquieting. The blackness, the longer one gazes into it, ceases to be black, but becomes a queer silver-blue, the threshold to secret visions; like Alice, I feel on the edge of a voyage through the looking glass, one I'm hesitant to take.

Truman Capote, "Music for Chameleons"

Larry Bell

Like a number of the other Light and Space artists, Larry Bell began as a painter, making works in the late 1950s that were, as he put it, "a sort of Abstract Expressionism." He moved quickly to a hard-edged style, working with flat diagrams of cubed spaces—just one shape executed in a clear color and placed against a large expanse of raw, shaped canvas. In these works Bell was playing a sophisticated two-dimensional/three-dimensional game, which was the first of the many ways he has given form over the years to his consuming passion for the square and the rectangle.

The writer Douglas Kent Hall has related a particularly poignant story about Bell's development as an artist:

> Bell tells of his early days at Chouinard Art Institute in Los Angeles, where he began with the compulsion of a fanatic to produce hundreds of geometric drawings a week—under the aegis of a life-drawing class taught by Herb Jepson. First ignored for this activity, then singled out as a result of it, Bell felt that his dedication to his "calling" had been recognized for the master stroke it was: "I didn't see anything except my own trip," Bell relates. Spurred on by what he terms Jepson's "metaphysical state of mind," Bell took off from what he understood that commitment of art to be—and sailed off on his own with it: "In my great joy and innocence I proceeded to explain to Jepson how it was that several weeks before I had finally understood what it was that

he was talking about, that drawing didn't have all that much to do with the nude figure but with the spontaneous personal relationship to the paper and whatever vehicles were necessary to get those energies out onto that paper.

"Jepson just stood there. He stood right in front of me, expressionless, looking me in the eye and he said, 'You know, there's this fellow you should talk to. You're one of the few people who have this vision.... You should see him.' It was my personal time. There was something I had discovered and it was special to me. I mean I had found magic in my art, and I was kind of guarding it. I was feeling great, better than I had felt in my life, and the work I was doing seemed extraordinarily good."

High on this new-found vision, Bell shortly thereafter completed a big new painting which he felt very good about. Elated and feeling it to be part of the whole process, he reported the Jepson story to his roommate, mentioning that he had been seeing this special "aesthetic advisor" to whom Jepson had sent him. "Aesthetic advisor, shit," his roommate stated. "You fucking idiot, he's a shrink. The school hired him to come and weed out the weirdos!"

At that point everything simply collapsed. Bell felt duped, unmasked. He went to the school, cleaned out all of his materials, and never returned. When asked if that was the end of his education, Bell replied, "No—that was the beginning."[1]

Bell's prescient shaped paintings, such as *My Montauk* (1960) and *Little Blank Riding Hood* (1962), came early in his career.[2] His first important group show was the *War Babies* exhibition, held at the Huysman Gallery in Los Angeles in 1961. His first one-man shows at the Ferus Gallery, Los Angeles, in 1962 and 1963, caught the attention of the national press.

Having already shaped his canvas, in 1961 Bell began painting simple geometric forms in one color on the shaped canvas, so that the cube shape of the canvas intensified the sense of volume in the painted form. His next major step came in 1962–63, when in works such as *Conrad Hawk,* he cut a square out of the center of the canvas and replaced it with glass. He then began adding mirrored surfaces to the paintings because he was intrigued with the illusion they added: "The shapes were simple and hard, so I thought I could get them even harder if I made them in glass [or mirror]. Then I realized that since I was making these "paintings" illustrations of volumes, I should probably just make the volumes, because it was the simplest way to do it, and the glass had the surface that I liked."[3] (The use of glass as a sculptural medium provided an apt answer to many of the sculptural questions that began to be asked in the 1960s, yet only a handful of artists have utilized it exclusively; its weight, fragility, and cost have precluded widespread experimentation.)

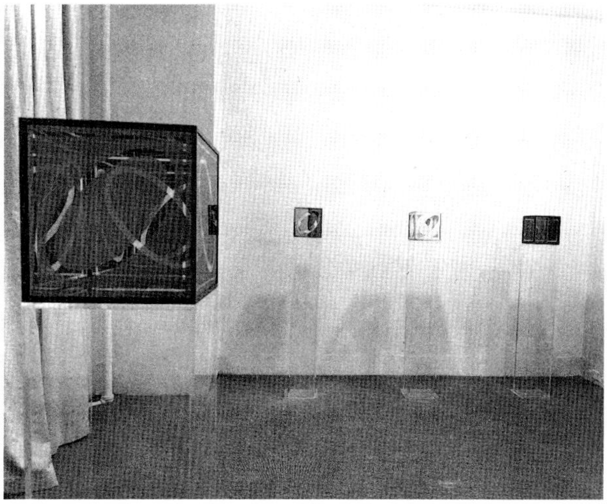

Larry Bell (b. 1939)
Exhibition, Pace Gallery,
New York, 1965

So, in 1962 Bell began his involvement with cubes, which has lasted up to the present. The cubes began as six-sided glass boxes banded in chrome, which bore on their surfaces multilayered etched and mirrored ovoids, bars, or checkerboards. These early cubes were small, intimate, often measuring no more than twelve by twelve inches or fourteen by fourteen inches. Exquisite, impeccable, fascinating as they were, they were still more like decorative objects than sculpture. The next step was to rid them of their surface imagery and to let them exist as pure, almost invisible entities made of what appeared to be clear glass. This step was an important one, but it was also the most precarious, because they ran the risk of being empty.

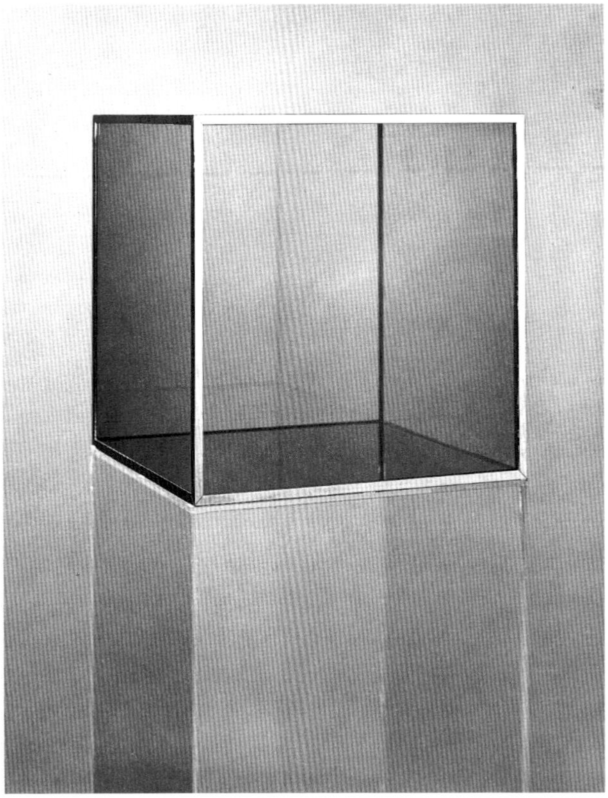

Ethereal, iridescent, as evanescent as soap bubbles, these new silver-rimmed cubes turned out to be fuller than before. Drawing the light from outside themselves, they contained it, hauntingly, within their walls. Sitting firmly on virtually invisible Plexiglas pedestals, they were gravity grounded. Instead of taking up space, they pulled space into themselves and kept it—a quality seldom seen in contemporary sculpture.

Bell's next step was to create rich, smoky cubes by coating glass in a specially designed vacuum chamber—a highly technical process that he has perfected over the years. In Taos, New Mexico, where the artist now lives, there is a "clean room": a sterile environment where he and his studio assistants work in gloves and surgical masks. It looks more like a cross between a NASA testing chamber and Frankenstein's lab than an artist's studio. Bell described his glass-coating process succinctly:

> *It's a simple commercial process called vacuum deposition. Essentially, you insert the glass and load the material (metallic Inconel and quartz) into a vessel, and you pump the air out of the vessel or vacuum chamber. In some precalculated proximity to the glass is a filament of tungsten metal that takes high heat; it is similar to the filament in a light bulb, which is also made of tungsten. When the pressure inside the vessel is low enough you pass a current through the filament. The material that's on the filament gets very hot and changes from a solid to a vapor; that vapor fills the tank and deposits on the glass in the form of a thin film or coating, which is also permanent.*
>
> *[The chamber] is a ten-foot-long tank that measures seven feet in diameter. I had to have my own equipment built simply because I could not gain regular access to a tank large enough to do my work. When I was coating the cubes I was using some apparatus I bought in a junkyard. It was exactly the same thing but just a smaller model. But I had learned enough from working with that older equipment to know what I wanted the new equipment to do. So I had it designed to be a lot more flexible and a lot easier to use.*[4]

The degree to which I am obsessed by a project reflects the degree of my need to know that which I have not known.

■ Larry Bell

Larry Bell
Untitled, 1964–65
Coated and engraved glass,
14 x 14 x 14 in.
(35.6 x 35.6 x 35.6 cm)
Collection of the artist

Since the mid-1960s, Bell's works have challenged the concept of the sculptural object. His newest work is directed both inward and outward, luring the viewer in with its reflective and illusory qualities while extending out into the viewer's space. Impeccably made, the pieces have no distracting surface incidents, except for the carefully controlled color, and thus they seem to appear and disappear with changes in perspective and light.

Bell is one of the Los Angeles artists of the 1960s whose work has been grouped under the label "Finish Fetish." The term, coined by John Coplans, was not intended derogatorily, but it does have the unfortunate connotation of slick superficiality. In reality, nothing could be further from the truth, and the complex ideas about color and perception explored by that group of artists are only now beginning to be fully understood.

Having come into prominence with his cubes, Bell refined them to highly finished perfection. Building his own machinery, devising his own techniques, he expanded and redefined processes originated by the aerospace industry. Although a sophisticated knowledge of technology played a crucial part in the execution of his pieces, it was never an end in itself. What Bell was concerned about was the subjectivity of perceiving color and light. Light is caught in the cubes—sometimes fleetingly—for the viewer to sense. The result is a highly introspective situation in which the viewer looks into or, paradoxically, through and beyond a piece to see it.

Bell's experimentation with the cubes, which he called the Terminal series, lasted until 1969. (Over the years he has continued to add a few works to the series.) A year prior to that he had first exhibited his standing walls, at the Vancouver Art Gallery. The step from the cubes to the walls was important, for in opening up the cubes Bell shifted the emphasis from the object to the environment. This change to freestanding walls required solving some tricky logistics: the panels, which are eight feet tall, can weigh as much as 250 pounds, making them difficult to handle both in the vacuum chamber and in the course of installation.

The walls sit firmly on the ground. For all their transparency and seeming fragility, they are quite substantial. Bell talks of having been strongly influenced by Ken Price's ceramic work—a statement that initially seems implausible. Yet it is the way Price's pieces "sit," how they respond to the gravitational pull, that fascinated Bell, and this quality is evident in his work as well. There is also the matter of color. Bell had begun to look seriously at the dark coloration of the cubes in his Terminal series, and he realized that a critical element of the work had to do with how the color emanated from the corners. He found that he no longer needed the full cube—he needed only a strong right angle.

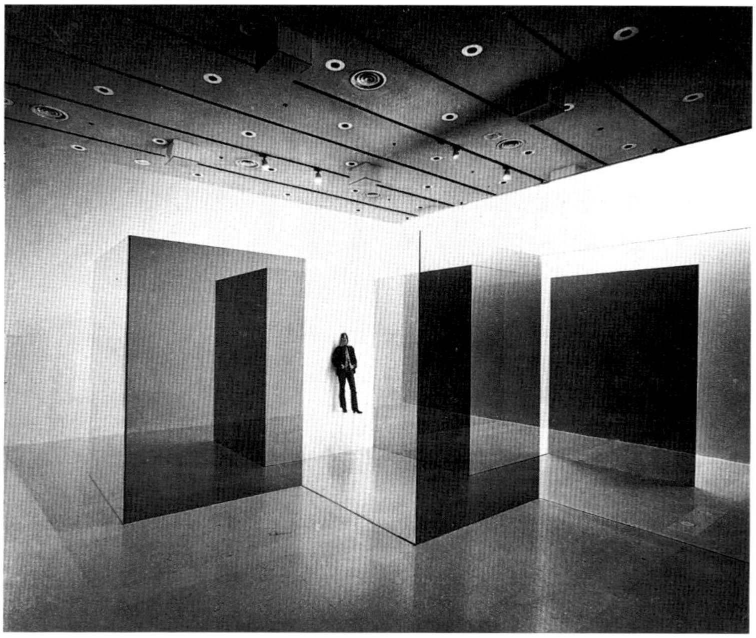

Larry Bell
Untitled, 1969
10 panels of 3/8-in. (1-cm) plate glass, 6 x 8 ft. (1.8 x 2.4 m.), each
Destroyed

Again we find that 1968–69 was a cusp period for yet another of the Light and Space artists. Clearly something was in the air; each of the artists was beginning to sniff it out in his or her own way, working independently yet learning from the others' work. Bell stated:

> In a lot of ways we were feeding off each other. It was like ten people solving the same problem—some weaker at a given point, and some stronger; then it would reverse out and the weaker ones would become strong and the stronger ones would become weaker for a while. All in all, you can look at the body of work by everyone as a single stroke activated by ten different artists. What really *separates* the individual practitioners is the quality of their blinding intensity.[5]

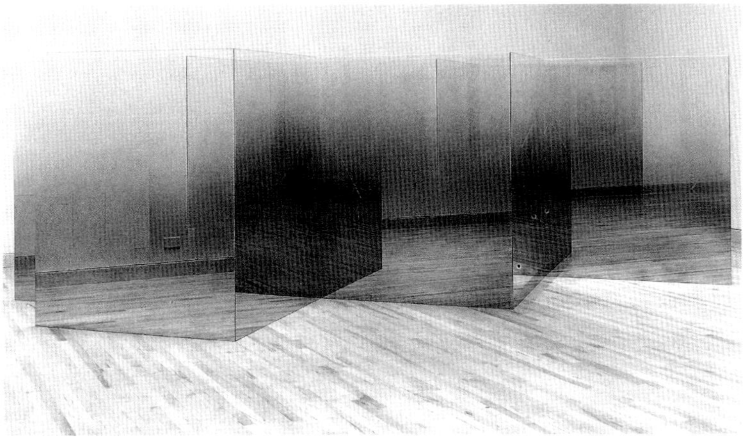

With Bell, this "blinding intensity" can be seen in the technical perfection of his works. When he decided to move from the well-known cubes to the walls and thus into space, he did so with finesse. The walls were now glass to glass; there was no metal frame or Plexiglas pedestal to stop the eye or contain the vision. Standing at right angles to each other, the walls are large panels of clear or smoky plate glass. Early on, they stood serenely alone. Later they zigzagged bravely across a space—sometimes in concert with its right angles and sometimes in opposition to them. The walls were most certainly *there;* they had density, weight, and gravity—*physical presence*—and they mirrored the viewer and the surrounding space on their surfaces. Yet as the viewer moved around them, they would intermittently appear to dematerialize, slipping into a kind of perceptual limbo. Possessed of an extraordinary illusory quality, they also became doors—a kind of crack in reality that seemed to beckon.

These new pieces were seen by some critics as contenders in the Minimalist Olympics, yet they were clearly not in the running. Bell never wanted his cubes and walls to be Minimalistic "primary structures" or to have a "nonhierarchical structure." They were far too colored, too romantic, too metaphysical, and too heavily laden with narcissistic content to play that game.

The first public presentations of Bell's walls were in the exhibitions *Los Angeles 6,* at the Vancouver Art Gallery (March 31–May 5, 1968), and *14 Sculptors: The Industrial Edge,* at the Walker Art Center, Minneapolis, in 1969. In these two shows, the environment became a crucial aspect of the work for the first time. The ambient light and shadow affected the walls in a way that it had never done with the cubes. Bell's work articulates a sense of place through pure sensation and perception. He aspires to a kind of perceptual awakening on the part of the viewer, an awakening achieved through the creation of an idealized place "out there"—a place that, however physically present, is experienced perceptually.

Glass is Bell's addiction and passion. But in the late 1960s, when he was producing his cubes in an endless procession, he seemed to be blocked, unable to extend his illusions. By this time many of his peers who worked with Light and Space had begun seriously questioning all their concerns—a questioning that eventually led them in the direction of room-environment pieces and site-specific work. In 1969 and in the early 1970s Bell began investigations in these areas as well, producing both in his studio and in a few museums a series of room environments that radically affected his thinking. These forays into large-scale experimental works were not always successful (they often lacked the sense of space and fine tuning that were always evident in Bell's glass work), but they represented a major step nonetheless, finally breaking the stranglehold that objects seemed to have on him.

Larry Bell
Untitled
Room size: 15 x 40 ft. (4.6 x 12.2 m.)
Installation, The Tate Gallery,
London, 1970

Installation
in *Larry Bell, Robert Irwin, Douglas Wheeler,* Tate Gallery, London
May 5–31, 1970

In one of his first situational works Bell experimented with a large black room, first executed in his studio, then in the *Spaces* exhibition at the Museum of Modern Art, New York, in 1969–70. It was shown shortly thereafter at the Tate. Bell said of this piece:

> *It was a very-low-level-light room that was painted black. There were some tubes suspended in the room that reflected a light source from outside the room. In the original piece I had a fifteen-by-forty-foot room divided up the middle with a wall sticking out.*
>
> *There was only one entrance. It was all black: ceiling, floors, everything. Down across the wall about five or six feet from the floor opposite the opening I hung some aluminized Pyrex tubing at different height levels. Then there was a framing spot projecting a beam of light onto a piece of light tape that was set back from the entrance to the room. At the point where the wall met the ceiling was where the piece of tape was.... Around the corner was the light source, so that the only light that entered this space was the ambient light that spilled off this piece of white paper tape. The rods reflected the light coming off the white tape.*
>
> *The idea was that you stepped into the room, and when your eyes accustomed themselves somewhat to the darkness, the only thing you'd see was the line way at the back. As you stepped in and moved toward the line, you were moving away from the light source—so the line appeared to keep moving away from you in direct proportion to how far away you were from the light source.*

The piece was disconcerting and, because of the low light level, somewhat anxiety provoking.

Installation
Oakland Museum, Oakland, California
January 23–March 11, 1973

Installation
Fine Art Gallery, University of California, Irvine, 1974

In two other room-environment pieces Bell abandoned the idea of darkness as a controlling factor and chose to work with sound instead. At the Oakland Museum he divided a large, gray, concrete room into fifths by hanging sound-deadening blankets and quilts from the ceiling—leaving a square of empty space at the center. He also hung inexpensive moving quilts on the wall to further soften the sound. He then recorded several hours of what he calls "random notes" on his twelve-string guitar and put the recordings onto four tape loops, placed with a player and a speaker in each of the four corners of the room. Each speaker had a different tape continuously repeating on it. One was a two-minute tape, one was thirty seconds, one was fifteen seconds, and so on. The museum person who started the piece in the morning was instructed to turn the tapes on differently each day so that they were never played in the same pattern. Museum visitors would walk around the gallery and hear varying tonal patterns. Those who chose to actively participate in the piece could lean into the central space, which was just big enough to stick their heads into, and, by moving their heads, they could compose the sound into different patterns. It was a curiously intriguing experience.

The guitar seemed an interesting thing to play around with, because nobody else was doing stuff like that.... I was making it quite clear that it had nothing to do with music. It just had to do with a learning experience—with trying to break free. I was using access to a museum gallery to do that.

The piece was done at a particularly desperate time in my life. I was wanting to make a change in the kinds of things I was doing and presenting. I liked the things I did, but I didn't like myself very much. I didn't like delivering the kinds of things that were expected of me, which meant always showing the glass cubes—which were real hot in my career at the time.

Sound had not yet been universally accepted as an art medium, and Bell's willingness to involve himself with it early on is an interesting example of his risk-taking capacity. However, as he said: "If it was bad, I didn't care. I wanted the public to see the screw-up, because to present just what was expected of me was unacceptable, so I just decided that I didn't care if it was bad—because in my mind the other thing was worse."

Having learned from the Oakland piece, Bell was given another opportunity to do new work in a public space at the University of California, Irvine. Working with a floor plan of the gallery, Bell laid out a sound installation in advance. But when he tried to install it, he discovered that the air-conditioning system in the gallery was so loud that the room was already acoustically full.

Originally, I was going to build a sort of megaphone, an acoustical amplifier for the footfalls of the people walking through the space. It was going to be set up in a sort of a channelway, where you walk in from either side, but you had to walk in a certain pattern through the space to get out through the other side. I was going to put a system in there that would amplify the sounds of your own feet—and zap them back to your ears. This would be done without any electrical stuff at all—with just a sounding board. The idea was that after three or four people got in there—all of a sudden it would sound like there were a lot of people in there because all you'd hear were feet coming right at your ears.

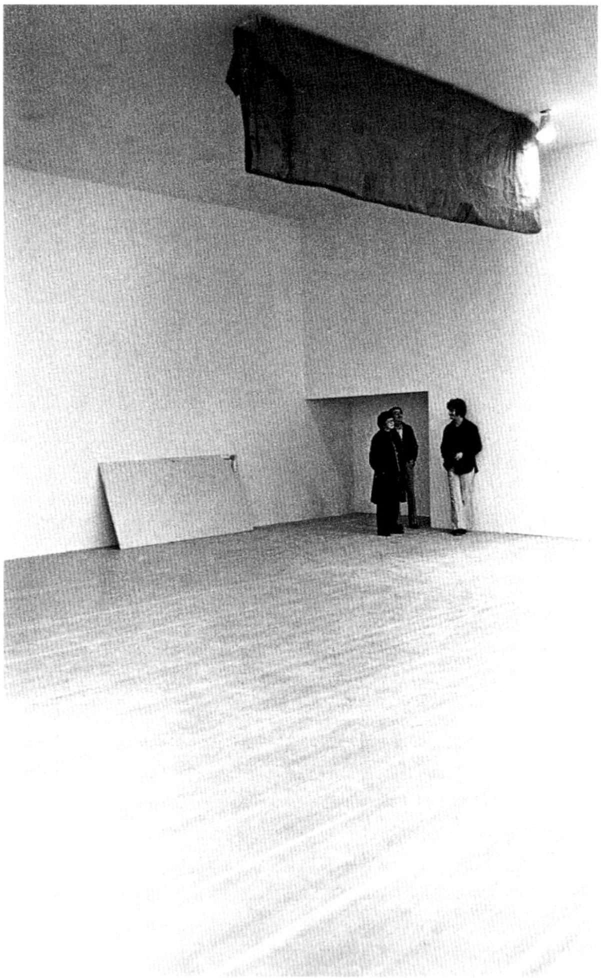

Larry Bell
Untitled
Installation, Fine Art Gallery,
University of California,
Irvine, 1974

Once he realized that the air conditioning would be the most predominant sound in the room, Bell began to experiment with materials that were lying around the gallery area.

> *We took pieces of Sheetrock and leaned them at different angles against the wall, covering the air-conditioning duct. In some cases we took Masonite and nailed it over the duct with one side down and the other side open, so that when the air currents pushed it, it fluttered a little bit. Then we took out all of the moving quilts except one. One of them I just sort of liked hanging there, because it divided the room on a vertical axis—so we just left it there. Then I took some Sheetrock and covered one of the openings, because there was too much light coming in. We just leaned it up against the opening, so that you could only get in from one side. Originally, before I got there, I had them construct a light-and-sound baffle to muffle those effects before you entered the room. It was already constructed when I realized the original piece wouldn't work. I had to decide whether to rip it out or leave it, so I left it. So when you went through the light-and-sound baffle you entered an empty room with all that shit leaning against the wall—and that was it! That was the piece!*

> *Maybe we could have pushed the Sheetrock aspect of the piece—I mean, there were a number of possibilities for the Sheetrock to lean against the wall, but finally it wasn't about the Sheetrock, it was about what the air sounded like, and so when finally the composition was interesting to me and I couldn't find out what to alter anymore—that was it.*

It is difficult, even with hindsight, to make any determinations about the Oakland and Irvine pieces—whether they were empty or full, whether they accomplished what Bell was attempting to do. Perhaps the most interesting question they raise is whether a public museum or gallery should be used for untried experiments. But bear in mind that works of an experiential nature can never be finalized in any space except the space for which they are intended. With that as a given, there will always be an element of experimentation—a risk that is often worth taking. The Irvine piece in particular was important to Bell, but the faculty and students were angry about it—a response that disappointed the artist, who felt they should have been more open to experimentation.

> *I learned a lot from that piece, because by taking those materials that were lying around—by just doing that, I really freed myself from a whole bunch of feelings about what an installation is supposed to be. That was a very liberating experience for me.*

> *You see, sound* does *fill the space visually.... The addition of any kind of theatrics to a given space—an auditorium, a room, a gallery, a space like that—does fill it up.... The space initially is a kind of neutral playground, and the artist does something—a sound work or a visual work or whatever—in there, and in doing so, he changes the space each time. Because you change what the room is by the addition of any element in there, and by the audience (the only people who are already interested). Now: they can like it or not like it or say that the room doesn't make any difference. The fact is that it has been changed simply by that artist coming into it and dealing with something that has to do with the perception of the space. That includes everything in the space—whether it is sound or a visual phenomenon.*

This process of liberation can now be seen as having led Bell both to *The Iceberg and Its Shadow* and to *Solar Fountain.*

***The Iceberg and Its Shadow*, 1975**
Santa Barbara Museum of Art, Santa Barbara, California
and many other museums, 1975–77
On loan to the Massachusetts Institute of Technology, Cambridge, since 1978

Bell's real breakthrough came with his monumental work *The Iceberg and Its Shadow*, which comprises fifty-six panels of three-eighth-inch-thick glass, some rectangular, some trapezoidal. The work is big, rising to one hundred inches at its highest points. Each panel weighs approximately two hundred fifty pounds; the entire work weighs more than thirteen thousand pounds. Some of the huge panes of glass are clear, the others are a rich smoky gray; along their bottoms or tops drift wisps of blue. Their edges, beveled at the top, create a hard, clear, prismatic line of light that flicks along the full length of the work. The clear panes are the iceberg and the gray ones, the iceberg's shadow. The title for the piece evolved, Bell says, when he "began to think about the idea of the piece being like an iceberg, because there were so many inherent structural combinations that at any one time you would only be seeing the tip." In spite of its size, *The Iceberg* is based on human scale and thus is not psychologically overwhelming. The panes are no wider than the artist's arms can reach, and the top can be touched by stretching on tiptoe. The immaculate surfaces and elegance of *The Iceberg* give it a sense of wholeness and clarity totally unlike normal day-to-day experience.

This important work came about partially as a happy accident. Glass is breakable and costly. As Bell had panes of glass fused together or prepared for coating, there was inevitably some damage. As a result he was left with a number of large sheets that were cracked, chipped, or had their corners broken off. He gathered these up and sent them to a glazier to have the corners mitered. When they returned, Bell found that he now had a series of trapezoids. As he began to experiment with them, he found that his visual vocabulary was radically extended. He started creating pieces that began and ended gently, gradually angling up from the floor until they reached the tip of the iceberg.

Experimenting further, he scattered wisps of sapphire blue across the top or bottom of the panes. The reintroduction of color is an important aspect of *The Iceberg and Its Shadow*. The cubes have a soap-bubble color that forms an important part of their presence and suggests an exquisite metaphor. Originally Bell had left color out of the freestanding walls, as Barbara Haskell noted:

> In Bell's boxes, the changing, reflected images create a highly active surface. This, combined with the color modulations, gives Bell's surfaces a high degree of visual complexity. For this reason, Bell eliminated color in his glass walls, as he said, "There were so many complex relationships occurring inside the pieces and with their environment that to have added color would have caused chaos."[6]

More than likely, Bell's hesitation about using color was related less to chaos than to newness: he wasn't ready to reintroduce color yet. However, once set on his course with *The Iceberg*, he seemed to understand how to utilize color subtly and with great impact. The elusive, fugitive blue in *The Iceberg* is almost sensed rather than seen. At first virtually invisible, the color suddenly becomes strong as sunlight plays across the work or as the viewer turns a corner and catches the color by surprise. Bell explained: "I was interested in using a blue that reminded me of many different things. The blue is very close to the ultraviolet band of the visual spectrum, and it's a similar kind of blue to the material used in cheap Mexican dinnerware—glass plates and glasses.

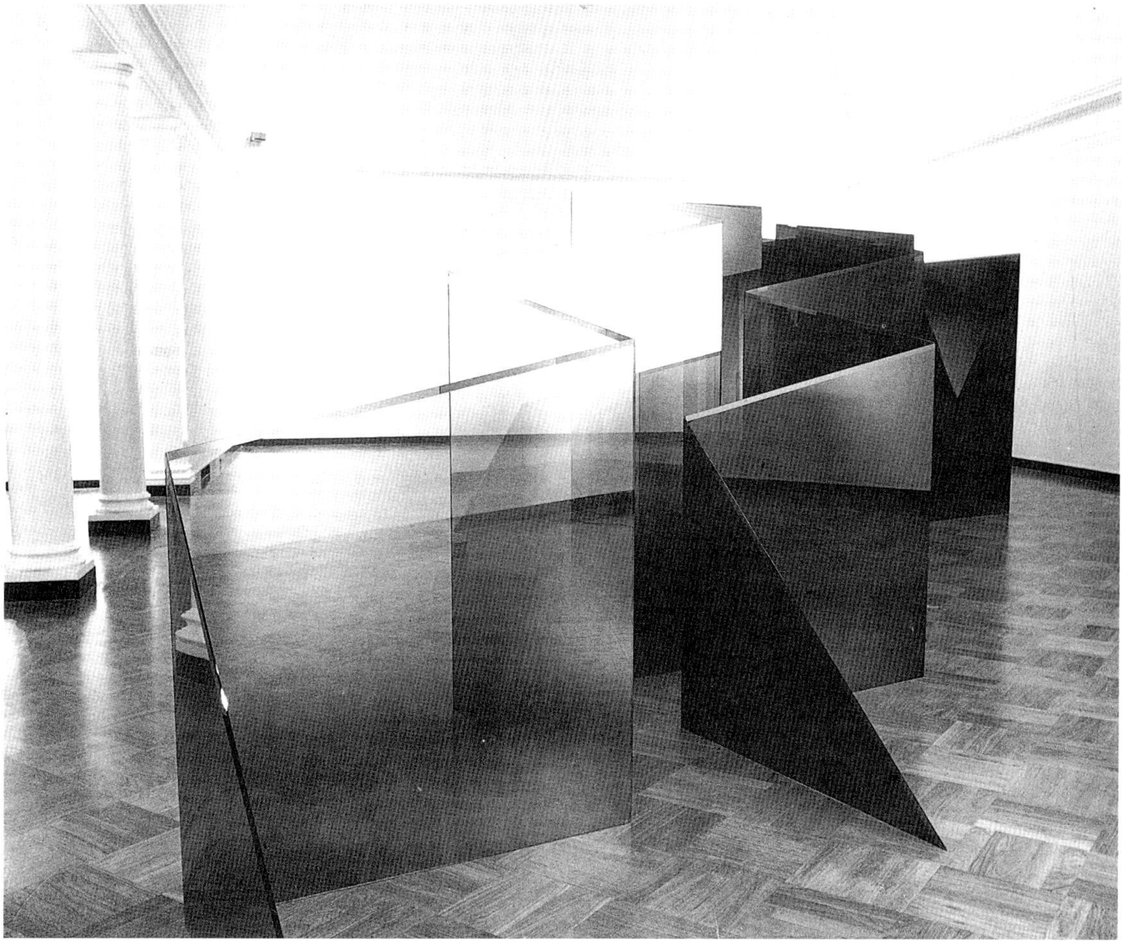

Larry Bell
The Iceberg and Its Shadow, 1975
56 panels of 3/8-in. (1-cm) clear and gray glass, coated with Inconel and quartz; width: 60 in. (152.4 cm), heights varying from 57 to 100 in. (144.8 x 254 cm)
Installation, Santa Barbara Museum of Art, Santa Barbara, California, 1976
Now in the collection of the Albert and Vera List Family, on loan to Massachusetts Institute of Technology

It also reminded me of some opals that I brought back from Australia—the same blue was inherent in those colors."[7]

The seemingly endless number of combinations afforded by the fifty-six panels of *The Iceberg and Its Shadow* will take years to explore. From 1975 to 1977 it was installed in museums and universities in Fort Worth, Saint Louis, Santa Barbara, and Corpus Christi. The work was purchased by the Albert and Vera List Family Collection and placed on long-term loan to the Massachusetts Institute of Technology. Since 1978 it has been installed again and again in various manifestations—as a learning experience both for the artist and for students at the university.[8]

Bell works better with a piece in its physical form than in a drawing or conceptual stage, and he is adamant about the importance of relatively permanent installations:

> *I am looking for a permanent base for my installations. I am looking for a platform that's less transitory than simply exhibiting an idea for something. I would like my pieces to hang around for a while. Prior to the experience with MIT, essentially all I have ever really done has been to participate in those kinds of transitory, show-biz museum or gallery installations, and that is all great fun... but when the piece is gone it's gone, and I have no way of going back to refer to it. So I am aiming to place pieces where they'll sit around for awhile, and hopefully set up the conditions that will allow me to move back into them if I want to... over a period of time.*
>
> *I need perspective on a piece, and I only get that perspective by going back to it three or four times, so that I can learn from it and assimilate the information.*
>
> *The truth is—a piece is never really resolved—you know? A crucial aspect of any project is the fact that if the exhibition is of a transitory nature—then the concept will be a transitory concern. If you've got ground rules that preclude considerations that have to do with any kind of longevity for the installation, then you don't have that as a root base to work with, and if that isn't inherent in the piece—that's all there is to it—you can't make sand out of air.*[9]

Solar Fountain, in conjunction with Eric Orr, 1974–78
Denver Center for the Performing Arts
installed 1981–83

Bell works hard and is dedicated to what he does. He is also quick to give credit to other artists who have influenced him or have provided collegial support. After *The Iceberg and Its Shadow*, his next major Light and Space venture was *Solar Fountain*. This piece, for which ground was broken in the summer of 1981, sits on a three-and-a-half-acre site in downtown Denver, on the grounds of the Denver Center for the Performing Arts. *Solar Fountain* is remarkable for several reasons. It is Bell's first exterior sculpture, and it extends his visual vocabulary by making use of ephemeral elements such as sunlight and fog. It also set a highly interesting precedent in that it was a challenging and successful collaboration with Eric Orr.

I see art as a learning experience completely individual, void of the criteria of quality; each projected, externalized effort reflects only my ability to see the parameters of the work chosen.

■ Larry Bell, in Christopher Knight, *Los Angeles Herald Examiner*, November 23, 1980.

Writing in April 1978, Bell discussed both the collaboration and the premise of the fountain:

> *Eric's main concerns in the past had been in mysterious sensate environments and strange metaphysical iconography. My preoccupation had always been with extremely simple kinds of physical relationships incorporating glass as a substrate to change the ambient and jovial conditions of the light in a given space. I never felt my work was particularly metaphysical or mysterious; on the contrary, I felt that it was always simple and obvious.*

Eric had an ongoing interest in certain noble metals, gold in particular because of its metaphysical implications. The only thing I knew about gold was that it was a fine reflector of the infrared. So his interest in gold from the metaphysical standpoint and what little I knew about gold from my experience mixed together to form one of the elements to be incorporated into our collaboration, that element being heat.

Eric had some experience with a scientist-engineer who had developed a piece of apparatus that was used industrially by the citrus industry to keep the orange trees from freezing. The apparatus produced a very fine water mist or fog. Now we had two elements to our collaboration, heat and fog.... We simultaneously considered the concept of a fountain with the heat evaporating the fog.[10]

Solar Fountain sits like an apparition on top of a deep, round reflecting pond. (It is called *Solar Fountain* because it actually utilizes more sunlight than water.) A circular vessel some thirty-seven feet in diameter and ten feet tall, it is made of huge panes of plate glass, stabilized visually and physically at each joint with trapezoidal "flying buttresses" of the same glass. Inside the vessel is a fog-making device.

Solar Fountain possesses some of the same illusory and reflective qualities as *The Iceberg and Its Shadow*. Both transparent and solid, it seems to dematerialize under certain lights. Coated with what appears to be gold, the piece reflects light near the infrared region of the spectrum, producing heat and affecting the particle content of the fog. The early morning sun activates the fog machine. At high noon the sun illuminates the interior of the fountain, making it particularly visible. At that time the gold panels reflect into the swirling fog that fills the interior and then drifts outward, eventually disappearing on the wind. The noon heat causes moisture to evaporate, and rainbows form where the moisture condenses once again. At the end of the day, when the sun has gone down, the fog disappears and the machine shuts off.

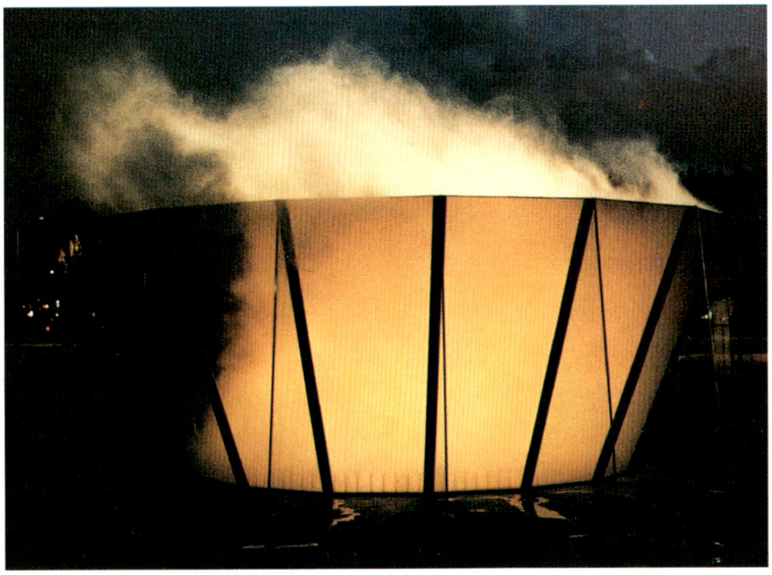

Larry Bell and Eric Orr
Solar Fountain, 1983
Coated glass, fog-making device, diameter: 37 ft. (11.3 m.); height: 10 ft. (3.1 m.)
Permanent installation, Denver Center for the Performing Arts

Bell had begun making room-environment works with trepidation, and after *Solar Fountain* was finally finished in 1983, he stopped making them (with the notable exception of his *Leaning Room*).

The considerations that have to go into making those kind of room installations are heavy. You don't ever forget what you have learned from each experience, but at the same time, you really have to work at it to be a participant in that game—especially when you are talking about competing with the caliber of installations by people such as Bob Irwin and Jim Turrell. Those guys have been focused on that kind of work as their total trip*. It's pretty hard to consider yourself any kind of a contender unless you are really working on it, and doing it well. Those guys are the best there is, and that's all there is to it.*

The chances are that I won't do any more of those things, because I am not that interested in learning it all again. I can't see those kinds of changes coming up in my work, because I like what I am doing right now, and it is suiting my needs at this time. I really like *the nature of my involvement now.*

Leaning Room II
in _Individuals: A Selected History of Contemporary Art, 1945–1986_
Temporary Contemporary, Museum of Contemporary Art, Los Angeles
December 10, 1986–January 10, 1988
Installation based on _Leaning Room,_ 1970

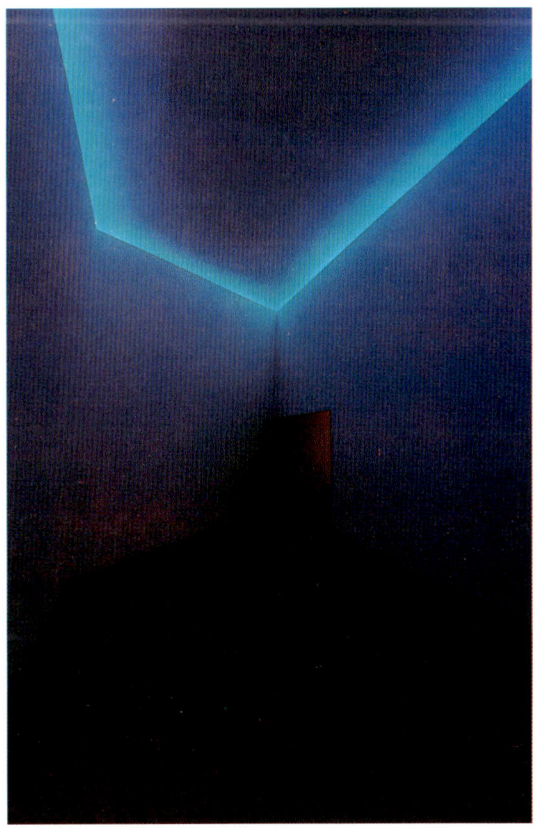

Larry Bell
Leaning Room II
Installation, Temporary Contemporary, Museum of Contemporary Art, Los Angeles, 1986–88

Beckoned by its intriguing shape, the participant entered Bell's *Leaning Room* (also known as *The Blue Room*) expectantly, having approached it through a long, dark corridor and past a bend as emphatic as a right angle but not as sharp. Where the narrowed point of *Leaning Room* ended, opposite its entrance, the joining of the wall with the ceiling was marked by a sharply drawn line of blue fluorescent light that whipped down one side, across the end of the room, and up the other side, stopping before the room twisted, allowing a spill of light from the entryway to create the second powerful phenomenon in the work.

Upon entering the room, all was blackness—except for the brilliance of the cobalt

Their rims are five-sided prisms that throw looping patterns of light and shadow on the wall behind them, so that the pieces themselves are nearly dematerialized. They seem to be at least partially influenced by Irwin's discs from 1968—thus nicely completing the circle of influence. Less subtle than Irwin's discs and not as refined in terms of his use of materials, Valentine's Rings achieve their ephemeral quality with a great economy of means. Transparent rather than opaque, they had a greater eloquence and coloristic diversity than anything he had yet made.

In 1968 something crucial happened: Valentine developed a casting process that enabled him to create sculpture on human rather than tabletop scale. Like the small early works, the new pieces were still exhibited on clear Plexiglas pedestals, but their uppermost edges were several feet above the viewer's line of sight. Delicate, transparent, seemingly fragile, they appear nearly clear at the top, where they slip into nothingness. The new scale and transparency established the works as integral to the setting rather than as separate objects. This breakthrough was to propel him into creating environmental art.

For the past half-dozen years, Valentine's work has been among the most important solid-object sculpture on the West Coast, and of those who have stuck with the ageless precept of an irreducible object, among the best sculpture in the country. These judgements should overshadow the important, but secondary fact that Valentine is a premier technician among those artists working in resin. He has managed, in spite of problems with heat, weight, and the danger of impurities, optics as clear and pure as those of his colleagues, while retaining the convincing mass of major sculpture.

But his major achievement has been the development of substantial sculpture during the Sixties, bringing together the presence of physical mass in palpable kinesthetic space and the "advanced" optical/perceptual properties, precursing such artists as James Turrell, Michael Asher, later Robert Irwin, and Ron Cooper's newest work.

■ **Peter Plagens, *DeWain Valentine: Sculpture* (New York: Denise René Gallery, 1973), n.p.**

In 1969 Valentine's work became even larger. Having made a number of major technological advances, he was now able to create works that were architectural in scale. These large curved slabs, some eight feet tall, are almost more walls than sculptures; defined by the space they are in, and defining that space in return, they become part of an architectural dialogue. Deliciously thin and vibrantly hued, they were executed in gleaming colors such as turquoise and deep rose. With these works Valentine moved closer to the concerns of colleagues such as Larry Bell, and he became interested in "transparency, reflection, light, and space" as manifested in room-environment works and site-specific pieces.

From 1969 to 1973 Valentine created some of his most significant work to date, the Circle Forms. These comprise concave circles, concave and convex circles, and those that are convex or concave on one side and flat on the other. (The double concave pieces act like colored magnifying glasses, bending, shaping, enlarging everything seen through them.) These works are glorious in color: yellow, pink, blue-green, violet, lavender. Some are one-color castings; others are two-color works in combinations such as pale rose and robin's egg blue. Valentine is fascinated with the sea and the sky, with the colors of the spectrum, with the reflective qualities of light: "What I would still ultimately like to be able to do is to take a big saw and cut out a piece of the sky and say, 'Here it is!' or a piece of the sea and say, 'Here *it* is—look at this!' Polyester offered me a medium whereby I could deal with that transparent colored space and objectify it—put it out as a common object."

Many of Valentine's works are pristinely simple; others are complex, almost baroque. Included in the second group are cast-polyester-resin works with clear centers and smoky swirls of color at their edges. In others the smoky color drifts through the entire form. Some of these works are no more than twenty-three inches in diameter; others are nearly six feet tall but no more than five inches deep. One of the most remarkable is the deep violet *Concave Circle,* which weighs thirty-five hundred pounds and stands six feet tall. As John Lloyd Taylor noted: "The piece has a slight floating or suspended effect. Its volume, scale and visual weight, combined with its sheer elegance, pristine surface and nearly flawless interior color mass, establish this work as one of the more consequential moments in contemporary sculpture."[4]

Valentine continued to produce object works in the early 1970s, but in 1970 and 1971 he also began to make drawings for several different kinds of nonobject works. Many of these were not realized until 1974–75, several years after their conception; others have still not been realized. As with most of the other Light and Space artists, Valentine's nonobject works were not widely exhibited, photographed, or published, which hinders full comprehension of his development.

One early work, never realized, was a klieg-light piece called *March 1–31, 1969,* which was part of a Conceptual art exhibition curated by Seth Siegelaub (the show took the form of a catalog). Valentine proposed placing 236 klieg lights at each of the four corners and along the sides of Central Park in New York. The lights would create a gigantic *Light Slab,* which would not only mark the edges of the park but also establish a slab of light within it.

In an interview with John Coplans published in 1970, Valentine discussed environmental spaces that dealt with light and colored space.[5] In October of that year Valentine started working on his living and studio spaces. Virtually all of the Light and Space artists have immaculate dwellings or studios, with white walls, extraordinary light, and as little furniture as possible. For these artists the studio is often a laboratory, a physical manifestation of the way they see. It is there that the initial testing is frequently done: walls are put up and taken down, lights are shifted, skylights added, corner coving changed, floors sanded and finished, often in white. Irwin will sit for hours observing leaves make shadows on the wall. Nordman will sit silently in the dark and watch the outside world through the one-way glass of her barren storefront studio. Valentine, in his loft, will watch sunlight from the skylights change the shadows on a new glass piece, enhancing its color.

From 1967 until 1991 Valentine's studio, one block from Venice Beach, was a pure white cube. The floor was white tile; the furniture was white; the tables, transparent glass. His work was (and still is) everywhere—along the walls, on the landing, down the hall. "The living space *is* the work," Valentine said.

> *Building it was an educational process for working with total space; making spaces within spaces; the way light was used; and so forth. This space is directly related to where my head was at that time [1970] in terms of my work. Before then I had lived in the studio for three years and never built a wall. My head wasn't there. Building this space gave me a foot into working with a surrounding kind of space. All the recent Space and Light situations are directly related to that way of thinking.*[6]

Catenary Light and _Cantilevered Spectrum_
69 Market Street, Venice, California, 1970–91
Recreated for _West/East: First-Generation Environmental Sculpture_
P.S.1, Institute for Art and Urban Resources, Long Island City, New York
exhibition proposed for 1981 but never realized

For many years these two room-environment pieces were installed in Valentine's studio, each in its own separate room in the working portion of the studio, behind the living area. As I entered *Catenary Light,* normal daylight fell away, and it took me some time to get used to the dark stillness of the room. The space was large—thirty feet square—and the walls, floor, and ceiling were pure white. The experience was akin to that of walking into a movie theater for a Saturday mati-

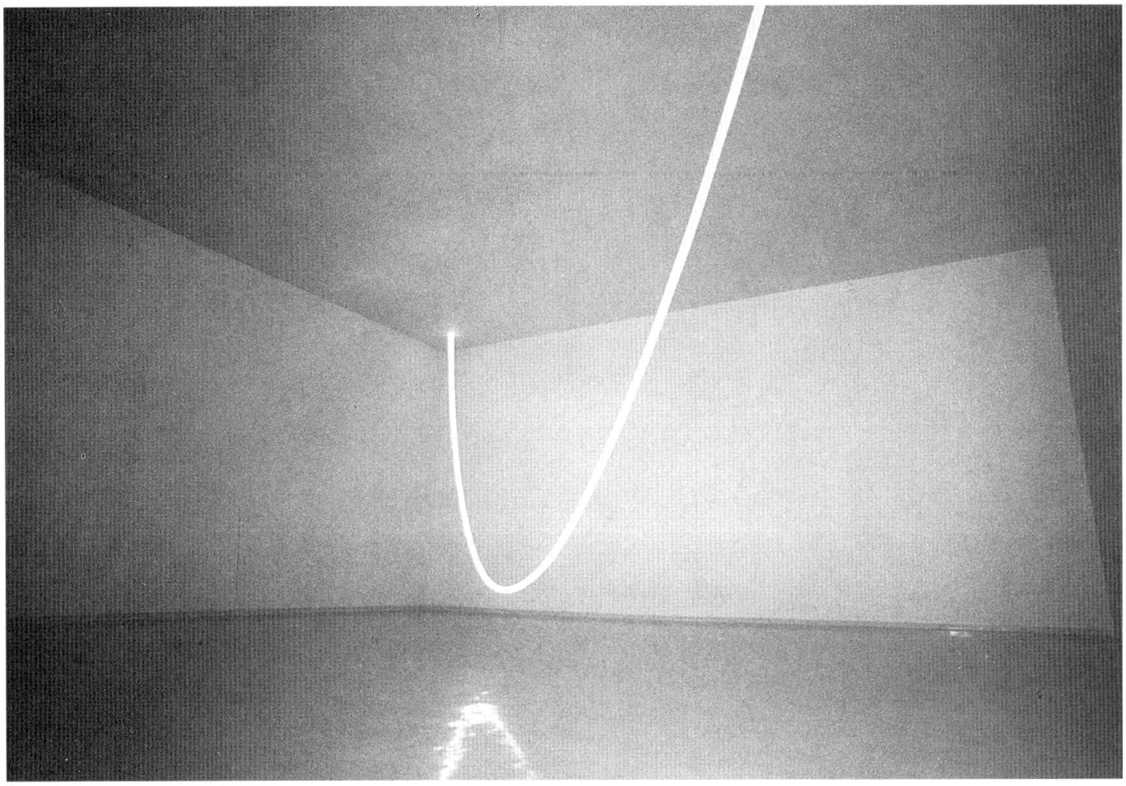

nee: it took a while for my pupils to adjust. The darkness was enfolding; it began to take on a visual roundness and a sensed or "felt" color, which was a warm black with blue halation near the light source.

A glowing line of light ran out of the darkness, curving diagonally from one corner to another. It started at the ceiling, slid three-quarters of the way to the floor, and then returned to the ceiling on the corner diagonally opposite. It cut the room into two triangles of thick, grainy darkness, which lightened near the arc and became fuzzy at the edges. The corners were indistinct and soft, yet the room was clearly readable as a square. The effect was curiously dreamlike, like being surrounded by a painting rather than looking at one.

Catenary Light takes its title from the catenary curve. If you hold a chain—or a Slinky—at both ends, the bend in the middle is a catenary curve. The crucial thing about *Catenary Light* is that even though it was powerful and unique, its means were simple: a hole drilled into the ceiling at either corner of the diagonal allowed light to travel down the acrylic rod, curve, and flow upward again until it reached the other end of the tube at the opposite corner.

At the same time that he had conceived the klieg-light piece for Central Park, Valentine had been working with photographs and drawings related to a gigantic wall of light he wanted to place off the breakwater at Venice Beach:

> *I was making drawings of works using a combination of klieg lights and laser beams. I kept wanting to find a way to make a laser beam bend, and there is no ostensible way to do that. Then it flashed in my head that in junior high school I had done some light pieces with fiberglass that would later be termed "fiber optics"—but I didn't know it had a name then. But that way, using the principles of fiber optics, I could light a piece of Plexiglas tubing and make the*

Opposite
DeWain Valentine
Catenary Light, 1971
Acrylic rod and daylight;
room size: 13 x 30 x 30 ft.
(4 x 9.1 x 9.1 m.)
Installation, Valentine's studio,
Venice, California

light bend . . . so . . . it just clicked into my head that I could make a line, and make it curve, and also make it illuminated—by using acrylic rod. And then the natural extension of that was to deal directly with daylight and use that rod as a vehicle to bring the daylight in—and to make a drawing.

Catenary Light was Valentine's first natural-light piece. In an interview with Melinda Wortz, he discussed other possibilities that he eventually had discarded. The final work was accomplished with pure daylight:

> Wortz: And you didn't use any applied color in that piece?
>
> Valentine: *I have modified it with color, but color imposed on it becomes identifiable as a particular color, while the color of daylight is much more unusual than any modification of color.*[7]

Whereas *Catenary Light* was dark, *Cantilevered Spectrum* was light. Whereas the first room was square, this room was rectangular, measuring forty by sixty feet. The piece ran horizontally at eye level across the longest wall. A thick plane of Plexiglas protruded several feet from a narrow horizontal slot cut through the studio wall to the outside; it was anchored at either end to the side walls of the room. The participant entered the room to find himself bathed in a rosy pink light—a color derived from blood coursing through his eyeballs—and facing a cantilevered plane of rainbowed light.

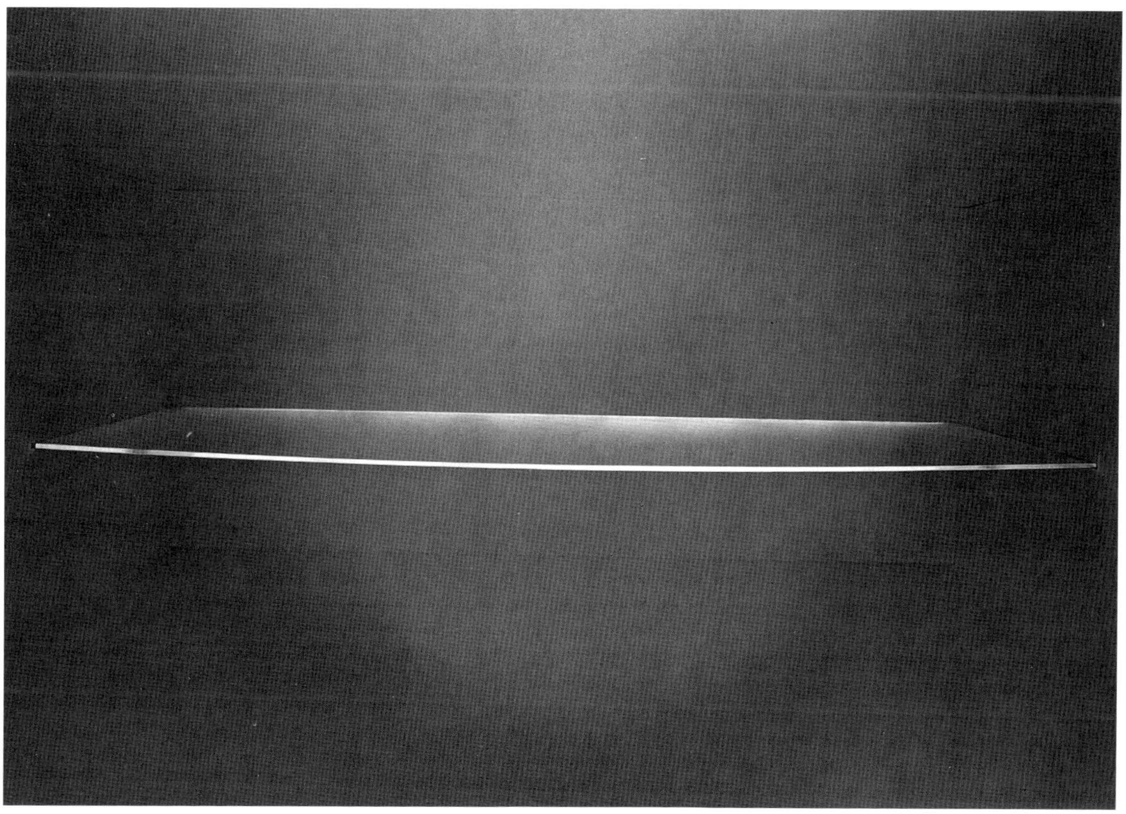

DeWain Valentine
Cantilevered Spectrum, 1972
Plexiglas and daylight, room size:
12 x 40 x 60 ft.
(3.6 x 12.2 x 18.3 m.)
Installation, Valentine's studio,
Venice, California

Skyline Installation
Barnsdall Park, Los Angeles, 1973

Spectrum Horizon
Long Beach Museum of Art, Long Beach, California
February 23–September 17, 1975

Valentine's next room-environment works were *Skyline Installation* and *Spectrum Horizon. Skyline* was essentially a large camera obscura, which transmitted images such as trees and architectural elements in from the outside and projected them onto a specially designed screen. *Skyline* was the far simpler of the two installations, but it was notable due to the fact that it transmitted images from the corners and cornices of the Frank Lloyd Wright building in which it was housed.

Spectrum Horizon was more sophisticated and more complex, but it was built on the same principle and was also a kind of camera obscura. In this piece Valentine had the ocean to contend with: *Spectrum Horizon* was installed in a room with a three-sided bay window that faced the sea. The catalog essay for *Spectrum Horizon* described the piece's technical aspects: "Very simply, the artist has blocked up with masonite a bank of windows which face the ocean. A small aperture near the center of each of the four masonite panels projects outdoor light onto a scrim of polyethylene coated with window frosting, extending the whole length of the gallery."[8]

Valentine also explained the process:

> *I stretched a large piece of polyethylene film on a giant stretcher that went from floor to ceiling, wall to wall. I frosted the back side of it with glass frosting. The whole piece worked like a rear projection screen. I covered the [existing] windows and then put apertures in them to bring in the images from the outside, and then between the windows and the screen I painted a spectrum with transparent colors on a transparent piece of film. The spectrum was suspended in the middle, between the two apertures and the [existing] windows and the screen, so that the spectrum was also projected on the screen.... There were about twenty-four* inches *between the strip of spectrum and the screen, and five* feet *between the windows and the screen.*

The main window was parallel to the screen; the two side windows were at a forty-five-degree angle to it. As the viewer walked into the room from the right-hand side, an image appeared, projected from the left-hand window. The effect was like that of a camera obscura; the image being projected was transferred, in its entirety but upside down, to the scrim. In addition, an apparitional spectrum hovered in the center of a four-panel scrim. As the viewer moved toward the center, the image changed into one projected by the front window. As the viewer moved to the left, the perspective slowly changed again and became the image emanating from the right-hand window. As time passed and the earth rotated, light also passed through the slot at a different time, so that over time it cast spectra of color in various places around the room.

As Valentine has noted: "The nice thing about the Long Beach piece was that the back faced the sea, so the sea sparkled on the screen all the time, and at night you could see the lights in the harbor and the boats moving."

***Curved Wall Spectrum*, 1971–74**
San Jose Museum of Art, San Jose, California
March 4–29, 1974

Curved Wall Spectrum was proposed as a project for San Jose in 1971, and the drawings for it were completed then; the project itself was exhibited at the San Jose Museum of Art three years later. The museum was in the process of rebuilding and had a large space that was going to be torn down, which they turned over to Valentine.

What Valentine did was construct an entire room, twenty-five feet square and twelve feet high. The walls were built with two-by-fours and drywall, then painted pure white. A false ceiling was made of stretched muslin, something like a stage flat. Valentine then built another wall, curved like a ship's hull, and covered it with form-fitting drywall. This wall was a half circle measuring twenty-four feet from end to end, with a slot of six inches between each side of the curve and the room's wall. Valentine described the work:

> *Behind the convex curve, along the back wall which has a southern orientation, are windows that you cannot see, but which allow daylight into the room. Two panels, four by twelve feet, are attached to the curved wall on either side at the back. On each of these panels I painted a spectrum which went from red-violet at the top to blue-violet at the bottom, with magenta-orange-red-green-blue in between. When sunlight struck the panels, it bounded around the corner and gradually diminished as it diffused along the convex curve out into the room. The color was mostly in the corners, where you got the whole reflection.*

The piece changed all day long: it was bright on the west side in the morning when the light came from the east and intense in the afternoon when light came from the west and flooded the east side, but it was brightest of all at midday. In her interview with Valentine, Wortz quoted him about this work: "It is a very elusive experience of color. The color appears to be coming through transparency, but it really isn't. For me, somehow, it's more magical that it's reflected rather than being really colored."[9] There *was* a magical quality to this work. The air seemed infused with pinpoints of rainbow color, as if the space had been airbrushed.

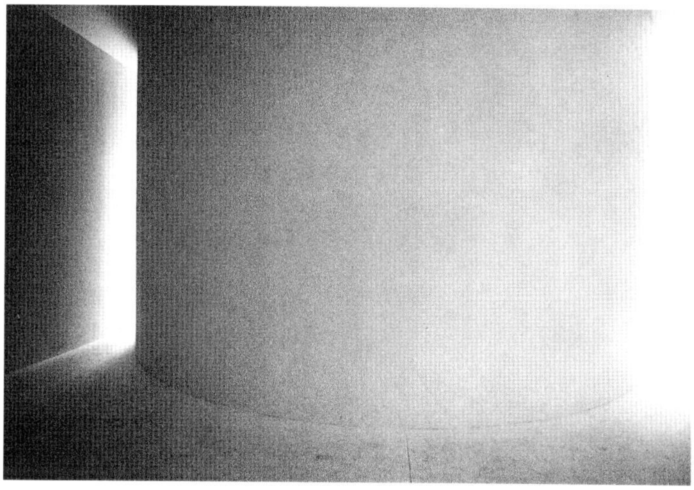

DeWain Valentine
Curved Wall Spectrum, 1971–74
Drywall, muslin, room size:
12 x 25 x 25 ft. (3.6 x 7.6 x 7.6 m.)
Installation, San Jose
Museum of Art, San Jose,
California, 1974

Valentine's architectural forms are as much "vessels or carriers of metaphysical meaning" as the rocks and trees, flowers and pastures in a Martin Johnson Heade or Fitz Hugh Lane painting. That intimations of the built environment have replaced nature is not surprising, but both exhibit a strong sense of place in which meaning is revealed. Transcendental philosophy attempted to ascertain the essence of "being" through nature, but since nature is not man-made, it keeps us at a certain distance. Architectural structures, however, are determined by man's own actions in concert with natural law. And these are the vessels that Valentine creates.

■ **Christopher Knight, *DeWain Valentine: New Work* (Los Angeles: Los Angeles County Museum of Art, 1979), n.p.**

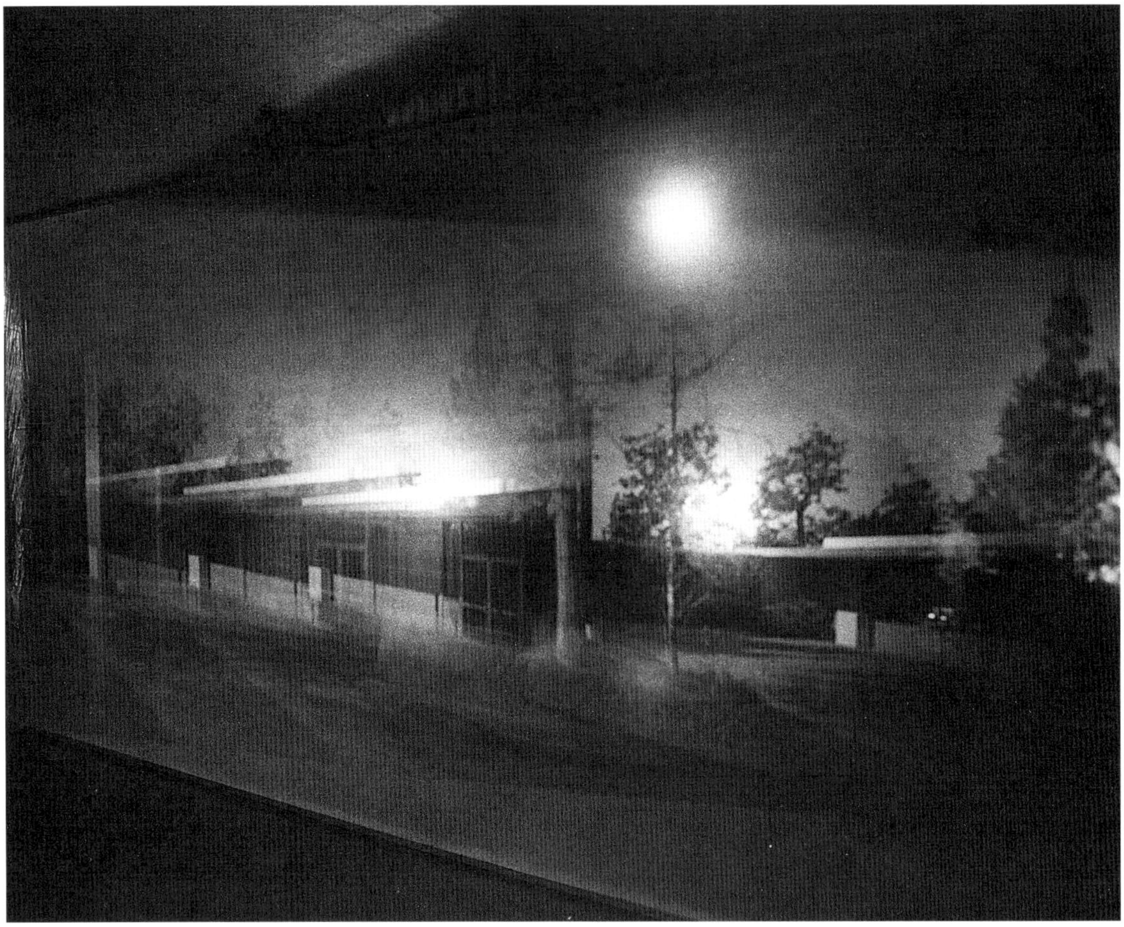

Sky Garden
Art Galleries, California State College, Northridge
November 4–30, 1975

With *Sky Garden,* Valentine executed a work that utilized both rear projection and a camera-obscura technique, but was larger and even more compelling than *Spectrum Horizon.*

The Northridge work was twelve feet high by sixty-five feet long. Valentine covered the room's windows with black plastic, then spaced seven holes, five-eighths of an inch in diameter, across the wall. Four virtually identical outside views were juxtaposed and moved across the flat screen, which was transparent plastic frosted with vinyl spray. The projected image was uncannily clear. The viewer could see people moving across the screen, trees moving in the breeze, and the buildings of the campus, all projected in cinematic fashion. Jean-Luc Bordeaux commented about the work:

> The scene varied according to one's position in the room and relationship to the screen. The banal trees of the Northridge patio and the students walking routinely across it suddenly appeared on the screen like a ballet of changing forms, and the fragmented and distorted perspective of the surrounding buildings added a dramatic note varying in intensity throughout the day. The projection of the sun itself was seen on the screen as seven round spots which moved from left to right during the course of the day—a direct manifestation of the turning of the earth on its axis, and a concrete visual track of the passing of time.[10]

Thus, time was a factor in the new work as it had never been before, adding a new dimension to Valentine's concern with ephemeral phenomena.

DeWain Valentine
Sky Garden
Black plastic, plastic screen,
room size: 12 x 65 x 25 ft.
(3.6 x 19.8 x 7.6 m.)
Installation, Art Galleries, California
State College, Northridge, 1975

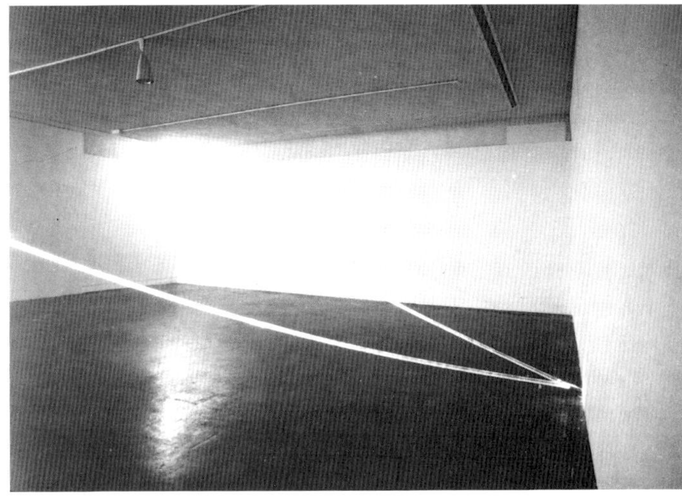

V Line **and** ***Cantilevered Planes***
La Jolla Museum of Contemporary Art, La Jolla, California
June 27–August 5, 1975

Right
DeWain Valentine
V Line
Acrylic tube, diameter: 1 in. (2.5 cm); room size: 9 x 12 x 24 ft. (2.7 x 3.6 x 7.3 m.)
Installation, La Jolla Museum of Contemporary Art, La Jolla, California, 1975

Below
DeWain Valentine
Cantilevered Planes
Acrylic and daylight, room size: 12 x 52 x 19 ft. (3.6 x 15.8 x 5.8 m.)
Installation, La Jolla Museum of Contemporary Art, La Jolla, California, 1975

Few of the artists discussed here have had the opportunity to refine and re-present their concepts. Valentine has been unusually fortunate in this. His exhibition in La Jolla allowed him to present variants of *Catenary Light* and *Cantilevered Spectrum,* as well as the space to execute *V Line.* All three were spectacular examples of Valentine's Light and Space environments. Powerful, geometric, intense, they were also romantic and magical. The viewer was enveloped by the light-infused colored spaces. It was difficult to ascertain how the ambience had been created, but at the same time it seemed important not to break the spell by attempting to analyze it. Though seemingly uncomplicated, the pieces required a great deal of preparation, as Fran Preisman noted:

> Many architectural alterations were necessary to carefully control the viewing space. Several walls were constructed to block off superfluous daylight and to reduce outside disturbances, and various apertures in the ceiling and walls were cut at charted positions to capture dense concentrations of light. Ideally these controls should create a dark contemplative environment in which to experience the phenomena of suspended light. The whole light approach is very simple and direct.[11]

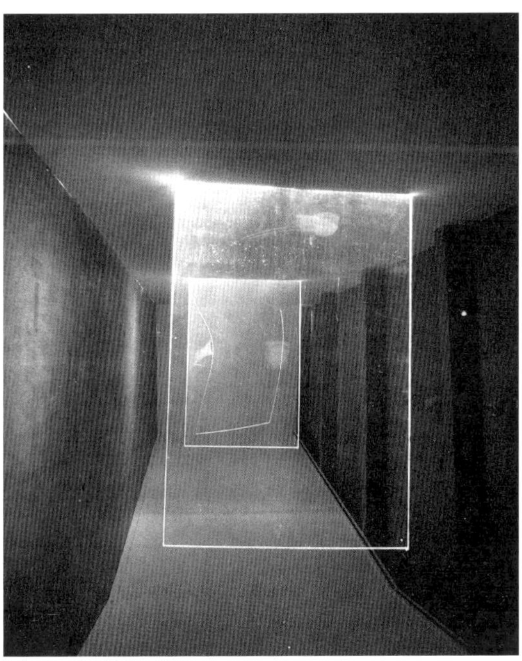

Cantilevered Planes was considerably different from Valentine's previous cantilevered works. Here the acrylic sheets were installed vertically rather than horizontally. However, it was still their edges that intrigued: charged with daylight, the outer edges of each sheet were as vividly defined as if rimmed with neon. As the viewer entered the darkened room, which was suffused with eerie blue light, he encountered two planes of light that seemed to float in midair. Brightly glowing at their edges, these mysterious planes looked like drawings in space. An illusion of a third plane was created by the reflection of the first plane on the second.

Technically, the piece was achieved in much the same way as *Cantilevered Spectrum.* Planes of acrylic were fitted into a slit in an outside wall, and their corners were attached by guy wires linked to the ceiling and floor. Daylight was picked up by the planes and transmitted to their edges.

What I was interested in was . . . almost a semitranslucent feeling, where you could *feel* the space. That was something I was very much interested in these pieces—that you could feel the space—as a substance—rather than simply as something to look through. Ultimately the whole space became a container of transparent color and light.

■ DeWain Valentine

The Wave* and *Water Columns
proposed for Center for Fine Arts, Miami, 1985

Like many other Light and Space artists, Valentine has created proposals for works that have not been built. One of the most beautiful of these is a proposed three-room work with two key sculptural elements titled *The Wave* and *Water Columns.* The entry room to the piece would have two columns, each measuring twelve feet high by two feet in diameter. These would be ceremonial columns, standing guard at the entrance. Proceeding past the columns, the participant would enter a diamond-shaped space completely dominated by a breathtaking work, created of green glass, that would be eight feet tall, eight feet wide, and only one and a half inches deep. The most extraordinary element of this work would be a circular room, eight feet tall, built completely of glass. Flooded with natural light from above, it would have a glass ceiling and a glass skylight, which would direct beams of light around and through the cut edges of the sea green glass. A "step system" of glass would line the walls—further deflecting and reflecting light. The chamber itself would be built like Valentine's glass *Pacific Waterwall,* made for Pacific Enterprises. The room would be entered through a triple arch of glass—again ceremonial—and the viewer would be immediately bombarded by the brilliance of light and the briny color of the glass.

***Waterwall,* 1988**
***Diamond Waterwall,* commissioned 1988;**
installed at 950 South Flower Street, Los Angeles, 1989
***Pacific Waterwall,* commissioned 1988;**
installed 1990 at the First Interstate World Center,
633 West Fifth Street, Los Angeles

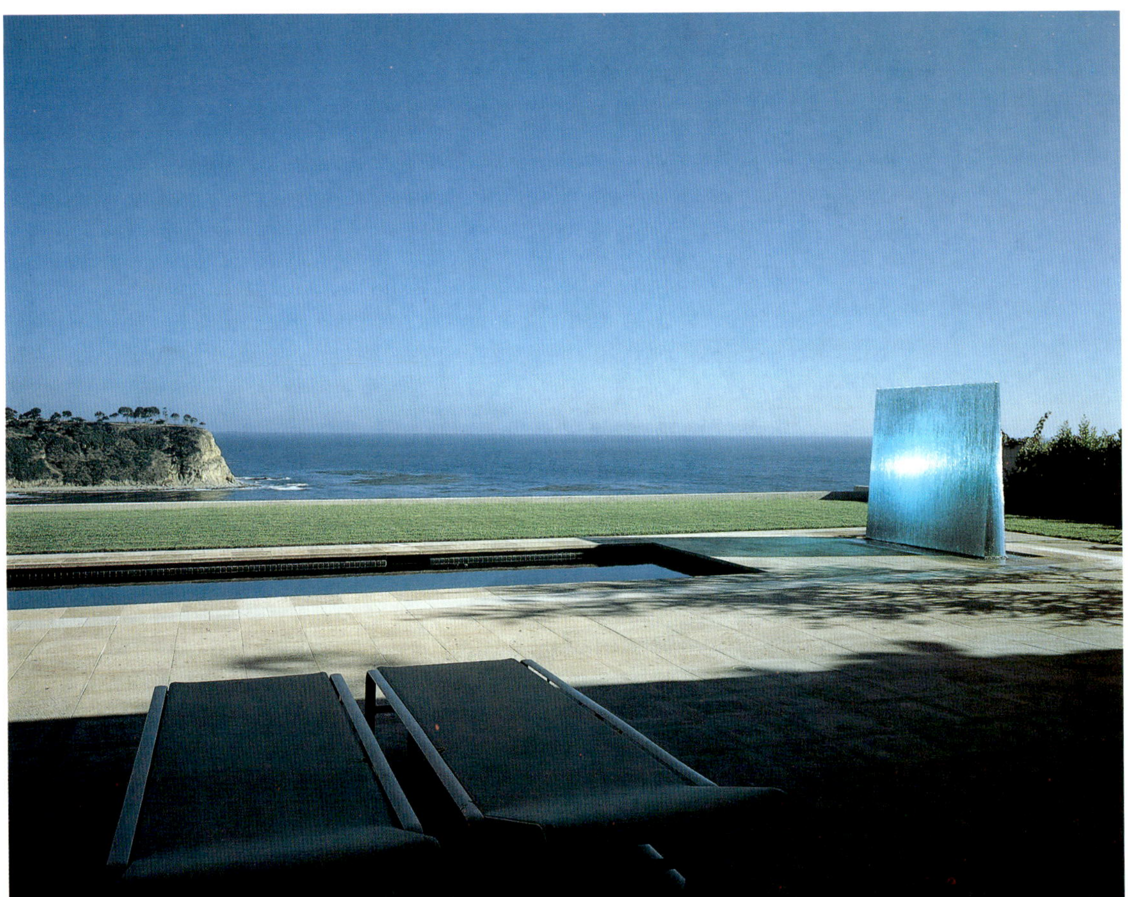

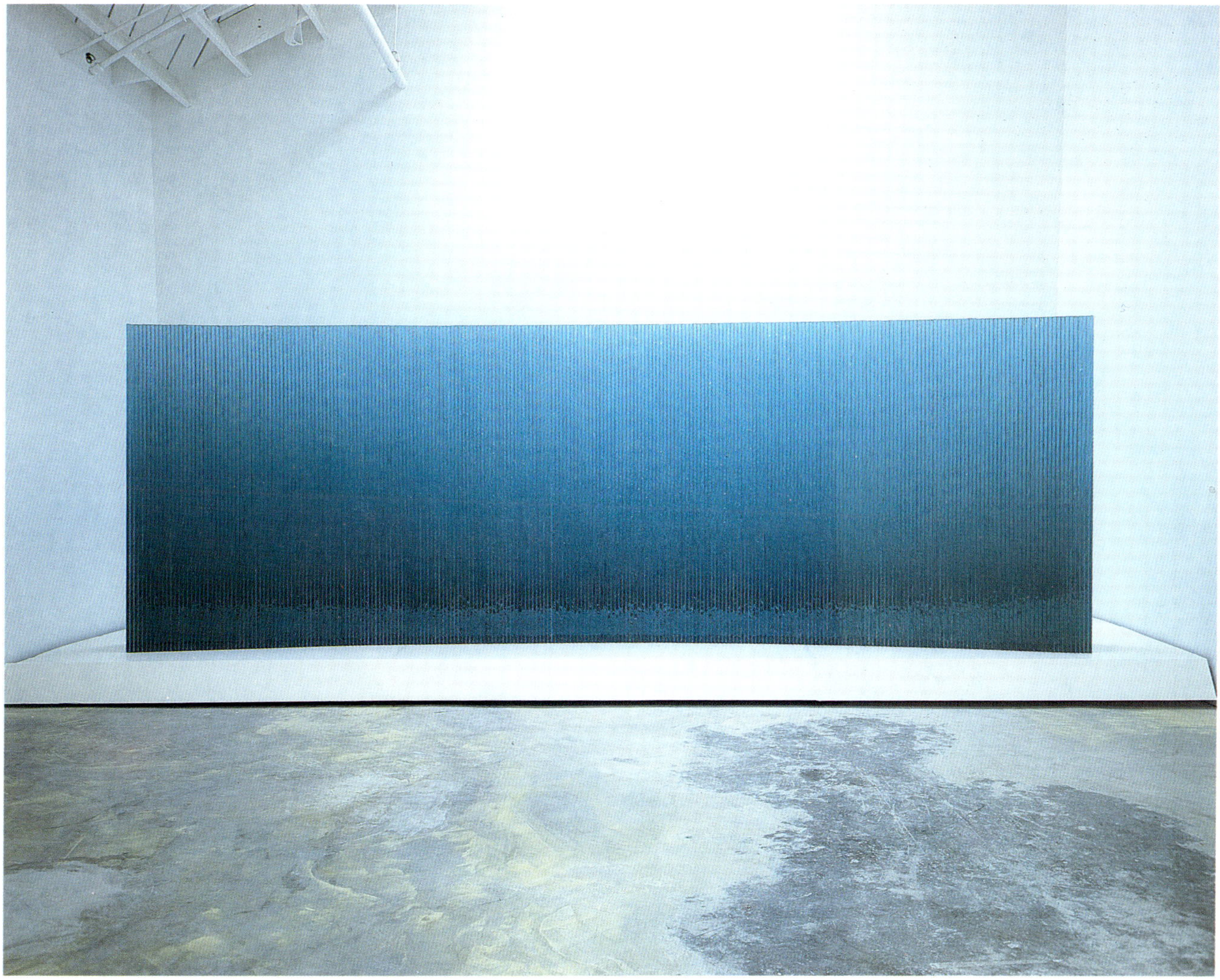

Opposite
DeWain Valentine
Waterwall, 1988
Glass, bronze, 72 x 72 x 12 in.
(182.9 x 182.9 x 30.5 cm)
Mr. and Mrs. Robert Columbato,
Los Angeles

Above
DeWain Valentine
Pacific Waterwall, 1988–90
Laminated glass,
6 ft. 10 in. x 19 ft. x 24 in.
(2.1 m. x 5.8 m. x 66 cm)
Pacific Enterprises,
Los Angeles

Valentine, who is more closely related to a purely sculptural tradition than most of the other Light and Space artists (with the exception of Nauman), has recently moved into a more specifically sculptural realm, yet his shimmering, translucent sculptures are clearly the inheritors of information gathered from decades of Light and Space work. Valentine's new, large-scale works still evidence Light and Space concerns, but they are implemented in a decidedly sculptural fashion.

Waterwall, a fountain commissioned by Mr. and Mrs. Robert Columbato, is installed outside at the end of a swimming pool. There it receives the myriad rays of light that dance on the pool's sparkling surface and also absorbs constantly changing color and light from the nearby sea. *Waterwall* makes its own light as well, as water from its center flows over the deep sea green glass and silently ripples down the planes of the monolith.

Diamond Waterwall, commissioned by Forest City Properties Co. for the Metropolitan (a mixed-use rental community in the South Park neighborhood of downtown Los Angeles), is also an exterior piece, installed in a courtyard between the high-rise buildings of the

Metropolitan's office complex. This huge diamond-shaped work, which weighs more than eleven tons, seems almost ethereal, and its sparkling water provides a visual and psychological respite from the bustle of the downtown traffic.

Pacific Waterwall, commissioned by Pacific Enterprises, is easily Valentine's most impressive sculptural work to date. Measuring six feet ten inches by nineteen feet and weighing more than five tons, this enormous glass sculpture is installed in the fifty-first-floor reception area of a corporate office. Its phosphorescent green glass sparkles like seawater, and the piece serves as a highly successful metaphor for a fountain—a real fountain being logistically difficult to realize so many stories up. A gigantic curving sculpture, made of hundreds of strips of one-foot-by-six-foot strips of glass, *Pacific Waterfall* is translucent rather than transparent, and it has a murkiness deep in its interior spaces that effervesces into twinkling light as it reaches the surface.

Susan Kaiser Vogel

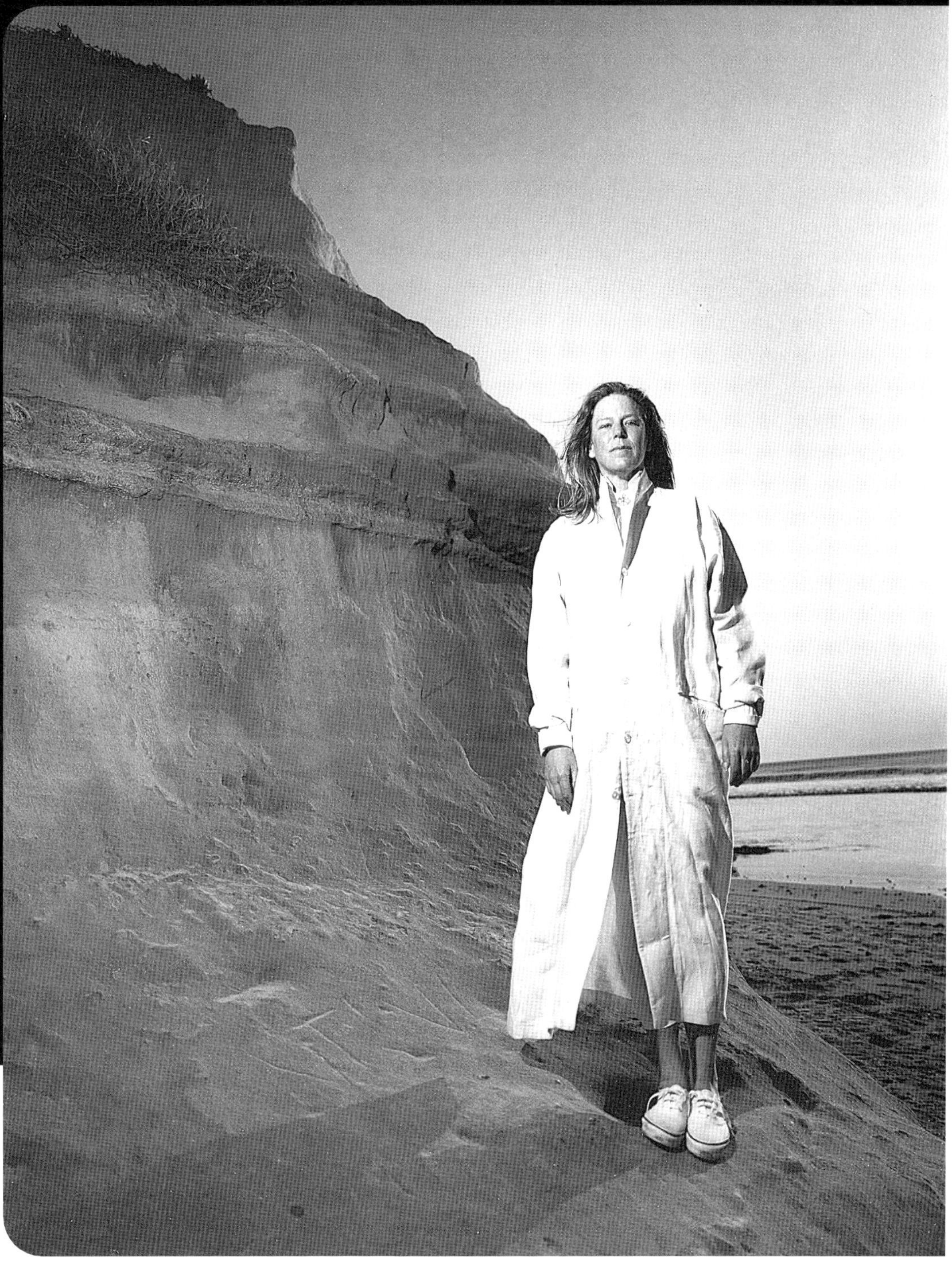

Once the experiential dimension of one's own sensory enclosure has been reached, reflection on one's existence has been reached, reflection on one's existence returns to the act of dwelling and to the dwelling itself. Heidegger asserted that you can think about the existence of a human being starting from his or her habitat. Therefore, consciousness of self can then proceed to the *appropriation* of the outside. This can signify the transformation of something outside the self into one's own property, in such a way that we can speak of a time and place "appropriate" to the person who transformed his or her way of living and his or her own home.

Germano Celant

Susan Kaiser Vogel

One interesting aspect of the Light and Space artists is that they appear to have spawned no direct heirs. There are, however, a few artists—particularly Susan Kaiser Vogel, Hap Tivey, Lita Albuquerque, and Peter Erskine—whose works are somewhat different visually from those by their senior colleagues but whose philosophical premises are similar. All are generally conceded to be "on the bus" (to borrow Ken Kesey's term for inclusion by general consensus). Recognition often comes slowly to West Coast artists, partially because there are so few people writing about art on the West Coast (until recently, magazine coverage has been shockingly absent). Senior members of the West Coast art community are frequently just beginning to be acknowledged as the younger ones are coming up, and that has resulted in a kind of generational telescoping.

Vogel spent ten years out of the country before returning to UCLA to get her M.F.A. As a result, she was not out of school until her forties, and she has not yet created a large body of work, though what she has done so far is mature and impressive. Her early friendships with Ron Cooper, Laddie Dill, Ed Moses, Eric Orr, and DeWain Valentine provided the same important support and collegiality that artists such as Irwin, Orr, Turrell, Valentine, and Wheeler had shared a full decade earlier.

In 1977 Vogel was in the process of putting together her obligatory M.F.A. exhibition. For some time she had been making organic shapes in handmade paper, which she would dye black and hang against a wall. The process of making these works appealed to her, but she felt that she was graduating without having learned anything profound about her art: "It was the process of birth, life, and death that fascinated me—not the works. I didn't know what to do with those pieces. What did become clear, however, was that the metaphor of impermanence was very important to me. The conceptual aspect of the impermanence of the pieces was what interested me—not how they looked on the gallery walls."[1]

Upset with the body of work that she was slated to show for her M.F.A. exhibition, Vogel began to examine what she thought worked in her paper sculpture and what didn't. Sitting in UCLA's sculpture garden in front of the art department shortly before her show was to be installed, she began suddenly to see it differently:

> *I had been watching people walk through this courtyard, which is constructed of pink brick. Its dimensions were about one hundred fifty by two hundred feet. As a student I had watched people walking in that area for three years, and they never walked through the courtyard—they would always walk around it instead of walking across it at a diagonal. Suddenly I had a vision: I wanted to build something that would bring people and life to that space that had never been there before. . . . I wanted to create a brick structure there. I wanted to give people an entirely new experience that didn't already carry the dead weight of familiarity with it.*

Within three days—with the help of a structural engineer and more than three tons of bricks—Vogel began to create *Blue Flame.*

Blue Flame
Frederick S. Wight Art Gallery, University of California, Los Angeles, 1977

It took well over a month to build the piece.

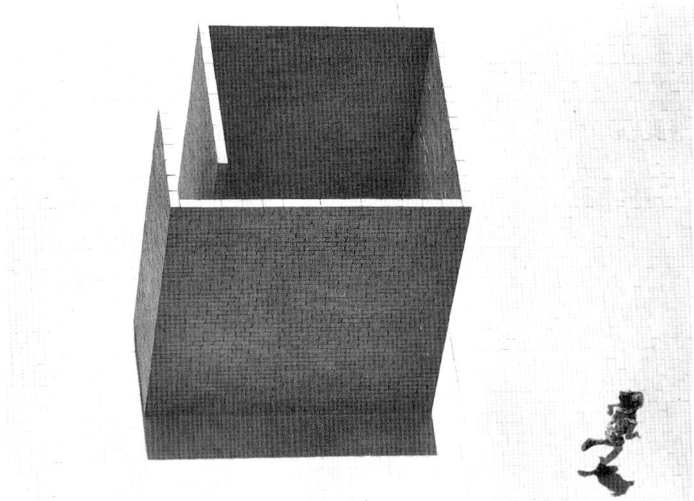

Susan Kaiser Vogel
Blue Flame
Ultra Marine Blue pastel on brick, north wall: $10^{1/2}$ x $10^{1/2}$ ft. (3.2 x 3.2 m.)
Installation, University of California, Los Angeles, 1977

> *I had forklifts out there—and eight skids of bricks, which weighed more than three tons. I built the structure without mortar. I put mastic butter between each brick, so that you could see only brick to brick, like the grid of a human nervous system rather than a visible mortar system.*
>
> *The process of putting up the work was very meditative. It took me a week and a half to build the structure, and four weeks to color it with three thousand sticks of Grumbacher 46F Blue. I wanted the surface to be made of a temporary and ethereal material, so that the chalk would soak into the brick and then gently drift down to the floor of pink bricks below.*

The work was stunning: a maze ten feet six inches in height and length, it was taller than a human could reach, and at one point it turned back into itself at a right angle. It was richly, passionately hand colored, brick by brick by brick. Its blue was the color of an ocean sky just before sunset. The underlying warmth of the terra-cotta bricks colored the blue, just as the sun's rays warm the color of the sky. Inside the construction, looking up, one saw only a cloud-filled square and Oscar Wilde's "little tent of blue that prisoners call sky."[2]

In the gallery where Vogel's exhibition would properly have gone, she built a pure white room with exactly the same dimensions as *Blue Flame.* Installed in it was a ten-foot-six-inch-tall sculpture of blue-chalked bricks exactly two feet wide. This was the missing link that closed up the maze in the courtyard outside.

A crucial aspect of the piece was its demise. It was lovingly taken down brick by brick. The polyethylene that had protected the courtyard was carefully removed, but an outline of *Blue Flame* remained—created by colored dust from the chalk that had sifted down during the three months of the piece's short life. Vogel's relationship with the piece was a fervent romance: "As the chalk began to blow away, it was like a flame slowly dying out. It was a complete experience for me. I had all the processes in life accounted for. I will never forget it as long as I live—it was like a great love affair."

Death in Venice
901 Pacific, Venice, California, 1978

Death in Venice was the second major piece Vogel created after graduating from UCLA. Having lived in her studio at 901 Pacific for some time, she began to feel increasingly trapped by the studio itself and disenchanted with the art community. She sealed off her exquisitely constructed studio, as if to wall herself up within it. The overtones were chilling, as Peter Clothier noted: "As in Thomas Mann's novel, life-death and art-reality are here shown to be two-way streets."[3]

Vogel described her work:

> *I made a triptych of glass created of three different-size panes or sections in place of the whole storefront. The windows were subtly, differently banded by polished aluminum strips, black aluminum strips, and strips of anodized aluminum. They were purposefully of different sizes to create a deftly balanced frame for the frontal wall. A single row of painted gold bricks ran upward vertically at the door. As you looked at the window from almost any angle, you received a multiplicity of reflected images from the buildings across the street. I also built a replica of Michelangelo's* David *almost five feet high and placed him on the roof of the building across the street so that he could look down on my building. (I had the greatest sculpture of all time—from the standpoint of human idealism—looking down on my work.)*
>
> Death in Venice *was a response to all the evils in the world. I lived behind it. I was blocked—walled in. Behind the storefront I put up a gorgeous wall of blue bricks.*[4]
>
> *I colored it again, but this time I colored it with* many *multicolored blue pastel chalk sticks, not just monochromatic blues. I built it so that it rolled over to you slightly at the top, then tilted back. It was not a straight wall. It was really beautiful, simply because it didn't reach all the way to the ceiling and light would pour in from over the top, from the front window.*

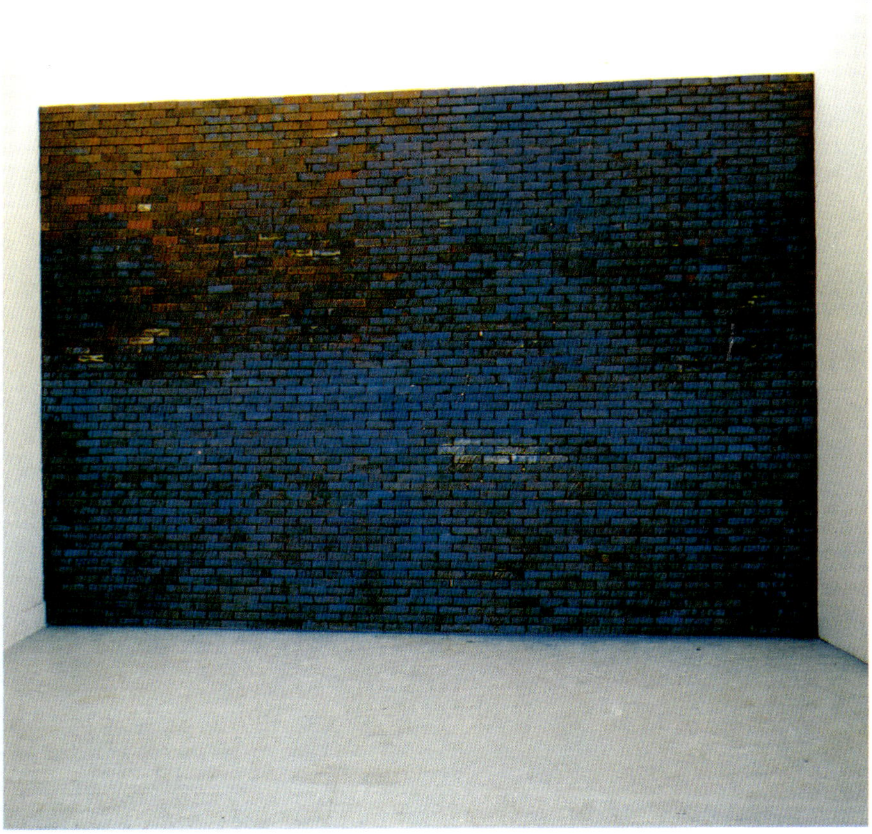

Susan Kaiser Vogel
Death in Venice
Glass, bricks
Installation, Vogel's studio, Venice, California, 1978

I also took out the sleeping loft, but I left the stairs that led up to the loft. When you got up to the level of the loft, the light at the top, at the ceiling, was rainbowlike. There, the horizon line of your eyes was the horizon line of the piece. I put a tatami mat in there to sleep in—it was very, very powerful.

Out on the street, cars were going back and forth, and at times their lights bounded around the room and did all kinds of wonderful things. Also, the streetlights would pour in this really wonderful yellow light at night.

There was even more to the piece. Vogel, who had sealed the bricks together with mastic, intentionally left out some of the mortar in the head joints in order to create the pattern of a star chart of the winter sky. From inside the building the constellations—spread out across the thirteen-by-nine-foot wall—twinkled and flickered as automobile lights flashed against the panes of the storefront window.

As with *Blue Flame,* the entire life cycle of the work became integral to it:

When I finally took Death in Venice *down brick by brick, I let all the silt and chinks fall to the ground, as I had with* Blue Flame. *On both sides of the wall, there was silted, colored dust that was a metaphor for the manner in which time erodes all things. I very delicately walked across the silt and chinks in a tiny little path, carrying the bricks out the door, so that I never disturbed it.*

In the very last photograph I took of the work, the sunrise was coming in through the window. As the wall between the studio and the outside windows finally came down and all the light poured in through the window, you could see a kind of landscape on the floor created from the colored silt and tiny fragments of brick. Then I shot it at night. The golden light from the street was glaring in, making the darkness gold. It was like a Martian landscape with just a few footprints in it—like the footprints of the first man who landed on the moon. I titled it Midnight on Mars.

One August day I was coming down from the hard, bitter region of whiteness, where gusts of sleet were swirling and storms were building up. I knew that all too soon various things would keep me from returning to that celestial country of jagged ridges dancing in the open sky; to the illusion of high and low places in the white cornices that were etched against the blue-black abyss overhead and slowly crumbled in the midafternoon silence; and to the slopes carved with ridges and glistening with ice where grapeshot suddenly explodes with the smell of sulfur. Once again I had wanted to sniff the greenish breath of a crevasse, explore a boulder's surface, slip between crumbling rocks, secure a rope, test the rise and fall of an uncertain wind, listen to the sound of steel on ice and the little crystalline clumps tumbling toward the pitfall of a hidden crevasse— a death trap powdered and draped with gems. I wanted to make a track in the diamonds and the flour, entrust myself to two strands of hemp, and eat prunes in the center of space.

■ **René Daumal, *Mt. Analogue: A Novel of Symbolically Authentic Non-Euclidean Adventures in Mountain Climbing*, trans. Roger Shattuck (Baltimore: Penguin, 1974), p. 118.**

The work was monumental, impressive, and not a little frightening. Clearly, Vogel was working within the arena of Light and Space. She was also among the first of those artists to add color to her pieces (as opposed to creating works out of colored light—as Turrell, for example, was doing). Additionally, with this work, there was an overriding sense of beauty for beauty's sake and a profound sense of metaphor. Melinda Wortz noted:

> Vogel's work demands time and perceptual attentiveness. From it we discover what we bring to looking, feeling, hearing; what these perceptual processes are at their fundamental nature when they become meditative, insightful activities. In Rinzai Zen practice meditators sit facing a blank wall. I strongly recommend Vogel's wall as the embarkation point for a personal, interior journey.
>
> The installation does not dominate its environment, but rather, makes everything that is there accessible to us in all its richness and beauty.[5]

Still Live
Four Corners, New Mexico, 1978–79

Perhaps after having metaphorically faced death, Vogel felt it necessary to affirm life. She chose to do so away from Venice and in a transitory fashion.

In Four Corners, at the point where four states meet, Vogel inscribed the following words one after another on the desert sands, to be dispersed by the wind and rain:

ALWAYS	FOREVER	SUBLIME
SURVIVAL	MUSCLE	CONSCIENCE
TRANSCENDENCE	MONEY	POWER

As she later noted:

> *Four Corners, New Mexico, is the most ancient seat of civilization in the Northern hemisphere. It is a strange place, with mystical, eroded earth, which looks more like a Martian landscape than anything I have ever seen. The sea had been there and gone, and the earth had drifted away.*
>
> *I got a geographic survey, which told me the exact place where those four corners met, and I created the work in exactly that spot.*
>
> *What I did was to take all the pigment I had been using and had it ground up by a steamroller. Then I put the powdered pigment into containers and took them out to the desert. I mixed the pigment with water, and then I drew the words that were interesting to me that had power. Each word as big as a football field, and it took tons of pigment just to do one word. And sometimes, just as I would get a whole word written, a big wind would come up and blow it all away. It was wonderful! Sometimes words would remain for days or weeks, and sometimes only for a few hours. But you knew that nature was always going to eventually take the work away with it.*

Point Conception, Leadwall,* and *Lead Barrier Reef
Fine Art Gallery, University of California, Irvine, 1979–80

Melinda Wortz noted about Vogel's Irvine show that it

> paired a five-foot-high wall, comprising pink pastel blocks, with a low wall constructed of large lead bricks. The two walls ran parallel to each other for thirty feet, the width of the gallery. Both were massive and seemingly ephemeral at the same time, literally rubbing off on people's fingers when touched. Their intriguing perceptual contradictions—mass against lightness, solidity against delicacy—were also inherent in the different perceived qualities of light and space.[6]

In 1979–80 Vogel was pregnant with her first child and she wanted to bring some of that experience into a major installation of her work.

> Point Conception *was all about.... the softness of motherhood and babies, and becoming a mother, and the fact that one of the biggest barriers we have to get over is the fear of projecting our future selves onto the world in the form of a child. I was scared and protective about being a mother—that's what the peach wall was all about.*
>
> *For obvious reasons, I was scared of people running up to my wall and touching it or backing into it. The thought was so horrible that I decided to put a lead barrier reef in front of the wall to protect it, because it was such an ethereal construction. I knew intimately about barrier reefs because I had lived in Hawaii for six years, and the first reef out was the reef that protected the whole cove that we lived in.*

In the 1980s my husband and I lived in Lewiston, California, just outside of Weaverville, on Star Route 1. It was there we decided to conceive a child. We had a house on the side of a creek. I built a redwood deck for the house that hung out over the water. I dammed up the creek with bricks and changed its course, so that it flowed and rippled under the deck and under the special bed I had built out there.

I conceived there, under the dappled trees to the sound of the breeze, with the sound of the stream and the sunlight pouring through the leaves. I wanted to hold onto that whole feeling, that sensibility, and so that is why I created the U.C. Irvine pieces, *Point Conception* and *Lead Barrier Reef,* the way I did. I was pregnant with my child, Rio, while I was working on *Point Conception.*

■ Susan Kaiser Vogel

Vogel made a strange construction of lead bricks that had originally been used for radiation protection. They were inordinately heavy, weighing thirty pounds each. Having become nicked and damaged, they had been transferred to ships to be used as ballast. The lead bricks also had alchemical associations, which became an element in Vogel's metaphor.

Some of the work's original meaning was lost because the gallery floors were not strong enough to support the immense weight of the lead wall. A compromise of sorts was reached: the final piece was a five-foot-two-inch-tall wall of peach bricks, dusted and softly scraped with peach-colored chalk; a one-brick-tall wall of lead bricks ran parallel in front of it. Inadvertently Vogel had made a work that was simultaneously of greater fragility and greater strength than the one she had originally conceived. Peter Clothier said of it:

> We're presented, then, with two horizons—or, rather two thresholds—which invite our eyes to penetrate the ambient light and space beyond them. The first, the lower, presents the greater obstacle. Its heaviness and darkness insist, both optically and psychologically, on a shift from our earthbound, gravitational weight in preparation for the now easier leap over a second, quasi-magical, chest-high, light-strong wall into the space beyond—a space made ethereal, in part by its physical separation from us, in part by its shimmering whiteness.[7]

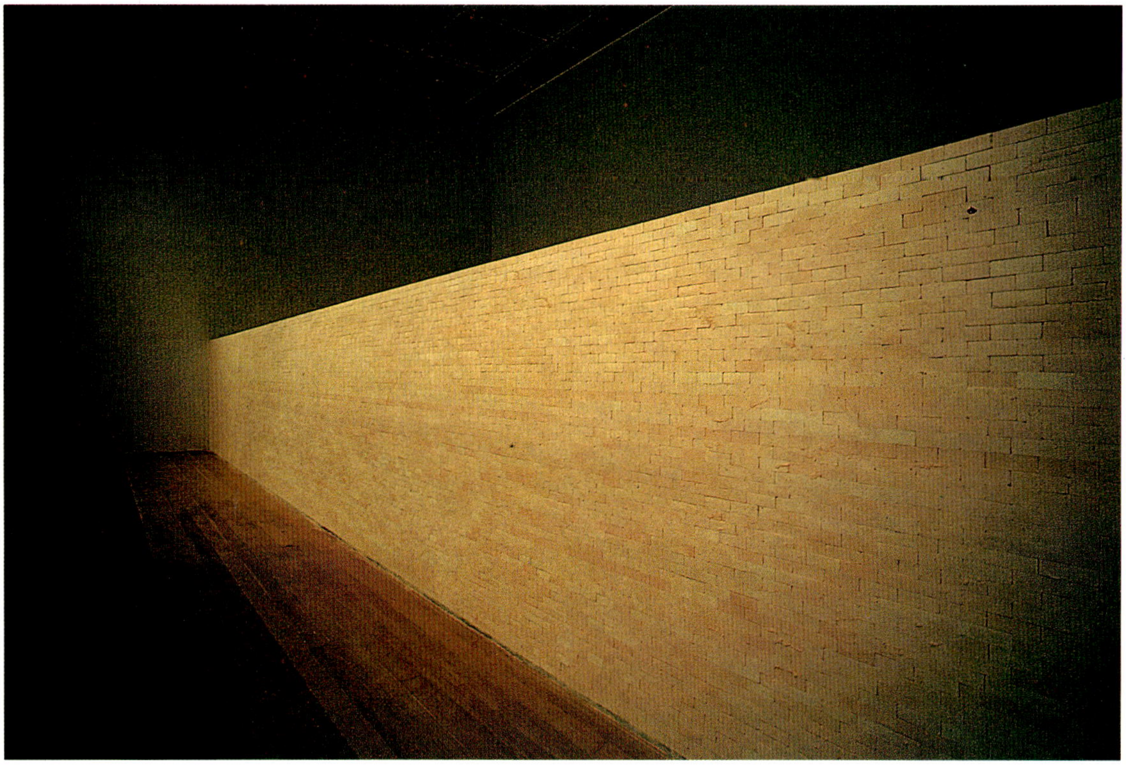

At the time that these pieces were being constructed, Vogel was fascinated by the structural implications of the human body and its place in the history of art. During the building of *Point Conception* and *Barrier Reef* she began to experiment with her sculpture. She activated it by orchestrating a performance in Irvine's gallery that incorporated a seventeenth-century Japanese flute piece by Kurasawa Kinko and a performance piece by the body builder Lisa Lyon. Lyon—clothed only in dull silvery graphite and accompanied by a bamboo flute—slowly performed a posed piece in front of Vogel's walls.

When I picked Lisa Lyon to work with my piece, it was at the time that she was working on her physical being as a statement of her soul. She feels beauty is very important in relation to the aesthetic statement of the soul. I didn't even know Lisa at that time; I had just seen her in a photograph. I realized she had taken that form and that medium of sculptural body building in order to make a statement about the body that was a legacy of a sense of perfection that reached its height in the Renaissance.

The use of Lisa also tied in with the use of the sculpture of David *on the roof of the building across the street in* Death in Venice. *I felt she was a perfect representation of beauty in the female form and that what she was doing in terms of defying gravity was a metaphor for what I was doing in an art medium, rather than with my body. I wanted to use her literally as a figure against my ground. I have always felt that my sculptures were like grounds of being. Without the human figure in interaction—whether individual figures in a crowd or Lisa, specifically, performing before them—they seem dull and lifeless.*

In the performance Richard Keeling played a work by Kurasawa Kinko. Lisa performed a series of very slow muscle movements to the sounds of music. It was like a still life becoming a living life for a moment, and then taking a fixed pose, and then making a transition to another one, and then taking a fixed pose again—so that it was a living, moving, breathing kind of thing. Everyone was overwhelmed by its beauty.

Susan Kaiser Vogel
Point Conception
Masonry bricks, lead bricks,
length: 30 ft. (9.1 m.)
Installation, Fine Art Gallery,
University of California, Irvine,
1979–80

About this curious yet compelling work, John Lombardi wrote:

> The piece was called *Contemporary Alchemy: Evolution Ritual* and was meant to evoke "the endless energy within woman." Staged over several hours in 22 poses that moved as imperceptibly as a glacier while sounds of rain, flapping clothes and random speech wove a "female" mood, it attempted to surpass even the most advanced notions of art: "The whole physical world is our bodies," Kaiser Vogel explains now, and what Lisa was doing, posing in gold paint, was "integrating" herself by becoming "real" before the audience's eyes, an image, a golden statue, confounding "reality" by *moving*. The perfection of her body, her narcissism, were "traps" where most of the audience got "caught," but these were only "way stations" on a journey to "clarity." "Lisa knew that to really see, you had to confront your own darkness—sexual, emotional and intellectual—and in those days she was fearless. In fact, she's the only person I've ever met—and I was with Tim Leary for five years—who could make darkness visible to everyone who saw her."[8]

Susan Kaiser Vogel
WoMan, 1981
Bronze, 76 x 18 x 1 in.
(193 x 45.7 x 2.5 cm)
Installation, San Francisco
Art Institute, 1982

WoMan and Companion (Space and Time)
in *White Tent: En Route to Mt. Analogue*
Santa Barbara Contemporary Arts Forum
Santa Barbara, California, 1981

This was one of the first installations at the newly formed Santa Barbara Contemporary Arts Forum.

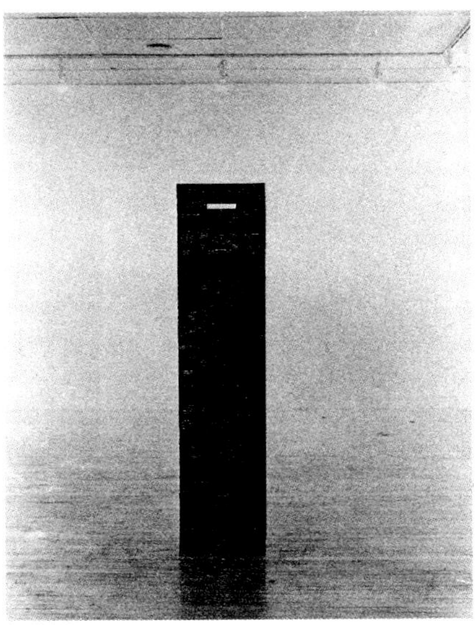

> Vogel's piece, fabricated especially for this exhibition with the technical assistance of Jack Brogan . . . [was] constructed of nearly 450 tiny one-by-three-inch high bronze bricks. The work is six feet two inches high, 18 inches wide and one inch thick. Sixty-nine inches from the floor, a beveled window or "eye" piece pierces the metal surface, opening its continuous mass to the space it occupies. . . . The artist lit the surrounding walls rather than the sculpture itself [and thus] . . . it basks mysteriously in ambient light without casting shadows.[9]

Deeply influenced by *Mt. Analogue*, written by the French Surrealist René Daumal in 1943, Vogel created a work that began to bare her inner and outer selves. This was not an easy undertaking at a time when personal content in art was still taboo and women's struggles made a great subject for feminist articles but were not yet that acceptable in the art-world mainstream.

In this work, cast in bronze, the bricks form a tall, thin, symbolic figure (the WoMan, Vogel) and her companion (Vogel's inner self)—within the "white tent" of the gallery. At first

I asked him, "What do you mean by 'analogical mountain climbing'?"

It's the art of. . . .

What is an art?

The value of danger:
temerity -----► suicide
Short of it, no satisfaction.

What is danger?

What is prudence?

What is a mountain?

For a mountain to play the role of Mount Analogue, I concluded,* its summit must be inaccessible, but its base accessible *to human beings as nature has made them. It must be* unique, *and it must* exist geographically. *The door to the invisible must be visible . . .* its persuasive significance [is] a *way uniting Earth and Heavens.

■ **René Daumal, *Mt. Analogue: A Novel of Symbolically Authentic Non-Euclidean Adventures in Mountain Climbing*, trans. Roger Shattuck (Baltimore: Penguin, 1974), pp. 42, 116.**

seeming to embody an exquisite Minimalism, this work could suddenly be perceived as metaphysically complex.

As thingness began to move into the works of Light and Space, it became apparent that what Douglas Wheeler called "the white-room syndrome" was not at all what it had seemed to be. There has always been content in works of Light and Space—content of a phenomenal sort, which is experiential rather than literal. Slowly but surely, as the 1980s unfolded, it became apparent to one artist after another that the most reductive aspects of this kind of work did not constitute its entirety. Although very often the works by many of these people were most powerful when they were most ethereal or ephemeral, the opposite also began to prove true. Now, however, the works were radically different from before—the exquisiteness of the experiential lessons could never be forgotten, and thingness had taken on a new metaphysical power.

This Side and Beyond, Plumb Blossom Domain
Malinda Wyatt Gallery, Venice, California, 1983

For this installation Vogel's wall was constructed of cement blocks, which she chose as one of the least expensive and most accessible building materials. She also wanted to convey the metaphor of "the building blocks of life." Rubbing individual blocks with chalk in a seemingly random fashion, she gave them a rich, almost gestural surface, which was highlighted by beams of sun through the gallery's skylights.

The wall was large: twenty-seven feet long and twelve feet tall. As in *Death in Venice,* light flowed over the top of it, softly, like a wave. In the center of the wall Vogel placed a window six feet four inches above the floor—above most viewers' line of vision. The blocks framed the window in a cruciform shape, imbuing the piece with a curious religiosity. Directly in front of the wall Vogel placed a strange, exquisite piece of wood rubbed with pigment the color of dark blood. This element seemed to complete the work, taking its shape from the window in the wall, from which it seemed to have fallen. Wortz's sense of the piece came close to that of the artist:

> [Vogel] titled the piece *Plumb Blossom Domain,* the blossom referring to the rich, red, faceted wooden jewel lying loose and vulnerable on the floor, in contrast to the tightly ordered mass of the wall. With its modular and cellular structure, Vogel conceives of the wall as a metaphor for the nervous system. It embodies the present. The second element in the installation, the blossom/jewel, isolated and fallen, referred to the past: lost youth, innocence, chastity. The window, in turn, opened to the future with clarity and brilliance.[10]

The artist was clearly moving toward greater visual and metaphorical complexity, which she achieved with even more rigorous economy of means in her next work.

Susan Kaiser Vogel
This Side and Beyond, Plumb Blossom Domain
Cement blocks, wood, wall: 12 x 27 ft. (3.6 x 8.2 m.)
Installation, Malinda Wyatt Gallery, Venice, California, 1983

The Master of High Drama **in Venice Biennale, June–September 1984 and in *No Nuclear Bombs* Japanese-American Cultural and Community Center, Los Angeles, 1985**

Presented in the context of largely minimal work by other Light and Space artists, Vogel's *Master of High Drama* seemed initially to share that minimalism. But it was, in fact, a chilling metaphor. Each of us is aware of the implications of the nuclear-bomb-releasing red button, wherever in the world it may be. In both installations of *The Master of High Drama,* Vogel wanted to make a powerful and universal statement about the possibility of nuclear warfare: "*The Master of High Drama* was my first twentieth-century icon. It was the first time that in addition to my individual aesthetic and psychic pre-occupations I achieved a universal symbol or metaphor."[11]

The Master of High Drama, though visually simple, turned out to be an extremely complicated piece to do in Venice. Following the technical advice of Jack Brogan, who is the fabrication wizard for most of the L.A. artists, Vogel shipped a freighter full of drywall from America to build a space to house her piece. The site assigned to her, off the Giudecca (which runs roughly parallel to the Grand Canal), was extremely difficult: it was not plumb, for one thing, and it was extremely dark and dingy. Its proportions were disastrous: it could have housed a small ship. The doors were sixteen feet tall, with skylights above them, and the corridor was one hundred fifty feet long, fifty feet wide, and fifty feet tall. Those were impossible proportions for just about any work, and Vogel's was small enough to fit in the palms of two hands.

Vogel and Brogan cleaned up the space, rebuilt it with drywall, and opened the skylight—which had been tarred over—so that a little slit of light came in at the front of the corridor and filtered down all the way to the back, where the red button, *The Master of High Drama,* was located.

This installation marked the first public showing of what Vogel refers to generically as her "heat signature recognition pieces."

> *I wanted to do a piece that dealt with the heat that comes from the body—or from a star when it is emitting energy.*
>
> *This button was* hot *when you put your hand on it. Very hot. In the darkened space at the Biennale you could put your hand up to it, and the light would reflect on your hand—it would then reflect the shadow of your hand and your whole body. If you stood in front of it, it would reflect the shadow of the entire silhouette of your body back onto the plane behind it. The heat aspect was very powerful.*

The implications of Vogel's metaphor were quickly understood, and this work was shown at the Japanese-American Cultural and Community Center in Los Angeles for the fortieth remembrance of Hiroshima, in a show entitled *No Nuclear Bombs.* In that installation as well were Vogel's *Mother and Child,* made of exquisitely rubbed and finished woods: the mother figure of deep ruby red and the child a tawny gold. Human size, they stood both as guards and as mute witnesses to the dread red button.

The Moon Room

former space of Malinda Wyatt Gallery, New York, 1986

Desiring a space she could control, Vogel rented a temporary site of her own that had been vacated by the regrettably short-lived Malinda Wyatt Gallery (where Vogel had held a crowded, not altogether resolved, yet highly interesting exhibition in early 1985).

> The Moon Room *was an extension of the other works I had done, but instead of being a whole volume, where the viewer is actually in the whole volume—the square and the squared circle became enormously interesting for me. When I did this in the East Village, I was dealing with the frontal plane again, and I wanted to project a light/energy field out through the storefront window onto the street. So I did the circle as a frontal image of light radiation. The circle was* The Moon Room. *I cut into the wall from behind, so that it emitted light from the plane in such a way that the wall, which functions and looks almost like a scrim, emits a light all the way down to the floor and over to the edge. There is a light box behind the drywall and a piece of glass behind the drywall, which is almost like a Larry Bell glass. It has a deposition of gold, which keeps the drywall from catching on fire—like the radiation shields on the helmets of men who go to the moon—it has a vapor deposition of gold, to keep them from getting their eyes burned.*

Somewhere along the line, Vogel began to examine her impulse to work abstractly, and the mid-to-late 1980s was a period of entrenchment for her. There were times when she produced no work (or at least none that was exhibited), but she was not idle. She began a serious study of sculpture through the ages, and then she started a study of her own sculptures, combining abstraction with figuration and using the body builder Lisa Lyon as a model—nearly a decade after Lyon's performance piece done in conjunction with Vogel's *Point Conception*. This sculptural work—which I have seen only in process—seemed curiously unresolved. Having earlier worked so successfully with the nude Lyon, Vogel seemed unable to let go of her as a muse in the new work and utilized her figure in too literal a way.

In the summer heat, in a steamy studio in Venice, California, I watched Vogel cover Lyon's body with malleable lead, shaping it over her body as if it were an armature. This was to be one of the figures for a work in progress entitled *Captives of Gravity: Figures Emerging from the Gravitational Plane* (1987–89), also known as *Even Sunshine Threatens Death*. Shown climbing upward, frantically attempting to defy gravity, the figure clawed its way up the side of a pit formed by Vogel's now-iconic bricks.

It was captivating, but it didn't work. Technically, the work was problematic—it was hot under the lead, and claustrophobic. More troublesome, however, was that the lead tended to soften and lose important nuances after Lyon crawled out from under it. The piece did not represent "consciousness becoming material," as Vogel wished—it was simply too literal. Yet something crucial was happening. "The state of consciousness has clarity at a precise moment," Vogel says. "I was unconscious at first—but now there is clarity. Every different state of art is a different state of consciousness. My consciousness then translates into material."

Susan Kaiser Vogel
Drawing for "The Bicameral Mind,"
1991
Giuseppe Panza di Biumo,
Varese, Italy

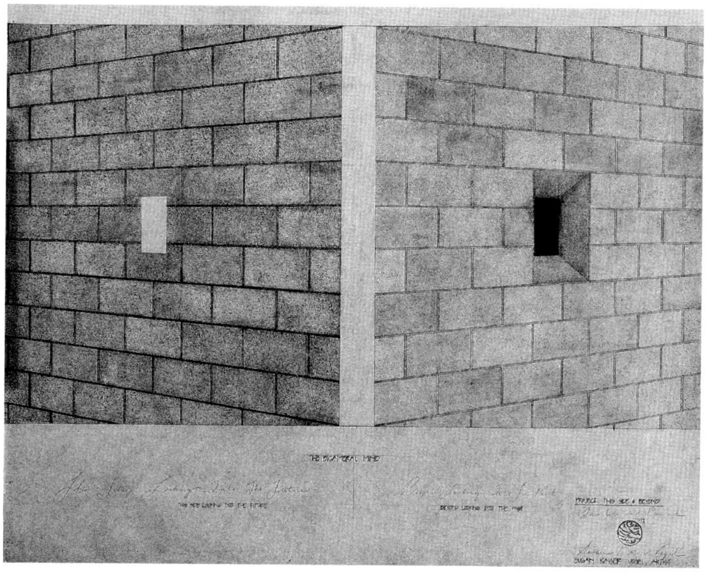

In the late 1980s Vogel received a copy of the *I Ching* as a gift, and after studying it for some time, she became profoundly interested in it. She threw the *I Ching* for eight successive days. "The same cards came up every time," Vogel says, "and there are only eight cards like that in black and white in the *I Ching*!" There is an order and a symmetry in Vogel's work that she saw in the *I Ching.* After having thrown the *I Ching* those eight times, she made a series of drawings representing precise states of mind that she wanted to turn into individual works. Vogel then began to write haiku for each of the eight responses, and she titled the entire group of poems *Eight Days in May.* Her notebooks are filled with aphorisms that arose as a result of this process—aphorisms such as "How you enter into where you are depends on your point of view," and "The symbol *is* the meaning."

Vogel has conceived of a work, also called *Eight Days in May,* made of hot steel or cold-rolled steel elements (one is black and one is white). The work is still in progress, and Vogel is also considering using brass in it, because brass takes patina beautifully in pinks, purples, and greens. She anticipates that the various elements in the work will be five-eighths of an inch thick and seven feet long. Each element will have a different coloration and slightly different dimensions, with the whole piece taking shape in eight rooms. The long metal bands will be inlaid into the drywall, located between the ceiling and the floor, with eleven feet five inches between them.

Also continuing to work with her trademark bricks, Vogel has used them to frame a metaphor as well as to create a sculpture. One of her newest works, *The Bicameral Mind*, is still in proposal form. Acquired by Count Panza, it is a two-sided sculpture. One wall has a white aperture, the other frames a black one—each is set dead center into a wall of brick. One side (the one with the aperture) looks into the future, the other looks into the past. Above, two skylights flood the space with sunlight. The light is most intense in the center of the room then drifts off, becoming thinner at the edges.

Susan Kaiser Vogel
Quiet Kan, October 1990
Drawing for installation, room size to be: $11^{2}/_{3}$ x $14^{1}/_{4}$ x 23 ft.
(3.5 x 4.3 x 7 m.)
Giuseppe Panza di Biumo,
Varese, Italy

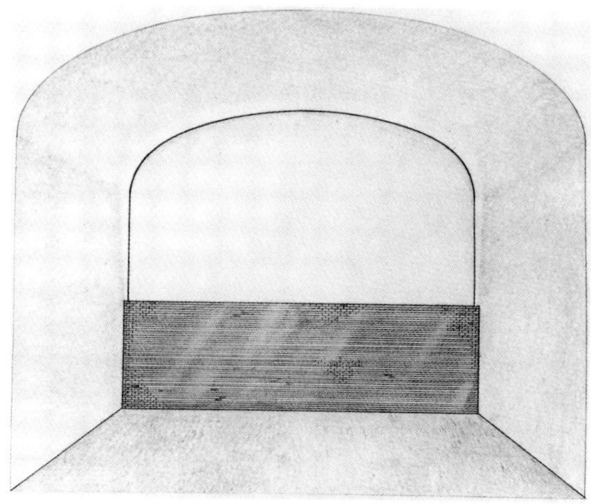

There are several other important pieces still in proposal form that were also acquired by Count Panza in 1991. These are all room-environment pieces created especially for his site in Varese. As in *The Bicameral Mind* the "walls" that make up the focal point of each piece are to be set out slightly from the walls that define the space. *Quiet Kan* is set out only three inches; *Red Scream* is set out eight feet; and *Stormy Sea with a Clearing in the Clouds* is set out ten feet from the load-bearing walls. Not figurative in any sense of the word, the works are exquisite abstractions. Vogel's expression "sensual minimalism" suits them well.

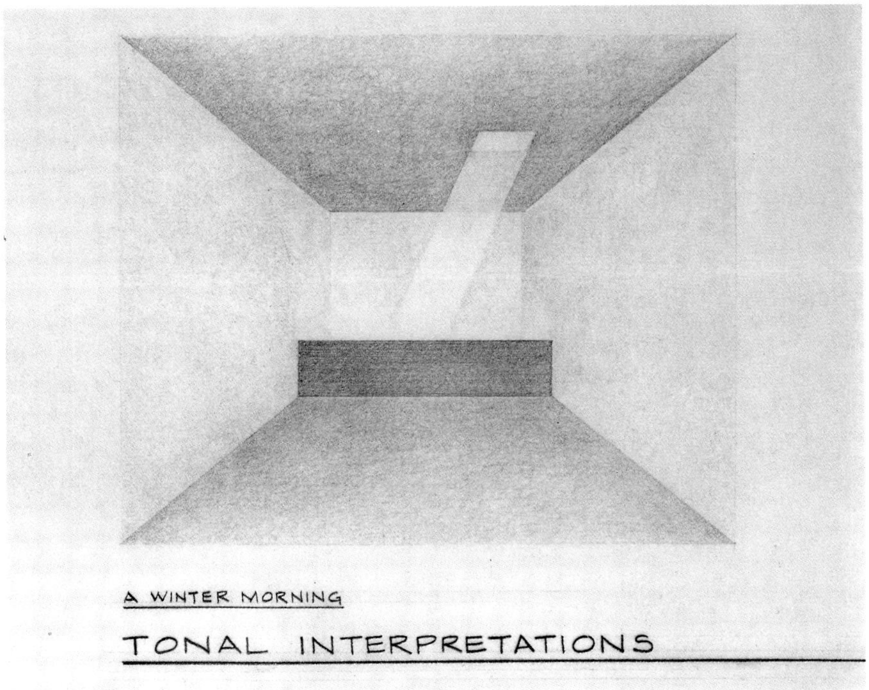

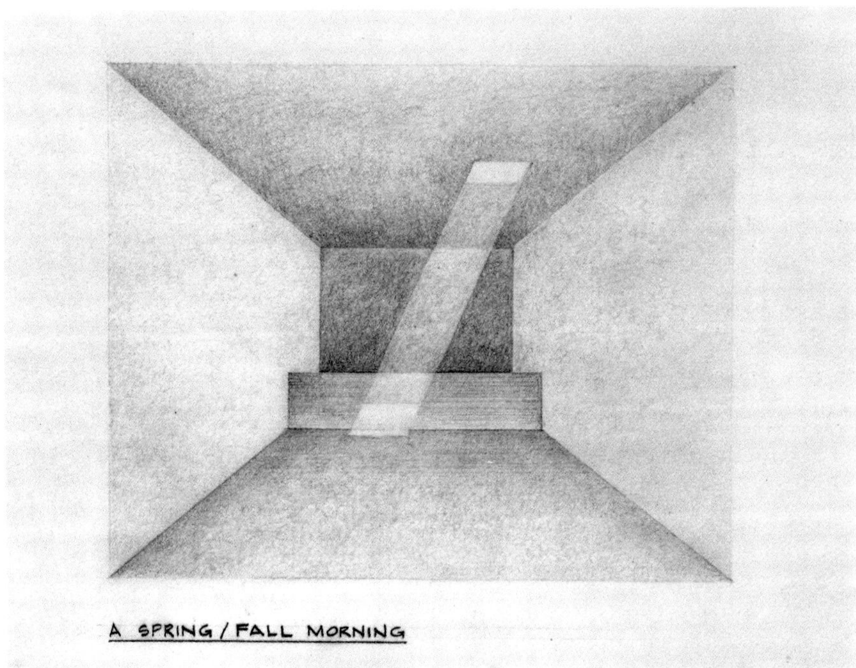

Susan Kaiser Vogel
Stormy Sea with a Clearing in the Clouds, 1991
Drawings for installation

Hap Tivey

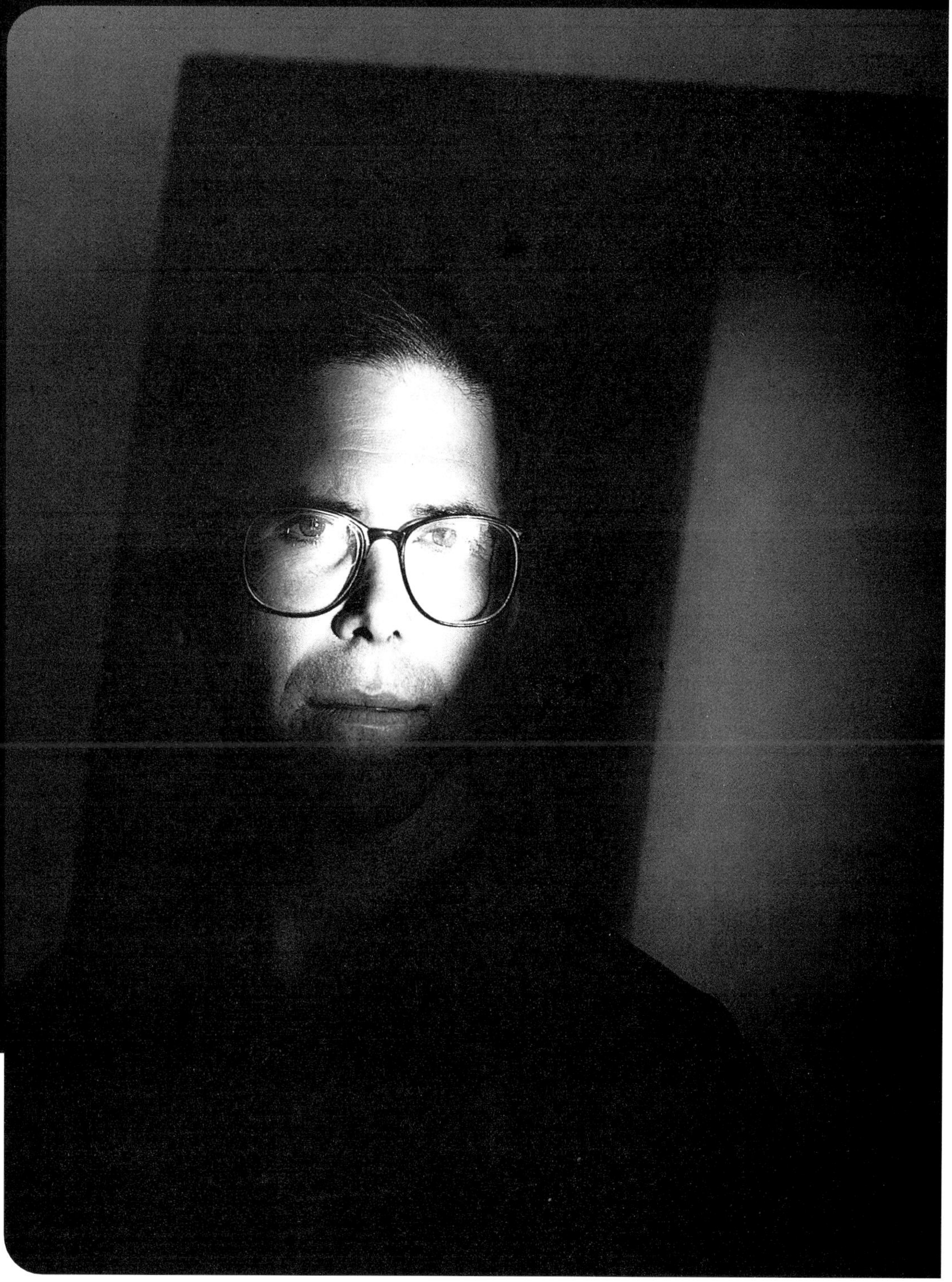

Wretched fear of wrong art haunts the city. Sloughed formalist trappings lie around the shelves of cut-rate book stores and They appear on the street newly garbed as adversaries—agents of the People. We're still rummaging through the old rules, feeling around the undergarments and side pockets for the right wrongness that proceeds from the tradition of the century. We're hoping for something tough, a subtle thing and capable, but this endless perfecting of art that's not wrong has led to outrageous alternatives; a pounding of water with heavy hammers, we try to thin it out in hopes that later we may use dilute versions in subtle experiments or perfumes. They demand it. New York has had the Force long enough to change the rule book and the code of ethics. Now that the old guard has joined the vigilante groups, it's a cold wind.

Hap Tivey, "Notice to the Force," 1976

Hap Tivey

Hap Tivey spent a year, 1974–75, in serious study at the Hofuku-ji Zen monastery in Japan. He had met Joshu Sasaki Roshi and begun practicing Rinzai Zen in 1967; the next year he met Sibayama Roshi and his disciple Gensho Fukushima. (Tivey also studied privately with Fukushima while the master was studying the bible at Claremont College in Southern California in 1977.) At the end of his year in Japan, Tivey returned to the United States and made the decision to live and make art in New York. His dedication to practicing Zen has had a profound effect on all aspects of his life and work, but it has manifested itself most specifically in the simplicity and purity of his art and in its spiritual, meditative qualities.

There is a gentle serenity to Tivey that sets him apart. At the time of our first meeting, in the mid-1970s, he seemed more a visitor from some forested planet than an inner-city dweller. During various periods of his life he has lived out of doors—in the desert, in a garden, in a tree-house in the mountains. But there is another, more conventionally cerebral aspect to Tivey as well: he entered Pomona College in 1965 as a physics major, with a scholarship from Lockheed Aircraft. He later changed his major from physics to math and eventually, during his last year in school, he moved from math to art.

As unusually diverse as those involvements may seem, they are compatible with current investigations into left-brain/right-brain thinking, which have proven that the right brain controls not only intuitive and artistic activities but math and spatial relationships as well. It seems almost as if Tivey has developed both his right brain and his left brain attributes to the same degree. He first conceives a work intuitively, then his capacity for discerning spatial relationships gives him what he needs to construct his works as environments, and his mathematical knowledge enables him to map out the complex sequences for the lighting that is so often a part of the work.

During the period of Tivey's first intense involvement with Zen, art experiences were also taking place in his life. In 1967 he began to study drawing with the sculptor John Mason; two years later he met Mowry Baden, an artist who creates situational sculptures to be participated in—often kinesthetically. At that point Tivey stopped painting and made stretched three-sided canvases that enclosed a space large enough be walked into. He had two shows of these large painting-sculptures while at Pomona College. Also during this time, with the Vietnam War raging, Tivey was classified as a conscientious objector. He moved to the California desert and began to work out his time doing alternative service at Angel View Crippled Children's Foundation. For the next two years Tivey "lived alone in a Datsun pickup truck in the desert, practiced Za-Zen and maintained correspondence with Gensho Fukushima in Japan."[1] He created Zen images on the sand dunes, which were taken by the wind.

Tivey's first complete gallery installation, *Black Room,* was composed with black light for the University of British Columbia in 1971. He described it as "black, like Ad Reinhardt's paintings were black."[2] That year Tivey met James Turrell, and after returning to Claremont Graduate School, Tivey "had an exhibition of light sculptures and built fire tunnels." He was a teaching assistant for Turrell at Claremont, compiling a resource text on light for Turrell's class and creating several searchlight works in conjunction with the older artist. Tivey also began private showings of his kerosene-lamp projections that year in his cabin on Mount Baldy, just north of Claremont.

Fire Pieces
various locations, including Vancouver; Boulder, Colorado; Pueblo, New Mexico; Tampa, Florida; Irvine, California; New York; and Miami, 1972–73

Tivey's first *Fire Pieces* were done in collaboration with James Turrell. The initial pieces utilized searchlights, which played off the surfaces of tunnels large enough to contain a number of people. Powerful, blinding, these pieces immersed the spectators in light. Subsequent pieces utilized phosphorous flares only, often in a simple configuration on the ground.

The *Fire Pieces* were all one-time light spaces created for a specific audience. Some of the flare pieces lasted for no more than ten minutes, and some were performed several times in one evening. Powerful because of their intensity and size (one tunnel piece was close to three stories high), these works were simple yet effective low-tech solutions to the problem of working with light on a very large scale. They gave both Tivey and Turrell something to work against in developing more durable pieces.

In 1972 Tivey met Douglas Wheeler, whose work, like Turrell's, was to have a deep effect on him. One year later Tivey built his *First Situation:* a "sixth-frequency" geodesic dome (a dome of this type has so many facets that it is almost spherical) with an enveloping low-light environment. Tivey's controlled use of light in such room-environment installations makes him, without question, a Light and Space artist. Though he now lives in New York, he was nurtured in

If Haskell was most profoundly affected by the sense of light, Melinda Wortz found the profundity of the piece to lie in a kind of denial of space, recalling "an intense purple-lavender color which is accompanied by a sense of rushing or collapsing space...the limitless void wherein bliss is experienced."[6] Wortz also noted:

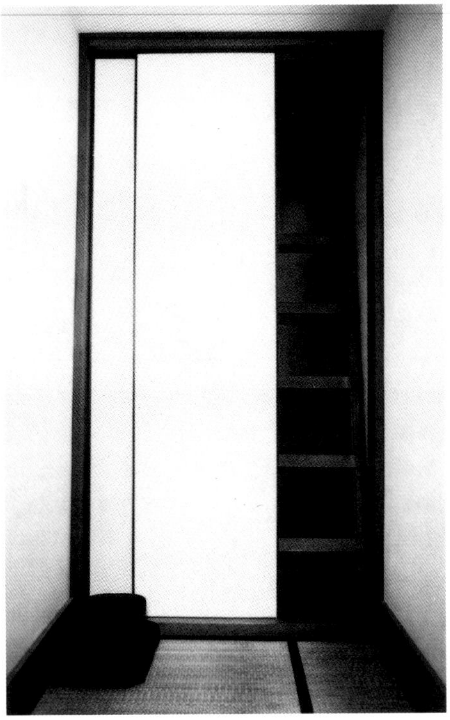

> Tivey thinks of his manipulations of space and color, and apparent and fabricated structure, as compositions, like music or even painting. The feeling of composition comes from the relationships between the viewer and the space, which are judged by density and color. He compares some of the different spatial sensations he is dealing with to the difference between closing one's eyes and then opening them to look at the sky.[7]

After participants had experienced the initial space, Tivey would take them back into the garden:

> *I used to spend about two hours with people.... We'd have tea and we'd talk and go on and look at one thing and then we'd have tea and talk and go look at another thing, and then we would have tea and talk again.... It was a kind of aesthetic service I was performing. I would talk with people for a while, and then I would decide what kind of a room I would show them next. I could tell quite a bit about them by then.*

When I made the light in the Pasadena studio, I would always think of it in three aspects: the *space* of the light, the *color* of the light, and the *density* of the light. So that, for example, some lights would have the kind of infinitude that the sky does, and then there would be the color of the light—which is obvious, and then there would be the density, which is something else altogether. It's difficult to program and it's difficult to predict... but if you have a certain adaptive period and then you lay a new stimulus over that, the combination of those two is what really created the experience.

■ Hap Tivey

The upper room in the Pasadena space was the most subtle. Here the participant sat, with his attention directed to three plain white walls. Behind the viewer was a platform and a number of exquisitely crafted wooden slats that went from floor to ceiling. One bore Oriental calligraphy that translated as "light has no back." The artist sat on the platform, and as he deftly made slight but very specific adjustments in the alignment of the slats, beams of tungsten light from a hidden source poured in between them. Sometimes almost yellow, sometimes blue, the intense light made bright lines on the walls. It also spilled into the ambient space, which was already colored with diffused light from the window in an adjacent room, adding to its intensity. These changes in the light and in the space itself were mysterious, intangible.

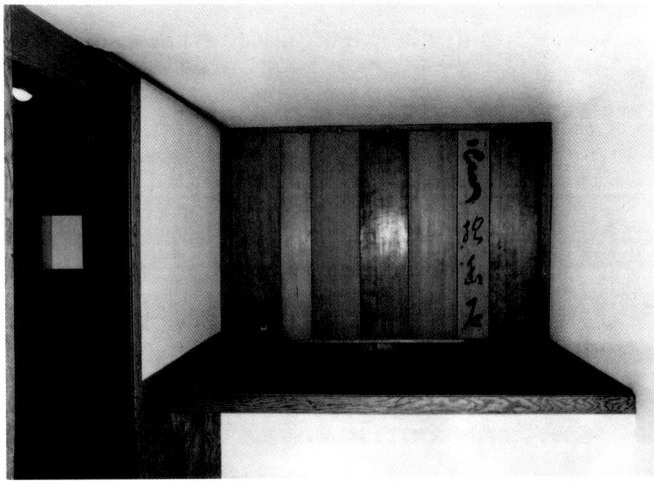

Opposite, top
Hap Tivey
Second Situation, 1973–74
Room below aperture room, with ladder connecting upper and lower rooms

Opposite, bottom
Hap Tivey
Second Situation, 1973–74
Upper room
Calligraphy reads
"Light has no back."

There were actually five rooms at the Dayton Street studio that contained light works, but most visitors took part in only two. (When participants went from the lower room with the Ganzfeld to the upper room, they passed through the three others as well.) The other rooms demanded such great sensitivity and preparedness that few perceived them, but for a select few Tivey would specify where in these intervening rooms they should sit and then present special pieces for them or direct them toward the pieces. One of these rooms had a window through which the participant could see the projection of light on the opposite wall. Another room contained a ladder to the upper and lower rooms and an enormous ground-glass window. The room could be altered by changing the space above it. In this piece, shapes of light would seem to hang on the window; in reality they were on the wall, four feet behind it. There was calligraphy on the vertical slats in these lower rooms as well, which translated as "white clouds on an ancient peak."

The generosity of a private donor enabled Tivey to construct the works and to keep the studio open for almost six months. Well over three hundred people participated in the work before he had to close it for lack of money to pay the rent. Because of the extreme complexity of this piece and because it took place before I was aware of the artist's existence, his description is particularly useful:

> *The Dayton Street studio in Pasadena was a complex of four light rooms and a garden, which acted as an intermission site between viewings. Of the two ground floor rooms, the Ganzfeld room was the most complex visual experience; the second room was a transition zone to the upper projection rooms, and its light character appeared only in night viewings. In the daytime, a twelve-foot translucent window flooded this room with sunlight, but at night a luminous shape projected through a portal in an upper wall. This portal also diffused light from the transition room window up into the second story in daylight, or acted as a viewing window at night. The principal light space of the ground floor, the Ganzfeld, was reached by way of a short flight of stairs and a narrow hall. A doorway opened from the hall, and the tatami mat floor seemed to become a cliff hanging over a void. It projected four feet into an egg-shaped, seamless and evenly lit room. A guest would sit near the edge of the mat on a cushion and face directly into the void. Beyond the viewer's body and the floor, no material surface could be seen, and although the room was bright and filled with color, the space seemed infinite in every direction. This space was shown to hundreds of guests during the six months it remained open, and no more than a dozen ever saw the same sequence of color changes that produced the optical field. The program was usually changed every week. A typical experience of the program might have run something like this:*
>
> *We're surrounded by sky-light blue, thin, atmospheric. The sky slowly bleaches toward gray; it seems to pulsate, turning almost foggy. The light flickers briefly, and a background of red faintly appears in the fog. Suddenly the space is deep viscous red, very close and dense. The room is not dark, but the air seems almost tangible. The red slowly thins and the view seems deeper, but the color doesn't change. A minute passes. The color flickers and shifts to a lighter violet, but not homogeneous; the field seems to break up into fragments of pink and blue: a lattice, a crystal structure. The blue disappears; the red is supersaturated fog again. It brightens to orange in two steps, and suddenly the room is thin blue sky again. We're relaxed and calm. The sky remains unchanged though gradually less intense in color. We return to the garden.*

After a brief orientation to normal space, we visit our next room. After stopping in the transition room to view an optical sculpture overhead, we climb a ladder into the second floor. The first room we enter lets us look back at the projection we saw in the room below, but our view is partial and the projection has apparently changed shape. We can take a cushion and watch a variety of these volumes of light transform. The last room is connected by an open doorway through which these projections are cast.

The last space is long and narrow with white walls and ceiling. The back wall is a series of wooden panels separated by gaps of one centimeter or less. We sit on cushions facing away from these panels and toward a blank wall. The overhead light turns off, and as we adapt to the dark we find the blank wall illuminated by lines of light. Thin shafts of light projected through the gaps of the boarded wall create this luminous field. The program for this room also changed every week, but a typical sequence of projections might have been as follows:

The dark room is silent, lit only by two parallel lines that run floor to ceiling at the center of the wall in front of us. They appear faintly green. The space between them is dark, but the wall is visible, as are the corners where this back wall meets the side walls. Two more lines slowly move along the ceiling overhead until they meet the far wall then down the corners to the floor. They are faintly red and not parallel, angling from several inches off the side walls to just half an inch off the corners. The central lines darken and the walls seem to squeeze inward to the red lines. These illusionary planes on either side glow red, the far wall a reddish haze. The volume of the room is vague. The lines on the ceiling vanish and the far wall becomes a glowing fog. One thick but faint line appears dividing this field; it glows bluish. First the left, then the right red line vanishes. The blue/white line becomes a solid column glowing in a darkness without dimension. The room is too dark to see corners or differentiate the floor. The column pulses and expands slightly as the color turns white then green. It brightens and divides into two parallel lines. The details of the room reassert themselves in our visual field; the light becomes lines on a field of faint color and finally, joined by the faint red lines at the corners, appears like a luminous Barnett Newman painting, wall to wall—floor to ceiling. We return to the garden and tea before leaving.[8]

Third Situation
Tivey's Spring Street studio, New York, 1976–82

Tivey built *Third Situation* in his New York space after he returned from Japan. Since I have never seen the Spring Street piece, I prefer to have Tivey describe it himself:

The Spring Street studio continued the tradition of private viewings begun at Dayton Street and provided opportunities for showing extraordinary perceptual spaces and luminous surfaces. Less complex than the Pasadena format, the New York studio utilized two rooms installed on one side of a large living loft and a 9-by-12-foot rear-projection screen installed in one wall. The light sequences and configurations used in the two rooms varied continuously for a period of about five years and further developed the exploration of infinite color and low-intensity color projection. The screen was illuminated from behind by a wide variety of sources and acted as a laboratory for experiments in infinite light spaces bounded by frame and front surface.

> *The first of the two rooms was the smallest Ganzfeld-showing space I could construct. It served as a prototype for the Irvine installation [*Fourth Situation*], but included a small attached chamber for a second person to sit just behind the viewer. The programs of color sequence varied from moderately dramatic shifts, shown to most guests, to aggressively intense perceptions, shown only to guests with previous experience. The most unusual color fields utilized contrasts of pure color and near ultra-violets.*
>
> *The second room incorporated an exterior window into the smallest projection chamber I could construct, which could still accommodate two viewers simultaneously. It employed low-wattage tungsten sources and a street lamp outside the building to create vertical linear fields of colors and shifted planes. The projections coming through sensitive slits could be manually manipulated, and the most stunning image and fields vibrated with the blood flow and muscular tension of the operator's hand. The Menil installation [which was on Sixty-ninth Street in New York and has recently been dismantled] evolved out of this room.*
>
> *The screen evolved as a result of my frustration in trying to find support in New York for pure light experiences. A collector of contemporary painting and photography saw the two rooms and declared they provided one of the outstanding visual experiences in his life; he sincerely recounted the intensity of the color and uniqueness of the space. He then eagerly asked, "What kind of art do you make?"*
>
> *I then began devising methods to "frame" light on a surface. The 9-by-12-foot screen hinged like an enormous door before a 2-foot-deep recess in the wall. Within the recess, hundreds of configurations of light sources were used to create both static and changing color fields. This process of an optical surface interrupting a projection or stream of light seemed the most technologically modern method of painting. Rather than use an unordered* source *and order the reflective* surface*—i.e., arrange the pigment—I chose to order the source and forgo the reflection. Later screen paintings combined both processes, but the original screen idea evolved into a number of installations—among them* The Asians *at Otis, the Old U.S. Customs House in New York, P.S. 1, and the School for Visual Arts.*[9]

Third Situation is in many ways similar to *Fourth Situation,* with one important exception: the viewing distance is deeper.

> *There are two rooms of light in New York. One of them [*Third Situation*] is similar to the room of light I built at Irvine, but it's built so that somebody can sit a long way away from that light if they are uncomfortable. And then, once they become comfortable, they can go up and sit in it. It's really critical for a lot of people to have that kind of introduction, because they are simply not ready to have that direct a confrontation with their senses, without an intermediary rationale of a gestalt of the space they are encountering. So part of the reason why the larger room at Irvine [*Fourth Situation*] was constructed the way it was was to bring people to the light or give them a hint of it. It was important to somehow put the structure of that light into an environment they were accustomed to or that they could understand, and that they could analyze or even subconsciously analyze.*

Fourth Situation
in *Hap Tivey,* Fine Art Gallery, University of California, Irvine
April 2–May 8, 1976

The showings of *Second Situation* at Tivey's Pasadena studio had been private, arranged only by mail, and news of the piece traveled primarily by word of mouth. In spite of that, more than three hundred people saw the work, though the only real documentation of it was a sensitive article by Melinda Wortz.[10] With the presentation of *Fourth Situation* at the University of California, Irvine (where Wortz had become the gallery director), the number of viewers was far greater. The work was seen by a large portion of the West Coast art community—well over one thousand visitors—and it was documented with a catalog and reviews in major art publications.[11] Its success made it clear that Tivey had become a serious California Light and Space contender, even though, ironically, he had at that point left for New York.

Fourth Situation consisted of two rooms and a foyer. Entering the first room, which was large and darkened, I saw a small Ganzfeld some eight feet in diameter. Emitting a pale green light

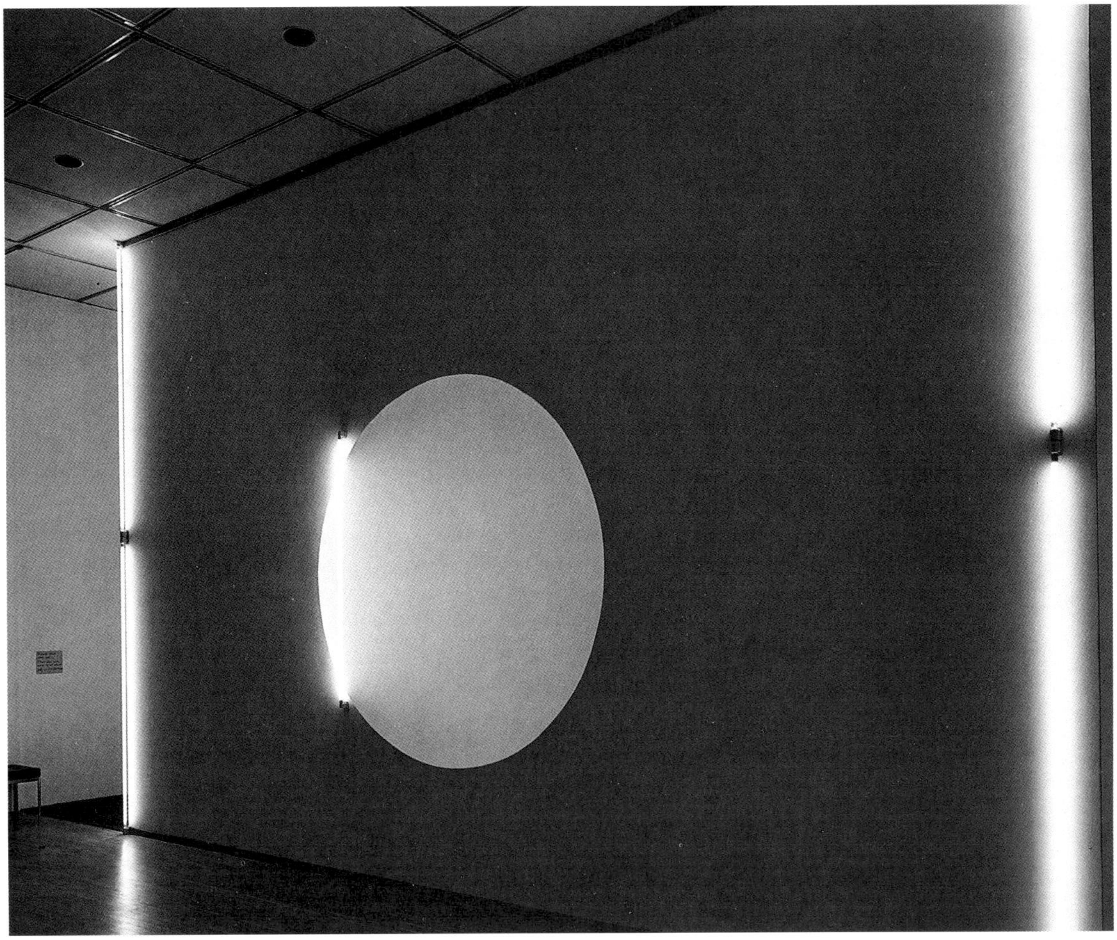

Hap Tivey
Fourth Situation
Ganzfeld room
Installation, Fine Art Gallery,
University of California,
Irvine, 1976

that appeared phosphorescent, the field seemed to hang on the wall like a circular painting. It was intersected on the left by a fluorescent tube that, in Constructivist fashion, pared off a portion of the circle while introducing an equally intense but qualitatively different light source. In reality the Ganzfeld was cantilevered and built into the wall from behind, although its undifferentiated space gave the impression that it was an aperture opening onto infinity.

Hap Tivey
Fourth Situation
Ganzfeld room
Installation, Fine Art Gallery, University of California, Irvine, 1976

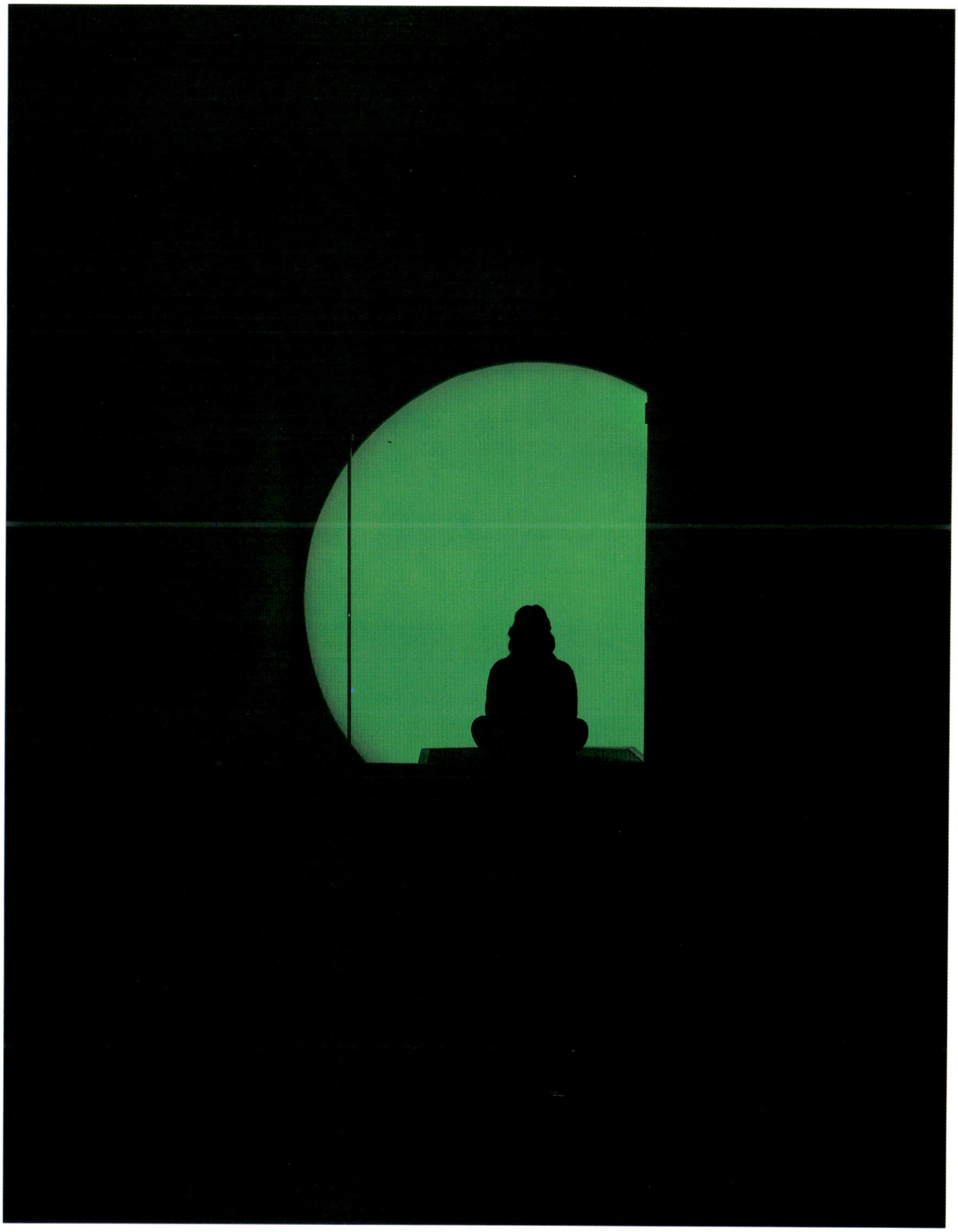

After experiencing that piece, which was enhanced by additional fluorescent tubes strategically placed on the opposite wall of the room and at the edge next to the adjoining gallery, I then removed my shoes and walked around the corner, where the room was sound dampened, silent. It contained the largest work. I ascended three low stairs to a felt-covered redwood platform, which formed the threshold of a large moon gate and extended slightly into the undifferentiated space. Having been asked at the entrance to the exhibition to remove my shoes and proceed alone into the final room, I was anticipating a silent, solitary experience, yet there was no real preparation for what was to come. Already moved and silenced by the work in the outside room, I sat cross-legged on the platform of the moon gate, silently waiting. What at first seemed to be a glowing white space of limitless depth was then slowly flooded with a pale green. Then, very gradually, it became a shimmering, iridescent apple green; finally, much later, a color as strange and vibrant as a green soap bubble surrounded me. I closed my eyes and rubbed them, then opened them again to find that the light had changed suddenly to magenta—not an ordinary magenta but some curiously potent variant that stained the air and the eyes. As I watched, the light gradually softened to violet and then washed out to pale pink. All along I was subliminally aware that it was not the light that I was seeing but some organic color inside my head. Lulled by the work's meditative qualities, quieted by its stepping-down process, excited by its sensate impact, I lost all sense of time.

The first impulse, once you relax in that light, is to go to sleep. And so to maintain that awareness, that flexibility, which I really wanted, there almost had to be that burst of the symphony, where the prince wakes up!

■ Hap Tivey

Tivey said of *Fourth Situation,* "It was the simplest and least sophisticated piece that I ever made," primarily because it was created to elicit a response from a broad array of people, rather than being structured for individual invitees, as in the Pasadena studio:

> *The mechanism was very simple. In the case of the* Fourth Situation, *the whole spectrum of light that the viewer saw was generated by one or two of the tubes being on at the same time as his retina was being bleached. In other words, the first thing that happens sets up, literally, a fugue of the response and the next stimulus. I think of those pieces as building music.*

In some ways Tivey found the Irvine work more difficult to effect than those in the Pasadena studio:

> *The* Fourth Situation *was harder because the viewer had to be able to come into it at any point [in the light sequence]. And, in order to make that work, the stimulus at any point had to mesh with the response of the next. For me, there was a beginning to the piece. I knew where the beginning and the end were. But for anyone else who went into it, they simply stepped in and it began immediately. The colors (such as that really brilliant pink or the bright mauve color) were partially a function of the afterimage of the color that preceded them, but they were also the function of a very subtle balancing of the fluorescent light that was coming all the way in from the other room.... There were only three basic lights in the work, but there were about twelve colors.*

Among the many statements I have received in the mail from Tivey over the years was one containing the following essay, written in 1977:

DISCONTINOUS NOTES REGARDING INSTALLATIONS OF LIGHT

1. Free light from materials.

A. One sees: (1) the transformations light undergoes when it encounters matter, i.e., from reflections, refractions, absorptions.

(2) Sources (another interpretation might be all one sees are sources, if transformations could be considered as secondary sources).

B. What we do not *see are things; we only assume the existence or character of things according to their light transformations, their source properties.*

C. Encountering light requires degrees of freedom from one's learned responses to things.

TO ENCOUNTER THE LIGHT CHARACTERISTIC ONE MUST MINIMIZE THE "THINGNESS" CHARACTERISTICS.

2. Encountering light is the sum result of physical light stimulating mind and mind ordering the stimulus and the analysis of the ordering.

A. The stimulation should exclude as much "thingness" as possible. The ordering pertains to the light, and the analysis of the ordering pertains to the light encounter, the mind order.

B. Analysis is optional for the aesthetics of the experience.[12]

The Asians
Otis Art Institute, Los Angeles
September 15–October 16, 1977

Proposal for *Asian Masters,* 1978
acquired by Giuseppe Panza di Biumo, Varese, Italy, 1988;
not yet constructed

The Asians
in *The Old Customs House Exhibition,*
organized by Creative Time, New York, 1979

The work that Tivey created for his exhibition at the Otis Art Institute utilized many of the same principles as *Second, Third,* and *Fourth Situations,* yet there were also substantial differences. First, the Otis work was structured so that several people could participate in it simultaneously in an open viewing situation. Second, the scale and presence of the piece were expanded, with many parts—only some of which could be perceived at any one time.

As viewers entered the darkened room, they confronted four large light screens (which Tivey referred to as *The Asians*). These screens were actually cinematic rear-view projection screens, which were fitted into triangular columns whose dimensions were determined by the existing architecture. The colors that emanated from these large screens ranged from white to yellow, pink, green, and blue, in varying intensities. Initially the experience of the light was engaging, but slowly, imperceptibly, it became overwhelmingly seductive and enveloping, as the colors blended and merged in the eye.

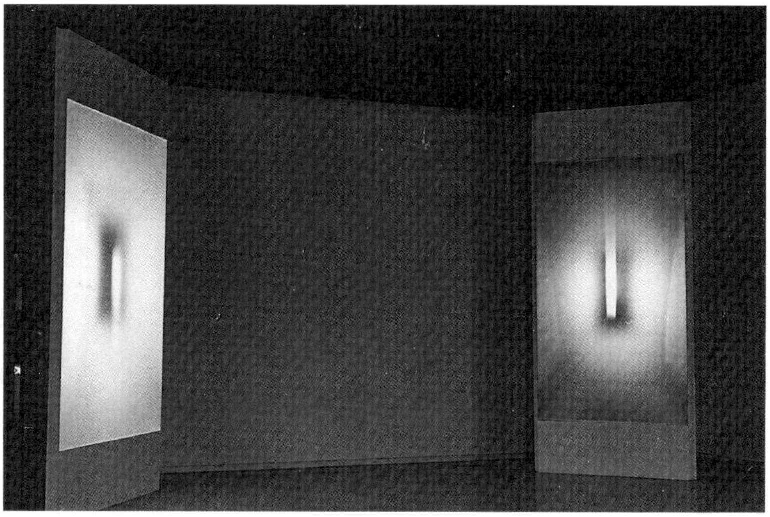

Stimulus and retinal bleach were continuously being overlaid on each other as the participant moved from one aspect of the piece to another. As Tivey noted, the light took on a presence of its own:

> *The images change shape and volume as one moves, thus asserting and denying the surface material. The issue of the images and their space then becomes a classic problem of an illusion of depth on a surface, as in traditional painting. The principal difference is the ability to see through the surface.*
>
> *The screen images are, essentially, not different from painting, when paint is considered a secondary source of light. Paint orders light, but one generally only encounters the "thingness" of the paint/surface rather than transformations of light. The screen material in these works is relatively neutral in that it presents a cross section of the structure of the light path, not a transformation of that structure. A cross sectional image from a perpendicular viewing angle appears differently than the same cross section from a oblique viewing angle. Consequently, a viewer*

moving in the room observes constantly changing images. The placement of the screens and their relative surface angles encourage continuous movement by denying any sense of center.[13]

The individual screens that made up the work constituted three individual "portraits" and a fourth that was a composite of all three, as Tivey explained: "In the Otis exhibition, the piece was very abstract. Each of the sections in the Otis piece was a portrait of an essence. If you looked directly into the individual screen segments of the work, they looked very much like my later screen paintings. If you walked around out of the screens and viewed it from the side, you actually saw planes—it was like planar geometry."

The viewers could move around the room in any order. One sequence was to move counterclockwise, starting with the smallest screen piece, created with sodium light, which was a very bright yellow—almost too intense to be directly observed. The next screen glowed with a curious white light, produced by white mercury lights. On the third screen, clear mercury lights caused an eerie blue glow. The fourth screen, which was the largest, was also the most complex. It combined all of the preceding lights, with the result that the sodium light became yellow, the white mercury light became green, and the clear mercury light became pink. Viewers were bathed in a glorious profusion of both real and perceived color.

Opposite
Hap Tivey
The Asians
4 screens, 6 x 10 ft. (1.8 x 3 m.), 8 x 10 ft. (2.4 x 3 m.), 4 x 10 ft. (1.2 x 3 m.), 14 x 10 ft. (4.3 x 3 m.)
Installation, Otis Art Institute, Los Angeles, 1977

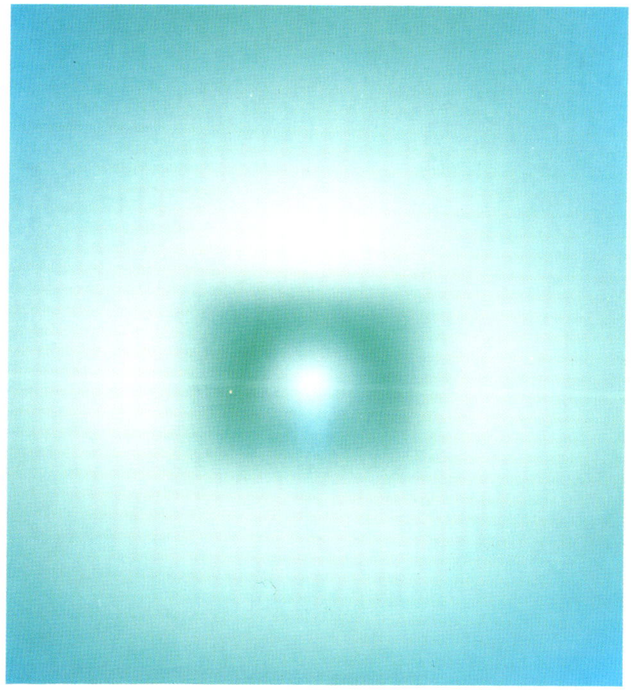

Right
Hap Tivey
Close-up of a screen in *The Asians*
Installation, Otis Art Institute, Los Angeles, 1977

The size and proportions of the individual screens varied greatly, and this variation was an integral part of the piece, as Wortz wrote:

> The order of encounters was suggested by the configuration of the entrance. The determining factor in the placement and proportions of the four units is the gallery's ceiling grid. Two of the triangular units [of the four in the show] are equilateral triangles; the other two are isosceles, having sides equal to one unit of ceiling grid, three and two units, two and two units, and five units. Thus, the first unit is half the size of the diagonally opposite structure, the fourth is the sum of the second and third, and so forth. In a similar manner the vertical and horizontal dimensions of the light screens are related—6 x 10', 8 x 10', 4 x 10', 14 x 10'—so that the third is half of the second, the fourth is the sum of the first and second, etc.... These proportions are sensed rather than overtly perceived by the viewer.... However, the felt order of this room is not like a gestalt. The relationships of a part to a whole are complex and cannot be perceived all at once.[14]

This sophisticated manipulation of spatial relationships extended Tivey's concepts, as he noted:

> *The Otis piece is much, much different from the New York and Pasadena pieces. My personal vision is no different in either of them, but in a way it's like someone who has been painting and then takes up sculpture—as though someone was painting in a Cubist fashion and then suddenly made a Cubist bronze. That's how far away the pieces are in my mind.... In the other works, a person was put into a situation where he confronted the light, and it confronted him in return, but the Otis piece was very abstract.*

The Asians led to an even more complex concept—*Asian Masters,* for which Tivey made drawings and a proposal in 1978. Ten years later Tivey described it as it will eventually be realized:

> *This gallery-oriented installation will use one room divided by a nylon scrim with four circular light cavities on one side and a screen with a projected image on the other. We enter the side with the cavities, which are formed by six-foot plastic hemispheres embedded in the walls, two on the left, two on the right. They are painted white, and the edges are ragged from coats of plaster, but the interior surfaces are perfect mat reflectors. Each [hemisphere] is a different hue of depthless color. Looking at the scrim wall, we see at the opposite end of the room a soft gold light and through it the source of the color—another screen stretched wall to wall, floor to ceiling some twenty feet beyond the scrim. The farthest plane is also gold light, but the center is a dark six-foot circle, like an eclipse of the light circles on either side of us. We can reach this screen by walking around either end of the scrim plane. Looking back at the light cavities from the eclipse side, the circles of hazy light fade in and out as our angle to the scrim changes, and their color seems to change as we adapt to the powerful influence of the sodium light behind the eclipse screen. The dark circle in the screen takes on a bluish cast with varying auras. Exiting, we encounter the light cavities once more, and their color seems to shift again as the influence of the screen diminishes. The light sources are a sodium street fixture, one thousand-watts high-pressure globe, and six fluorescent lights.*[15]

Tivey devoted two additional years of study to *The Asians* after he created the version at Otis. He executed two more versions of it in his Spring Street studio and another two at the Old Customs House, where he presented them publicly in New York for the last time.

Situated at the foot of Manhattan, the Old Customs House, with its grand scale and ponderous official architecture, temporarily played a role as the grande dame of alternative spaces. It took some forty-five minutes of roaming up and down the dreary stairways and in and out of the dark stone corridors and empty rooms before I found Tivey's two pieces. Finally, I spotted them under the grand arches at the top of the stairs, looming phosphorescently out of the dungeonlike gloom. The pieces, which were installed floor to ceiling where two arches intercepted a wall, were ten feet tall and consisted of two quarter-circles of light. The first work, *Lin Chi,* created of mercury-vapor lights mixed with blue fluorescent ones, was a circle bisected within a circle that glowed with an intense blue-green light. To the left stood another work, *Rinzai,* created of sodium-vapor and blue fluorescent light. Here the image, which subtly shifted from yellow to pale blue, was softened, indistinct. It, too, was installed within an arch, fitting it neatly, like a stained-glass window. The titles of the works, *Lin Chi* and *Rinzai,* are in themselves illuminating. *Lin Chi* is the name of a Chinese monk. *Rinzai* is his Japanese name and the name of the school of Zen he founded.

The relative isolation of the works in the building (which one assumes was intentional) made the viewing experience a private one. Because they were conceived as an integral part of the architecture, these were very satisfying pieces. Gentle yet profound, they were out of the way experiences that the viewer stumbled on rather than confronted immediately.

Sodium Exchange
Miami-Dade Community College, Miami
November 15–December 1, 1976

Queen's Grey Passage
P.S. 1, Institute for Art and Urban Resources, Long Island City, New York, 1976

Asian Eclipse
School of Visual Arts, New York, 1979

As with the multiple installations of different aspects of *The Asians,* works such as *Queen's Grey Passage, Sodium Exchange,* and *Asian Eclipse* were variations on a similar concept that was altered by its context.

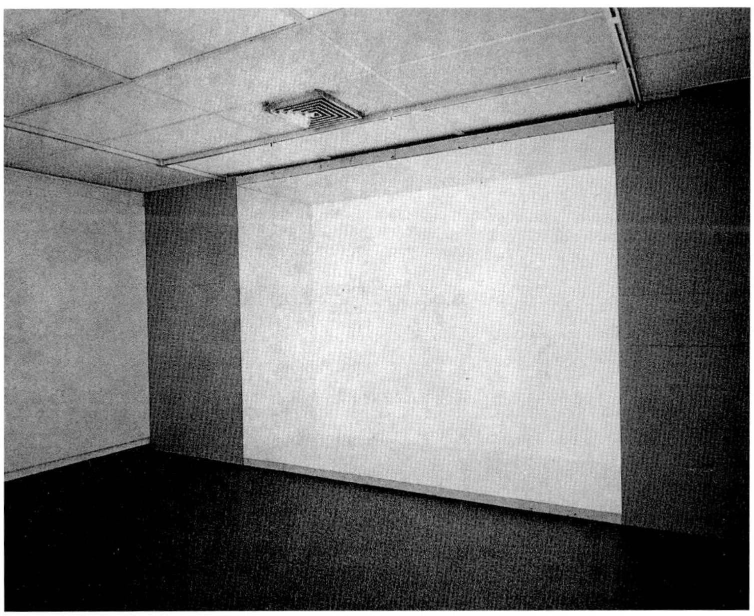

Hap Tivey
Sodium Exchange
South side of gallery, with sodium-vapor light and screen, room size: approximately 9 x 30 x 30 ft. (2.7 x 9.1 x 9.1 m.)
Installation, Miami-Dade Community College, Miami, 1976

Sodium Exchange was created by the transference of light emitted by energized sodium ions through the membrane of a rear-projection screen. In Tivey's view, *Sodium Exchange* was a figurative piece. The screen material was the same as that used at Otis, except that in Florida there was a single membrane dividing the entire room in half instead of a triangular unit in each corner of the room. The membrane was illuminated with a different kind of light on each side. One side was lit by a xenon projector (essentially a movie projector); the other side was lit by a sodium-vapor lamp.

The entrance opened onto a sixty-foot-long hall. Thirty feet to the right and to the left were two doorways. Yellow light spilled out of the one to the right; blue-white light came from the one on the left. The door to the right opened into a roughly square space about thirty by thirty feet. Inside the room, the wall to the right was framed by a two-foot-wide, two-foot-deep fascia. At the center of this alcove was a large white rectangle, mounted in front of two sodium fixtures, which saturated the room with yellow light. After the first minute in the space, retinal fatigue adjusted this color until it appeared as if the viewer was standing in a white, light-filled room with an alcove wall tinged with a yellow that shifted toward blue at the center. Opposite this alcove was a wall-to-wall screen framed in heavy construction-grade cardboard, which divided the sixty-by-thirty-foot room in half, creating the impression of two separate, thirty-foot spaces. Tivey later wrote about this piece, "When the light changes in one room, it causes changes in the other, and that change is reflected in the apparent saturation of the sodium light on the membrane or screen."[16]

Viewers on the other, xenon-lit side would walk in front of a projector, interrupting its light and casting their shadows on the screen; they would dance, roll around, becoming "the

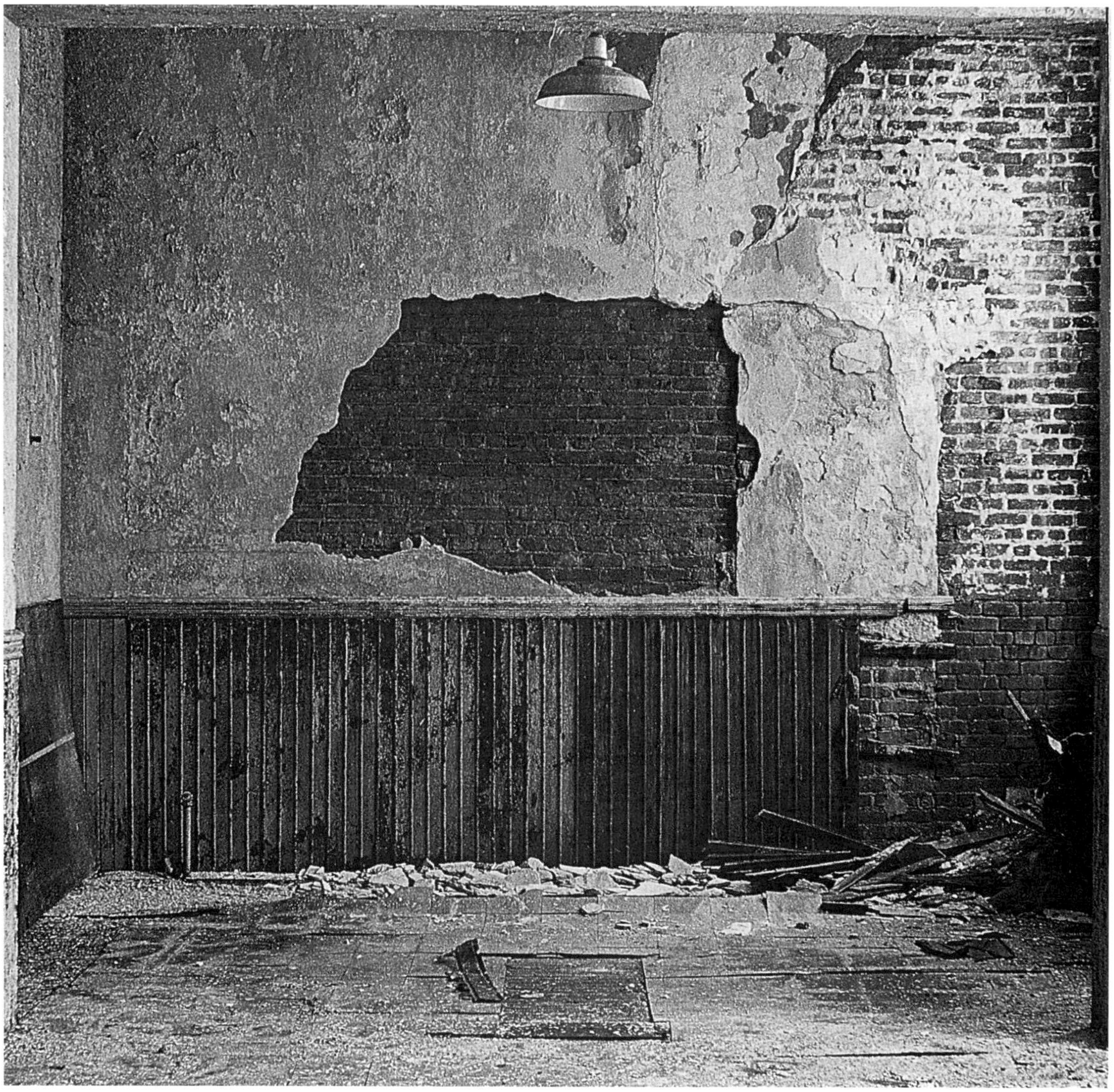

movie." To viewers on the sodium-vapor side the screen appeared a glowing blue, upon which danced figures the color of brown cardboard—projected from the space on the other side of the screen. *Sodium Exchange* had a curious psychological effect. The voyeurs gravitated toward the brightly lit sodium-vapor side, watching the shadows of people performing on the other side. The exhibitionists tended to cluster on the xenon side.

Hap Tivey
Queen's Grey Passage
Installation, P.S. 1, Institute for Art
and Urban Resources,
Long Island City, New York,
1976

When a viewer immersed in the sodium light returned to the hallway and then went into the second room, a retinal adjustment occurred. Entering the other door, the viewer saw a tall white box attached to the left wall; to the right was the opposite side of the same screen as seen in the other half of the room. A circular opening in the box projected xenon white light at the screen, which appeared to be a deep, empty gold; yet the viewer knew that less than a millimeter away someone else saw the same screen as a brilliant blue. This room, unlike the first room, appeared bathed in gold light but it was softer and caused very little retinal change. Some visitors perceived a subtle aura of blue-white on the cardboard frame just adjacent to the screen's edge; otherwise, the screen remained a vacant, infinite gold color.

The screen functioned much like the wall of a biological cell. "It's not an exact metaphor in any sense," Tivey wrote, "but this conveyance of light from each of the rooms to the other through the screen suggests to me the nature of information transferred via ion exchange across the semi-permeable membrane of a nerve."[17]

Other installations utilizing this same principle were *Queen's Grey Passage* at P.S. 1 and *Asian Eclipse* at the School of Visual Arts. The rooms at P.S. 1 have a certain tawdry yet poetic appeal, with their crumbling plaster, exposed structure, worn flooring, and accumulated debris. In *Queen's Grey Passage,* Tivey used his space there to create a haunting work of great magic and power, which he later described as follows:

> Queen's Grey Passage *revealed invisible views. When originally created at P.S. 1, it employed a short hallway with a coved interior and a glass windowed door, which could be looked into but not entered (a feature which could be omitted in later construction), and a 25' x 40' room divided by a rear projection screen. The window of the alcove/hallway superimposed a reflection of the brick wall and structural details of the hall's opposite wall onto an empty field of light colored rose/grey. No structure (walls, floor, ceiling, facets, etc.) would be seen by looking in the window. The only material image was the reflection of the physical world directly behind the viewer's head.*
>
> *Parallel to the visual hallway, a short functional hallway led us into a small room. This interior had been decaying for twenty-five years, and among the rubble of plaster, wood, and glass sat a single school chair. The entire room was painted neutral grey [by Tivey]—every surface. Overhead an antique institutional light fixture [grey] still hung from the ceiling, but emitted no light. The light filling the room came from one entire wall, which was a rear projection screen. On the screen appeared a mirror-image of the grey room in every detail, but reversed, as if the wall shifted not only the position of objects but the grey values of light as well. The image was a black and white negative of the room. The light fixture and its negative reflection were at the centers and thus shifted only grey values.*
>
> *After a few minutes, the image of the fixture began to brighten. Behind the screen [on the projector's side], a mercury street light had been turned on and was building in intensity. Gradually, the entire negative image faded from view as the screen became a bright pink fog. The room now seemed to have a huge window that looked out onto a cloud and in that cloud one could just discern a tiny fragment of the room's negative image. Wherever we walked, the fragment followed, and we realized that the fragment in the pink fog was just that bit of the room directly behind our head. Wherever we stood, our only view of the phantom room was that fragment of the room we could never see. Abruptly, the pink brightness vanished and the negative mirror room returned to the screen.*[18]

Asian Eclipse was also a figurative work, yet in it (as in all of Tivey's situational work) the interaction of the participant with the piece itself was what created the image. *Asian Eclipse* was a self-portrait environment, with the light from mercury-vapor and sodium-vapor lamps combined to make a double image. When a viewer entered the room, the light source was interrupted, and two figurative images appeared in two different kinds of light—one in gold, the other in silver. One image appeared head on, the other in profile. Tivey explained:

> *The source of light occupied one corner of the room; half mercury vapor, half sodium vapor. The frontal and profile images appeared in glowing Rothko-like light in two paintings behind the screens. Each image was a shadow in gold and silver leaf. When illuminated by both the mercury and the sodium sources, they appeared as white, or "fog" figures in Rothko/light fields. As the viewer passed between the light source and the image, one of the two sources would be blocked out, and the resulting figures would change color and seem to stand out of the screen. The personality splits and confronts itself; one portrait in light, one in darkness.*[19]

Cincinnati International Airport
Carl Solway Gallery, Cincinnati, 1980

Extending the figurative element implicit in *Asian Eclipse* and in the suggested landscapes of his screen paintings (also done in 1980), Tivey began, in 1980, to execute works whose content was "real" but whose form continued to be abstract. Utilizing light, screen, frosted glass, fluorescent tubes, and metal mesh, Tivey created a light "portrait" of the Cincinnati airport. This work had its roots deep in the Constructivist tradition. Brilliant white, green, and blue in coloration, it created the visual effect of an airport seen at night, when its outlines are defined solely by light. Tivey incorporated aspects of landscape in the form of abstract representations of the "patchwork quilt" seen from the air: tilled fields, property lines, and so on. A gigantic three-dimensional drawing, the "lines" of the work were executed in fluorescent tubing and wire mesh. Light gave it color, and the use of both clear and frosted glass gave it the painterly qualities of opacity and transparency.

Tivey saw the airport as a kind of metaphor for travel through time and space: "The airport is the window to the life of the world, the doorway between safe *terra firma* and the infinity of space/time. The airport is the twentieth-century collective painting created to be recognized by those off the earth: an enormous graphic of light. The installation is an abstraction of a landscape which is itself an abstraction."[20]

The scale of the Cincinnati installation invites comparison with the Nazca lines in Peru—not simply because the lines are seen by some as landing strips but because of the clear implication that they were meant to be seen from the air. Contemporary art seldom engages this "extra-terrestrial" vision, but there are clear precedents in Turrell's *Roden Crater Project*, Robert Smithson's *Spiral Jetty*, Christo's *Running Fence*, some of Claes Oldenburg's cross-country monuments, and Isamu Noguchi's famous head, *Sculpture to Be Seen from Mars.*

Screen Paintings

Blum/Helman Gallery, New York, October 1978 and September 1979
Landau Alexander Gallery, Los Angeles, 1979
Margo Leavin Gallery, Los Angeles, 1980

At the same time that he was creating environmental works, Tivey (who had stopped painting in 1969) was also exploring the quality of light in a new kind of painting. Sometime in 1977, at the time of his Otis show, Tivey began to create works in which the same rear-projection screen used in his situational pieces was used as a surface or cover for the paintings—part of whose imagery lay underneath. Tivey thus presented the painting as a surface of light rather than a surface of pigment.

The first of the screen paintings, which were shown at Blum/Helman Gallery in 1978 and at Landau Alexander Gallery in 1979, were shadow boxes over which Tivey stretched the screen and in which he placed baroque columns of once-molten aluminum. As the ambient or directed light played on the boxes, it hit the aluminum and bounced back through the screen, giving the work a soft glow. These paintings were lyrical, amorphous, foglike, with suggested images that drifted in space. Their frosted colors were slate gray, steel gray, silver, and a luminous pale gold. Hovering in the same curiously fascinating space between the literal and the abstract that characterizes Tivey's other work, they intrigued because of their poetic suggestiveness, yet they also frustrated because one did not know quite how to categorize them.

A later series, shown at Blum/Helman in 1979 and at Margo Leavin Gallery in 1980, represented a major development. Some of the paintings, no longer tentative and no longer pure abstractions, now blossomed with hinted-at images in blushing violets, lavenders, cherry pinks, and pale terra cotta. Others bloomed in blues and greens. Their titles such as *Hood* (Mt. Hood?) and *Red Wall* (which refers, as the critic Torr Seidler noted,[21] to the red ceramic wall that contains Ryoan-ji, one of the best known of the Japanese sand gardens) help elucidate their meaning. Even more important, they grew in size, and with size came power. Many of them were now diptychs. Whereas his early screen paintings measured no more than thirty by thirty-six inches, *Red Wall* was 9 1/2 feet high by 12 1/2 feet long. The works now engulfed the viewer, causing a real confrontation.

As he sees it, Tivey's role in the room-environment pieces and in the screen paintings is to provide an "idealized general moment" within which the art experience can take place:

> *Most art, even one's own, has a very limited experiential availability, so the experience for most becomes a matter of juxtaposing oneself for a moment with some physical condition—paint on canvas, in some room of some building, between hours of a specified date. This situation also exists with most unique experiences—performance, concerts, sunsets.*
>
> *Stonehenge, for example, creates within a slowly changing yet theoretically repeatable matrix, a series of moments unique to any observer and less obviously, unique to the universe. Any observer juxtaposed with rare days and good conditions may experience remarkable moments of the sun and the earth. Sun, earth, stones generate real and unique moments (non-repeatable); the matrix creates an idealized general moment recurrently available to anyone with the proper time and attitude. Consider the phenomena religious and/or esthetic experience.*[22]

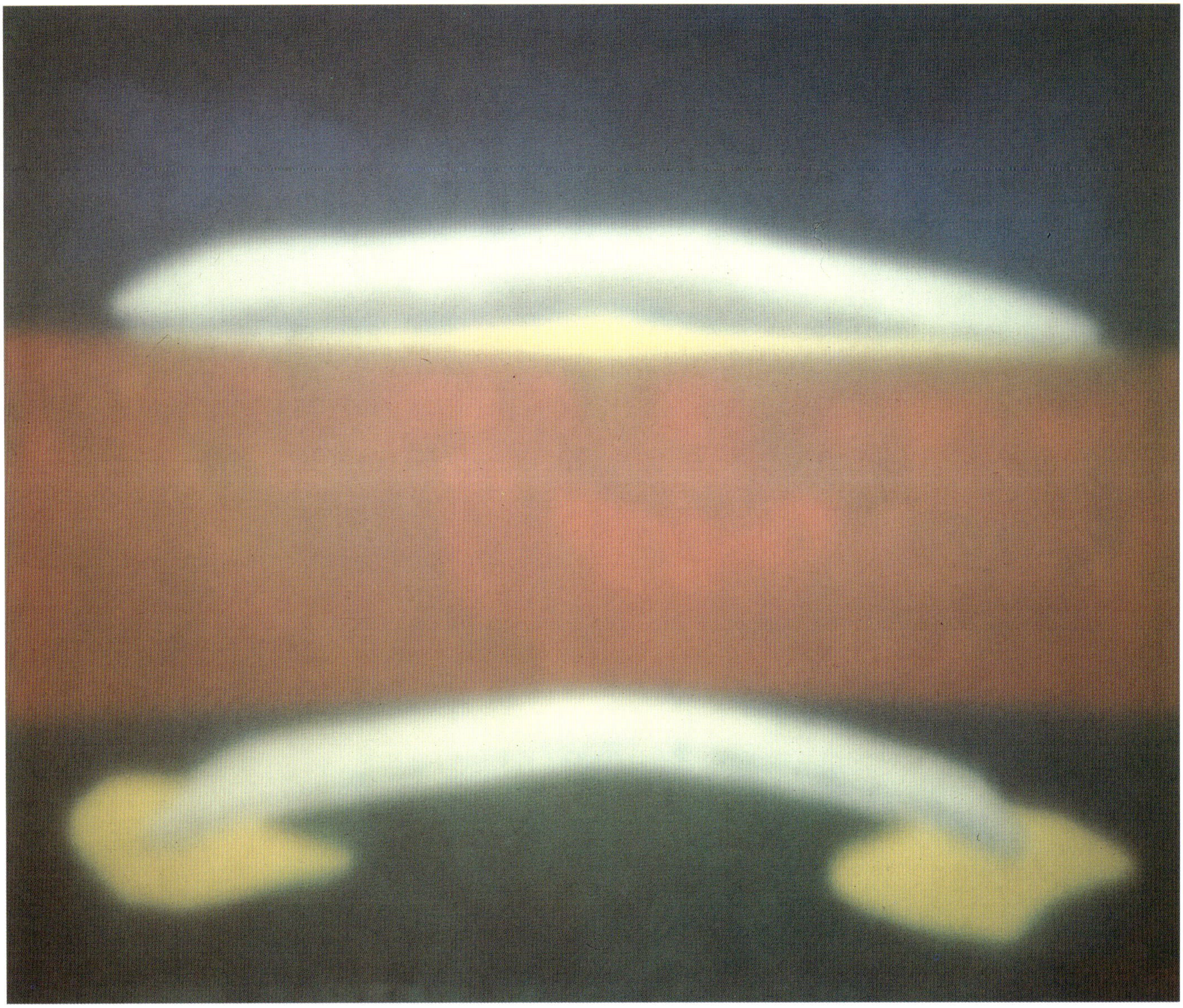

Installation
Christophe de Menil residence, Sixty-ninth Street, New York
installed 1981, dismantled when residence was sold

On the third floor of a New York apartment was a room with a handsome lap pool, a cushion-filled gazebo designed by the architect Frank Gehry, and a stunning, meditative room-environment piece by Hap Tivey.

The central focus of Tivey's work was the bathing chamber (the tub of which was built of black granite), which was installed in a room behind the pool area. The participant entered the darkened bathing area in this room and slipped into the water, then discovered that the tub extended below the existing floor level and was deep enough to create a curiously soothing sensation of weightlessness.

Hap Tivey
Red Wall, 1979
Mixed media, 114 x 138 in.
(289.6 x 350.5 cm)
Private collection

As the light sequence began in the room, the participant saw light projections either on a facing wall and the ceiling or in the mirrorlike reflection of the water's surface, which appeared black. A tall window in one corner transmitted light from the bathing chamber to the adjacent pool room. The light sequence began with dim light from the pool window, and darkened as the window was gradually masked off mechanically. As the lights were gradually quenched, the room darkened further and the walls disappeared; light bars seemed to hang in the air.

The work was serene, meditative. For Tivey, it conveyed a sense of spiritual passage and had definite allegorical elements: *The Path* (the yellow beams of light that pour across the ceiling and down the wall into a corner of complete darkness); *The Gate* (a post and lintel configuration of shimmering blue-green); and *The Guardians* (two vertical elements viewed separately as the other projections darken). It was a curiously mystical environment to encounter on the third floor of a private residence, but it was profoundly successful.

In 1988 Count Panza purchased six or seven of Tivey's proposals for works conceived to be constructed in a site-specific situation, including *Asian Masters.* As yet unconstructed, they exist only as Tivey's proposals, copies of which Tivey sent to me in January 1988 and which I present here in edited form.

Proposal for *Solar Cell,* 1987

At the end of a path taken through the forest, we find ourselves looking up at stone terracing on the hillside, and wide stone stairs. We may see the circular steel cap of a light tube just visible in the terracing, but only if someone has previously opened or aligned it. When closed, it blends with the stones.

Looking up to the hills, we see an arched doorway leading into the earth. The space recalls a mine entrance or a tunnel.

Ascending the stairs, we find that we have arrived at an arched hall of plaster and concrete. In this space the smooth walls and ceiling area provide a continuous surface of natural white. Sloping gently upward into the hill, the floor is covered in large, rough tiles the texture and color of dark stone. Eventually this hall leads into a circular chamber with the same smooth white surface. One small stone separates the level of the hall tiles from those of the circular chamber. The view backward, out from the hall from the inner room, reveals only sky, as the hill falls away from the opening and all intruding foliage has been cleared away. The inner room is five meters in diameter, and the ceiling is a dome with a radius of curvature of two-and-one-half meters. Aside from the tile floor and the stone step at the hall entrance, the room has only three other features:

Directly across from the hallway entrance, a stone shelf is cantilevered out from the wall, just above the floor. Smooth at the top and front edge, the otherwise rough stone is a light color and is just large enough for a person of medium height and austere habits to sleep.

A second feature appears at the apex of the domed ceiling: a six-inch-diameter hole in the surface, which appears as an eccentric ellipse to an observer seated on the bench. It is much brighter than the room, because it is actually at the end of a tube made up of successively larger cylinders that connect the ceiling to the surface and the hillside above and allow skylight to penetrate the chamber. Mounted on the top of this tube is an adjustable mirror device that can be aligned to direct either sunlight or moonlight into the chamber.

Proposal for *Three-Quarter Sphere*, 1987

Installed in the antechamber of Three-Quarter Sphere *are two doors and two spherical light discs. The discs are fitted flush to the wall and are painted the same flat white. Deep hemispheres of plastic, the discs create an infinite sense of space and color in the darkened room. They appear as if they were windows looking out on a cloudless sky. Their color is variable and ranges from pale gold to vibrant green and blue, depending on the mixtures of light from the fluorescent sources in the walls of this chamber. These same mixtures create the color and space in the larger spherical chamber as well. Observers of the discs outside the sphere see these colors objectively in a neutral space. They will appear to be very different when seen in the total environment of the sphere.*

A stairway leads from the antechamber to the floor of the sphere, which now takes on the shape of a great, round room. The plane of the floor seems to hang suspended in space, and the participant makes contact with it only at the doorway. Near the edge of the platform is a comfortable chair. When one is seated in the chair, one's feet do not quite reach the floor. The feeling is one of being seated at the edge of a great precipice. The depthless surrounding light soothes and relaxes. When one leans back, the field of vision becomes completely nonmaterial; the field of vision has, in a sense, disappeared, and one sees only light. By reflected comparison one realizes this space, and its corresponding light, are more than one saw in the disc in the preceding room. The more immediate sensation is a composite of the physical light and the mind. The color and space begin to transform as soon as one starts the program by pressing a button on the arm of the chair. The color is, at times, foglike; at others it is hard crystalline, both in density and dimension, as the color shifts.

The antechamber offers a gradual return to material perceptions, as we leave the sphere, and the light discs recall that infinite sense of space and color that are now framed in the wall.

At the end of the 1980s and into the 1990s Tivey found himself concentrating in several different areas: he perfected his magical light sculptures and developed them as glowing sculptural objects; he continued to work on light spaces on paper, preparing for a time when they could be built; and he built a teahouse in Paris for Claude Picasso. The teahouse, which has many echoes of Tivey's Pasadena work, is a deeply rewarding experience.

Tivey's sculptures are powerful objects. Making use of techniques learned from the many versions of *The Asians,* he now creates works that have a fabricated sculptural cavity and one or more luminous planes. Within the cavity is a fluorescent bulb and a system of planes that fill the cavity with colored light. The luminous planes are created by the use of Tivey's now trademark rear-projection screen on stainless-steel mesh. Light within the cavity is projected onto the front screen of light. Eerie and otherworldly, according to Tivey these sculptures make clear that "Line can be released from surface and seen as a continual field of energy."

Recently, Tivey wrote to me: "I no longer try to convince New Yorkers of the excellent experiences available with pure light. I maintain my simple studio in the country with one room for projections and meditation."

Hap Tivey
Teahouse, 1990
Claude Picasso, Paris

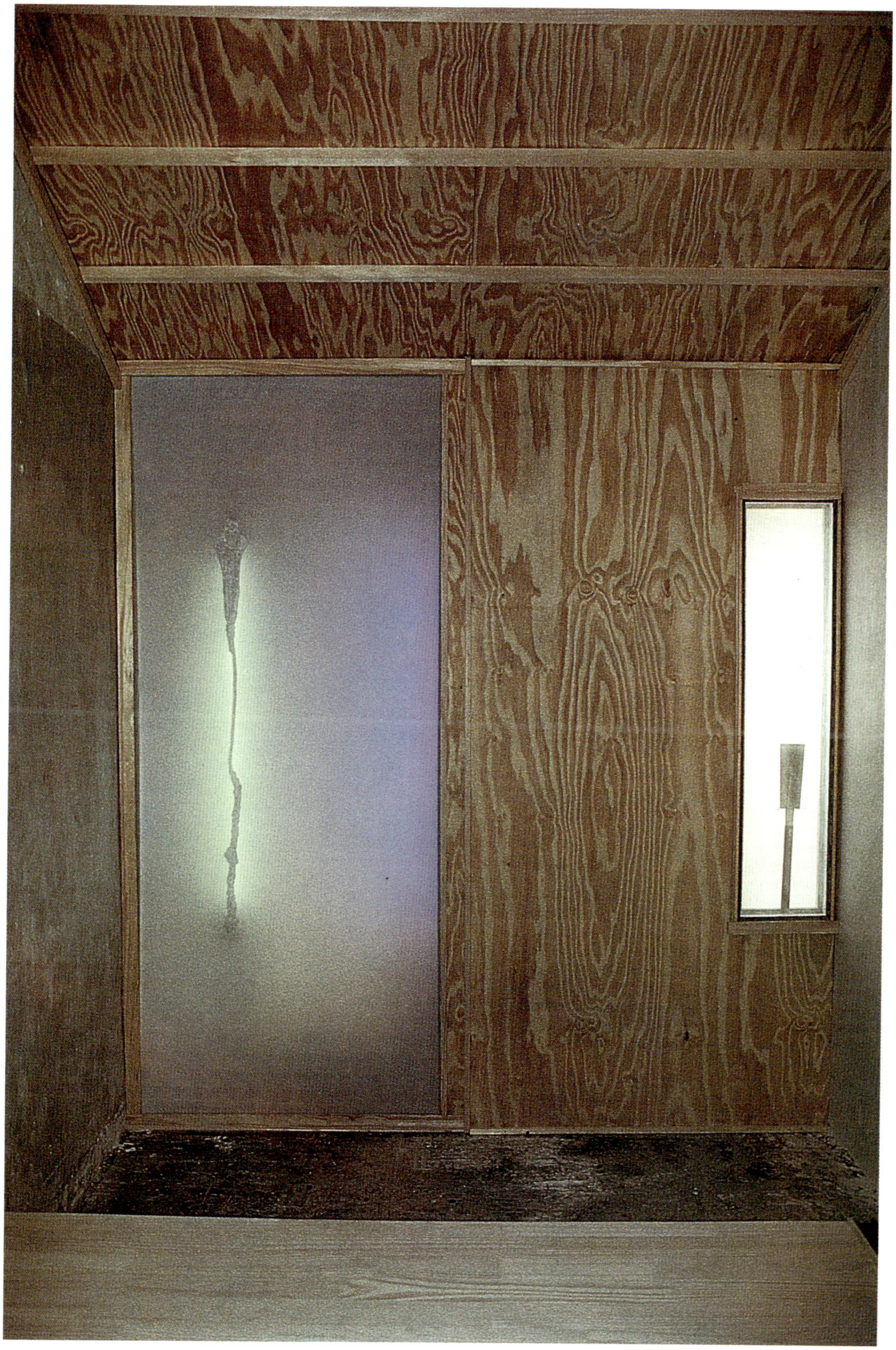

Afterword

As this book took final shape, ready at last to have its premises carved in stone, it became clear that the names of a few more artists had to be entered on the roster of Light and Space artists. The first four must be added because they were *there*—involved early on with some of the premises of light or space (but not both and not for long). The second two have taken the ideas of the Light and Space artists and gone on to transform them into something else—but something that is clearly related.

The first is Edward Moses, who created works of Light and Space in his Venice studio during the 1960s. Only a few people saw them, but he certainly did them as early as or perhaps earlier than anyone else. He showed this kind of work publicly only once, at Mizuno Gallery in 1970, and then he returned to painting, to become a true "painter's painter"—and one whose works were informed by his excursions into the realm of Light and Space.

The second artist is Ron Cooper, who created what he called "Light Traps," in which the light appears suspended in space. Cooper was interested right at the beginning in transparency and reflection, and his experiments in Light and Space led him to use resin and fiberglass cloth, which he overlapped in as many as thirty layers to create large, square "paintings" that literally glowed with trapped light. Cooper's best-known works in the Light and Space realm were even more ephemeral pieces that evolved from these Light Traps. They were conceived as corner works in which two or more fluorescent tubes were strategically juxtaposed with sheets of plate glass so that light bounced off them and intermingled, creating the illusion of a solid volume. Having experimented with perception in these Light and Space works, Cooper became fascinated with the way we see; he then turned to work that examined the photographic process and eventually he moved on to making bronze sculpture.

Mary Corse is something of an enigma in terms of her relationship to Light and Space art. After careful consideration, I decided not to include her in the main body of this text, not because she is not a superb artist—because she is—but because she is primarily a painter rather than an artist concerned with room environments or site-specific installations. Working with glass microspheres, Corse creates paintings that are almost eerie in their intensity: inordinately bright, luminous canvases made by mixing crushed glass with acrylic paint, which she then smooths to a brilliant sheen. Powerful lights trained on her canvases create a glistening "pure whiteness," which fragments into halated spectrum colors as the viewer passes by. Corse is long overdue for serious critical consideration—but this book is not the place for it.

Tom Eatherton has been around for as long as anyone can remember, but for some strange reason he has not been an active part of the Light and Space dialogue. (He has, however, been written about well, though sparsely.) Eatherton received his B.A. at the University of California at Los Angeles in 1957. He worked and exhibited as a painter from 1957 to 1967 and exhibited his first room-environment light works in his studio in 1967. Eatherton is an artist of quiet, methodical strength, whose works are balanced and clear.

Eatherton's first permanent commission is *Unity,* created for Los Angeles County's Metropolitan Rail System. Made for the Blue Line station at Seventh and Flower streets, the work runs 3,000 feet and uses some 5,000 points of light—both fiber optic tubes arranged in concentric circles and light points mounted on forty-two-inch "canvases" running parallel to the track. By Eatherton's count, there are thirty-two different kinds of circles and fifty "point sets" (dots of color that form an image).

The success of *Unity* and of *Panel* (1991), which was commissioned for the Edgemar complex (which houses the Santa Monica Museum of Art) has brought Eatherton unprecedented new visibility. I hope that this new attention will help establish his rightful place in the historical scheme of things.

A new generation of artists has come up whose works have been informed by the concepts of Light and Space but who are not Light and Space artists per se. Having "taken permission" from the artists discussed in this book, they have gone on to create works of their own that are markedly different from those made by their predecessors. The first of these artists is Lita Albuquerque, whose works are both alchemical and cosmological. From the beginning of her career one notable aspect of her work has been the use of brilliant color—in sharp contrast to the pristine all-whiteness of early Light and Space works. Using powdered pigments of intense red, yellow, and blue, Albuquerque taps into the cosmos. In some works she splatters stars and spiral nebulae across the surfaces of her paintings. In others, she encases or overlays her works with skins of gold leaf. In outdoor works she drifts the pigment across huge expanses of earth or uses it to ceremonially anoint earth and stones. Albuquerque's Tunisian heritage and her travels to the mystical "power spots" of the world have contributed to a vocabulary that gives her site-specific works great resonance and impact.

Albuquerque's 1991 work for Koll Corporation, located in the Los Angeles Civic Center, is a superb example of her site-specific work. Entitled *Site/Memory/Reflection,* it features a river of deep blue glass tesserae, a huge golden mandala, and a meditation chapel that reminds one of the small roadside churches in Greece. The chapel's interior chamber, which functions like a small ganzfeld, is a haven of calm and serenity in a busy downtown area. With *Site/Memory/Reflection,* Albuquerque has come into her own as an artist, combining the elements of beauty and mysticism within an architectural work on a powerful scale.

Peter Erskine also makes installations of great beauty and intensity. Deeply concerned with the preservation of the earth, he created an extremely ambitious work entitled *Secrets of the Sun: Millennial Meditations,* a site-specific piece (sponsored by the Frederick R. Weisman Art Foundation) that he first exhibited in Rome's Imperial Forum in the spring of 1992. He then launched it on a world tour that began with an exhibition organized by the Cultural Affairs Department of the city of Berlin, as part of the Berlin Olympics Committee for the Berlin Olympics 2000.

Using sunlight, text, and sound, in *Secrets of the Sun,* Erskine attempted to address the whole range of nature, from its most elemental embodiment as pure light to its most complex expression in the global ecology. The sun's transformed colors flooded the ancient chambers of the Forum and Trajan's marketplace with red, purple, peach, sky blue, green, and lemon yellow. A requiem mass played slowly in the background while a solemn voice intoned the names of dying and extinct species of animals.

■ ■ ■

It has been nearly thirty years since the very first glimmers of Light and Space work twinkled faintly on the horizon. At the beginning of the 1960s it was impossible to anticipate what course this work would take or to predict its vast implications. Now it seems apparent that, as the artists have insisted all along, Light and Space art is not a movement—rather, it is a mind set. Over the years the artists we have been discussing have grown further apart aesthetically rather than closer together. What they have been dealing with has been a philosophy—a method that can be applied to a multiplicity of aesthetic developments. The critical and popular acceptance of the experiential approach that constitutes this philosophy has seemed to develop with painful slowness. Nonetheless, new concepts of art making and of perception first posited by the Light and Space artists have been embraced by one artist, one critic, one viewer after another until virtually all our ways of seeing have been called into question and all our concepts about the nature of art have been radically challenged. That has been no small accomplishment.

Notes

Introduction

Epigraphs: Maurice Merleau-Ponty, *The Primacy of Perception,* trans. Carleton Dallery, ed. James M. Edie (Evanston, Ill.: Northwestern University Press, 1964), p. 14.

Irwin and Turrell, in Maurice Tuchman and Jane Livingston, *A Report on the Art and Technology Program of the Los Angeles County Museum of Art, 1967–1971* (Los Angeles: Los Angeles County Museum of Art, 1971), p. 131.

1 Robert Irwin, statement made at the seminar "The Spirit in Art," Graduate Union Theological Seminary, Berkeley, California, April 21, 1979, pp. 25–26 in the unpublished transcription by Craig Vista Svare.

2 Axel Madsen, *Hearts and Minds* (New York: Quill, Morrow, 1977), p. 62.

3 Gaston Bachelard, *Poetics of Space,* trans. Maria Jolas (Boston: Beacon, 1969), p. 201.

4 Kazimir Malevich, "Cubism and Futurism to Suprematism: The New Painterly Realism, 1915," in *Russian Art of the Avant-Garde: Theory and Criticism,* ed. John Bowlt (New York: Viking, 1976), p. 132.

5 *The Avant-Garde in Russia, 1910–1930: New Perspectives,* ed. Stephanie Barron and Maurice Tuchman (Los Angeles: Los Angeles County Museum of Art; Cambridge, Mass.: MIT Press, 1980), p. 186.

6 Boris Brodsky, "El Lissitzky," ibid., p. 92.

7 Michel Seuphor, *Piet Mondrian: Life and Work* (New York: Harry N. Abrams, 1956), p. 158.

8 Willoughby Sharp, *Light/Motion/Space* (Minneapolis: Walker Art Center, 1967), p. 4.

9 Melinda Wortz, *California Perceptions: Light and Space, Selections from the Wortz Collection* (Fullerton: California State University Art Gallery, 1979), p. 10.

10 Hal Glicksman, interview with Marge Goldwater, in Goldwater and Glicksman, *Los Angeles in the Seventies* (Fort Worth: Fort Worth Art Museum, 1977), p. 5.

11 Lucy Lippard has applied this idea to architecture too: "The most important architects today are not those whose works can be exposed in one-man shows but those whose collective conscience is changing the quality of life in often invisible and rarely touted ways." (Lucy R. Lippard, "The Inside Picture from the Outside," in Debra Burchett, et al., *Architectural Sculpture,* 2 vols. [Los Angeles: Los Angeles Institute of Contemporary Art, 1980], vol. 1, p. 25.)

12 Melinda Wortz, "Architects of Emptiness," ibid., p. 37.

13 Robert Irwin, interviews with author, 1972–91. This is also the source for the Irwin quotations in the sidebars.

Robert Irwin

Epigraphs: Rainer Maria Rilke, *The Duino Elegies,* trans. David Young (New York: W. W. Norton, 1978), p. 11.

Robert Irwin, interviews with author, 1972–91. Unless otherwise indicated, all quotations by the artist in the text and sidebars are from this source.

1 Paul Klee, in Maurice Merleau-Ponty, *The Primacy of Perception,* trans. Carleton Dallery, ed. James M. Edie (Evanston, Ill.: Northwestern University Press, 1964), p. 183.

2 Irwin, in Jan Butterfield, "The State of the Real: Robert Irwin Discusses the Activities of an Extended Consciousness, Part 1," *Arts Magazine* 46 (Summer 1972): 48.

3 Ibid., p. 49.

4 Ibid.

5 Ibid.

6 Robert Irwin, statement made at the seminar "The Spirit in Art," Graduate Union Theological Seminary, Berkeley, California, April 21, 1979, p. 59 in the unpublished transcription by Craig Vista Svare.

7 Ibid.

8 Livingston, in Maurice Tuchman and Jane Livingston, *A Report on the Art and Technology Project of the Los Angeles County Museum of Art, 1967–1971* (Los Angeles: Los Angeles County Museum of Art, 1971), p. 131.

9 Ibid., p. 128.

10 Ibid., p. 126.

11 Ibid., p. 129.

12 Ibid., p. 130.

13 Irwin and Turrell, ibid., p. 128.

14 Irwin, ibid., p. 139.

15 Irwin, "Spirit in Art," n.p.

16 After Turrell left the project, Irwin and Wortz carried on an extended dialogue, which continues to be of great importance to them both. Wortz eventually left his job as a project scientist for Garrett Aerospace and is now a clinical psychologist, president of the Gestalt Therapy Association of Los Angeles, and past president of the Biofeedback Society of California. His patients include many in the art field. Through Irwin he met the critic Melinda Terbell, who had been writing and collecting in the areas in which Wortz and Irwin had become involved. Terbell and Wortz later married, and she earned a doctorate from the Graduate Union Theological Seminary in Berkeley.

17 One important exception should be mentioned here: the collaboration between Larry Bell and Eric Orr that began in the late 1970s and has continued into the present. Even this association appears to be more collegial than collaborative, born more out of friendship than any similarity of intent. Each artist's primary body of work is vastly different in process and materials from their collaborative project *Solar Fountain,* which appears to have developed out of a momentary convergence of paths rather than an inherent desire to collaborate. For a more complete discussion of their involvement, see the chapter on Bell in this volume and the essay by Melinda Wortz in *Larry Bell: New Work* (Yonkers, N.Y.: Hudson River Museum, 1981), pp. 17–18.

18 Irwin, in Thomas Albright, "Robert Irwin: 'Everything I've Done in the Last Five Years Doesn't Exist,'" *Artnews* 76 (Summer 1977): 53.

19 Jan Butterfield, "An Uncompromising Other Way," *Arts Magazine* 48 (June 1974): 54–55.

20 Jan Butterfield, "Reshaping the Shape of Things; Part 2: The Myth of the Artist," *Arts Magazine* 47 (September–October 1972): 30.

21 Hilton Kramer, "A Career That Rejected Studio Art," *New York Times,* May 8, 1977, sec. 2, p. 25.

22 Ira Licht, *Robert Irwin* (Chicago: Museum of Contemporary Art, 1975), p. 12.

23 Larry Rosing, "Robert Irwin at Pace," *Art in America* 63 (March–April 1975): 87.

24 An earlier version of this text appeared in Butterfield, "Uncompromising Other Way."

25 An earlier version of this text appeared in Jan Butterfield, "Robert Irwin: On the Periphery of Knowing," *Arts Magazine* 50 (February 1976): 72.

26 Ibid.

27 Albright, "Everything I've Done," p. 53.

28 Roberta Smith, "Robert Irwin: The Subject Is Sight," *Art in America* 64 (March–April 1976): 69.

29 Ibid., p. 72.

30 Irwin, in Butterfield, "State of the Real," p. 48.

31 Mark Stevens, "The Dizzy Decade," *Newsweek,* March 26, 1979, p. 88.

32 Robert Irwin, "Notes toward a Model," in *Robert Irwin* (New York: Whitney Museum of American Art, 1977), p. 31.

33 Ibid.

34 For more information on Irwin's work and theories, see Lawrence Weschler, "Robert Irwin's Whitney Project: Retrospects and Prospects," *Journal* (Los Angeles Institute of Contemporary Art), no. 15 (July–August 1977): 14–20; and Weschler's biography of Irwin, *Seeing Is Forgetting the Name of the Thing One Sees: A Life of Contemporary Artist Robert Irwin* (Berkeley and Los Angeles: University of California Press, 1982).

35 An earlier version of this text appeared in Jan Butterfield, "The Enigma Suffices: Robert Irwin, *Room with Twin Skylights,*" *Images and Issues* 1 (Winter 1980–81): 38–40.

36 The Dallas commission was implemented through a matching-funds grant as part of the National Endowment for the Arts' Works of Art in Public Places program.

37 Janet Kutner, "Rusty Knife Slices New Plaza, but It's Cause to Rejoice," *Dallas Morning News,* September 19, 1981.

38 Irwin, in Jan Butterfield, "Robert Irwin: The Name of the Game Is Context," *Calendar* (University Art Museum, Berkeley, Calif.) 1 (March 1979): 1.

39 Irwin, in "The Talk of the Town: Seeing," *New Yorker,* September 30, 1985, p. 27.

40 Robert Irwin, *Being and Circumstance: Notes toward a Conditional Art* (Larkspur Landing, Calif.: Lapis, 1985), p. 33.

41 Ibid., pp. 26–27.

42 Kenneth Baker, "A Purveyor of the 'Phenomenal,'" *San Francisco Chronicle,* October 20, 1985.

43 Jean E. Feinberg, "Perceiving the Garden: Robert Irwin at Wave Hill," brochure (New York: Wave Hill, 1987), n.p.

44 Jean E. Feinberg, *Perceiving the Garden: Robert Irwin at Wave Hill,* catalog (New York: Wave Hill, 1987), p. 29.

45 Calvin Tomkins, "The Art World: Knowing in Action," *New Yorker,* November 11, 1985, p. 147.

46 Alan G. Artner, "Persistent Images," *Chicago Tribune,* May 17, 1987, sec. 13.

James Turrell

Epigraph: James Turrell, interviews with author, 1979–91. Unless otherwise indicated, all quotations by the artist in the text and sidebars are from this source.

1 Turrell, in Julia Brown, ed., *Occluded Front: James Turrell* (Larkspur Landing, Calif.: Lapis; Los Angeles: Museum of Contemporary Art, 1985), p. 42.

2 One suspects that Turrell now somewhat regrets this, for as a result there have been questions about his dating of his pieces. (He is the only artist in this volume who dates his work from its alleged conception rather than its first exhibition.) One argument in his defense is the fact that there were precious few opportunities in the late 1960s and early 1970s for any of these artists to exhibit; little interest had yet arisen in them, and there was no money to execute works on a large scale. Therefore, many of these artists have unrealized works from that early period.

Although I tried on numerous occasions to view *The Mendota Hotel Stoppages,* it was never the right time for me to do so, according to Turrell. As a result, I saw neither that work nor any sketches for more extensive pieces that might have existed then.

3 "The Talk of the Town: Light," *New Yorker,* December 15, 1980.

4 Turrell, in Maurice Tuchman and Jane Livingston, *A Report on the Art and Technology Program of the Los Angeles County Museum of Art, 1967–1971* (Los Angeles: Los Angeles County Museum of Art, 1971), p. 140.

5 Edward De Wilde, "Jim Turrell's Light Spaces," in *Jim Turrell* (Amsterdam: Stedelijk Museum, 1976), n.p.

6 This work invites comparison with Douglas Wheeler's wall works shown at the Pasadena Art Museum in 1968, at the Fort Worth Art Museum in 1969, and at the Ace Gallery, Los Angeles, in 1970 (though Wheeler used neon rather than fluorescence, and his floating planes were plastic rather than wood). Turrell's piece was not actualized until his Stedelijk exhibition in 1976 (though it is dated 1969, the date of its conception); it has posed some very real and as yet unanswered questions. Wheeler's dates are easily documentable; Turrell's are not. There appear to be dating ambiguities with Turrell's sky pieces as well. Count Panza discusses their actualization as post-1973—Turrell dates them 1972 in the book *Occluded Front* (1985).

7 Charles Baudelaire, *Paris Spleen,* trans. Louise Varèse (New York: New Directions, 1970), p. 5.

8 Ross Wetzsteon, "Do Not Go Gentle into That Good Light," *Village Voice,* November 19, 1980, p. 95.

9 Mark Stevens, "Turrell's 'Celestial Vault,'" *Newsweek,* February 10, 1986, p. 71.

10 Fred Hapgood, "Roden's Eye," *Atlantic 260* (August 1987): 52.

11 Turrell, in Jan Butterfield, "A Hole in Reality: Roden Crater Project," *Images and Issues 1* (Fall 1980): 54.

12 Ibid., p. 56.

13 Jacob Needleman, *A Sense of the Cosmos: Science and Ancient Truth* (New York: E. P. Dutton, 1965), pp. 24–25.

14 Dodie Kazanjian, "Vogue Arts," *Vogue* 181 (May 1991): 168.

Maria Nordman

Epigraph: Rainer Maria Rilke, *The Duino Elegies,* trans. David Young (New York: W. W. Norton, 1978), p. 29.

1 Nordman, in Barbara Haskell and Hal Glicksman, *Maria Nordman: Saddleback Mountain* (Irvine: University of California, 1973), n.p.

2 Maria Nordman, "Workroom 1971," *Interfunktionen* (Cologne), no. 12 (Summer 1975): 99.

3 *Bijutsu Techno* (Tokyo) 31 (April 1979): 58–59.

4 Arata Isozaki, "The Notion of Space/Time in Japan." In *Ma: Space/Time in Japan,* ed. Seigow Matsuoka (New York: Cooper-Hewitt Museum, 1978), n.p.

5 My discussion here of Nordman's Studio Pieces is an expanded version of an essay I wrote in 1979 with her cooperation. It appeared in the brochure accompanying her piece in the exhibition *Andre, Buren, Irwin, Nordman: Space as Support,* at the University Art Museum, Berkeley, in 1979.

6 Corinna Ferrari, "Lux Lucus," *Domus,* no. 593 (April 1979): 179.

7 Peter Plagens, "Maria Nordman," *Artforum* 12 (February 1974): 41.

8 Germano Celant, *Das Bild einer Geschichte 1956/1976: Die Sammlung Panza di Biumo* (Düsseldorf: Kunstsammlung Nordrhein-Westfalen, Kunstmuseum und Kunsthalle; Milan: Electa, 1980), pp. 295, 296.

9 Nordman, in Haskell and Glicksman, *Saddleback Mountain,* n.p.

10 Ibid., n.p.

11 Alfred Frankenstein, "Nordman's Hidden Work of Magic," *San Francisco Chronicle,* November 15, 1975.

12 Aniela Jaffe, "Symbolism in the Visual Arts," in *Man and His Symbols* (New York: Doubleday, 1964), p. 249.

13 Maria Nordman, *De Sculptura: Works in the City* (Munich: Schirmer/Mosel, 1986), pp. 11–12.

14 Maria Nordman, *Data* (Milan), April–June 1977, p. 52.

15 Nordman, conversation with author, November 1979, Santa Monica, California.

16 Nordman, *De Sculptura,* p. 98.

17 Ibid., p. 26.

18 Ibid., p. 71.

19 Melinda Wortz, "Maria Nordman, *315 N. Alameda/166 N. Central,*" *Artforum* 22 (October 1983): 82.

20 Gabriella Mills, "Nordman Transforms Abandoned Gas Station," *Contemporary* (Los Angeles Museum of Contemporary Art), Spring 1984, p. 4.

21 Ibid.

22 Sam Francis, *Aphorisms* (Larkspur Landing, Calif.: Lapis, 1985), n.p.

23 Marga Bijvoet, "Maria Nordman: Reflections on the Waves," *Artweek,* March 9, 1985, p. 1.

24 Stephan Schmidt-Wulffen, "Maria Nordman: Folkwang Museum, Essen," *Flash Art,* no. 123 (Summer 1985): 60.

Douglas Wheeler

Epigraph: Robert Morris, "The Present Tense of Space," *Art in America* 66 (January–February 1978): 73.

1 Turrell's and Irwin's exhibitions preceded Wheeler's by only eight and four months, respectively.

2 John Coplans, *Doug Wheeler* (Pasadena, Calif.: Pasadena Art Museum, 1968), n.p.

3 Ibid.

4 William Wilson, "Wheeler's Electronic Age Art in Pasadena Exhibition," *Los Angeles Times,* June 3, 1968.

5 *Time* magazine, discussing what it termed "the ineluctable serenity in the artist's work," stated in 1968 that Irwin's disc paintings and their accompanying environmental installation were like "a nun at a cocktail party."

6 Wheeler, interviews with author, 1979–81 and 1992. Unless otherwise indicated, all quotations by the artist are from this source.

7 Peter Plagens, "Los Angeles," *Artforum* 8 (March 1970): 83.

8 Michael Compton, "UK Commentary," *Studio International* 179 (June 1970): 268.

9 Michael Compton, "Controlled Environments: Larry Bell, Robert Irwin and Doug Wheeler at the Tate," *Art and Artists* 5 (May 1970): 45.

10 Robert Melville, "Bare Walls at the Tate," *New Statesman,* May 15, 1970, p. 709.

11 *Punch,* May 27, 1970, Punch Choice section.

12 Tom Marioni, "Out Front," *Vision* (Oakland, Calif.), no. 1 (September 1975): 11.

13 Many Light and Space artists have executed new versions of an existing concept, adapting a piece slightly in each situation to meet the demands of a particular site. But the only other occasion I can think of when an artist was able to work in exactly the same arena again, so the resonances of the first piece could be compounded, was Irwin's *Room with Twin Skylights, Facing Wall Removed* (1980). He installed it in what had been his old studio space in Venice, where he had created many pieces over the years.

Bruce Nauman

Epigraph: From "The Bruce Nauman Story," 1968, a broadside by Shelby "Hindu" Kennedy and Don Whitaker, Bruce Nauman Artist File, San Francisco Art Institute Archives.

1 Peter Plagens, "Roughly Ordered Thoughts on the Occasion of the Bruce Nauman Retrospective in Los Angeles," *Artforum* 11 (March 1973): 55.

2 Nauman, in Jane Livingston and Marcia Tucker, *Bruce Nauman: Work from 1965 to 1972* (Los Angeles: Los Angeles County Museum of Art; New York: Whitney Museum of American Art, 1972), p. 31.

3 Livingston, ibid.

4 Nauman, ibid., p. 22.

5 Nauman, in Willoughby Sharp, "Nauman Interview," *Arts Magazine* 44 (March 1970): 25.

6 Plagens, "Roughly Ordered Thoughts," p. 55.

7 Nauman, in Sharp, "Nauman Interview," p. 23.

8 Nauman, interviews with author, 1979–81. Unless otherwise indicated, all quotations by the artist in the text and sidebars are from this source.

9 Marcia Tucker, "PheNAUMANology," *Artforum* 9 (December 1970): 42.

10 Bruce Nauman, *Yellow Triangular Room (Installation with Yellow Lights)* (New York: Leo Castelli Gallery, 1973), exhibition mailer.

11 Nauman, in Livingston and Tucker, *Bruce Nauman,* p. 13.

12 Robert Pincus-Witten, "Bruce Nauman: Another Kind of Reasoning," *Artforum* 10 (February 1972): 31. A footnote to this discussion indicates that the "Wow" concept was adopted from the terminology of the artist Mel Bochner.

13 Michael Auping, "Bruce Nauman's *Yellow Triangular Room,*" *Artweek,* March 5, 1975.

14 Bruce Nauman, *Flayed Earth, Flayed Self (Skin Sink)* (Los Angeles: Nicholas Wilder Gallery, 1974), n.p.

15 Bruce Nauman, "False Silences," *Vision* (Oakland, Calif.), no. 1 (September 1975): n.p.

16 Melinda Wortz, "Los Angeles: Black Art and Mannerist Geometry," *Artnews* 75 (December 1976): 82.

17 "Artwalk," *Los Angeles Times,* November 5, 1976.

18 Bruce Nauman, "The Consummate Mask of Rock," 1975, typescript, Bruce Nauman Artist File, San Francisco Art Institute Archives.

19 Bruce Nauman, *Diamond Mind II* (New York: Sperone Westwater Fischer, 1976), n.p.

20 Among them were Mona da Vinci, "Bruce Nauman," *Artnews* 76 (March 1977): 142–43; and Kenneth Baker, "Bruce Nauman at Castelli, Sonnabend and Sperone Westwater Fischer," *Art in America* 65 (March–April 1977): 111–12.

21 Nauman, in Frank Zoretich, "Tunnel Vision," *Impact* (*Albuquerque Journal* magazine), March 8, 1988, p. 4.

22 Ibid.

23 Walch, ibid.

Eric Orr

Epigraph: Eric Orr, unpublished typescript in author's collection.

1 Thomas McEvilley, "Journeys in and out of the Body: Proto-Materialism of Eric Orr," *Images and Issues* 2 (Spring 1981): 18.

2 Orr, interviews with author, 1979–91. Unless otherwise indicated, all quotations by the artist in the text and sidebars are from this source.

3 Orr, in Janet Kutner, "Dallas/Fort Worth: Capricious Places," *Artnews* 76 (December 1977): 104.

4 Ibid., p. 102.

5 McEvilley, "Journeys," p. 19.

6 Ibid.

7 Ibid., p. 20.

8 Thomas McEvilley, "Negative Presences in Secret Spaces: The Art of Eric Orr," *Artforum* 20 (Summer 1982): 62.

9 Eric Orr and Thomas McEvilley, wall label, Los Angeles County Museum of Art, 1980; also made available to gallery visitors, Neil G. Ovsey Gallery, June–July 1981.

10 Ibid.

11 Hunter Drohojowska, "Pick of the Week," *LA Weekly,* June 12, 1981, p. 62.

12 Orr, in Jan Butterfield, "Eric Orr: Works from the Shadow Side," unpublished typescript in author's collection.

13 Ibid.

14 Jeff Kelley, "Eric Orr, Neil G. Ovsey Gallery," *Artforum* 22 (April 1984): 89.

15 McEvilley, "Negative Presences," p. 61.

Larry Bell

Epigraph: Truman Capote, "Music for Chameleons," in *Music for Chameleons* (New York: New American Library, 1981), pp. 8–9.

1 Douglas Kent Hall, "Lunch with Dr. Lux," *Artlines* (Taos, N.Mex.) 5 (November 1980): n.p.

2 *My Montauk* was included in Bell's major exhibition at the Pasadena Art Museum in 1972, and *Little Blank Riding Hood* was part of *The Last Time I Saw Ferus,* an exhibition at the Newport Harbor Art Museum, Newport Beach, California, in 1976.

3 Bell, in Janet Kutner, "Larry Bell's Iceberg," *Arts Magazine* 50 (January 1976): 63.

4 Ibid., p. 64.

5 Bell, interviews with author, 1976–80. Unless otherwise indicated, all quotations by the artist in the text and sidebars are from this source.

6 Barbara Haskell, *Larry Bell* (Pasadena, Calif.: Pasadena Art Museum, 1972), p. 23.

7 Larry Bell, "Larry Bell: A Statement," 1976, typescript, Santa Barbara Museum of Art, Santa Barbara, California, 1976.

8 For a fuller discussion of *The Iceberg and Its Shadow,* see Jan Butterfield, "Larry Bell: Transparent Motif," *Art in America* 66 (September–October 1978): 95–99.

9 Bell, ibid.

10 Bell, in "Bell-Orr *Solar Fountain,*" *Domus,* no. 581 (April 1978): 52.

11 Margaret Mittlebach, "From Famine to Feast in the City of Light," *LA Reader,* July 24, 1987, pp. 14, 15.

DeWain Valentine

Epigraph: Melinda Wortz, *DeWain Valentine* (Honolulu: Honolulu Academy of Art and Contemporary Arts Center, 1985), p. 8.

1 Robert Irwin's transparent prismatic columns, made in 1970–71, may have been influenced by Valentine's eight-foot prismatic column shown in maquette form at Ace Gallery, Venice, California, in 1968. Since Irwin and Valentine lived across the street from each other in Venice, it seems reasonable to suppose that Irwin was familiar with Valentine's work.

2 John Lloyd Taylor, "DeWain Valentine," *Art International* 17 (September 1973): 23.

3 Valentine, interviews with author, 1979–81. Unless otherwise indicated, all quotations by the artist in the text and sidebars are from this source.

4 Taylor, "Valentine," p. 23.

5 John Coplans, "An Interview with DeWain Valentine," in *DeWain Valentine: Recent Sculpture* (Pasadena, Calif.: Pasadena Art Museum, 1970), n.p.

6 Valentine, in Melinda Wortz, "DeWain Valentine: An Interview," *Journal* (Los Angeles Institute of Contemporary Art), no. 1 (May 1974): 17.

7 Ibid., p. 19.

8 Melinda Wortz, *DeWain Valentine: Documentation of "Spectrum Horizon" Installation* (Long Beach, Calif.: Long Beach Museum of Art, 1975), n.p.

9 Valentine, in Wortz, "Interview," p. 20.

10 Jean-Luc Bordeaux, "DeWain Valentine: Light Explored," *Art in America* 67 (December 1979): 103.

11 Fran Preisman, "DeWain Valentine, Seizing Light," *Artweek,* July 26, 1975, p. 3.

12 Wortz, *Valentine: Documentation,* p. 2.

Susan Kaiser Vogel

Epigraph: Germano Celant, "Bonds between Art and Architecture," trans. Camilla Sbrissa, in Mark Rosenthal, ed., *Andre, Buren, Irwin, Nordman: Space as Support* (Berkeley, Calif.: University of California Press, 1979), p. 19.

1 Vogel, interviews with author, 1987–91. Unless otherwise indicated, all quotations by the artist in the text and sidebars are from this source.

2 Oscar Wilde, "The Ballad of Reading Gaol," in *The Annotated Oscar Wilde* (New York: Clarkson N. Potter, 1982), p. 32.

3 Peter Clothier, "Moving Downtown," *Art in America* 69 (May 1981): 49.

4 This was a very powerful and very intimate act, an act of "topoanalysis." Janet Kardon has noted that a number of artists deal with what Gaston Bachelard has called "Topoanalysis, . . . the systematic psychological study of the sites of our intimate lives." (Janet Kardon, *Siah Armajani* [Philadelphia: Institute of Contemporary Art, University of Pennsylvania, 1985], p. 51.)

5 Melinda Wortz, "A Perceptual Journey," *Artweek*, August 12, 1978, pp. 3–4.

6 Melinda Wortz, "Architects of Emptiness," in Debra Burchett et al., *Architectural Sculpture*, 2 vols. (Los Angeles: Los Angeles Institute of Contemporary Art, 1980), vol. 1, p. 29.

7 Peter Clothier, "Walls Are for Leaping," *Artweek*, February 2, 1980, p. 3.

8 John Lombardi, "Little Miss Dangerous," *Spy*, October 1991, p. 46.

9 Melinda Wortz, "Blowing in the Wind," *Artnews* 81 (March 1982): 134.

10 Melinda Wortz, unpublished article sent to the artist in 1983.

11 Vogel, unpublished statement for Malinda Wyatt Gallery, New York, 1985.

Hap Tivey

Epigraph: Hap Tivey, "Notice to the Force," *Journal* (Los Angeles Institute of Contemporary Art), no. 10 (March–April 1976): 10.

1 Tivey, in Melinda Wortz, *Hap Tivey: Fourth Situation* (Irvine: Fine Arts Gallery, University of California, 1976), n.p.

2 Hap Tivey, interviews with author, 1979–91. Unless otherwise indicated, all quotations by the artist in the text and sidebars are from this source.

3 Tivey, in Wortz, *Fourth Situation*, n.p.

4 Ibid.

5 Barbara Haskell, "Pasadena Studio, Second Situation," in *Sodium Exchange* (Miami: Miami-Dade Community College, 1976), p. 4.

6 Melinda Wortz, "Hap Tivey: A Studio Report," *Artweek*, August 10, 1974, p. 13.

7 Ibid.

8 Tivey, letter to author, January 1988.

9 Ibid.

10 Wortz, "Studio Report," p. 14.

11 Specifically, Sandy Ballatore, "Southern California: Hap Tivey at Irvine," *Art in America* 64 (July–August 1976): 111; and Elizabeth Perlmutter, "Dizzy in the Ganzfeld," *Artnews* 75 (Summer 1976): 140–42.

12 Tivey, letter to author, January 1988.

13 Tivey, in Melinda Wortz and Hap Tivey, "Asians: A Description," *Journal* (Los Angeles Institute of Contemporary Art), no. 16 (November 1977): 46.

14 Wortz, ibid., p. 39.

15 Tivey, letter to author, January 1988.

16 Ibid.

17 Ibid.

18 Ibid.

19 Ibid.

20 Tivey, letter to author, June 1987.

21 Tor Seidler, "Hap Tivey: Blum Helman Gallery," *Artforum* 18 (December 1979): 74.

22 Tivey, "Studio Notes," in letter to author, January 1988.

Acknowledgments

My involvement with the work of the artists in this book started in the mid-1960s and has expanded over the years. I have been radically changed by my investigations of their work as I have followed my own circuitous route toward some understanding of humankind's place in the universe and our capacity to effect change. My gratitude to these artists for their tireless patience is boundless. It is not easy to provide a formula for magic and harder still to submit one's psyche to the tape recorder, but they have all been willing to make the attempt. In some very real ways, we developed along parallel paths: I have slowly (and sometimes in spite of myself) become more intuitive, and they have learned to give words to their visual thinking. It has been a thoroughly symbiotic process.

I wish to thank the National Endowment for the Arts, which first provided me with travel funds and then twice gave me a critic's grant, thus substantially underwriting my initial investigations into California art. I offer this book as an expression of my ongoing desire to contribute to the much-needed documentation of the state's art.

My thanks also go to the Frederick R. and Marcia Weisman Foundation, for providing me with an emergency fellowship in the 1980s when my teaching stipend could not support my critical activity; and to Lyn Kienholz, of the California International Arts Foundation, which similarly provided me with a substantial grant. Lyn's hospitality and moral support also made possible my countless trips to Los Angeles when I was living in San Francisco. In addition, I am grateful to the San Francisco Art Institute for its patience when my travels cross country to view the projects documented here took me away from the classroom.

Thanks are due to Alberta Mayo, who typed two well-thumbed versions of the manuscript, and to Karel Birnbaum and Amy Handy, who typed many more. I also wish to thank Kathy Holland, whose initial editing helped save me from inaccuracies and non sequiturs; Philip Reynolds, who made sure that the endnotes and bibliography are as accurate as the fugitive and ephemeral sources permit; Jeremy Morgan, who wrestled with the editing of an early draft; and Sue Arnold, who edited the early version and whose virtually flawless editorial sensibility I have come to depend upon.

I am deeply indebted to the photographer Jim McHugh, whose superb portraits of the artists in this book enhance our understanding of them. I also owe a great deal to Frank Thomas, who so generously "staked" me to prints of photographs from the early 1960s when my funds ran out.

Nancy Grubb, executive editor at Abbeville Press, immersed herself in the art of light and space in order to condense some seven hundred manuscript pages to publishable size. Her unfailing ear for dialogue and her ability to "keep the movie running" while she was making massive cuts contributed substantially to this book. I also thank Scott W Santoro, whose complex and innovative design for this book has made it an art form in itself.

Finally, and most important, I am profoundly grateful to Robert E. Abrams, publisher and president of Abbeville Press, for his unwavering support of this book throughout the many years that intervened between its initial receipt at Abbeville and its publication.

Selected Bibliography

General Books and Catalogs

The Art Collection of Pacific Enterprises. Artists' biographies by Jan Butterfield. Los Angeles: Pacific Enterprises, 1990. Includes Bell, Nauman, Orr, Turrell, Valentine.

Brown, Julia, and Bridget Johnson, eds. *The First Show: Painting and Sculpture from Eight Collections, 1940–1980.* Los Angeles: Museum of Contemporary Art, 1983. Includes Bell, Irwin, Nauman, Nordman, Orr, Wheeler.

Celant, Germano. "Ambient/Art," in *La biennale di Venezia, Section of Visual Arts and Architecture, General Catalogue.* 2 vols. Venice: Alfieri Edizioni d'Arte, 1976. Includes Irwin, Nordman, Wheeler.

———. *Das Bild einer Geschichte 1956/1976: Die Sammlung Panza di Biumo.* Düsseldorf: Kunstsammlung Nordrhein-Westfalen, Kunstmuseum und Kunsthalle; Milan: Electa, 1980. Includes Bell, Irwin, Nauman, Nordman, Orr, Turrell, Wheeler.

Compton, Michael. *Larry Bell, Robert Irwin, Doug Wheeler.* London: Tate Gallery, 1970.

Coplans, John. *West Coast 1945–1969.* Pasadena, Calif.: Pasadena Museum of Art, 1969. Includes Bell, Irwin, Nauman.

Davis, Douglas. *Art and the Future: A History/Prophecy of the Collaboration between Science, Technology and Art.* New York: Praeger Publishers, 1973. Includes Bell, Irwin, Nauman, Turrell.

Foley, Suzanne. *Space, Time, Sound: Conceptual Art in the San Francisco Bay Area: The 1970s.* San Francisco: San Francisco Museum of Art, 1973. Includes Bell, Irwin, Nauman, Nordman.

Friedman, Mildred. *The Meaning of Place in Art and Architecture.* Cambridge, Mass.: MIT Press, 1983.

Goldwater, Marge, and Hal Glicksman. *Los Angeles in the Seventies.* Fort Worth, Tex.: Fort Worth Art Museum, 1977.

Heiss, Alanna, and Linda Blumberg. *Rooms: P.S. 1, June 9–26, 1976.* New York: Institute for Art and Urban Resources, 1977.

Hopkins, Henry T. *Painting and Sculpture in California: The Modern Era.* San Francisco Museum of Modern Art, 1977. Includes Bell, Irwin, Nauman, Nordman, Turrell, Valentine, Wheeler.

Isozaki, Arata. "The Notion of Space/Time in Japan." In *Ma: Space/Time in Japan.* Edited by Seigow Matsuoka. New York: Cooper-Hewitt Museum, 1978.

Knight, Christopher. *Art of the Sixties and Seventies: The Panza Collection.* New York: Rizzoli, 1988. Includes Bell, Irwin, Nauman, Nordman, Orr, Turrell, Wheeler.

Kompass 4: Westkunst USA = West Coast USA. Eindhoven, the Netherlands: Stedelijk van Abbemuseum, 1969. Includes Bell, Irwin, Nauman, Wheeler.

Kultermann, Udo. *The New Sculpture.* Trans. Stanley Baron. New York: Praeger Publishers, 1967. Includes Bell, Nauman, Valentine.

Lippard, Lucy R. *Six Years: The Dematerialization of the Art Object from 1966 to 1972.* New York: Praeger Publishers, 1973.

Sharp, Willoughby. *Light/Motion/Space.* Minneapolis: Walker Art Center, 1967.

Singerman, Howard, ed. *Individuals: A Selected History of Contemporary Art, 1945–1986.* Los Angeles: Museum of Contemporary Art; New York: Abbeville Press, 1986. Includes Bell, Irwin, Nauman, Turrell, Wheeler.

Tuchman, Maurice, et al. *The Spiritual in Art: Abstract Painting 1890–1985.* Los Angeles: Los Angeles County Museum of Art; New York: Abbeville Press, 1986. Includes Irwin, Nauman, Orr, Turrell.

——— and Jane Livingston. *A Report on the Art and Technology Program of the Los Angeles County Museum of Art, 1967–1971.* Los Angeles: Los Angeles County Museum of Art, 1971. Includes Bell, Irwin, Nauman, Turrell.

Wortz, Melinda. *University of California, Irvine, 1965–75.* La Jolla, Calif.: La Jolla Museum of Contemporary Art, 1975. Includes Bell, Irwin, Nauman.

———. *California Perceptions: Light and Space, Selections from the Wortz Collection.* Fullerton: California State University Art Gallery, 1979.

General Periodicals

Baker, Elizabeth C. "Los Angeles, 1971." *Artnews* 70 (September 1971): 27–39. Includes Bell, Irwin, Nauman, Turrell, Valentine.

Butterfield, Jan. "Context: Light and Space as Art." *Journal* (Los Angeles Institute of Contemporary Art), no. 32 (Spring 1982): 57–61.

Celant, Germano. "Arte Ambienale in California: Asher, Nauman, Irwin, Orr, Turrell, Nordman, Wheeler." *Domus,* no. 547 (June 1975): 52–53.

———. "Art Spaces." *Studio International* 190 (September–October 1975): 116–23. Includes Irwin, Nauman, Orr, Turrell, Wheeler.

Compton, Michael. "Controlled Environments: Larry Bell, Robert Irwin and Doug Wheeler at the Tate." *Art and Artists* 5 (May 1970): 45.

———. "UK Commentary." *Studio International* 179 (June 1970): 268–70. Includes Bell, Irwin, Wheeler.

Gendel, Milton. "If One Hasn't Visited Count Panza's Villa, One Doesn't Really Know What Collecting Is All About." *Artnews* 78 (December 1979): 44–49. Includes Bell, Irwin, Nauman, Nordman, Turrell.

Hart, Claudia. "Environments of Light: Ornament in Search of Architecture." *Industrial Design* 31 (March–April 1984): 22–27. Includes Bell, Irwin, Turrell.

Livingston, Jane. "Two Generations in L.A." *Art in America* 57 (January–February 1969): 92–97. Includes Irwin, Turrell, Wheeler.

Marioni, Tom. "Out Front." *Vision* (Oakland, Calif.), no. 1 (September 1975): 8–11. Includes Bell, Irwin, Nauman, Wheeler.

Melville, Robert. "Bare Walls at the Tate." *New Statesman,* May 15, 1970, p. 709. Includes Bell, Irwin, Wheeler.

Morris, Robert. "The Present Tense of Space." *Art in America* 66 (January–February 1978): 70–80.

Muchnic, Suzanne. "Advent of Avant-Garde." *Los Angeles Times,* July 2, 1980.

Perlmutter, Elizabeth. "A Hotbed of Advanced Art." *Artnews* 75 (January 1976): 44–46. Includes Bell, Irwin, Nauman, Turrell.

Piene, Nan R. "L.A. Trip." *Art in America* 58 (March–April 1970): 138–41. Includes Bell, Irwin, Turrell.

Plagens, Peter. "Site Wars." *Art in America* 70 (January 1982): 90–98. Includes Irwin, Orr, Turrell.

Restany, Pierre. "The Angeles Lizard." *Domus,* no. 627 (April 1982): 75. Includes Bell, Irwin, Nauman, Valentine.

Russell, David. "London." *Arts Magazine* 44 (Summer 1970): 53. Includes Bell, Irwin, Wheeler.

Seldis, Henry J. "Pasadena's Lopsided West Coast Survey." *Los Angeles Times,* November 30, 1969, p. 78.

Sharp, Willoughby. "New Directions in Southern California Sculpture." *Arts Magazine* 44 (Summer 1970): 35–38. Includes Bell, Irwin, Orr, Turrell, Wheeler.

Stevens, Mark. "California Dreamers." *Newsweek,* August 17, 1981, pp. 78–79. Includes Bell, Irwin, Orr.

Winer, Helene. "How Los Angeles Looks Today." *Studio International* 183 (October 1971): 127–31. Includes Bell, Irwin, Nauman, Valentine.

Larry Bell

Aldrich, Larry. "New Talent USA." *Art in America* 54 (July–August 1966): 22–69.

Ashton, Dore. "Art." *Arts and Architecture* 81 (June 1964): 8–9.

———. "New York Commentary: New Sculpture Fresh in Old Techniques." *Studio International* 169 (June 1965): 260–63.

———. "New York Commentary." *Studio International* 179 (March 1970): 118–19.

Bell, Larry. "Larry Bell: A Statement." 1976. Typescript, Santa Barbara Museum of Art, Santa Barbara, Calif.

———. "Bell-Orr *Solar Fountain.*" *Domus,* no. 581 (April 1978): 52.

Bengston, Billy Al. "Los Angeles Artists' Studios." *Art in America* 58 (November–December 1970): 100–109.

Bourdon, David. "Boxing up Space." *Village Voice,* February 18, 1966.

Burnside, Madeleine. "Larry Bell and Eric Orr." *Artnews* 77 (April 1978): 152–53.

Butterfield, Jan. "Larry Bell: Transparent Motif." *Art in America* 66 (September–October 1978): 95–99.

Coplans, John. "Three Los Angeles Artists." *Artforum* 1 (April 1963): 29–31.

———. "Circle of Styles on the West Coast." *Art in America* 52 (June 1964): 24–41.

———. "The New Abstraction on the West Coast, U.S.A." *Studio International* 169 (May 1965): 192–99.

———. "Larry Bell." *Artforum* 3 (June 1965): 27–29.

———. "Five Los Angeles Sculptors at Irvine." *Artforum* 4 (February 1966): 33–37.

Danieli, Fidel A. "Bell's Progress." *Artforum* 5 (Summer 1967): 68–71.

Friedman, Martin. "Fourteen Sculptors: The Industrial Edge." *Art International* 14 (February 1970): 31–40, 55.

Gabriel, Bertram. "New Mexico: The Mainstream and Local Currents." *Artnews* 81 (April 1982): 120–24.

Hall, Douglas Kent. "Lunch with Dr. Lux." *Artlines* (Taos, N.Mex.) 5 (November 1980): n.p.

Haskell, Barbara. *Larry Bell.* Pasadena, Calif.: Pasadena Art Museum, 1972.

Hargreaves, George. "Post-Modernism Looks beyond Itself." *Landscape Architecture* 73 (July–August 1983): 60–65.

Heartney, Eleanor. "Larry Bell at Shafrazi." *Art in America* 79 (July 1991): 124–25.

Hess, Thomas B. "You Can Hang It in the Hall." *Artnews* 64 (April 1965): 41–43, 49–50.

Kirby, Michael. "Sculpture as a Visual Instrument." *Art International* 12 (October 1968): 35–37.

Knight, Christopher. "Environment as Sculpture: The Intimate, Human Work of Larry Bell." *Los Angeles Herald Examiner,* June 14, 1981, sec. 3, p. 1.

Kozloff, Max. "São Paulo in Washington." *Nation,* February 28, 1966, pp. 250–52.

Kutner, Janet. "Larry Bell's Iceberg." *Arts Magazine* 50 (January 1976): 62–66.

Langsner, Jules. "Art Centers, Los Angeles: America's Second Art City." *Art in America* 51 (March–April 1963): 127–31.

Larry Bell: New Work. Essay by Melinda Wortz. Yonkers, N.Y.: Hudson River Museum, 1981.

Leider, Philip. "The Cool School." *Artforum* 2 (Summer 1964): 47.

———. "Gallery '68: High Art and Low Art." *Look* 32 (January 1968): 14–21.

———. "New York: *Spaces.*" *Artforum* 8 (February 1970): 69–70.

Mellow, James R. "Through the Looking Glass." *New York Times,* April 25, 1971.

Meyer, Jon. "Larry Bell." *Arts Magazine* 57 (September 1982): 29.

Montgomery, Cara. "Los Angeles Report." *Arts Magazine* 47 (May–June 1973): 53.

Muchnic, Suzanne. "Pulling the Walls over Our Eyes." *Los Angeles Times,* June 15, 1981, sec. 6, pp. 1–2.

Nadelman, Cynthia. "New York Reviews: Hudson River Museum." *Artnews* 80 (September 1981): 240–42.

Nordland, Gerald. "Los Angeles Newsletter." *Art International* 19 (December 1975): 29–37.

Perrone, Jeff. "Larry Bell, Eric Orr: Marian Goodman Gallery." *Artforum* 16 (April 1978): 64–65.

Peterson, William. "Smoke Rings, Shinto Shrines, Doktor Thrill and the Snake Lady." *Artnews* 79 (December 1980): 136–39.

Plagens, Peter. "Present-Day Styles and Ready-Made Criticism." *Artforum* 5 (December 1966): 36–39.

———. "Los Angeles: Five Artists, Ace Gallery." *Artforum* 10 (October 1971): 86–87.

———. "Larry Bell Reassessed." *Artforum* 11 (October 1972): 71–73.

Rickey, Carrie. "Six-Sided Constructions." *Art in America* 71 (April 1983): 150–53.

Rose, Barbara. "Los Angeles: The Second City." *Art in America* 54 (January 1966): 110–13.

Rush, David. "Larry Bell on New Work." *Artweek,* May 15, 1976, pp. 1, 16.

"See-Throughs." *Time,* February 9, 1968, pp. 40, 45.

Seldis, Henry J. "Viewer, Object Merge in Larry Bell Glasses." *Los Angeles Times,* April 16, 1972, p. 50.

Smithson, Robert. "Entropy and the New Monuments." *Artforum* 4 (June 1966): 26–31.

Tarshis, Jerome. "San Francisco." *Artforum* 8 (June 1970): 91–92.

Tillim, Sidney. "In the Galleries: Seven New Artists." *Arts Magazine* 38 (September 1964): 62.

Trini, Tommaso. "Larry Bell: Le pareti dell'infinito." (Larry Bell: Vacuum Vision.) *Domus,* no. 460 (March 1968): 42–44.

Tuchman, Phyllis. "American Art in Germany: The History of a Phenomenon." *Artforum* 9 (November 1970): 58–69.

Wight, Frederick S., ed. *Transparency, Reflection, Light, Space: Four Artists.* Los Angeles: Art Galleries, University of California, 1971.

Wilson, William. "Larry Bell: Heeding the Siren of Technology." *Los Angeles Times,* March 28, 1982.

"Work in Progress." *Esquire* 73 (December 1969): 210–17.

Robert Irwin

Albright, Thomas. "Robert Irwin: 'Everything I've Done in the Last Five Years Doesn't Exist.'" *Artnews* 76 (Summer 1977): 49–54.

Artner, Alan G. "Persistent Images." *Chicago Tribune,* May 17, 1987, sec. 13.

Ashton, Dore. "Art." *Arts and Architecture* 81 (June 1964): 8–9.

Atkins, Robert. "Robert Irwin." *Arts Magazine* 60 (December 1985): 102.

Baker, Kenneth. "A Purveyor of the 'Phenomenal.'" *San Francisco Chronicle,* October 20, 1985.

Barron, Stephanie. *The Museum as Site: Sixteen Projects.* Los Angeles: Los Angeles County Museum of Art, 1981.

Beardsley, John. *Earthworks and Beyond.* New York: Abbeville Press, 1984.

Berman, Avis. "Public Sculpture's New Look." *Artnews* 90 (September 1991): 102–9.

Butterfield, Jan. "The State of the Real: Robert Irwin Discusses the Activities of an Extended Consciousness, Part 1." *Arts Magazine* 46 (Summer 1972): 47–49.

———. "Reshaping the Shape of Things; Part 2: The Myth of the Artist." *Arts Magazine* 47 (September–October 1972): 30–32.

———. "An Uncompromising Other Way." *Arts Magazine* 48 (June 1974): 52–55.

———. "Robert Irwin: On the Periphery of Knowing." *Arts Magazine* 50 (February 1976): 72–77.

———. "Robert Irwin: World Without Frame." *Arts Magazine* 50 (February 1976): 72–77.

———. *Space as Support, Part 2.* Berkeley, Calif.: University Art Museum, 1979.

———. "Robert Irwin: The Name of the Game Is Context." *Calendar* (University Art Museum, Berkeley, Calif.) 1 (March 1979): 1.

———. "The Enigma Suffices: Robert Irwin, *Room with Twin Skylights.*" *Images and Issues* 1 (Winter 1980–81): 38–40.

Cameron, Dan. "High-Tech Redux." *Flash Art,* no. 141 (Summer 1988): 102–5.

Coplans, John. "Circle of Styles on the West Coast." *Art in America* 52 (June 1964): 24–41.

———. "The New Abstraction on the West Coast, U.S.A." *Studio International* 169 (May 1965): 192–99.

———. *Gene Davis, Robert Irwin, Richard Smith.* New York: Jewish Museum, 1968.

———. *Robert Irwin.* Pasadena, Calif.: Pasadena Art Museum, 1968.

Dillenberger, Jane, and John Dillenberger. *Perception of the Spirit in Twentieth-Century American Art.* Indianapolis: Indianapolis Museum of Art, 1977.

Dillon, David. "Fraud Halts Art Project in Dallas." *Los Angeles Times,* March 16, 1980.

Dreiss, Joseph. "Robert Irwin." *Arts Magazine* 49 (February 1975): 16.

Failing, Patricia. "MOCA." *Artnews* 82 (October 1983): 105–9.

———. "San Diego: Big Bird on Campus." *Artnews* 82 (November 1983): 132–33.

Feinberg, Jean E. *Perceiving the Garden: Robert Irwin at Wave Hill.* New York: Wave Hill, 1987.

Fischer, Hal. "Berkeley: 'Space as Support.'" *Artforum* 18 (October 1979): 64–66.

Fried, Michael. "New York Letter." *Art International* 8 (Summer 1964): 81–82.

Glenn, Constance, ed. *A View Through.* Long Beach: California State University Museum Studies Program and Art Galleries, 1975.

Hargreaves, George. "Post-Modernism Looks beyond Itself." *Landscape Architecture* 73 (July–August 1983): 60–65.

Hazlitt, Gordon J. "An Incredibly Beautiful Quandary." *Artnews* 75 (May 1976): 36–38.

Herrera, Hayden. "Manhattan Seven." *Art in America* 65 (July–August 1977): 50–63.

Hopps, Walter. *VIII São Paulo Bienal, United States of America.* Pasadena, Calif.: Pasadena Art Museum, 1966.

Hudson, Andrew. "Letter from Washington." *Art International* 10 (Summer 1966): 130–32.

Irwin, Robert. Statement of Position on Photographic Reproductions of His Paintings. *Artforum* 3 (June 1965): 23.

———. Letter to the Editor. *Artforum* 6 (February 1968): 4.

———. "Twenty Questions." *Vision* (Oakland, Calif.) 1 (September 1975): 38.

———. "The Hypothesis Is Simple." *Journal* (Los Angeles Institute of Contemporary Art), no. 15 (July–August 1977): 21–23.

———. "Notes toward a Model." In *Robert Irwin.* New York: Whitney Museum of American Art, 1977.

———. Statement made at the seminar "The Spirit in Art," Graduate Union Theological Seminary, Berkeley, California, April 21, 1979. Unpublished transcription by Craig Vista Svare.

———. *Being and Circumstance: Notes toward a Conditional Art.* Larkspur Landing, Calif.: Lapis, 1985.

"Irwin's Light Piece." *Artweek,* November 4, 1972, p. 3.

Joselit, David. "Lessons in Public Sculpture" (Stuart Collection, University of California, San Diego). *Art in America* 77 (December 1989): 130–34.

Kozloff, Max. "São Paulo in Washington." *Nation,* February 28, 1966, pp. 250–52.

Kramer, Hilton. "U.S. Art from São Paulo on View in Washington." *New York Times,* January 29, 1966, sec. 1, p. 22.

———. "Art: The Jewish Museum Assembles a Triptych of 60's Talent in Stripes, Disks and Shaped Canvas." *New York Times,* March 22, 1968, p. 56.

———. "A Career That Rejected Studio Art." *New York Times,* May 8, 1977, sec. 2, p. 25.

Kutner, Janet. "Rusty Knife Slices New Plaza, but It's Cause to Rejoice." *Dallas Morning News,* September 19, 1981, p. 10.

Langsner, Jules. "Los Angeles." *Artnews* 58 (Summer 1959): 23, 59–60.

———. "Art Centers, Los Angeles: America's Second Art City." *Art in America* 51 (March–April 1963): 127–31.

Leider, Philip. "The Cool School." *Artforum* 2 (Summer 1964): 47.

——— and Lucy R. Lippard. *Robert Irwin, Kenneth Price.* Los Angeles: Los Angeles County Museum of Art, 1966.

Levine, Edward. "Robert Irwin's Recent Work." *Artforum* 16 (December 1977): 24–29.

Licht, Ira. *Robert Irwin.* Chicago: Museum of Contemporary Art, 1975.

Licht, Jennifer. *Spaces.* New York: Museum of Modern Art, 1969.

Livingston, Jane. *Robert Irwin/Doug Wheeler.* Fort Worth: Fort Worth Art Center, 1969.

———. "Some Thoughts on 'Art and Technology.'" *Studio International* 181 (June 1971): 258–63.

McEvilley, Thomas. "Robert Irwin: Public Safety Building Plaza, Old Post Office." *Artforum* 22 (June 1984): 96.

———. "Robert Irwin: The Pace Gallery." *Artforum* 24 (January 1986): 87.

McGill, Douglas C. "Sculpture Goes Public." *New York Times Magazine,* April 27, 1986, pp. 42–45, 63–67, 85–87.

Mackintosh, Alistair. "Robert Irwin: An Interview with Alistair Mackintosh." *Art and Artists* 6 (March 1972): 24–27.

———. "Los Angeles Newsletter." *Art International* 19 (December 1975): 29–37.

"Place in the Sun." *Time,* August 30, 1968, pp. 38–41.

Plagens, Peter. "Robert Irwin's Bar Paintings." *Artforum* 17 (March 1979): 41–43.

Projects for PCA. Essay by Janet Kardon. Interview by Marcia Tucker. Philadelphia: Philadelphia College of Art, 1976.

"Robert Irwin: Interview." 50-minute video interview by Kate Horsfield, August 1976. Available through *Video Data Bank* (School of the Art Institute of Chicago), 1982.

Robins, Corinne. "The Circle in Orbit." *Art in America* 56 (November–December 1968): 62–69.

Rosenthal, Mark, ed. *Andre, Buren, Irwin, Nordman: Space as Support.* Berkeley and Los Angeles: University of California Press, 1979.

Rosing, Larry. "Robert Irwin at Pace." *Art in America* 63 (March–April 1975): 87.

Schwartz, Ellen. "'Floating' a Line in Space." *Artnews* 76 (Summer 1977): 52–53.

Solomon, Alan. "Is California Art the Equal of Eastern Art?" *San Francisco Chronicle,* July 18, 1965.

Smith, Roberta. "Robert Irwin: The Subject Is Sight." *Art in America* 64 (March–April 1976): 68–73.

———. "Matter Turned into Light and Space." *New York Times,* September 25, 1992, sec. C, p. 29.

Some New Art from Los Angeles. San Francisco: San Francisco Art Institute, 1964.

Stevens, Mark. "The Dizzy Decade." *Newsweek,* March 26, 1979, pp. 88–91, 94.

The Studs: Moses, Irwin, Price, Bengston. Los Angeles: Ferus Gallery, 1965.

"The Talk of the Town: Black Plane." *New Yorker,* June 6, 1977, pp. 28–29.

"The Talk of the Town: Seeing." *New Yorker,* September 30, 1985, pp. 27–29.

Tillim, Sidney. "In the Galleries: Seven New Artists." *Arts Magazine* 38 (September 1964): 62.

Tomkins, Calvin. "Like Water in a Glass." *New Yorker,* March 21, 1983, pp. 92–97.

———. "The Art World: Knowing in Action." *New Yorker,* November 11, 1985, pp. 144–49.

Turnbull, Betty. *The Last Time I Saw Ferus.* Newport Beach, Calif.: Newport Harbor Art Museum, 1976.

"The 'Vasari' Diary: Down the Granite Path." *Artnews* 81 (January 1982): 16–20.

Wasserman, Emily. "Robert Irwin, Gene Davis, Richard Smith." *Artforum* 6 (May 1968): 47–49.

Weschler, Lawrence. "Robert Irwin's Whitney Project: Retrospects and Prospects." *Journal* (Los Angeles Institute of Contemporary Art), no. 15 (July–August 1977): 14–20.

———. "Robert Irwin." *Matrix/Berkeley* 15 (University Art Museum), October–December 1979.

———. "Lines of Inquiry." *Art in America* 70 (March 1982): 102–9.

———. *Seeing Is Forgetting the Name of the Thing One Sees: A Life of the Contemporary Artist Robert Irwin.* Berkeley and Los Angeles: University of California Press, 1982.

Wight, Frederick S., ed. *Transparency, Reflection, Light, Space: Four Artists.* Los Angeles: Art Galleries, University of California, 1971.

Wilson, William. "Couple of Bogey Men Add Luster to an Art Tradition." *Los Angeles Times,* July 11, 1966.

Wortz, Melinda. "Robert Irwin's Portal." *Artweek,* February 16, 1974, p. 3.

———. "Perceptual Reorientations." *Artweek,* November 15, 1975, p. 7.

———. "Self-Scrutiny and Scrims." *Artnews* 75 (January 1976): 62–64.

———. "Surrendering to Presence: Robert Irwin's Esthetic Integration." *Artforum* 20 (November 1981): 63–69.

———. "San Diego: Robert Irwin, University of California." *Artforum* 22 (October 1983): 81–82.

Bruce Nauman

Abbildungsteil der Auftragswerke. Basel: Skulpturenausstellung Wenkenpart Riehen, 1980.

Armstrong, Richard, and Richard Marshall, eds. *The New Sculpture 1965–1975: Between Geometry and Gesture.* New York: Whitney Museum of American Art, 1990.

Auping, Michael. "Bruce Nauman's *Yellow Triangular Room.*" *Artweek,* March 5, 1975.

"The Avant-Garde: Subtle, Cerebral, Elusive." *Time,* November 22, 1968, pp. 70–77.

Baker, Kenneth. "New York: Bruce Nauman, Castelli Gallery." *Artforum* 9 (April 1971): 77–78.

———. "Bruce Nauman at Castelli, Sonnabend and Sperone Westwater Fischer." *Art in America* 65 (March–April 1977): 111–12.

Barnitz, Jacqueline. "In the Galleries: Bruce Nauman." *Arts Magazine* 42 (March 1968): 62.

Beatty, Frances. "Nauman's Art Downtown." *Art World,* November 20, 1976, p. 9.

Bell, Jane. "Bruce Nauman: Leo Castelli; Sperone Westwater Fischer." *Artnews* 81 (May 1982): 168–70.

Benezra, Neal. "Empowering Space: Notes on the Sculpture of Bruce Nauman." In *Affinities and Intuitions: The Gerald S. Elliott Collection of Contemporary Art,* pp. 58–91. Chicago: Art Institute of Chicago; London: Thames and Hudson, 1990.

"Bruce Nauman" (Interview). *Avalanche,* 1971, no. 2, pp. 22–31.

"Bruce Nauman, Galerie Schmela, Düsseldorf." *Heute Kunst/Flash Art,* no. 25 (March 1979): 12.

Bruggen, Coosje van. *Bruce Nauman.* New York: Rizzoli, 1988.

———, Dieter Koepplin, and Franz Meyer. *Bruce Nauman Drawings, 1965–86.* Basel: Museum für Gegenwartskunst, 1986.

Burchett, Debra, et al. *Architectural Sculpture.* 2 vols. Los Angeles: Los Angeles Institute of Contemporary Art, 1980.

Burton, Scott. "Time on Their Hands." *Artnews* 68 (Summer 1969): 40–43.

Butterfield, Jan. "Bruce Nauman: The Center of Yourself." *Arts Magazine* 49 (February 1975): 53–55.

Calas, Nicolas. "Bodyworks and Porpoises." *Artforum* 16 (January 1978): 33–37.

Carluccio, Luigi. "Un tempo per l'arte americana d'oggi." *Bolaffiarte* (Turin, Italy) 3 (February 1972): 42–44.

Cohrs, Timothy. "Bruce Nauman: Drawings." *Artnews* 86 (November 1987): 200.

Danieli, Fidel A. "The Art of Bruce Nauman." *Artforum* 6 (December 1967): 15–19.

da Vinci, Mona. "Bruce Nauman." *Artnews* 76 (March 1977): 142–43.

Davis, Douglas. "Veni, Vidi, Video." *Newsweek,* April 13, 1970, pp. 98–99.

———. "Man of Parts." *Newsweek,* March 1, 1971, p. 70.

Domingo, Willis. "New York Galleries." *Arts Magazine* 45 (March 1971): 55–56.

Frankenstein, Alfred. "A Survey of Nauman Ties All Together." *San Francisco Chronicle,* January 7, 1973.

———. "A Confrontation with the Modern Era." *San Francisco Chronicle,* September 12, 1976.

Gilardi, Piero. "Da New York." *Flash Art* (Rome), no. 5 (1967): 1–2.

Glueck, Grace. "Art Notes: Bruce Nauman, No Body but His." *New York Times,* April 1, 1973, sec. 2, p. 24.

Gold, Barbara. "Corcoran Biennial: New Sensibility in Washington." *Arts Magazine* 43 (April 1969): 28–31.

Goldberg, Roselee. "Space as Praxis." *Studio International* 190 (September–October 1975): 130–35.

Gopnik, Adam. "Bits and Pieces." *New Yorker,* May 14, 1990, p. 145.

Greenspun, Roger. "Screen: Palette of Art." *New York Times,* April 14, 1972, p. 23.

Handy, Ellen. "Bruce Nauman/Judy Tomkins/Keith Haring." *Arts Magazine* 60 (January 1986): 134.

Hughes, Robert. "Vapid Wunderkind." *Time,* April 16, 1973, p. 61.

Joselit, David. "Lessons in Public Sculpture" (Stuart Collection, University of California, San Diego). *Art in America* 77 (December 1989): 130–34.

Junker, Howard, and Ann Ray Martin. "The New Art." *Newsweek,* July 29, 1968, pp. 56–63.

Kozloff, Max. "Nine in a Warehouse." *Artforum* 7 (February 1969): 38–42.

Kramer, Hilton. "At the Whitney: In Duchamp's Footsteps." *New York Times,* March 30, 1973.

———. "Avant-Garde Academician." *New York Times,* April 8, 1973, sec. 2, p. 25.

Kurtz, Stephen. "Reviews and Previews: Bruce Nauman." *Artnews* 68 (September 1969): 20.

Larson, Kay. "Spectator Sport." *New York,* July 29, 1991, pp. 50–51.

Leider, Philip. "'The Properties of Materials': In the Shadow of Robert Morris." *New York Times,* December 22, 1968, sec. 2, p. 31.

———. "New York." *Artforum* 8 (February 1970): 68–70.

Lichtenstein, Therese. "Arts Reviews: Bruce Nauman." *Arts Magazine* 59 (January 1985): 36.

Linker, Kate. "Bruce Nauman, Leo Castelli Gallery, Sperone Westwater Gallery." *Artforum* 23 (January 1985): 86–87.

Lippard, Lucy R. "Eccentric Abstraction." *Art International* 10 (November 1966): 28, 34–40.

Livingston, Jane, and Marcia Tucker. *Bruce Nauman: Work from 1965 to 1972.* Los Angeles: Los Angeles County Museum of Art; New York: Whitney Museum of American Art, 1972.

Lyon, Christopher. "Bruce Nauman: Sperone Westwater." *Artnews* 87 (December 1988): 145.

McCann, Cecile N. "Bruce Nauman." *Artweek,* January 6, 1973, pp. 1, 12.

McCormick, Carlo. "Bruce Nauman: Sperone Westwater, Leo Castelli." *Flash Art,* no. 120 (January 1985): 42.

Monte, James, and Marcia Tucker. *Anti-Illusion: Procedures/Materials.* New York: Whitney Museum of American Art, 1969.

Moore, Alan. "Of Mutable Space." *Artweek*, December 22, 1973, pp. 5–6.

———. "Bruce Nauman, Leo Castelli Gallery." *Artforum* 13 (April 1975): 79–80.

Müller, Grégoire. *The New Avant-Garde: Issues for the Art of the Seventies.* New York: Praeger Publishers, 1972.

Nauman, Bruce. *Floating Room.* New York: Leo Castelli Gallery, 1973.

———. *Flayed Earth, Flayed Self (Skin Sink).* Los Angeles: Nicholas Wilder Gallery, 1974.

———. "False Silences." *Vision* (Oakland, Calif.), no. 1 (September 1975): n.p.

———. "The Consummate Mask of Rock." Typescript, Bruce Nauman Artist File, San Francisco Art Institute Archives, 1975.

———. *Diamond Mind II.* New York: Sperone Westwater Fischer, 1976.

Nemser, Cindy. "Subject-Object: Body Art." *Arts Magazine* 46 (September–October 1971): 38–42.

Nisselson, Jane E. "Contemporary Sculpture at MoMA." *Skyline* 2 (Summer 1979): 10.

Nittve, Lars. "Quartetto." *Artforum* 23 (September 1984): 107–8.

Oxenaar, Rudolf, et al. *Bruce Nauman, 1972–1981.* Otterlo, the Netherlands: Rijksmuseum Kröller-Müller, 1981.

Parent, Béatrice. "Le Néon dans l'art contemporain." *Chroniques de l'art vivant* 20 (May 1971): 4–6.

Perreault, John. "Reviews and Previews: Bruce Nauman." *Artnews* 67 (March 1968): 22.

———. "Art." *Village Voice,* December 2, 1971.

Perrone, Jeff. "Bruce Nauman, Leo Castelli Gallery Downtown, Sonnabend, Sperone Westwater Fischer." *Artforum* 15 (January 1977) 58–60.

Peterson, William. "Smoke Rings, Shinto Shrines, Doktor Thrill and the Snake Lady." *Artnews* 79 (December 1980): 136–39.

Pincus-Witten, Robert. "New York." *Artforum* 6 (April 1968): 63–65.

———. "Bruce Nauman: Another Kind of Reasoning." *Artforum* 10 (February 1972): 30–37.

Plagens, Peter. "Roughly Ordered Thoughts on the Occasion of the Bruce Nauman Retrospective in Los Angeles." *Artforum* 11 (March 1973): 55–59.

———. "Bruce Nauman, Nicholas Wilder Gallery." *Artforum* 12 (March 1974): 85–86.

Pohlen, Annelie. "Bruce Nauman: Galerie Fischer, Museum Haus Esters." *Artforum* 22 (May 1984): 95–96.

Price, Jonathan. "Video Art: A Medium Discovering Itself." *Artnews* 76 (January 1977): 41–47.

Princenthal, Nancy. "Bruce Nauman: Sperone Westwater and Leo Castelli." *Artnews* 84 (January 1985): 137.

Raffaele, Joe, and Elizabeth C. Baker. "The Way Out West: Interviews with Four San Francisco Artists." *Artnews* 66 (Summer 1967): 38–41, 66–67.

Ratcliff, Carter. "New York Letter: Spring." Parts 1, 2. *Art International* 15 (April and May 1971): 25–28, 31, 69; 32–39, 45.

———. "New York Letter." *Art International* 16 (February 1972): 32–34, 52–56.

———. "Adversary Spaces." *Artforum* 11 (October 1972): 40–44.

———. "Bruce Nauman at Castelli Greene Street and Sperone Westwater." *Art in America* 73 (March 1985): 151.

Rauh, Emily S. "Among Recent Acquisitions." *Saint Louis Art Museum Bulletin* 7 (March–April 1972): 4–6.

———. "Bruce Nauman." In vol. 3 of *Modern Painting, Drawing and Sculpture Collected by Louise and Joseph Pulitzer, Jr.* 4 vols. Cambridge, Mass.: Fogg Art Museum, 1972.

Russell, John. "Art." *New York Times,* November 12, 1976, sec. C, p. 18.

———. "A Contemplative Chicago Show." *New York Times,* July 29, 1979, sec. 2, p. 31.

Schjeldahl, Peter. "New York Letter." *Art International* 13 (September 1969): 70–73.

"Self-Portrait." *San Francisco Chronicle,* June 2, 1974.

Sharp, Willoughby. "Nauman Interview." *Arts Magazine* 44 (March 1970): 22–27.

———. "Body Works." *Avalanche,* no. 1 (Fall 1970): 14–17.

Simon, Joan. "Breaking the Silence." *Art in America* 76 (September 1988): 140–49, 203.

Smith, Barbara T. "Nauman's Floating Room." *Artweek,* February 3, 1973, p. 3.

Smith, Bob. "Nauman Interview." *Journal* (Los Angeles Institute of Contemporary Art), no. 32 (Spring 1982): 35–38.

Smith, Roberta. "Sculpture at the Whitney: The Radical Years." *New York Times,* March 9, 1990, sec. B, p. 1.

———. "Extremes of Sculpture in Three Nauman Shows." *New York Times,* March 16, 1990, sec. C, p. 32.

———. "At the Modern, Works Unafraid to Ignore Beauty." *New York Times,* October 18, 1991, sec. C, p. 1.

Stiles, Knute. "William Geis and Bruce Nauman." *Artforum* 5 (November 19, 1966): 65–66.

Stitelman, Paul. "Bruce Nauman at the Whitney Museum." *Arts Magazine* 47 (May–June 1973): 54–55.

Tarshis, Jerome. "San Francisco." *Artforum* 9 (February 1971): 85–87.

Tucker, Marcia. "PheNAUMANology." *Artforum* 9 (December 1970): 38–44.

Warren, Ron. "Bruce Nauman." *Arts Magazine* 59 (December 1984): 39–40.

Wilson, William. "Bruce Nauman's Unsettling Art Given a Masterful Touch." *Los Angeles Times,* March 23, 1970, sec. 4, p. 6.

Wortz, Melinda. "Los Angeles: Black Art and Mannerist Geometry." *Artnews* 75 (December 1976): 80–83.

———. "Measurements of Time and Structures for Experience." *Artweek,* November 1, 1980, p. 5.

———. "Irrational Geometry." *Artnews* 80 (Summer 1981): 147–48.

Young, Joseph E. "Los Angeles." *Art International* 14 (Summer 1970): 111–15.

Zoretich, Frank. "Tunnel Vision." *Impact* (*Albuquerque Journal* magazine), March 8, 1988, pp. 4–7.

Zwinger, Susan. "Video as Attitude in New Mexico." *Artweek,* July 16, 1983, p. 18.

Maria Nordman

Albright, Thomas. "California Reviews, San Francisco: Sealed Rooms and Open Studios." *Artnews* 75 (January 1976): 60–62.

———. "Starting the Longest Day in a Museum." *San Francisco Chronicle,* June 23, 1979.

Atkins, Robert. "Light Paints a Museum." *Artweek,* July 28, 1979, pp. 1, 20.

Bijutsu Techno (Tokyo) 31 (April 1979): 58–59.

Bijvoet, Marga. "Maria Nordman: Reflections on the Waves." *Artweek,* March 9, 1985, p. 1.

Brenson, Michael. "Maria Nordman's Exhibition of Permanent Transience." *New York Times,* November 30, 1990.

Butterfield, Jan. "Maria Nordman: One Day Only, Dawn to Dusk." *Space as Support, Part 4.* Berkeley, Calif.: University Art Museum, 1979.

Celant, Germano. "Urban Nature: The Work of Maria Nordman." *Artforum* 18 (March 1980): 62–67.

Ferrari, Corinna. "Lux Lucus." *Domus,* no. 593 (April 1979): 52–53, 179.

Fischer, Hal. "Berkeley: 'Space as Support.'" *Artforum* 18 (October 1979): 64–66.

Frankenstein, Alfred. "Nordman's Hidden Work of Magic." *San Francisco Chronicle,* November 15, 1975.

Goldwater, Marge. *Maria Nordman, Texas.* Fort Worth: Fort Worth Art Museum, 1980.

Haskell, Barbara, and Hal Glicksman. *Maria Nordman: Saddleback Mountain.* Irvine: University of California, 1973.

Larson, Kay. "On the Line." *New York,* November 19, 1990, pp. 117–18.

Maria Nordman. *Data* (Milan), April–June 1977, pp. 52–53.

"Maria Nordman." Genoa, Italy: Saman Gallery, March–April 1979.

"Maria Nordman: Dawn to Dusk." In *Calendar* (University Art Museum, Berkeley), June 1979, p. 1.

Mills, Gabriella. "Nordman Transforms Abandoned Gas Station." *Contemporary* (Los Angeles Museum of Contemporary Art), Spring 1984, p. 4.

Nordman, Maria. "Workroom 1971." *Interfunktionen* (Cologne), no. 12 (Summer 1975): 99–105.

———. *De Sculptura: Works in the City.* Munich: Schirmer/Mosel, 1986.

Onorato, Ronald J. *Maria Nordman: Trabajos en la ciudad de ondas.* La Jolla, Calif.: La Jolla Museum of Contemporary Art, 1985.

Overy, Paul. "The Biennale: A Show of Compromises." *New York Times,* July 25, 1976, sec. 2, p. 24.

Plagens, Peter. "Decline and Rise of Younger Los Angeles Art." *Artforum* 10 (May 1972): 79–81.

———. "Maria Nordman." *Artforum* 12 (February 1974): 40–41.

Rosenthal, Mark, ed. *Andre, Buren, Irwin, Nordman: Space as Support.* Berkeley, Calif.: University of California Press, 1979.

Russell, John. "A Contemplative Chicago Show." *New York Times,* July 29, 1979, sec. 2, p. 31.

Saunders, Wade. "Los Angeles: Maria Nordman on Washington Boulevard." *Art in America* 67 (December 1979): 119–20.

Schmidt-Wulffen, Stephan. "Maria Nordman: Folkwang Museum, Essen." *Flash Art,* no. 123 (Summer 1985): 60.

Shapiro, David. "A View of Kassel." *Artforum* 16 (September 1977): 56–62.

Terbell, Melinda. "Los Angeles: Cups, Ballet, Funny Video." *Artnews* 72 (December 1973): 72–73.

Wilson, Simon. "Current and Forthcoming Exhibitions: The Venice Biennale." *Burlington Magazine* 118 (October 1976): 723–27.

Wortz, Melinda. "Sculpture: Maria Nordman." *Journal* (Los Angeles Institute of Contemporary Art), no. 24 (September–October 1979): 68–70.

———. "Maria Nordman, *315 N. Alameda/166 N. Central.*" *Artforum* 22 (October 1983): 82.

Eric Orr

Baker, Kenneth. "Painting with Some Sinister Substance." *San Francisco Chronicle,* April 12, 1986.

Bell, Larry. "Bell-Orr *Solar Fountain.*" *Domus,* no. 581 (April 1978): 52.

Boettger, Suzaan. "Eric Orr at Scott Hanson." *Art in America* 76 (May 1988): 186.

Brenner, Douglas. "L.A. Dream House." *Architectural Record* 173 (February 1985): 134–41.

Burnside, Madeleine. "Larry Bell and Eric Orr." *Artnews* 77 (April 1978): 152–53.

Elements: Five Installations. New York: Whitney Museum of American Art at Equitable Center, 1987.

Eric Orr. Santa Monica, Calif.: James Corcoran Gallery, 1988.

"Eric Orr." *New Yorker,* January 28, 1991, p. 60.

"Eric Orr, Cirrus Gallery." *Artforum* 13 (December 1974): 83.

Filler, Martin. "One Step Beyond." *House and Garden* 157 (September 1985): 134–35, 236–37.

Gardner, Colin. "The Artist as Shaman." *Artweek,* January 28, 1984, p. 3.

Garver, Thomas H. "Los Angeles: Eric Orr, Howard Fleming." *Artforum* 8 (March 1970): 84–85.

Hoffman, Fred. "Sacred Associations." *Artweek,* November 3, 1979, p. 1.

Hugo, Joan. "Mediating Substance and Thought." *Artweek,* November 6, 1982, p. 3.

"Interview with Eric Orr." *Artlines* (Taos, N.Mex.), August 1982.

Kelley, Jeff. "Eric Orr, Neil G. Ovsey Gallery." *Artforum* 22 (April 1984): 88–89.

Knight, Christopher. "Evolution from Environmental Artist to Painter." *Los Angeles Herald-Examiner,* April 22, 1984.

Kutner, Janet. "Dallas/Fort Worth: Capricious Places." *Artnews* 76 (December 1977): 102–6.

Larsen, Susan C. "New Editions: Eric Orr." *Artnews* 78 (September 1979): 45.

Larson, Kay. "The Good, the Bad, and the Young." *New York,* January 12, 1981, pp. 56–58.

McEvilley, Thomas. "Journeys in and out of the Body: Proto-Materialism of Eric Orr." *Images and Issues* 2 (Spring 1981): 18–20.

———. "Eric Orr, Neil G. Ovsey Gallery." *Artforum* 20 (September 1981): 82–83.

———. "Negative Presences in Secret Spaces: The Art of Eric Orr." *Artforum* 20 (Summer 1982): 58–66.

Muchnic, Suzanne. "Shining in Contemporary Light." *Los Angeles Times,* November 26, 1979.

———. "Pulling the Walls over Our Eyes." *Los Angeles Times,* June 15, 1981.

———. "Eric Orr at Ovsey Gallery." *Los Angeles Times,* October 22, 1982.

———. "Eric Orr Yokes Power with Rare Sophistication." *Los Angeles Times,* April 26, 1984.

"Multiples and Objects and Artists' Books." *Print Collector's Newsletter* 11 (November–December 1980): 180–81.

Nittve, Lars. "Stockholm: Eric Orr, Anders Tornberg Gallery." *Artforum* 24 (February 1986): 117.

Orr, Eric, and Thomas McEvilley. *Eric Orr: A Twenty-Year Survey.* San Diego: San Diego State University Art Gallery, 1984.

Perrone, Jeff. "Larry Bell, Eric Orr: Marian Goodman Gallery." *Artforum* 16 (April 1978): 64–65.

Pincus, Robert. "Reviews: Orr at Ovsey Gallery." *Los Angeles Times,* January 20, 1984.

———. "Resonances in Light, Dark." *Los Angeles Times,* October 9, 1984.

Plagens, Peter. "Eric Orr, Cirrus Gallery." *Artforum* 13 (December 1974): 83.

"Power Objects in Zero Mass." *Artforum* 20 (June 1982): 117.

"Silence and the Ion Wind." *Los Angeles Times,* December 5, 1980.

Wilson, William. "Eric Orr: Light, Space Exhibit of LACMA." *Los Angeles Times,* December 5, 1980.

Wortz, Melinda. "The Wonder and Value of Light." *Artweek,* October 30, 1976, pp. 3–4.

———. "Los Angeles: Glass with a New Slant." *Artnews* 80 (February 1981): 186–87.

Young, Joseph E. "Los Angeles." *Art International* 14 (October 1970): 76.

Hap Tivey

Ballatore, Sandy. "Hap Tivey: *Fourth Situation.*" *Artweek,* April 24, 1976, pp. 1, 16.

———. "Southern California: Hap Tivey at Irvine." *Art in America* 64 (July–August 1976): 111.

Bell, Jane. "Hap Tivey (Blum-Helman)." *Artnews* 78 (January 1979): 158.

Carlson, Prudence. "Hap Tivey at Blum-Helman." *Art in America* 67 (March–April 1979): 154–55.

Henry, Gerrit. "Hap Tivey at Blum-Helman." *Artnews* 78 (November 1979): 187.

———. "Hap Tivey at Diane Brown." *Art in America* 73 (January 1985): 140–41.

Muchnic, Suzanne. "The Galleries." *Los Angeles Times,* May 30, 1980.

Nisselson, Jane. "Hap Tivey: Apollonian Gold and the English Fog." *Arts Magazine* 54 (December 1979): 138–39.

Perlmutter, Elizabeth. "Dizzy in the Ganzfeld." *Artnews* 75 (Summer 1976): 140–42.

Seidler, Tor. "Hap Tivey: Blum-Helman Gallery." *Artforum* 18 (December 1979): 74–75.

Sodium Exchange. Essay by Barbara Haskell. Miami: Miami-Dade Community College, 1976.

Tivey, Hap. *From the Dayton Street Studio.* Pasadena, Calif.: Studio Notes, 1974.

———. "Notice to the Force." *Journal* (Los Angeles Institute of Contemporary Art), no. 10 (March–April 1976): 10.

Wortz, Melinda. "Hap Tivey: A Studio Report." *Artweek,* August 10, 1974, p. 13.

———. *Hap Tivey, Fourth Situation.* Irvine: Fine Arts Gallery, University of California, 1976.

———. "Experiencing the Ephemeral." *Artweek,* October 8, 1977, pp. 1, 16.

———. "Los Angeles: The Zen Science of Light." *Artnews* 76 (November 1977): 200–206.

——— and Hap Tivey. "Asians: A Description." *Journal* (Los Angeles Institute of Contemporary Art), no. 16 (November 1977): 46–49.

James Turrell

Adcock, Craig. "Anticipating 19,084: James Turrell's *Roden Crater Project.*" *Arts Magazine* 58 (May 1984): 76–85.

———. "Perceptual Edges: The Psychology of James Turrell's Light and Space." *Arts Magazine* 59 (February 1985): 124–28.

Altman, China. "A Wonderful Puzzlement." *Tech Talk* (Massachusetts Institute of Technology) 27 (February 1983): 1, 5.

Antin, David. "Art and the Corporation." *Artnews* 70 (September 1971): 23–26, 52–56.

Art + Architecture + Landscape: The Clos Pegase Design Competition. Foreword by Helene Fried. Essay by Martin Filler. San Francisco: San Francisco Museum of Modern Art, 1985.

"Arts: One of a Kind." *People,* January 7, 1985, pp. 46–54.

Beardsley, John. *Earthworks and Beyond.* New York: Abbeville Press, 1984.

Boettger, Suzaan. "San Francisco: James Turrell, Capp Street Project." *Artforum* 23 (September 1984): 118–19.

Brown, Julia, ed. *Occluded Front: James Turrell.* Larkspur Landing, Calif.: Lapis; Los Angeles: Museum of Contemporary Art, 1985.

Burns, Sarah. "Illusions." *New Art Examiner* (Chicago) 8 (November 1980): 21.

Bussel, David. "James Turrell: Meditations on Self-Illumination." *Flash Art,* no. 154 (October 1990): 147.

Butterfield, Jan. "A Hole in Reality: Roden Crater Project." *Images and Issues* 1 (Fall 1980): 53–57.

Castelli, Tommaso Trini. "Nella stanza del'arte." *Casa Vogue* (Milan), no. 79 (February 1978): 50–67.

Cecil, Sarah. "New Editions." *Artnews* 84 (March 1985): 67.

Cope, Maurice E. *James Turrrell: "Jida": An Installation.* Newark: University Gallery, University of Delaware, 1984.

Coplans, John. *Jim Turrell.* Pasadena, Calif.: Pasadena Art Museum, 1967.

———. "James Turrell: Projected Light Images." *Artforum* 6 (October 1967) 48–49.

Curtis, Cathy. "Light as Art: It's a Heavy Experience." *San Francisco Examiner,* June 3, 1984.

Daval, Jean-Luc, ed. *Skira Annual* 77. Geneva: Editions d'Arte Albert Skira, 1977.

Davis, Douglas. "View from Hill and Main." *Newsweek,* October 27, 1969, p. 111.

De Wilde, Edward. *Jim Turrell.* Amsterdam: Stedelijk Museum, 1976.

Failing, Patricia. "James Turrell's New Light on the Universe." *Artnews* 84 (April 1985): 70–78.

Feliciano, Hector. "Taking the Plunge into Heavy Water." *Los Angeles Times,* June 6, 1991.

Gablik, Suzi. "Dream Space." *Art in America* 75 (March 1987): 132–33, 153.

Glowen, Ron. "Light Illusions." *Artweek,* April 3, 1982, pp. 4–5.

Glueck, Grace. "Whitney Museum Sued over 1980 'Light Show.'" *New York Times,* May 4, 1982, sec. C, p. 16.

Hammond, Pamela. "James Turrell, Light Itself." *Images and Issues* 3 (Summer 1982): 52–56.

Hapgood, Fred. "Roden's Eye." *Atlantic* 260 (August 1987): 47–52.

Hazlitt, Gordon J. "Art Review: Questions That Amuse, Delight." *Los Angeles Times,* November 29, 1976.

Hughes, Robert. "Poetry out of Emptiness." *Time,* January 5, 1981, p. 81.

James Turrell, Light and Space: An Exhibition. Introduction by Melinda Wortz. Commentaries by James Turrell. New York: Whitney Museum of American Art, 1980.

Junker, Howard, and Ann Ray Martin. "The New Art." *Newsweek,* July 29, 1968, pp. 56–63.

Kazanjian, Dodie. "Art." *Vogue* 181 (May 1991): 164–77.

Koplos, Janet. "James Turrell." *New Art Examiner* (Chicago) 8 (October 1980): 21.

Larson, Kay. "New Landscapes in Art." *New York Times Magazine,* May 13, 1979, pp. 30–38.

———. "The Agony of Ecstasy." *New York,* November 17, 1980, pp. 90–93.

———. "Dividing the Light from the Darkness." *Artforum* 19 (January 1981): 30–33.

———. "The Good, the Bad, and the Young." *New York,* January 12, 1981, pp. 56–58.

———. "The Flash of Truth." *New York*, October 27, 1986, pp. 106, 124–25.

———. "What on Earth." *New York*, June 4, 1990, pp. 66–69.

Levin, Kim. "James Turrell." *Arts Magazine* 55 (December 1980): 5.

Lewis, James. "James Turrell: Open Space for Perception." *Flash Art*, no. 156 (January–February 1991): 110–13.

———. "The Artist and His Volcano." *Connoisseur* 221 (February 1991): 48–51, 100.

Livingston, Jane. "Some Thoughts on 'Art and Technology.'" *Studio International* 181 (June 1971): 258–63.

Lucebert. "James Turrell." In *Voor vridenden dierne en gedichten*, pp. 88–89. Amsterdam: Van Lanschot Bankiers, 1979.

Marmer, Nancy. "James Turrell: The Art of Deception." *Art in America* 69 (May 1981): 90–99.

Miedzinski, Charles. "James Turrell: The Capp Street Project." *Artweek*, June 16, 1984, p. 1.

———. "Affirmations of Perception and Spirit." *Artweek*, January 25, 1986, p. 1.

Millin, Laura J., ed. *James Turrell: Four Light Installations*. Seattle: Real Comet Press, 1982.

Morschel, Jurgen. "Jim Turrell." *Das Kunstwerk* 29 (July 1976): 92.

Muchnic, Suzanne. "Shining in Contemporary Light." *Los Angeles Times*, November 26, 1979.

———. "Gonna Carve a Mountain." *Los Angeles Times*, April 1, 1984.

Perreault, John. "Literal Light." In *From Aten to Laser (Art News Annual 35)*, ed. Thomas B. Hess and John Ashbery. New York: Macmillan Co., 1969.

Radice, Barbara. "A Piece Made in the Sky." *Data* (Milan), February–March 1977, pp. 40–43.

Ratcliff, Carter. "James Turrell's 'Deep Sky.'" *Print Collector's Newsletter* 16 (May–June 1985): 45–47.

Rose, Barbara. "Gallery without Walls." *Art in America* 56 (March–April 1968): 67–71.

Russell, John. "Art." *New York Times*, October 31, 1980, sec. C, p. 22.

———. "An Earthwork Looks to the Sky." *New York Times*, January 5, 1986, sec. 2.

Schuyt, Michael, Joost Elffers, and George R. Collins. "Jim Turrell, Roden Crater Project." In *Fantastic Architecture*, pp. 50–51. New York: Harry N. Abrams, 1980.

Sharp, Willoughby. "Rumbles." *Avalanche*, no. 1 (Fall 1970): 2–3.

Shinoda, Morio. "Performance of the Celestial Sphere." *Bijutsu Techno* (Tokyo) 34 (April 1982): 151–55.

Sobchack, Vivian. "Williamstown: James Turrell, Williams College." *Artforum* 30 (October 1991): 132.

Stevens, Mark. "Turrell's 'Celestial Vault.'" *Newsweek*, February 10, 1986, pp. 70–71.

"The Talk of the Town: Light." *New Yorker*, December 15, 1980, pp. 29–31.

Tarbell, Roberta K. "Newark: Jim Turrell, University of Delaware Gallery." *Artnews* 83 (April 1984): 137.

Tilroe, Anna. "De schatkamers van Panza." *Avenue* (Amsterdam), October 1979, pp. 14–21.

Turnbull, Betty. *The Last Time I Saw Ferus*. Newport Beach, Calif.: Newport Harbor Art Museum, 1976.

Turrell, James, et al. *Mapping Spaces: A Topological Survey of the Work by James Turrell*. New York: P. Blum, 1987.

"Turrell's Medium Is Perception." *Contemporary* (Los Angeles Museum of Contemporary Art), Fall 1983, p. 1.

Viladas, Pilar. "Interiors: The New Modernism, Speaking in Metaphors." *Progressive Architecture* 64 (September 1983): 108.

Von Meier, Kurt. "Los Angeles." *Art International* 11 (November 1967): 54–57.

Wetzsteon, Ross. "Do Not Go Gentle into That Good Light." *Village Voice*, November 19, 1980, p. 95.

Zimmer, William. "Now You See It, Now You . . ." *Artnews* 80 (February 1981): 225.

DeWain Valentine

Albright, Thomas. "L.A., N.Y.: Gallery Shows from Two Cities." *San Francisco Chronicle*, August 16, 1969.

Alliata, Vicky. "West Coast: Nella terra del duemila si chiama Venezia la città dell'arte." *Bolaffiarte* (Turin, Italy) 51 (June–July 1975): 41–44.

Bordeaux, Jean-Luc. "Un Musée américain en pleine croissance." *Connaissance des arts* 286 (December 1975): 64–73.

———. "DeWain Valentine: Light Explored." *Art in America* 67 (December 1979): 102–6.

Danieli, Fidel A. "Two Showings of Younger Los Angeles Artists." *Artforum* 5 (October 1966): 24–26.

———. "DeWain Valentine." *Art International* 13 (November 1969): 36–39.

De Benedetti, Carla. "Valentine De Vein fa scultura." *Abitare* 143 (March 1976): 20–21.

DeWain Valentine: New Work. Essay by Christopher Knight. Los Angeles: Los Angeles County Museum of Art, 1979.

DeWain Valentine: Recent Sculpture. Pasadena, Calif.: Pasadena Art Museum, 1970.

"DeWain Valentine" (*Skyline Installation*). *Journal* (Los Angeles Institute of Contemporary Art), no. 4 (February 1975): 51.

Frank, Joseph. "Denver." *Artforum* 3 (September 1964): 50.

Frank, Peter. "Reviews and Previews: DeWain Valentine." *Artnews* 72 (March 1973): 76.

Friedman, Martin. "Fourteen Sculptors: The Industrial Edge." *Art International* 14 (February 1970): 31–40, 55.

Garver, Thomas H. *DeWain Valentine: Recent Sculpture*. Vancouver: Fine Arts Gallery, University of British Columbia, 1969.

Hastings, Nora. "DeWain Valentine." *Western Plastics*, November 1974.

Hazlitt, Gordon J. "Venice, Unique among the World's Bohemias." *Artnews* 79 (January 1980): 94–98.

Hoffman, Fred. "Los Angeles: DeWain Valentine." *Artforum* 18 (January 1970): 77–78.

Hugo, Joan. "The Behavior of Materials." *Artweek*, October 18, 1979, p. 7.

Kozloff, Max. "Whitney Annual: Sculpture, Whitney Museum." *Artforum* 7 (February 1969): 64.

Kubiak, Richard. *DeWain Valentine: Dayline*. Santa Barbara, Calif.: Santa Barbara Museum of Art, 1977.

Lindsley, Carol. "Plastics into Art." *Art in America* 56 (May–June 1968): 114–15.

Livingston, Jane. "Los Angeles: *Plastics, L.A.*" *Artforum* 6 (May 1968): 65–66.

———. "Artist's Dialogue: DeWain Valentine—Light on a Glass Horizon." *Architectural Digest* 43 (Fall 1986): 178.

Montgomery, Cara. "Los Angeles Report." *Arts Magazine* 47 (May–June 1973): 53.

Opliger, Curt. "New Images, New Materials." *Artforum* 7 (December 1968): 14–16.

Passoni, Franco. *Art and Plastics.* Milan: Industria Pubblicazioni Audiovisivi, 1975.

Plagens, Peter. "Los Angeles: Five Artists, Ace Gallery." *Artforum* 10 (October 1971): 86–87.

———. *DeWain Valentine.* La Jolla, Calif.: La Jolla Museum of Contemporary Art, 1975.

———, ed. *DeWain Valentine Sculpture.* New York: René Denise Gallery, 1973.

Preisman, Fran. "DeWain Valentine, Seizing Light." *Artweek,* July 26, 1975, p. 3.

Restany, Pierre. *Le Plastique dans l'art.* Monte Carlo: Editions André Sauret, 1973.

———. "USA 76: The Year of Recycling." *Domus,* no. 565 (December 1976): 52–54.

Taylor, John Lloyd. "DeWain Valentine." *Art International* 17 (September 1973): 21–24, 76.

Valentine, DeWain. *Proposal.* New York: Seth Siegelaub, 1969.

Wortz, Melinda. "DeWain Valentine: An Interview." *Journal* (Los Angeles Institute of Contemporary Art), no. 1 (May 1974): 17–19.

———. *DeWain Valentine: Documentation of "Spectrum Horizon" Installation.* Long Beach, Calif.: Long Beach Museum of Art, 1975.

———. *DeWain Valentine.* Irvine: Fine Arts Gallery, University of California, 1979.

———. "Los Angeles: Glass with a New Slant." *Artnews* 80 (February 1981): 186–87.

———. *DeWain Valentine.* Honolulu: Honolulu Academy of Art and Contemporary Arts Center, 1985.

Susan Kaiser Vogel

Barrili, Renato. "Post Minimalismo, Susan Kaiser Vogel." *Periodici d'arte contemporaneo,* 1985.

Clothier, Peter. "Walls Are for Leaping." *Artweek,* February 2, 1980, p. 3.

———. "Bricks, Brushes, and Barbells." *Art in America* 69 (May 1981): 58–61.

Gary, Robin. "Blue Flame Ignites Feelings." *Playgirl* 21 (November 1977).

Groot, Paul. "Closed Quotes." *Artforum* 23 (September 1984): 107.

Menzies, Neal. "A Metaphysical Monolith." *Artweek,* January 9, 1982, p. 5.

Muchnic, Suzanne. "Future: More Than a Wistful Look at a Bomb." *Los Angeles Times,* July 23, 1985.

Wortz, Melinda. "A Perceptual Journey." *Artweek,* August 12, 1978, pp. 3–4.

———. "Los Angeles: Meditations on Death." *Artnews* 77 (November 1978): 153–62.

———. "Blowing in the Wind." *Artnews* 81 (March 1982): 134–40.

———. "Plum Blossom Domain." Typescript, 1983.

Douglas Wheeler

Coplans, John. *Doug Wheeler.* Pasadena, Calif.: Pasadena Art Museum, 1968.

———. "Doug Wheeler: Light Paintings." *Artforum* 7 (September 1968): 40–41.

Foote, Nancy. "The Apotheosis of the Crummy Space." *Artforum* 15 (October 1976): 28–37.

8e biennale de Paris: Manifestation internationale des jeunes artistes. Paris: Idea Books, 1973.

Livingston, Jane. *Robert Irwin/Doug Wheeler.* Fort Worth: Fort Worth Art Museum, 1969.

"Place in the Sun." *Time,* August 30, 1968, pp. 38–41.

Plagens, Peter. "Los Angeles." *Artforum* 8 (March 1970): 83–84.

———. "Doug Wheeler: Riko Mizuno Gallery." *Artforum* 13 (September 1974): 88.

Seldis, Henry J. "Artwalk." *Los Angeles Times,* April 26, 1974.

Stockwood, Jane. *Harper's Bazaar,* May 1970, p. 19.

Wilson, Simon. "Current and Forthcoming Exhibitions: The Venice Biennale." *Burlington Magazine* 188 (October 1976): 723–27.

Wilson, William. "Wheeler's Electronic Age Art in Pasadena Exhibition." *Los Angeles Times,* June 3, 1968.

Wortz, Melinda. "Doug Wheeler: Drawings." *Artweek,* April 20, 1974, pp. 5–6.

Young, Joseph E. "Los Angeles." *Art International* 14 (March 1970): 83–90.

Index

(Page numbers in *italic* refer to illustrations.)

G

H

I

J

K

L

M

N

O

P

Q

R

S

T

Credits

Text

Charles Baudelaire, *Paris Spleen,* copyright © 1970 New Directions Pub. Corp. Reprinted by permission of New Directions.

Gaston Bachelard, *The Poetics of Space.* Copyright © 1958 by Presses Universitaires de France, translation copyright © 1964 by The Orion Press. Used by permission of Viking Penguin, a division of Penguin Books USA Inc.

Photography

The artists' portraits that open each chapter were photographed by Jim McHugh using Polaroid Positive/Negative film Type 55.

The photographers and the sources of photographic material other than those indicated in the captions are as follows (numbers refer to pages):

Courtesy Asher/Faure Gallery, Los Angeles: 13; Marianne Barcellona, New York: 136; Larry Bell: 32–33, 188; Courtesy Larry Bell: 178; Peter Bermingham: 87; Henry Blackham: 202; Ben Blackwell: 57; Courtesy Blum Helman Gallery, New York: 240; Michael Burns and Susan Kaiser Vogel: 213; Steven Burns: 185; Jan Butterfield: front cover, lower right, 23, 37, 44, 103; © Giorgio Colombo, Milan: 217 top, 139; M. Lee Fatheree: front cover, upper left; Gus Foster: 182; Tom Fox: 48; Howard Harrison: 177; Rob Lewine, Los Angeles: 161; Los Angeles County Museum of Art: 11; The Los Angeles Institute of Contemporary Art: 106; Courtesy Los Angeles Municipal Art Gallery: 156; Andrei P. Lovinescu, Milwaukee, Courtesy John Lloyd Taylor, Milwaukee: 191; Malcolm Lubliner: 26, 28, 120 bottom, 121 top, 155 ; Malcolm Lubliner, Courtesy Ace Gallery, Los Angeles: 121 bottom; Susan Kaiser Vogel: 207; Courtesy Malinda Wyatt Gallery, Venice, Calif.: 47; Courtesy Riko Mizuno, Los Angeles: 124; Peter Moore, courtesy Leo Castelli Gallery: 134, 135; Museum of Contemporary Art, Chicago: 39; Museum of Contemporary Art, Los Angeles: 81; Courtesy Neil G. Ovsey Gallery, Los Angeles: 166; Courtesy Pace Gallery, New York: 12; Eric Pollitzer, Hempstead, N.Y.: 141; Larry Reynolds: 165; Warren Silverman, New York: 41; Gian Sinigaglia, Fotografo, Milan, Italy: 20, 36, 38, 74, 138; Courtesy Skystone Foundation, Flagstaff, Ariz.: 86; Sonnabend Gallery, New York: 14; Stedelijk Museum, Amsterdam: 69, 70, 72 bottom, 75, 85; Courtesy Stuart Collection, La Jolla, Calif.: 149; © 1979 Craig Vista Svare. All rights reserved: 107, 108 top and bottom, 109; © Tate Gallery, London: 180; Jean-Luc Terradillos: 92 top and bottom, 93 top and bottom; Frank J. Thomas, Los Angeles: 35, 97, 98, 99, 119 top, 120 top, 139, 195; Walter Mariam Uolde: 162, 163; Gilles van Niel: 169; Tom Vinetz: 187 bottom; Courtesy Daniel Weinberg Gallery: 21; Courtesy Doug Wheeler: 125 top and bottom, 127; Oliver Wick: 79, 83; Gaston Wicky, Zurich, Courtesy Turske & Turske, Zurich, and the Skystone Foundation, Flagstaff, Arizona: 88, 89; Donald Woodman © 1988: 150.